General editor: Andrew S. Thompson

Founding editor: John M. MacKenzie

When the 'Studies in Imperialism' series was founded by Professor John M. MacKenzie more than thirty years ago, emphasis was laid upon the conviction that 'imperialism as a cultural phenomenon had as significant an effect on the dominant as on the subordinate societies'. With well over a hundred titles now published, this remains the prime concern of the series. Cross-disciplinary work has indeed appeared covering the full spectrum of cultural phenomena, as well as examining aspects of gender and sex, frontiers and law, science and the environment, language and literature, migration and patriotic societies, and much else. Moreover, the series has always wished to present comparative work on European and American imperialism, and particularly welcomes the submission of books in these areas. The fascination with imperialism, in all its aspects, shows no sign of abating, and this series will continue to lead the way in encouraging the widest possible range of studies in the field. 'Studies in Imperialism' is fully organic in its development, always seeking to be at the cutting edge, responding to the latest interests of scholars and the needs of this ever-expanding area of scholarship.

Crowns and colonies

Manchester University Press

SELECTED TITLES AVAILABLE IN THE SERIES

WRITING IMPERIAL HISTORIES
ed. Andrew S. Thompson

EMPIRE OF SCHOLARS
Tamson Pietsch

HISTORY, HERITAGE AND COLONIALISM
Kynan Gentry

COUNTRY HOUSES AND THE BRITISH EMPIRE
Stephanie Barczewski

THE RELIC STATE
Pamila Gupta

WE ARE NO LONGER IN FRANCE
Allison Drew

THE SUPPRESSION OF THE ATLANTIC SLAVE TRADE
ed. Robert Burroughs and Richard Huzzey

HEROIC IMPERIALISTS IN AFRICA
Berny Sèbe

Crowns and colonies

EUROPEAN MONARCHIES AND OVERSEAS EMPIRES

Edited by
Robert Aldrich and Cindy McCreery

MANCHESTER UNIVERSITY PRESS

Copyright © Manchester University Press 2016

While copyright in the volume as a whole is vested in Manchester University Press, copyright in individual chapters belongs to their respective authors, and no chapter may be reproduced wholly or in part without the express permission in writing of both author and publisher.

Published by Manchester University Press
Oxford Road, Manchester M13 9PL
www.manchesteruniversitypress.co.uk

British Library Cataloguing-in-Publication Data
A catalogue record for this book is available from the British Library

ISBN 978 1 7849 9315 3 hardback
ISBN 978 1 5261 5602 0 paperback

First published 2016

Paperback published 2021

The publisher has no responsibility for the persistence or accuracy of URLs for any external or third-party internet websites referred to in this book, and does not guarantee that any content on such websites is, or will remain, accurate or appropriate.

Typeset by Out of House Publishing

CONTENTS

List of figures—vii
List of contributors—ix
Acknowledgements—xii

1 European sovereigns and their empires 'beyond the seas'   1
 Robert Aldrich and Cindy McCreery

2 The British royal family and the colonial empire from the
 Georgians to Prince George   *Miles Taylor*   27

3 Two Victorias? Prince Alfred, Queen Victoria and
 Melbourne, 1867–68   *Cindy McCreery*   51

4 Kaiser Wilhelm II and the limits of the royal prerogative in
 German South-West Africa   *Matthew P. Fitzpatrick*   77

5 Orangists in a red empire: salutations from a Dutch queen's
 supporters in a British South Africa   *Susie Protschky*   97

6 Sultans and the House of Orange-Nassau: Indonesian
 perceptions of power relationships with the Dutch   119
 Jean Gelman Taylor

7 The return of the throne: the repatriation of the Kandyan
 regalia to Ceylon   *Robert Aldrich*   139

8 Kingitanga and Crown: New Zealand's Maori King
 movement and its relationship with the British monarchy   163
 Vincent O'Malley

9 The Maharani of Kutch and courtly life before and
 after Indian Independence   *Jim Masselos*   177

10 Colonies, monarchy, empire and the French *ancien régime*   194
 François-Joseph Ruggiu

11 Napoleon III and France's colonial expansion: national
 grandeur, territorial conquests and colonial embellishment,
 1852–70   *Emmanuelle Guenot*   211

12 The British, the Hashemites and monarchies in
 the Middle East   *Matthieu Rey*   227

CONTENTS

13 An empire for a kingdom: monarchy and Fascism in
    the Italian colonies   *Alessandro Pes*   245

14 'So brave Etruria grew': dividing the Crown in early colonial
    New South Wales, 1808–10   *Bruce Baskerville*   262

15 A new monarchy for a new commonwealth? Monarchy and
    the consequences of republican India   *H. Kumarasingham*   283

16 Waiting to die? The British monarchy in Australia,
    New Zealand and Canada, 1991–2016   *Mark McKenna*   309

Index—325

FIGURES

1 Statue of Queen Victoria outside Government House, Port-Louis, Mauritius. Photograph by Robert Aldrich, June 2015 *page* 2
2 Sculpture in wood representing Queen Victoria, by an unidentified West African artist, probably late nineteenth century. © Pitt Rivers Museum, University of Oxford (1965.10.1). Reproduced with permission 12
3 Postcard c. 1911, 'Coronation Durbar, Delhi. The King-Emperor and Queen-Empress presenting themselves to their people' Ernest Brooks, photographer. 690.P. Beagles postcards, collection of Robert Aldrich 19
4 The Great Seal of New Zealand, from *The Illustrated London News*, 21 June 1845. Source: Private Collection, Look and Learn/ Illustrated Papers Collection/Bridgeman Images, LIP1095609. Reproduced with permission 38
5 Portrait of Queen Victoria and Maharajahs. Reproduced with permission of Maharana of Mewar Charitable Foundation, Mewar Palace, Udaipur, Rajasthan, India 42
6 'Fireworks in the Yarra Park, in celebration of the visit of HRH the Duke of Edinburgh', engr. Samuel Calvert, wood engraving, *Illustrated Melbourne Post*, 27 December 1867. State Library of Victoria, IMP27/12/67/177 55
7 'Union Bank of Australia', wood engraving, *Illustrated Australian News for Home Readers*, 26 November 1867. State Library of Victoria, IAN26/11/67/SUPP/4 57
8 'Illuminations in Melbourne: Messrs. Sands and M'Dougall, Collins Street', wood engraving, *Illustrated Melbourne Post*, 27 November 1867. State Library of Victoria, IMP27/11/67/5 59
9 *Oorkonde* for Queen Wilhelmina from a Women's Committee, Johannesburg, July 1909. Koninklijk Huisarchief, The Hague, A50 VIIIe 11. Reproduced with permission 98
10 *Oorkonde* from the Nederlandsch Zuid-Afkrikaansche Vereniging (Dutch South-African Society) for Queen Wilhelmina's inauguration, 1898. Koninklijk Huisarchief, The Hague, A50 XIVb 91. Reproduced with permission 108
11 Cover page of the *oorkonde* from the Cape Town Women's Committee for Juliana's birth, 1909. Koninklijk Huisarchief, The Hague, A50 VIIIe 12. Reproduced with permission 109
12 Second page of the 1909 Cape Town Women's Committee *oorkonde* 110
13 Detail from the third page of the 1909 Cape Town Women's Committee *oorkonde*. Koninklijk Huisarchief, The Hague, A50 VIIIe 12. Reproduced with permission 111

LIST OF FIGURES

14 Dagger and sheath (*kris*), Javanese, late nineteenth century, iron, wood, brass (a–b) 48.8 × 14.6 × 2.8 cm (overall), National Gallery of Victoria, Melbourne, Purchased, 1974, image code 53033. Reproduced with permission — 126

15 Sultan Hamengku Buwono VII of Yogyakarta (r. 1877–1921) with gold betel set from his royal regalia. Photographer Kassian Cephas, restored by Durova, Tropenmuseum, part of the National Museum of World Cultures, image code: 60001455. Wikimedia Commons, licensed under CC BY-SA 3.0 — 127

16 Gusti Raden Ajeng Siti Nurul Kusumowardani, daughter of Mangku Negara VII of Surakarta, dances in the Noordeinde Palace, The Hague, as a wedding gift to Princess Juliana and Prince Bernhard, 28 December 1936. Leiden University, KITLV Digital Image Library, image code 53255. Reproduced with permission — 132

17 The regalia of the King of Kandy in the National Museum, Colombo. Photograph by Robert Aldrich — 144

18 Queen Elizabeth II, the Maori Queen, Te Arikinui Dame Te Atairangikaahu, Prime Minister Jim Bolger and Douglas Graham (Minister in Charge of Treaty of Waitangi Negotiations) at the signing of the Waikato Raupatu Claims Settlement Act, Auckland, 4 November 1995. Source: EP/1995/4375B/33A-F, Alexander Turnbull Library, Wellington, New Zealand. Reproduced with permission — 173

19 The late Maharani Kunverba of Kutch. Photograph by Jim Masselos — 182

20 Photograph of King Faisal I and associates at the celebration of Iraq becoming a member of the League of Nations; Royal Palace, Baghdad, 6 October 1932. American Colony (Jerusalem), G. Eric and Edith Matson Photograph Collection, Library of Congress Prints and Photographs Division, Washington, DC, Wikimedians of Levant – GLAM Project. Wikimedia Commons — 239

21 1792 wax impression of the obverse of the Great Seal of New South Wales (1791 to 1817). Source: State Library of New South Wales, a1316004, Safe 1/4c. Reproduced with permission — 266

22 1792 wax impression of the reverse of the Great Seal of New South Wales (1791 to 1817). Source: State Library of New South Wales, a1316003, Safe 1/4c. Reproduced with permission — 267

CONTRIBUTORS

Robert Aldrich is Professor of European History at the University of Sydney. His recent publications include *The Routledge History of Western Empires* (edited with Kirsten McKenzie, 2013) and *Cultural Encounters and Homoeroticism in Sri Lanka: Sex and Serendipity* (2014). He is currently completing an Australian Research Council-funded study of the deposition and banishment of indigenous rulers by colonial authorities in the nineteenth and twentieth centuries.

Bruce Baskerville is completing a doctoral thesis at the University of Sydney on the cultural history of the Crown in Australia. He has worked in cultural heritage management around Australia and has been Site Manager of the Kingston & Arthur's Vale Historic Area on Norfolk Island. He is currently working on a study of commemorative plaque programmes in New South Wales.

Matthew P. Fitzpatrick is Associate Professor in International History at Flinders University, Adelaide. He is the author of *Purging the Empire: Mass Expulsions in Germany, 1871–1914* (2015) and *Liberal Imperialism in Germany: Expansionism and Nationalism, 1848–1884* (2008). Recently he has been a Humboldt Fellow at the Westphalian Wilhelms University of Münster in Germany. He is currently working on a monograph on Kaiser Wilhelm II's role in German foreign and colonial policy prior to the First World War.

Emmanuelle Guenot has recently completed a doctoral thesis at the University of Sydney on the decolonisation of the five French Indian territories (1954–62). It examined France's marginal colonial dependencies in India, Franco-British colonial rivalries and 'subaltern' colonial power in India.

H. Kumarasingham is Researcher at the Max Planck Institute of European Legal History in Frankfurt and Senior Research Fellow at the Institute of Commonwealth Studies, University of London. Prior to this he was Smuts Fellow in Commonwealth History and Politics at the University of Cambridge. His latest book is *A Political Legacy of the British Empire: Power and the Parliamentary System in Post-colonial India and Sri Lanka* (2013), and he recently edited for Cambridge University Press *Constitution Maker: Selected Writings of Sir Ivor Jennings* (2015).

Jim Masselos is Honorary Reader in History at the University of Sydney. He is the author of *Towards Nationalism* (1974), *Indian Nationalism* (1991) and *The City in Action: Bombay Struggles for Power* (2007). He has co-authored *Beato's Delhi* (2000) and *Dancing to the Flute: Dance and Music in Indian Art* (1997) and has edited or co-edited numerous works on South Asia.

Cindy McCreery is Senior Lecturer in the Department of History at the University of Sydney. Her recent publications examine naval sociability in the

LIST OF CONTRIBUTORS

nineteenth-century Asia-Pacific region (2014) and the role of the sea in shaping the Australian settler experience (2013, 2015) as well as colonial responses to Prince Alfred's royal tours (2013). She is currently writing a monograph on Prince Alfred's global voyages in HMS *Galatea* (1867–71) and the role of British princes and navy officers in shaping responses to the nineteenth-century British empire.

Mark McKenna is Professor and Australian Research Council Fellow in the Department of History at Sydney University. He has published widely in Australian history, including the history of republicanism and monarchy, indigenous history, the contemporary commemoration of war, environmental history and biography, including a two-volume biography of the Australian historian Manning Clark, *An Eye for Eternity: The Life of Manning Clark* (2011, 2015). He is currently writing a book on historical consciousness in Australia through twelve places.

Vincent O'Malley is a New Zealand historian who has written extensively on the history of Maori relations with European settlers (Pakeha) and colonial governments. He is the author most recently of *The Meeting Place: Maori and Pakeha Encounters, 1642–1840* (2012) and *Beyond the Imperial Frontier: The Contest for Colonial New Zealand* (2014). He was the 2014 J. D. Stout Research Fellow at Victoria University of Wellington. He is currently working on a history of the Waikato War.

Alessandro Pes is Lecturer in Contemporary History at the University of Cagliari. With Valeria Deplano, he is the editor of *Quel che resta dell'impero: la cultura coloniale degli Italiani* (2014); he is also the author of *Bonificare gli Italiani: la Società Bonifiche Sarde tra risanamento e colonizzazione nell'Italia fascista* (2013) and *La Costruzione dell'impero fascista: Politiche di regime per una società coloniale* (2010). His current research focuses on the social and cultural aspects of the Italian decolonisation.

Susie Protschky is Senior Lecturer in the History Programme at Monash University, Melbourne. She is a historian of modern Dutch colonialism and visual culture. Her first book was *Images of the Tropics: Environment and Visual Culture in Indonesia* (2011), and she is the editor of *Photography, Modernity and the Governed in Late-Colonial Indonesia* (2015). She is currently preparing a monograph entitled *Photography, Monarchy and Empire in Indonesia*.

Matthieu Rey is Lecturer in the Modern History of the Arab World at the Collège de France, Paris, and has been a fellow at the Middle East Institute at the National University of Singapore and the French Institute of the Near East in Damascus. He has written on the history of Iraq and Syria for various publications and edited a special issue of the journal *Vingtième Siècle* on *Militaires et pouvoirs au Moyen-Orient* (2014). He is currently completing a history of Syria from the nineteenth to the twenty-first century.

François-Joseph Ruggiu is Professor of History at the University of Paris-Sorbonne. Originally a specialist of early modern European societies, he has recently oriented

LIST OF CONTRIBUTORS

his research towards the study of seventeenth- and eighteenth-century colonial societies, especially of the elites. He has co-edited, with Cécile Vidal, *Sociétés, colonisations et esclavages dans le monde atlantique: historiographie des sociétés américaines des XVIe–XIXe siècles* (2009); and, with Pierre Singaravélou and Claire Laux, *Au sommet de l'empire: les élites européennes dans les colonies du début du XVIe siècle au milieu du XXe siècle* (2009). He is currently writing an imperial history of the French colonies from the mid-sixteenth to the mid-nineteenth century.

Jean Gelman Taylor is Honorary Associate Professor of History in the School of Humanities and Languages at the University of New South Wales, Sydney, where she taught Indonesian and South-East Asian History for twenty years. Her most recent publications include a new edition of *The Social World of Batavia: European and Eurasian in Colonial Indonesia* (2009) and *Global Indonesia* (2013). She is co-editor of *Culture and Cleanliness: Histories from Indonesia* (2011).

Miles Taylor is Professor of Modern History at the University of York, and from 2008 to 2014 was Director of the Institute of Historical Research at the University of London. He is the author of numerous works on British political history, and, most recently, co-editor with Charles Beem of *The Man behind the Queen: Princes Consort in History* (2014). He is currently working on a book, *The Sovereign People: Parliament and Representation in Britain since 1750* as well as a study of Queen Victoria and India.

ACKNOWLEDGEMENTS

Most of the chapters in this volume were presented in earlier versions, among other papers, at a conference on 'Crowns and Colonies: Monarchies and Colonial Empires' held at the University of Sydney in June 2014. We would like to thank the School of Philosophical and Historical Inquiry at the University of Sydney for providing funding for the conference as well as for some of the illustrations in this book.

Robert Aldrich acknowledges with gratitude a Discovery Grant from the Australian Research Council which has funded his research into colonialism and monarchies.

Briony Neilson provided invaluable assistance in organising the conference and putting together this volume, and we would like to thank her most warmly for her work. We would also like to thank Trevor Matthews for preparing the index, Nicholas Keyzer for assistance with the illustrations, and James Drown for collating the proofs.

The chapters in this book have all been peer-reviewed, and we would like to acknowledge colleagues at the University of Sydney and other institutions for their critical reading and useful comments. In particular, we thank Chris Hilliard, Kirsten McKenzie, Mark Seymour and Nigel Worden for their generous assistance.

CHAPTER ONE

European sovereigns and their empires 'beyond the seas'

Robert Aldrich and Cindy McCreery

The word 'empire' conjures up both the idea of a dynastic lineage of emperors and empresses and the idea of a collection of conquered territories, particularly overseas colonies. Indeed, many colonial empires were ruled over by the crowned heads of metropolitan powers. Some of the Holy Roman Emperors in early modern Europe reigned over Spanish colonial possessions in the Americas; later, such nineteenth-century rulers as Her Britannic Majesty Queen Victoria, the Empress of India, and her contemporary, Emperor Napoleon III of France, became sovereigns over lands scattered around the world (see Figure 1). By the early twentieth century, Spain had virtually no more colonies and France had no more emperor (though it did have an even more extensive overseas empire than at the time of Napoleon III), but monarchs such as the Queen of the Netherlands and the Emperor of Germany ruled far-flung domains. This book explores the multiple and evolving connections between European monarchs and their colonies. It argues that during much of the history of colonialism there existed a direct and important link between most colonial empires and the institutions of monarchy.

Ruling over the world's largest empire, the British sovereign's relationship with the colonies was of special moment. That relationship was dramatically on display at the time of the monarch's coronation, and such ceremonies provide a unique perspective on the sovereign's role as paramount rulers of colonial empires.

British imperial coronations, 1937 and 1953

On 12 May 1937, George VI was crowned 'King of the United Kingdom of Great Britain, Ireland and the British Dominions beyond the seas' and Emperor of India. A commemorative publication issued by *The Times*, in London, spoke of the monarchy as the most important single institution of common interest to all the peoples of the Empire. It

1. Statue of Queen Victoria outside Government House, Port-Louis, Mauritius. Photograph by Robert Aldrich, June 2015

recalled that an imperial conference in 1926 had declared that the peoples of Britain and its dominions – Canada, Australia, New Zealand, South Africa, the Irish Free State and Newfoundland – were 'united by a common allegiance to the Crown' and noted that, according to the 1931 Statute of Westminster, 'any alteration in the law touching the Succession to the Throne or the Royal Style and Titles shall hereafter require the assent as well of the Parliaments of all the Dominions as of the Parliament of the United Kingdom'. The newspaper conceded that different parts of the Empire had varying legal and emotional links with the monarch. In the princely states of India, 'the Coronation of the King-Emperor does not possess that special significance which attaches to it in respect of British India', that is, the portion of the subcontinent directly governed by the British, but the princes nevertheless

> are bound to the King-Emperor by treaty relations, and they recognise in him the personal embodiment of the paramount power of the Crown. Moreover, for them as monarchs, within their own sphere, the institution of monarchy has a more than ordinary appeal, and they have a strong interest in its maintenance and in the increase of its prestige.

In the formal colonies – the bulk of the British outposts in Africa, the Caribbean, and the Atlantic, Indian and Pacific Oceans –

> the attitude of the native peoples towards the King is, in most of the colonial possessions of His Majesty, in a sense, a much more personal one than is that of any other section of His Majesty's subjects. They look to him as their supreme ruler and they trust to him that their welfare and protection will be secured. They make little distinction between His Majesty and His Majesty's Government.[1]

Those words not only underlined the personal links that were thought to bind both settlers *and* colonised peoples to their monarch but also alluded to the complex constitutional issues of what exactly royal rule meant overseas; in passing, *The Times* noted moves to increasing self-government in Southern Rhodesia, Ceylon and Burma, evidence that the relations between Britain and its empire, and between sovereign and subjects, were not immutable. For the moment, however, the newspaper concentrated on the pageantry of the coronation, witnessed by the prime ministers of the dominions, troops brought to London from around the British Empire (singling out the Royal Canadian Mounted Police, 'fine figures in scarlet tunics', and the 'dark-skinned officers and men of Indian regiments, in the many uniforms and sometimes strange headdresses') and the indigenous maharajahs and sultans sitting in Westminster Abbey alongside European royals from Belgium, Norway, Sweden and Denmark.

> Here, too, were the Indian Princes, robed in the rich fabrics of the East, their sparkling gems not insignificant against those of the [British] regalia. Among them were the popular Maharajah of Bikaner, who has behind him so great a record as a soldier [in the First World War], administrator, and statesmen; the Prince of Berar, representing his father, the Nizam of Hyderabad …; the Maharajah Gaekwar of Baroda, with the Maharani

at his side; and those keen polo players, the Nawab of Bhopal and the Maharajah of Jaipur.

The commemorative publication reported, too, on the King's address to his people on the evening of the coronation, in which he said: 'I felt this morning that the whole Empire was in very truth gathered within the Walls of Westminster Abbey.'

A celebratory booklet was also published in India, offered 'as an humble tribute, a token of the loyalty and affection of the citizens of the Indian Empire' to George VI. The text, no doubt written largely by and for Britons and an Anglophile Indian elite, welcomed the new king 'to the throne of the greatest Empire that the world has seen'. The publication included an article by Winston Churchill on 'India and the Constitution', in which Churchill, then in the political wilderness but gaining attention with his warnings about Fascism, said that 'the British monarchy and constitution, spread as they are in different forms throughout the self-governing dominions, stand at this time as the most obvious bulwark against arbitrary rule, tyrannies and dictatorships of all kinds'. Churchill's allusion to Japanese aggression in Manchuria, Italian conquest of Ethiopia and Hitler's demands for the restitution of Germany's colonies were the snatch-and-grab moves that Britain had abjured, he stated, for 'far gone are the army days of Queen Victoria'. The Indian booklet, like ones printed for the coronation elsewhere in the empire, offered readers detailed accounts of the investiture, descriptions of the regalia, biographies of members of the royal family, a piece on the 'spiritual significance of the Coronation', and recollections of the grand Delhi Durbar of 1911. Indians themselves remained almost completely absent in the pictures and among the authors, though the publication contained advertisements for an Ayurvedic doctor, the Jewel of India Perfume Company, Ajanta Beauty Products ('hundred per cent Indian') and 'Squibb's Ague Specific – a gift from Heaven to fight the fevers, malaria & influenza'.[2]

Few who cheered at the coronation of King George VI would have foreseen that just over a decade later Britain would quit India and that the monarch would thus lose his title of 'Emperor of India'. Soon Burma and Sri Lanka would follow India and Pakistan into independence. Finally, the reign of the King's daughter and successor, Elizabeth II, would see Britain withdraw from most of its remaining colonies by the mid-1960s. Still, at Elizabeth II's coronation in 1953, the mood was imperially festive. Churchill, now Prime Minister, provided a link to the interwar years, and the engaging young monarch was lauded as the perfect figure for the dawn of a new Elizabethan age. The Queen, in an address, evoked 'the living strength and majesty of the Commonwealth and Empire: of societies old and new, of lands and races different in history and origins, but all, by God's will, united in spirit and in aim'. On her coronation day, the prime ministers of the newly independent countries, such as Jawaharlal Nehru from India and D. S. Senanayake from Ceylon, joined those from the old dominions. Once again, there were other royals in Westminster Abbey. In the procession across London, a particular favourite was the tall Queen Salote of Tonga, who declined to have the roof of her carriage raised despite the rain (perhaps to the dismay of the Malay Sultan of Kelantan, who shared the carriage with her).[3] And once again there were commemorative publications, the *Official Souvenir Programme* from Penang, for instance, listing the English, Indian, Chinese and Malay names of the coronation celebration committee, giving the schedules of Hindu, Buddhist and Muslim services of thanksgiving, and recording an 'all-community luncheon (by invitation) to prominent citizens' at the exclusive Penang Club. There were school processions, the erection of a triumphal arch by the Penang Muslim Community, parades of the Royal West Kent Regiment and the Gurkha Pipe Band, a cocktail party hosted by the Royal Navy and a ball at the grand Eastern and Oriental Hotel. The souvenir noted that the dukes of Clarence, Connaught, Gloucester and Kent, as well as the Prince of Wales, had visited the Malay states and that the sultans of Johore, Selangor, Kelantan and Perak had made the journey to London for the coronation of Elizabeth II 'and will, thereby, make even closer the personal ties which bind Her Majesty to the Rulers and the Malayan peoples'.[4]

Sixty years on, Queen Elizabeth's abiding dedication to the Commonwealth is well known, but the 'realms and territories' (in the current formulation of the monarch's title) over which her successor shall be crowned will constitute a diminished portfolio of imperial holdings. He will become the sovereign not of the catch-all 'domains beyond the seas' but, more specifically, will be proclaimed King of Canada (the title was a Canadian innovation already in 1937) and King of Australia – a title instituted in 1973 – that is, unless these two former dominions and New Zealand do not first become republics. The British monarchy has survived the virtual end of empire, but it would be hazardous to predict whether the formal ties that make the sovereign the head of state of such diverse countries as Australia and Papua New Guinea will endure into the reigns of Elizabeth II's heirs. Nevertheless, for a very long time, not only in Britain but also in other countries, the institutions of monarchy and overseas empire have gone together.

CROWNS AND COLONIES
European monarchs and their overseas empires

In the mid-1700s, virtually every polity in the world was, in some way, organised according to monarchical principles, with rule exercised by a figure who inherited his or her rights, or had wrested them from a predecessor and hoped to pass them on to family members of the dynasty. Even in the late nineteenth century, republican governments remained an exception (largely in the Americas and in France, Switzerland and San Marino) in a world where crowned heads reigned and ruled. Many monarchs ruled extensive domains, either continental or overseas, that encompassed a wide variety of peoples, cultures and territories. In the early years of the twentieth century, the Russian Emperor ruled over Baltic, Central Asian and Siberian peoples, the Chinese Emperor's administration extended to the lands of the Uighurs and Tibetans, and the Japanese Emperor claimed the Ryukyu Islands, Taiwan and Korea. Though he had no overseas empire, the Habsburg ruler established his rights over a quasi-colonial Bosnia. The British, Dutch, Belgian, German, Italian, Danish, Portuguese and Ottoman rulers claimed overseas territories. Some empires had existed, in varied configurations, for centuries, while others, such as the German, Italian and Japanese overseas empires, were recent acquisitions but, their leaders hoped, were destined for eternity. If, as Jane Burbank and Frederick Cooper have remarked, most polities in world history could be seen as empires, so too most, even in the early 1900s, were monarchies.[5]

In fact, by the late 1800s, having an empire appeared to be a necessity for a country to achieve great-power status, whence the expansionism of newly unified Germany and Italy and renascent Japan, and the aspirational expansion of the King of the Belgians. Having a monarch was also a sign of being a 'proper' country, as shown with the appointment of kings (often in the first instance German princes, some of whom were relatively poor with little if any remaining territory of their own) for such European countries that gained independence in the nineteenth century as Greece, Belgium, Romania and Bulgaria. Even after the turn of the century, new dynasties assumed thrones in Norway, Yugoslavia and, as late as 1928, Albania. The republicanism of France, Switzerland, San Marino, the USA and the countries of Central and South America (though both Mexico and Brazil episodically had emperors and several European monarchies still held territory in the Americas) was an anomaly, though it is noteworthy that all of the American republics had emerged from colonial wars of independence. In short, colonies were, for the most part, the territories of monarchical states. A monarch was not necessary for colonial rule, as the cases of France and the USA and their overseas domains prove, as does the continued existence of overseas empires after the end of the Portuguese monarchy, but monarchism was the more usual form of rule at home, in Europe and elsewhere, and in the colonial empires.

Monarchism, in some ways, sat well with imperialism. A monarch's power spread to the moving frontiers of his or her realm, wherever they might be, and kingship easily allowed for diverse vassal states to exist under the Crown, so long as their rulers and subjects pledged fealty to the paramount ruler. There were antecedents to early modern European royal houses ruling empires overseas. In the twelfth and thirteenth centuries, for example, the French Lusignan family expanded its territorial control beyond parts of France and England to include the kingdoms of Jerusalem, Cyprus and Cilicia. A monarch could pose as a central figure unifying disparate peoples and lands, a personage above internecine political debates, ethnic clashes and cultural quarrels. Mongol, Mughal and later Ottoman rulers built multi-ethnic empires whose wide geographical reach and long-term success was due, at least partly, to the emperor's central power being balanced by a general toleration of diverse religious and cultural practices.[6] Even when constitutional monarchies had replaced absolutist ones, the sovereign retained the presence of a demigod, sometimes anointed (in the Western tradition) with sacramental oils or blessed with the mandate of Heaven and thus holding a sacral position recognisable to many in Africa, Asia and Oceania. The wealth, and the pomp and pageantry, of monarchy projected the primacy and potency of the sovereign. Monarchs were international celebrities heralded in proclamations and newspapers (and later in newsreels). Subjects in those countries of Europe and elsewhere that remained largely hierarchical and deferential, as most societies were, bent their knees to majesties and royal highnesses. The presidents of France or the USA might find it awkward to square the circle of absolute rule overseas with the principles of liberty, equality and fraternity, or the precepts of Bills of Rights, at home. Without the encumbrances of republicanism, colonial monarchs faced fewer contradictions between their rule at home and abroad, even though such critics as J. A. Hobson pointed out the differences between what the British proclaimed for British subjects at home (and whites in the Empire) and native subjects abroad.[7]

The success of rule at home often had important implications for monarchs' rule overseas. It is perhaps not coincidental that when the German Kaiser, the Ottoman Sultan and the Habsburg Emperor lost the First World War, they also lost their thrones and their continental and overseas empires, as did the Italian King after the Second World War. Crowns and colonies went together – but not always. The Portuguese kept their empire after overthrowing their king in 1910; the Japanese lost their empire, but the Emperor kept his throne in 1945. After the Bolshevik revolution, and the murder of the Tsar, the Soviets nevertheless effectively reconstituted the old tsarist empire (though it disaggregated with the disintegration of the Communist system), while the Chinese Communists have held on to the old Qing Empire (minus Taiwan). Thrones might survive, but extensive colonial empires were less liable to do so.[8] Decolonisation deprived the Belgian King of his domain in central Africa, Belgium's only true colony, in 1960, and the Dutch Queen lost the vast East Indies in the 1940s and Suriname in the 1970s. King Juan Carlos, after Spanish withdrawal from north-west Africa in the transition from Francoism, inherited only two enclaves in Morocco (as well as Spain's oldest colony, the Canary Islands), and King Felipe still rules over those two Mediterranean cities, Ceuta and Melilla, standing opposite British Gibraltar. The Danish monarch continues to rule over largely autonomous Greenland and the Faeroe Islands, and the Dutch King rules over six island territories in the Caribbean Sea. The British Queen reigns over fourteen British 'overseas territories' – from Anguilla in the Caribbean to St Helena in the Atlantic and minuscule Pitcairn in the Pacific.[9] She is also Head of State of sixteen states in addition to the United Kingdom (and she was Head of State of several other decolonised states that have now become republics). Queen Elizabeth II is also Head of the Commonwealth, nominally presiding over an association that encompasses most of Britain's former colonies.

The chronicle of the links between monarchies and overseas empires is, thus, a long and complex history, extending from the *prises de possession* of new territories in the Americas under European monarchs in the late 1400s and early 1500s down to ongoing rule, in name, over residual colonial possessions around the world. This volume explores some of the dimensions of the relationship between European monarchies and their overseas empires. It does not claim to be a comprehensive examination of those multiple connections over many centuries and around the colonised world. Rather, it provides, through a series of individual case studies, analysis of the major themes that shaped this relationship. These include the often difficult but always dominant relationship between European monarchs and indigenous rulers, questions about what royal rule actually meant in the Empire and how the position and power of the Crown changed over time and place, the strategies by which that royal rule was imprinted on the colonies, the personal links between monarchs and their overseas domains (including the increasingly important phenomenon of royal tours) and questions about the place of 'imperial crowns' today and in the future. The chapters consider a wide range of source material, including traditional diplomatic correspondence and official speeches, private diary entries, loyal addresses, gifts (painted and photographic portraits, local craft items such as East Indian *kris* [daggers] and betel-nut sets), urban decorations such as illuminated transparency pictures and gas-lit symbols, and royal regalia such as crowns, thrones and jewellery, as well as newspapers and woodcut engravings from illustrated periodicals. Collectively, the sources demonstrate that crowns and colonies mattered not just to elites but to ordinary people too, although their relevance was by no means static and attitudes could and did change sharply over time.

Colonial and indigenous rulers

As their soldiers conquered overseas domains, European sovereigns came into conflict with other, indigenous rulers – kings, maharajahs, sultans, emirs, chieftains – who almost always owed their positions to inheritance or conquest (and in the latter case, with the intention of passing their positions on to their scions). Some of the local rulers were killed, either in battle or in summary executions: Moctezuma in Spanish America is a prime example. Others who resisted colonial incursions were deposed, the invaders replacing them with more pliable rulers. Alternatively, indigenous dynasties were abolished, as, for example, by the British in Ceylon in 1815, India in 1858 and Burma in 1885. When they left dynasties in place, the colonialists worked by cooperation and coercion to transform rulers into loyal feudatories. Such emoluments as recognition of traditional legal and religious prerogatives, the budgeting of privy purses, the giving of gun salutes – the number carefully calculated to reflect the perceived grandeur and loyalty of each prince – and the awarding of royal honours helped draw many of the Indian princes into the British orbit. Some, however, proved recalcitrant, and the British did not hesitate to depose those they considered inconvenient, such as the rulers of Punjab and the maharajahs of Baroda and Indore.[10] Colonists could also virtually create new monarchies, promoting local and not-so-local figures to kingship over extended areas demarcated by the foreigners, as occurred notably when the British extended recognition to the King of Bhutan in 1907.[11] As Matthieu Rey's chapter in this collection shows, the British were also largely responsible for the creation of modern Iraq and the institution of a foreign (Hashemite) monarchy there after the First World War. And the French promoted the ruler of Luang Prabang to be the King of Laos.[12] In protectorates (as opposed to formal colonies), ranging from Morocco and Tunisia, Vietnam, Cambodia and Laos under French control to the Indian princely states, Malay sultanates and

African chiefdoms under British overlordship, local rulers continued to reign, though they ruled only under the watchful eye and interventionist hand of the colonial masters. Here formal and informal European agents played an important role in both advising local rulers and reporting on their behaviour to imperial authorities.[13]

However, the relationship between colonial and indigenous rulers and peoples is far from straightforward. In the early modern Americas, European armies overran and largely annihilated local polities, including the empires of the Incas and Aztecs, marginalising local populations through the establishment of European settlements. In Asia, however, the situation was different. There, 'courtly encounters', as Sanjay Subrahmanyan puts it, lay at the heart of European and non-European relations.[14] European monarchs delegated their powers to commissioned captains and chartered companies, but the balance of power between indigenous and foreign rulers, especially in the early periods of European expansion, was often weighted in favour of the indigenous rulers: the French King, Louis XIV, sent an embassy to the court of the Siamese King in Ayutthaya; the Dutch paid court to East Indian sultans; and the British (and others) sought advantages from Indian princes who could accord them trading rights, territorial concessions and prized commodities. Many of the Asian rulers, notably the Chinese Emperor, carefully weighed up the disadvantages as well as advantages of engaging in Western trade and remained mindful of the political as well as economic challenges posed by Europeans. As a result, European maritime trade with China was restricted for much of the early modern period to a single port, Canton (Guangzhou). More drastically, the Japanese Shogun, on behalf of the Emperor, confined the Dutch – for over two centuries the only Europeans allowed to trade in Japan – to the tiny artificial island of Dejima just off Nagasaki. For centuries, Asian 'potentates' addressed the Europeans as their equals (or inferiors), bargained for armaments and other supplies in return for the spices or silks that the Europeans so coveted, deftly and successfully played off one European group against another, and alternately welcomed and rebuffed foreign traders and missionaries.[15]

Even after the Europeans had secured colonial authority, local rulers – even some of the subjugated elites in the Americas – often maintained a considerable degree of their customary power and status, representing traditional culture in the eyes of their erstwhile subjects, continuing to manoeuvre and negotiate with the new colonial masters. The colonial rulers overseas might 'hollow out' local crowns, depriving surviving dynasts of much of their real power, but this was not true everywhere.[16] In cases of indirect rule, European overlords could delegate powers to indigenous rulers and make them into intermediaries between imperial authorities and the masses of local people. Many still commanded the loyalty of their 'native' subjects, and displacement of indigenous sovereigns ran the risk of sparking campaigns of resistance or movements of royalist restoration. In Burma, for example, the surviving members of the royal family continued to be viewed with enormous veneration by local people, and their thrones and other accoutrements of royal status maintained their symbolic power long after the British sent the monarch into exile and the palace treasures were dispersed.[17] Other local rulers became the trustworthy feudatories of which the Europeans hoped to take advantage, eventually serving (as in the case of the Indian princes) as a counterweight to nationalists.[18]

The relationship between settler populations and distant monarchs could also be complex. While professing their loyalty, settlers regularly chafed at colonial administration, yearning both for the protection provided by 'mother countries' and for ever greater degrees of self-government. This led to the severance of imperial connection in campaigns by the descendants of settlers, of course, in the USA and the Latin American states, but moves for autonomy by settler groups were endemic. Certain expatriate populations, such as some Irish in the British Empire, nursed ancestral opposition to monarchs who governed them, and the Boers submitted to overarching British rule in South Africa only after their military defeat. Like indigenous groups, imported populations – slaves, indentured labourers, convicts – did not all have good reason to cheer the monarchs who reigned over them, and republican and anti-colonial groups found fertile soil throughout the empires.[19] Yet a surprising number of diverse colonial groups nevertheless supported European monarchs. Many Irish Catholics in Australia cheered Queen Victoria's son Alfred on his tour of 1867–68, just as Boers had cheered him in South Africa. As well, African, Malay, Indian and Chinese groups welcomed him as a representative of his mother, who was widely revered as a monarch who cared for all of her 'children' throughout the British Empire. As late as 1947, the visit of the royal family to South Africa was welcomed by black African groups keen to assert their political rights.[20] As Charles Reed points out, educated and progressive men of colour in British colonies often seized upon royal tours as an opportunity to advance their community's claims for greater political participation.[21] Indigenous people in particular turned to Queen Victoria, who never toured her colonies, to communicate their disadvantage and seek redress from the wrongs wrought by colonial administrations.[22] They also used the figure of the monarch to display themselves. In West Africa, for example, the creation of carved wooden portrait figures of Queen Victoria appears to reflect both loyalty to the Queen as well as pride in Aku (and, in particular, Aku women's) identity (see Figure 2).[23]

Royal tours could also showcase local discontent with imperial rule. Gandhi's non-cooperation movement gained further international attention during the Prince of Wales's 1921 tour of India, when, as occurred in Allahabad and several other Indian cities, the Prince was greeted not by cheering crowds but by virtually no one. As Chandrika Kaul points out, royal tours could consolidate existing loyalty, but they could not create it when it was absent – or contested.[24]

As the apex of colonial structures, the European monarchs thus occupied complex positions vis-à-vis indigenous rulers and their subjects. Some indigenous rulers were incorporated into the power structures (albeit with limited powers) and rewarded. Most of the Indian princes and sultans in the East Indies (with the notable exception of the Sultan of Yogyakarta) remained loyal to the paramount colonial

2. Sculpture in wood representing Queen Victoria, by an unidentified West African artist, probably late nineteenth century. © Pitt Rivers Museum, University of Oxford (1965.10.1). Reproduced with permission

rulers. Jean Gelman Taylor's chapter in this book shows the respectful connections between the Dutch rulers and the East Indian sultans and rajahs. When successful, this formed a client network of what Colin Newbury refers to as 'chieftaincy and over-rule' in the empire.[25] Those who were not so cooperative were disposed of; Lord Curzon during his tenure as Viceroy of India deposed fifteen princes, generally on grounds of maladministration. Chieftains in Africa, such as the Asante King, and Oceania (the King of Samoa) were assimilated into colonial power structures, though there, too, obedience was expected.[26] Resistance could be punished severely. As Richard Price notes, in southern Africa, the British (or their auxiliaries) hunted down and eventually imprisoned or killed many of the amaXhosa chiefs who had fought them for decades on the Eastern Cape frontier, as well as their old enemy the Zulu King, Cetshwayo.[27]

Royal powers and prerogatives

The exact role of the Crown in colonies is a complicated and confusing issue. New territories might be possessed in the name of a king or queen, but such pronouncements did not clarify what the status of the new domains would be, what prerogatives the monarch would have or how administration would be exercised. Theories, laws and institutions of colonial governance changed markedly over time and place, not surprisingly so, considering the chronological and geographical breadth of empires. The early modern Spanish empire, as a case in point, was part of a 'composite monarchy' in which the monarch, at the time of the Spanish Habsburgs, ruled over Spain, the Netherlands, parts of Italy and parts of eastern Europe as well as a vast American empire. In addition, Charles V was elected Holy Roman Emperor in 1519. Charles V royally stated that 'we are lord [señor] of the West Indies, Islands and mainland of the Ocean Sea, both discovered and to be discovered, and they are incorporated into our Royal Crown of Castile'. According to a papal bull of 1493, the territories conquered overseas were 'united with and incorporated into the Crown of Castile and León', which, as J. H. Elliott notes, technically made the colonies a Castilian empire of monarchs who were also the kings of Aragon on the Spanish peninsula. Occasionally, the ruler was referred to, though not officially, as 'Emperor of the Indies' or 'Emperor of America'. Territories that the Spanish sovereign had gained by inheritance or marriage were treated on an equal footing as the Spanish domains, but those that had come under his rule by conquest were ruled by separate laws. Yet, according to decrees from the Spanish Junta in 1809, 'the vast and precious dominions which Spain possesses in the Indies are not properly colonies ... but an essential and integral part of the Spanish Monarchy', and thus were allowed to send deputies to the Junta assembly – though those 'Indies' colonies would not remain in Spanish hands for much longer.[28] Indeed, in colonial Mexico, Spanish viceroys deliberately fashioned themselves in the image of the King, employing the symbolism of monarchy to cement their imperial authority.[29] In India, too, British viceroys deployed royal pageantry to underscore their role as representatives of the monarch. At times, though, individual viceroys represented themselves as quasi-monarchs to further their own glory, as when Lord Curzon attempted in Delhi in 1903 to 'crown himself a virtual Maharaja', eight years before George V's coronation as King-Emperor at a similar durbar on the same spot.[30]

François-Joseph Ruggiu's contribution to this volume shows the changing and unclear relationship between the French Crown of the *ancien régime* and France's overseas domains, with a king who was sovereign but who delegated administration through letters patent to governors, *intendants* and chartered companies. Similarly in the case of the British and Dutch empires, until the 1800s much imperial rule was subcontracted to East and West Indies companies, though the way they exercised their rights, as was exposed in the Hastings trial in Britain in the late 1700s, often created controversy. In later manifestations of Empire, the rights of the Crown continued to be uncertain. Matthew P. Fitzpatrick shows here how constitutional law in Wilhelmine Germany was less than crystal clear about whether the colonies were an integral part of Germany and what prerogatives the Kaiser might retain, and events in Africa in the early years of the twentieth century would show that he might or might not use those powers even against the advice of the government. Still later, as Alessandro Pes demonstrates in his chapter, although Mussolini had Vittorio Emanuele III grandly proclaimed Emperor of Italian East Africa, in practice, the Italian Fascist government overshadowed the monarchy in the colonies even when a member of the royal family was appointed Governor-General of Abyssinia. The complexities of monarchy and colonialism, and of the sometimes surprising siting of real and ceremonial power, may be illustrated through the example of early nineteenth-century Brazil. The Portuguese Prince Regent, threatened by the advance of Napoleon's armies in 1807, decamped from Lisbon to Rio de Janeiro, turned a colonial capital into a royal court and, for over a decade, ruled a European state's empire from a colonial seat in South America.[31]

The question of the sovereign's rights continued to engage politicians and constitutional lawyers – imperialists as well as anti-colonial activists – right through the history of decolonisation, though after the 1940s this was primarily a preoccupation of the British. The exact role of the British monarch (ex-emperor), and his governor-general (ex-viceroy) in India and Sri Lanka continued to animate discussions in the last years of Empire and afterwards.[32] Such real or ceremonial royal rights as assenting to legislation, accrediting ambassadors, awarding decorations, naming the holders of certain offices, convening and proroguing parliaments were all at issue. The monarch, through a governor or governor-general, continued to possess 'reserve powers', exercised almost always on the advice of an elected local government. But the dismissal by the Governor-General of the Whitlam government in Australia in 1975 created both a constitutional crisis and rising antipathy to the monarchy and in particular its representative in Australia – though, as it turned out, the Governor-General in Canberra had made no approach to Buckingham Palace for advice before he dismissed Prime Minister Gough Whitlam. The viceregal assent to legislation in Commonwealth countries where the Queen remains Head of State constitutes one of the abiding prerogatives of the monarchy, though almost never exercised in person. Even the question of continued awarding of imperial honours – the knighthoods so prized by many in the colonies – has occasionally flared up, as when the Australian Prime Minister Tony Abbott, who had recently revived the dormant practice of awarding knighthoods, was ridiculed in 2015 for successfully proposing that the Duke of Edinburgh be made a Knight of the Order of Australia.

Such incidents may appear tempests in imperial teacups, but they point not only to continuing connections between some European monarchies and far-flung domains but also to the issue of the extent of Crown rights, an issue that is particularly pertinent in countries such as Australia and New Zealand. In Australia, Aboriginal demands for land rights have partly turned on the question of colonial appropriation of land in the name of the Crown.[33] In New Zealand, as Vincent O'Malley shows in his chapter in this volume, the fact that a treaty was signed between the Crown and the Maori has created a special bond between the British monarch and the indigenous population, and has inflected discussions about the place of Maori in New Zealand public life.

The constitutional role of the monarch has been a key part in the history of colonial takeovers and decolonisation. Two chapters in this collection illustrate that centrality in Australia. Bruce Baskerville, examining the history of the Great Seal of New South Wales, explores a still debated question of whether the Crown is 'divisible' – whether the monarch ruled over one realm or many, and to what extent Crown powers and prerogatives applied uniformly – with particular reference to a mutiny against royal authority in early colonial Sydney. Mark

McKenna, looking at the Australian (as well as Canadian and New Zealand) debates pitting proponents of a constitutional monarchy against republicans in recent decades, considers the various rationales employed for retaining or dispensing with the Crown in present-day Australia, with arguments ranging from residual cultural and affective attachment to the throne to ones justifying or contesting the legal powers reserved to the monarch and her representative. McKenna argues that one of the reasons for Australia keeping the monarchy is that, ironically, in many ways it has become 'irrelevant' to national life. By contrast, Baskerville reveals the complex meanings the symbols of monarchy held at an earlier time for two opposing groups of British settlers on the Australian continent.

The fate of the monarchy in decolonised countries, however, was not just an issue for British settler societies. Indeed, as H. Kumarasingham demonstrates in his chapter, intense debates took place in both Britain and India in 1947–49 concerning a variety of possible post-Independence roles for the Crown in the subcontinent. These discussions reveal competing ambitions for a post-imperial monarchy. India's decision to become a republic and its desire still to remain in the Commonwealth meant that the British monarchy had to adapt in order to survive as a unifying symbol within the Commonwealth.

India became a republic in 1950, only three years after independence, although other ex-colonies retained the monarchy for far longer periods. The Queen continued to reign as head of state in Ceylon from its independence in 1948 until 1972, when a republic was declared and the name of the country changed to Sri Lanka, and Mauritius became a republic only in 1992, twenty-four years after independence. Various other former colonies also became republics at some point after independence, though local political dynamics generally determined the change, and there is no clear pattern in chronology or ideology. The remaining independent countries that recognise the Queen as head of state are either the old settler dominions or islands or territorial enclaves in the West Indies and South Pacific. Indeed, in 2009, St Vincent and the Grenadines rejected republicanism through a referendum. In the present-day Commonwealth, republics far outnumber the 'Commonwealth realms' of which the Queen is individually head of state; adding complexity to the post-imperial federation is the fact that Brunei, Lesotho and Swaziland have hereditary monarchs of their own, and there is an elected king of Malaysia. The Queen's position as Head of the Commonwealth – with the monarch also serving as head of state for some of the member countries – is nevertheless an anomaly in post-imperial politics. No other colonial-era monarch remains head of state of any of that country's former colonies.

Royals in the colonies

Royal power imprinted itself on the colonies in numerous symbolic ways. In the case of the British, Edwin Lutyens' grand Raj capital of New Delhi formed a stage for the performance of what Jan Morris has called the 'theatre of empire', and the Gateway to India in Bombay (Mumbai) was erected as the triumphal arch for the arrival of the King-Emperor in 1911.[34] Majestic Government Houses and viceregal lodges rose all around the British Empire, and statues of Queen Victoria and later sovereigns stood in public squares. The royal cipher adorned structures from monumental government secretaries' buildings to modest postboxes. British governors overseas flew customised flags in their role as representatives of the Crown, and both colonists and indigenous people rose to their feet for 'God Save the King'. The monarch's face appeared on local currency and stamps, and war memorials were put up to commemorate soldiers who had died 'for King and Country'. The monarch's birthday was celebrated with fanfare, and loyalty toasts were drunk to the sovereign. In the name of the King, laws were proclaimed and honours awarded. The monarch created orders and decorations – the Order of St Michael and St George, the Order of the British Empire, the Order of the Star of India, the Order of the Indian Empire – to honour worthy settlers and natives, the sashes, badges and certificates visible signifiers of royal acknowledgement for loyal service; occasionally, the monarch elevated a colonial to the peerage. The monarchy was thus visible and knowable in empires – indeed, the manifestations of the monarchy were vital tools of both imperial propaganda and colonial policy.

The iconography of monarchy in the colonies – and, of course, the parallel imagery employed by non-royal states – provided a way to reaffirm both imperial paramountcy and the personal role of a sovereign. Walter Bagehot noted in the 1860s that the British monarch was 'at the head of the pageant of life'. So too, as David Cannadine has remarked, pageantry was an integral part of Empire.[35] Seeing the face of a sovereign on a coin or a bust, even on a fly-bill or advertisement, reminded Europeans in the colonies and the colonised themselves of connections with a faraway figure who was said to be law-giver, guarantor of national unity and integrity and protector of native peoples. Yet it is worth noting that many of the most spectacular demonstrations of monarchical power and imperial rule took place during periods of growing resistance to Empire both in the colonies and at home. One way rulers attempted to downplay nationalist claims for independence was to reassert imperial splendour – even, and sometimes most fervently, at the end of Empire. This is perhaps most obvious in British India, where, for example, the splendid new imperial capital, New Delhi, was completed just, as the architectural historian Nikolaus Pevsner noted, 'five minutes before closing time'.[36]

The relationship between individual monarchs and their colonies was varied. Kaiser Wilhelm II was little interested in or concerned by colonies, happy almost to ignore them unless they sparked some troubling incident. Napoleon III, by contrast, as Emmanuelle Guenot details in her chapter, had a deep interest in extending France's colonial empire, in sponsoring grand public works projects in the colonies and in imagining himself as the head of an 'Arab kingdom' in North Africa. King Leopold II of the Belgians made colonialism his own personal project, contracting Henry Morton Stanley to scout out territory in central Africa and setting up the International African Association. In 1885, Leopold II established the Congo Free State, with himself as Head of State, a domain over seventy times the size of Belgium; he essentially ran the Congo in a bout of megalomania as a private colony, relinquishing it to the Belgian state only in 1908 after an international scandal about the brutalities of concessionary companies and maladministration by the King's functionaries.[37] As Miles Taylor demonstrates in his chapter, from the late eighteenth century, British monarchs were far more involved with their colonies than the existing historiography suggests. Queen Victoria gloried in the title of Empress of India, which was created for her in 1876, and she devoted much attention to imperial affairs, especially, as Taylor notes, in the areas of church and military appointments and in her concern for indigenous peoples and their rulers. Her personal interest may be indicated through a few examples here: her attachment to her *munshi* (Indian servant) Abdul Karim, her fondness for the deposed Sikh Maharajah, Duleep Singh, her attempts to learn Hindi, her collection of imperial *objets d'art*, her serving as godmother to the daughter of the exiled Maharajah of Coorg.[38] It is indeed almost impossible to see Victoria without her empire, to separate her reign from Britain's imperial heyday.

Monarchs engaged with colonies in various ways and to differing degrees, and one of the most significant was royal tours. In early modern history, European monarchs never braved the dangerous voyages to their distant possessions, and, somewhat curiously, a reigning Dutch monarch never visited a Dutch colony, even during the later stages of the Empire. Queen Victoria never journeyed to the Empire either, but she did dispatch her sons and grandsons on royal tours, as Cindy McCreery shows here in her chapter on the global tour of Prince Alfred in the 1860s, one of the first examples of such an imperial royal progress. Napoleon III twice went to Algeria (in 1860 and 1865); the first

Belgian royal, Prince (later King) Albert visited the Congo in 1909; and the Italian King, Vittorio Emanuele III, visited Somalia in 1934 and Libya in 1938.[39] The British tours were especially important in displaying monarchy in the colonies, and time and again British royals went on the road to visit the sovereign's domains. From the 1860s until it became independent in 1947, there were eleven visits by members of the royal family to Ceylon, and then Queen Elizabeth II herself arrived in 1954 as part of a grand tour of her empire just after the coronation.

Colonial tours presented an opportunity for members of the royal family to preside at festivities, to open parliaments, to meet their subjects, to familiarise themselves with colonial life – and for the men, usually to engage in some big-game hunting. Their travels were increasingly followed by huge audiences at home, in the colonies and, via press reports, around the world. Certainly one of the most splendid occasions of British imperial rule was the grand durbar of 1911, at which King George V, accompanied by Queen Mary, crowned himself Emperor of India and accepted formal acknowledgements of fealty proffered by dozens of Indian princes (see Figure 3).[40]

Such manifestations of the monarchy gave to residents of the colonies – settlers, migrants and indigenous people – the chance to see a

3. Postcard c. 1911, 'Coronation Durbar, Delhi. The King-Emperor and Queen-Empress presenting themselves to their people' Ernest Brooks, photographer. 690.P. Beagles postcards, collection of Robert Aldrich

royal, or better yet a sovereign, in person or at least to know that the monarch, or a member of the monarch's family, was treading the soil of their country. Gazed on as celebrities, followed with near religious devotion, fêted in public ceremonies, by their visits even minor royals were thought to embody and strengthen the personal bonds between the monarchs and the subjects of the sovereign. Even when colonies became republics, as many African and Asian colonies of Britain did in the post-war period, minor royals remained valuable dignitaries to preside over independence ceremonies.[41] During the colonial era, no greater occasion could be choreographed for the manifestation of the Crown than a royal visit or a grand viceregal ceremony. Yet local responses were multifaceted. Royal tours also provided opportunities for local civic groups to show off their town, city, colony and, above all, themselves, to outshine their neighbours and rivals, and even, on occasion, the monarch. In 1867–68, for example, the Australian colony of Victoria prioritised representations of itself before those of the visiting Prince Alfred – or, indeed, Queen Victoria.

Moreover, travel took place along a two-way street. The occasional exotic prince had appeared at a European court in early modern history – a Vietnamese prince was brought to the court of Louis XVI in 1787, for instance – but from the late nineteenth century a procession of non-Western royals visited Europe. As Jean Gelman Taylor shows in her chapter, East Indian princes journeyed to the Netherlands and were warmly welcomed at the royal court. They often bore elaborate gifts for the Dutch monarch and members of the royal family, gifts that were reciprocated with presents for the East Indian sultans. Here was not only an example of ritual gift-giving and the expression of loyalty but also the affirmation of the status of the East Indian rulers as royals in their own right, figures of historic legitimacy, recognised authority and spiritual and social power. Maharajahs, among other colonial royals, meanwhile came to Britain, occasionally in exile, sometimes as diplomats or students, frequently on grand tours to the imperial capital and visitors to the sights of Europe.[42] Maharanis came too. Jim Masselos here offers a case study of one princely Indian figure, the Maharani of Kutch, whose life moved between several worlds: India and Britain, princely state and independent republic, the segregated world of female purdah as well as mixed public life.

Objects as well as people moved between metropoles and colonies, including the Great Seals discussed by Baskerville and the Indonesian gifts explored by Taylor. Susie Protschky gives another example of an object that testifies to connections between monarchs and colonies, the elaborate letters of felicitation (*oorkonden*) sent by descendants of Dutch migrants to South Africa to the Dutch Queen on such occasions as her birthday, jubilee or the birth or christening of an heir to the throne. Such letters witness, too, the residual identification between the Afrikaners and the land of their ancestors through the person of the Queen. In yet another example of material objects, Robert Aldrich traces the history of the regalia of the King of Kandy, the symbols of a deposed king in Ceylon captured as booty by the British in 1815, taken to Britain and ultimately returned to Ceylon in the 1930s, the restitution a marker both of the proclaimed generosity of the British monarch to his loyal subjects and the signifier, for some in Ceylon, of a budding nationalist identity.

During the late nineteenth and early twentieth centuries, the age of modern empires and monarchies, there was a rising current of republicanism in many European countries, evidenced most clearly by the overthrow of Napoleon III in France in 1870 and the King of Portugal in 1910. Republican movements also existed in the colonies; in the case of the British realm, not only most dramatically in Ireland, but also in such dominions as Australia, though there they generally gained the support only of small minorities of the population.[43] In India, however, republicanism was supported by prominent nationalists such as Jawaharlal Nehru in the 1920s as a way to escape British influence, while in the French mandate of Syria, nationalists campaigned for the same form of government – an independent republic – as existed in the 'mother country'. Republican movements targeted, as well, the 'puppet' monarchs retained in power by colonial authorities, as was the case for many Vietnamese protesting against the 'feudal' powers and privileges (though they had been severely reduced since the French takeover) of the Emperor of Annam. In particular, radical movements, such as the Communist parties that were set up in many colonies by the 1930s, were resolutely anti-monarchical in orientation.

Nationalist campaigns in the colonies did not always aim at full independence but sometimes had as their objective self-rule or home government.[44] Anti-colonialism and decolonisation also did not mean the end of all the indigenous royal houses over which 'paramount' colonial powers had ruled. Some feudatories retained their thrones after the imperialists departed, such as King Sihanouk in Cambodia (who would be on and off the throne for decades afterwards), the King of Laos (until a *coup d'état* in 1975) and the King of Tonga. The Sultan of Morocco became its king when that country gained independence from France. Haile Selassie, Emperor of Ethiopia, was forced into exile by the Italians in 1936, then returned to his throne after Ethiopian nationalists and Allied forces defeated Fascist Italy on the Horn of Africa; he remained ruler until overthrown in a coup in 1974. 'Sub-national' monarchies remained in power in many of the former colonies. They include, notably, the emirs of the Gulf states and the nine hereditary sultans of what is now Malaysia, one of whom is elected, on a rotating basis, for a five-year term as head of state. In sub-Saharan Africa, traditional regional rulers, such as those in Nigeria and Uganda, and such other figures as the paramount Zulu chief in South Africa, retain official or quasi-official positions. As Jean Gelman Taylor points out here, the Sultan of Yogyakarta is hereditarily the governor of that province of independent republican Indonesia. Although Prime Minister Indira Gandhi deprived the Indian princes of their official titles and privy purses in 1971, the maharajahs and other princes, such as the traditional Maharana of Udaipur, who now styles himself the 'Custodian' of the House of Mewar in Rajasthan, retain wealth, influence and celebrity; in 2015, a twenty-three-year-old economics graduate was thus installed as the most recent Maharajah of Mysore.

There have also been ongoing links between royal figures, ex-viceroys and former colonies. Lord (Louis) Mountbatten, as the last Viceroy of British India and the first Governor-General of independent India, as well as uncle of the Duke of Edinburgh and a close friend of Queen Elizabeth, spanned both official and royal circles. His subsequent involvement as a mediator between the Indian and British governments from the late 1940s until the mid-1960s demonstrates the importance of personal relationships in fostering good relations between former colonies and ex-imperial powers. When these personal relationships ended, however, as with the death in 1964 of Mountbatten's old ally the Indian Prime Minister Jawaharlal Nehru, so did much of the influence of the old guard.[45]

Conclusion

For longer or shorter spans of time, many European monarchies were imperial monarchies, their sovereigns ruling over disparate and distant possessions, in the case of the British stretching from Great Britain and next-door Ireland to islands on the other side of the globe. The sovereign stood at the centre of an imperial nexus, for it was in the name of the sovereign that territories were claimed and colonies were ruled. The sovereign was everywhere visible – in names affixed to laws and decrees issued on viceregal authority, on coinage and in stamps, in triumphal arches and illuminated transparency decorations erected for royal tours and in the grandeur of colonial capitals. Even in the absence of a sovereign on colonial soil, this was, however, a real presence. Despite their diminishing authority in a modernising and more democratic Europe, through the colonial age, monarchs were far from devoid of real and symbolic power. For Bagehot, the monarch remained 'a visible symbol of unity'.[46] Queen Elizabeth II's words to the Commonwealth after her coronation in 1953, quoted earlier, struck a chord, either harmonious or dissonant, with leaders increasingly less willing to accept the verities of the colonial order. By the time Elizabeth became queen, the monarchs of Italy and Germany (and Japan) had no remaining colonies, the Dutch Queen had lost the 'emerald necklace' of the Indonesian islands, the last formal ties between Iceland and the Danish Queen had been severed, the Belgian King had only seven more years of tenure as an imperial ruler in Africa, and Portugal's colonies had no king though it would take another twenty years for those colonies to gain independence. In the colonial period, monarchs mattered to colonies. Colonies also mattered to monarchs, giving them status, international power and, at least in principle, the fealty of subjects. There were also material rewards. It was perhaps not coincidental that the great 105 carat Koh-i-noor diamond, taken from Maharajah Duleep Singh of the Punjab, was incorporated into the crown worn by the consorts of Edward VII, George V and George VI. The beginning of European overseas imperialism in the late 1400s and early 1500s was, through no coincidence, connected to the rise of absolutist, unified monarchies in Europe – the royal *reconquista* in mainland Spain leading the way for the work of the *conquistadores* overseas, the establishment of empires in the Americas and Asia under the aegis of the powerful Tudor and Stuart monarchs in newly unified Britain, the carving out of 'New France' preparing the way for the absolutist monarchy of the Bourbons, the expansion of Portugal mirroring the interests and ambitions of Prince Henry 'the Navigator' and the Manueline dynasty, the trade of the Dutch East India Company providing the wealth and gravitas of the *stadhouder* of Holland. Some of the overseas empires survived the tumult of the late eighteenth century, but new monarchs also wanted their colonies – Napoleon I's thwarted conquest of Egypt, Charles X's takeover of Algiers and Napoleon III's subsequent colonial manoeuvres in western Africa, the southern Pacific and Indochina were all signs of the international aspirations of the monarchs. Still later, the Kaiser of a unified Germany and the King of a united Italy jousted for their share of the colonial spoils.

The end of empire did not exactly coincide with the end of European monarchies, as the reach of Queen Elizabeth II's imperial mantle shows. However, it is perhaps not coincidental that there was a coalescence in the dual mid-twentieth-century phenomena of anti-colonial nationalism and the critique of monarchy as a dynastic form of government over a multitude of far-flung, subjected peoples. Both thrones and empires had seen their better days.

Notes

1 *Crown and Empire: The Coronation of King George VI, May 12, 1937* (London: Times Publishing Co., 1937).
2 *King George VI Coronation Souvenir: India's Tribute to the King-Emperor* (Calcutta: Art Press, 1937).
3 Christopher Lloyd, *Ceremony and Celebration: Coronation Day 1953* (London: Royal Collection, 2003).
4 *Penang Settlement: Coronation Celebrations – Official Souvenir Programme* (Penang: Settlement Coronation Celebrations Committee, 1954).
5 Jane Burbank and Frederick Cooper, *Empires in World History: Power and the Politics of Difference* (Princeton, NJ: Princeton University Press, 2010).
6 Jim Masselos (ed.), *The Great Empires of Asia* (London: Thames & Hudson, 2010).
7 J. A. Hobson, *Imperialism: A Study* (New York: Gordon Press, 1975), pp. 6–7. First published 1902.
8 See Peter Conradi, *The Great Survivors: How Monarchy Made it into the Twenty-First Century* (Richmond: Alma, 2012); A. W. Purdue, *Long to Reign? The Survival of Monarchies in the Modern World* (Stroud: Sutton, 2005); and Roger Kershaw, *Monarchy in South-East Asia: The Faces of Tradition in Transition* (London and New York: Routledge, 2001).
9 Robert Aldrich and John Connell, *The Last Colonies* (Cambridge: Cambridge University Press, 1998).
10 Caroline Keen, *Princely India and the British: Political Development and the Operation of Empire* (London: I. B. Tauris, 2013).
11 Michael Aris, *The Raven Crown: The Origins of Buddhist Monarchy in Bhutan* (Chicago, Ill.: University of Chicago Press, 1994).
12 Grant Evans, *The Last Century of Lao Royalty: A Documentary History* (Chiang Mai: Silkworm Books, 2009).
13 Richard Price, *Making Empire: Colonial Encounters and the Creation of Imperial Rule in Nineteenth-Century Africa* (Cambridge: Cambridge University Press, 2008).
14 Sanjay Subrahmanyam, *Courtly Encounters: Translating Courtliness and Violence in Early Modern Eurasia* (Cambridge, Mass.: Harvard University Press, 2012).
15 See, among other works, Gang Zhao, *Qing Opening to the Ocean: Chinese Maritime Policies, 1684–1757* (Honolulu, HI: University of Hawai'i Press, 2013); John E. Wills, Jr. (ed.), *China and Maritime Europe, 1500–1800: Trade, Settlement, Diplomacy, and Missions* (Cambridge: Cambridge University Press, 2011); and Adam Clulow, *The Company and the Shogun: The Dutch Encounter with Tokugawa Japan* (New York: Columbia University Press, 2014).
16 Nicholas B. Dirks, *The Hollow Crown: Ethnohistory of an Indian Kingdom* (Ann Arbor, Mich.: University of Michigan Press, 1993).
17 Thant Myint-U, *The Making of Modern Burma* (Cambridge: Cambridge University Press, 2001).
18 Ian Copland, *The Princes of India in the Endgame of Empire, 1917–1947* (Cambridge: Cambridge University Press, 1997). Indian chiefs were not the only rulers with reservations about independence; hereditary chieftains, for instance, opposed independence of a Fiji that they feared would be dominated by a majority Indian population.
19 Hilary Sapire, 'Ambiguities of Loyalism: The Prince of Wales in India and Africa, 1921–2 and 25', *History Workshop Journal*, 73: spring (2012), 37–65.
20 Cindy McCreery, '"Long May He Float on the Ocean of Life": The First Royal Visit to Tasmania in 1868', *Tasmanian Historical Studies*, 12 (2007), 19–42; 'Telling the Story: HMS *Galatea*'s Voyage to South Africa, 1867', *South African Historical Journal*, 61:4 (2009), 817–37; Hilary Sapire, 'African Loyalism and Its Discontents: The Royal Tour of South Africa, 1947', *Historical Journal*, 54:1 (2011), 215–40.
21 Charles Reed, *Royal Tourists, Colonial Subjects, and the Making of a British World, 1860–1911* (Manchester: Manchester University Press, 2016), Chapter 4: '"Positively Cosmopolitan": Britishness, Respectability, and Imperial Citizenship'.

22 Sarah Carter and Maria Nugent (eds), *Mistress of Everything: Queen Victoria in Indigenous Worlds* (Manchester: Manchester University Press, 2016).
23 Zachary Kingdon, 'The Queen as an Aku Woman? Reassessing "Yoruba" Queen Victoria Portrait Figures', *African Arts*, 47:3 (2014), 8–23.
24 Chandrika Kaul, 'Monarchical Display and the Politics of Empire: Princes of Wales and India 1870–1920s', *Twentieth-Century British History*, 17:4 (2006), 464–88.
25 Colin Newbury, *Patrons, Clients, and Empire: Chieftaincy and Over-rule in Asia, Africa, and the Pacific* (Oxford: Oxford University Press, 2003).
26 See, for example, D. A. Low, *Fabrication of Empire: The British and the Uganda Kingdom, 1890–1902* (Cambridge: Cambridge University Press, 2009).
27 Richard Price, 'One Big Thing: Britain, Its Empire, and Their Imperial Culture', *Journal of British Studies*, 45:3 (2006), 602–27, at p. 621.
28 J. H. Elliott, *Empires of the Atlantic World: Britain and Spain in America, 1492–1830* (New Haven, Conn.: Yale University Press, 2006), pp. 120, 378.
29 Alejandro Cañeque, *The King's Living Image: The Culture and Politics of Viceregal Power in Colonial Mexico* (London and New York: Routledge, 2004).
30 Kaul, 'Monarchical Display and the Politics of Empire', p. 469.
31 Kirsten Schultz, *Tropical Versailles: Empire, Monarchy, and the Portuguese Royal Court in Rio de Janeiro, 1808–1821* (London and New York: Routledge, 2001).
32 Philip Murphy, *Monarchy and the End of Empire: The House of Windsor, the British Government and the Post-war Commonwealth* (Oxford: Oxford University Press, 2013); H. Kumarasingham, *A Political Legacy of the British Empire: Power and the Parliamentary System in Post-colonial India and Sri Lanka* (London: I. B. Tauris, 2013).
33 Maria Nugent, '"The Queen Gave Us the Land": Aboriginal People, Queen Victoria and Historical Remembrance', *History Australia*, 9:2 (2012), 182–200; Lisa Ford, *Settler Sovereignty: Jurisdiction and Indigenous People in America and Australia, 1788–1836* (Cambridge, Mass.: Harvard University Press, 2010).
34 Jan Morris, *The Spectacle of Empire: Style, Effect and the Pax Britannica* (London: Faber & Faber, 1982).
35 Walter Bagehot, *The English Constitution* (London: Kegan Paul & Co., 1873; first published 1867), p. 68; David Cannadine, *Ornamentalism: How the British Saw Their Empire* (London: Penguin, 2002).
36 Nikolaus Pevsner, 'Building with Wit: The Architecture of Sir Edwin Lutyens', *Architectural Review*, 109 (April 1951), 219, quoted in Gavin Stamp, 'New Delhi: A New Imperial Capital for British India', *The Court Historian: The International Journal of Court Studies*, 17:2 (2012), 189–207, at p. 194.
37 Adam Hochschild, *King Leopold's Ghost: A Story of Greed, Terror, and Heroism in Colonial Africa* (Boston, Mass.: Houghton Mifflin, 1998).
38 Sushila Anand, *Indian Sahib: Queen Victoria's Dear Abdul* (London: Duckworth, 1996); Shrabani Basu, *Victoria and Abdul: The True Story of the Queen's Closest Confidant* (Stroud: History Press, 2010); and Michael Alexander and Sushila Anand, *Queen Victoria's Maharajah, Duleep Singh, 1838–1893* (London: Phoenix, 2001).
39 Robert Aldrich and Cindy McCreery (eds), *Royals on Tour: Pageantry and Politics in Colonies and Metropoles* (Manchester: Manchester University Press, forthcoming).
40 See Julie F. Codell (ed.), *Power and Resistance: The Delhi Coronation Durbars* (Ahmedabad: Mapin Publishing, 2012); and Sunil Raman and Rohit Agarwal, *Delhi Durbar 1911: The Complete Story* (New Delhi: Lotus Collection, 2012).
41 Murphy, *Monarchy and the End of Empire*, pp. 78–87.
42 Rozina Visram, *Ayahs, Lascars and Princes: Indians in Britain, 1700–1947* (London: Pluto, 1986).
43 Anthony Taylor, *'Down with the Crown': British Anti-monarchism and Debates about Royalty since 1790* (London: Reaktion, 1999).
44 On the French case, see Adria Lawrence, *Imperial Rule and the Politics of Nationalism: Anti-colonial Protest in the French Empire* (Cambridge: Cambridge University Press, 2013); and Frederick Cooper, *Citizenship between Empire and*

Nation: Remaking France and French Africa, 1945–1960 (Princeton, NJ: Princeton University Press, 2015).
45 Rakesh Ankit, 'Mountbatten and India, 1948–64', *International History Review*, 37:2 (2015), 240–61.
46 Bagehot, *The English Constitution*, p. 68.

CHAPTER TWO

The British royal family and the colonial empire from the Georgians to Prince George

Miles Taylor

In April 2014, the Duke and Duchess of Cambridge, and their son Prince George, touched down in Australia at the start of a ten-day tour. It was the first time on Australian soil for mother and child, although not for Prince William, who himself had been there in 1983 aged nine months. Indeed, Prince George belongs to the seventh generation of royals to visit Australia, a tradition that started with the tour in 1867–68 of Alfred, the Duke of Edinburgh and second eldest son of Queen Victoria. The present queen has visited on sixteen occasions since her accession in 1952 (six more visits than to New Zealand). Of her first visit in 1954 it is calculated that Queen Elizabeth II was seen by 75 per cent of all Australians.[1] The tour of Australia in 2014 came amidst a revival of royal popularity. Polling ahead of the Cambridges' tour revealed that support for an Australian republic had slipped to a thirty-five-year low, with only 42 per cent of those asked in favour of ending the status of constitutional monarchy (falling to only 28 per cent among the youngest voters). The heady days of 2013, when the outgoing governor-general, Quentin Bryce, could look forward in a major public lecture to a republican future, already seemed a long way off. As they did in New Zealand, where Prime Minister John Key admitted during the Cambridges' visit there that the time frame for changing his country's relationship with the British Crown had moved 'considerably further out'.[2]

There is nothing like a visiting royal to quell republicanism or at least to confuse the issues. At significant foundational moments of Australian history, a royal has been present. For example, the Duke of Cornwall and York came to open the first parliament of the Commonwealth of Australia in 1901. In 1934, the Duke of Gloucester took part in the centenary of British settlement of what had become the state of Victoria. At the end of 1987, in Sydney, Queen Elizabeth II unveiled a statue of Queen Victoria passed on to Australia by the

Republic of Ireland – the statue had been mothballed in 1948 after standing in Dublin for forty years – as preparations were under way for the commemoration of the bicentenary of the British establishment of a settlement in New South Wales.[3] What is true of Australia is true of the Commonwealth and the former colonies more generally. From beginning to end – from the 1780s when the Duke of Clarence (the future William IV) saw naval service in the American War of Independence and in the Caribbean, and so became the first prince to actually see the colonies, through to Prince Charles's presence at the ceremonies marking the British withdrawal from Hong Kong in 1997 – the British royal family seems to have served as the symbolic link between Britain and its dominions overseas.

Historians have at last caught up with journalists in the attention they now give to the British royal family overseas. The topic of royalty is notable by its omission from the original five volumes of the *Oxford History of the British Empire* (1998–99) and, before this collection, as an explicit topic in the Studies in Imperialism series published by Manchester University Press since 1984. Now there is a growing body of scholarly work that examines the role played by the Crown in Britishness overseas and the ideology of imperialism more generally. Coverage of the white settlement colonies has been strongest. There are studies of monarchy in South Africa,[4] Canada,[5] and Australia.[6] But there has also been analysis of the symbolism of monarchy in India,[7] and even Britain's Mediterranean colonies – for instance, Gibraltar – have got a look in.[8] Even so, we still know less about the Crown in New Zealand than we should – the lawyers have taken over somewhat.[9] And more work needs to be done on the West Indies.[10] The British Empire in East and South-East Asia remains relatively untouched, with the exception of recent work on royal 'beefeater' yeoman guards.[11] Much of this recent scholarship focuses on the phenomenon of the royal tour, although, particularly in the case of Ireland, there has been a deeper investigation of the constitutional and political relationship between the Crown and its dominions before 1914.[12]

For all its novelty, the new historiography of the Crown and the colonies rests upon some standard assumptions about the place of royalty in a secular, democratic and post-colonial world. With a few famous exceptions, most member-states of the modern Commonwealth of Nations are republics. So, looking back, historians tend to see the Crown as imposed upon the colonies without their consent. To explain the salience of the royal connection, historians turn to culture and ideology, taking as given that the Crown has only a symbolic rather than a real function overseas. Invoking an influential book of 1983, the idea of the British monarchy as an 'invented tradition' looms large in recent scholarship on the Crown at home as well as in the Empire.[13] So, too, does the presumption that the monarchy is part of the 'propaganda' of Empire, an argument that again has its roots in a study now over thirty years old.[14] That is to say, as Britain modernised from the 1870s as a democracy at home and an expanding empire overseas, the Crown became used as a ceremonial prop to distract working-class voters at home and colonial separatism overseas. The new imperialism of the prime-ministership of Benjamin Disraeli (1874–80) – for instance, his audacity in making Queen Victoria Empress of India – combined with the rolling out of the trappings of monarchy in the colonies and dependencies. Alongside the tours of the royal family, there was the export of the British honours system[15] and royal patronage of colonial exhibitions of arts and industry.[16] By the closing years of Queen Victoria's reign, colonial loyalty to the Crown, as measured by the jubilees of 1887 and 1897, appeared unquestioned. In the aftermath of her death, Queen Victoria became apotheosised as the undisputed symbol of empire – in the 'Victoria League' for example.[17] And the royal family stood at the apex of a global imperial patriotism in wartime as well: at the time of the South African War especially and again during the First World War.[18]

This is the older narrative that underpins much of the new work on the Crown and colonies. It is open to question in a number of ways. First, conventional scholarship on the Crown and colonies privileges the half century after 1870 as the most formative era of an imperial monarchy. But monarchy and empire existed in tandem long before the 1870s. Much like the rest of Europe, Britain from the sixteenth century onwards was a composite monarchy first and a colonial empire later, as historians of political thought have recognised in a series of significant studies.[19] The deeper roots of Britain's monarchical empire are to be found in the early modern era and in the context of the dynastic politics and commercial rivalry of European continental powers.[20] Second, although ostensibly about the monarchy, recent studies leave out entirely the agency of the Crown. It is assumed that British monarchs, unlike Kaiser Wilhelm II of Germany or Leopold II of Belgium, had no interest in the colonies themselves and were anyway bound by constitutional conventions and restraints on the exercise of their prerogative at home and in the empire. However, we know that the royal prerogative extended a long way into those parts of the state that were significant in colonialism: namely, the Church of England, the Army and the whole apparatus of crown colony government, including the governors-general and, in the case of Ireland and India, the viceroys. Yet hardly any attention has been devoted to this system of royal patronage or to the attitudes towards Empire of individual British monarchs.[21]

Finally, current work often gives us a one-dimensional picture of colonial and imperial loyalty, associating it primarily with deference to monarchy. Alternatively, expressions of loyalty to the Crown might be better understood as belonging to an older tradition of appeal to the monarch as above partisanship. The convention of petitioning the monarch for remonstrance, mercy or reform was prevalent in eighteenth- and nineteenth-century Britain, but has seldom been looked at in a colonial context.[22] So many parts of the British Empire had prior traditions of indigenous kingship and native monarchy into which the Crown became absorbed in ways that demand fuller investigation.

This chapter provides a short survey of the British Crown and its colonies with the monarchy put back in. It concentrates particularly on the late eighteenth century through to 1901, arguing that there was more continuity than is often supposed between the monarchical empire of the earlier era of war and revolution (c. 1688–1815) and the new imperialism of the late nineteenth century. By the time Disraeli made Queen Victoria Empress of India in 1876, the Crown had already worked itself into the structures of colonial empire, through the patronage it exercised in matters of Church and State overseas. The chapter then turns to look at how the Crown was resorted to by petitioners and delegations from the colonies and dependencies, suggesting that imperial loyalty was as much a political tactic as a gesture of submission. Finally, it is argued that the Crown was indeed part of the 'new imperialism' of the 1870s, not as theatre but rather as the centrepiece of attempts to revive the idea of the Empire as a federal union.

Monarchy and Empire under the Tudors, Stuarts and Georgians

There is a presumption in much of the recent work on monarchy and the British Empire that the symbolism of the Crown only became grafted onto the colonies in the later decades of the nineteenth century. A longer-term and pan-European perspective suggests otherwise. With the important exception of the Dutch republic, most modern European states were monarchies long before they became empires or developed colonial interests. Between the sixteenth and late eighteenth centuries, France, the United Kingdom of Denmark and Norway, Portugal and Spain expanded first as continental European and Eurasian powers (a process within Europe that included Austria, Russia and Prussia as well) and then added territory overseas in the Americas and Asia. In this way, empires grew out of multiple European kingdoms, themselves the product of dynastic marriages across smaller states, or even shared 'dual' monarchies as in the case of the Habsburg and Danish kingdoms. As early modern European monarchies expanded their realms overseas, as François-Joseph Ruggiu shows elsewhere in this volume for Bourbon France, they extended the sovereignty and style of royalty at home to the polities of the new distant settlements.[23] The evolution of the British imperial state was not so very different from the rest of Europe in this respect. The Tudor and Stuart monarchies authorised the early phases of the colonial empire, in so far as they granted royal charters to traders – the East India Company (1600) and the Hudson's Bay Company (1670) – and to settlers migrating to colonise the American seaboard, starting with the London Company and the Plymouth Company (both 1606). Under Elizabeth I and James I (and VI of Scotland), the Crown acquired territory in its own name through a planned policy of overseas plantations, starting in Ireland, and, less successfully, through land claims made on its behalf by entrepreneurial explorers such as Francis Drake ('New Albion' on the west coast of the North American continent).[24] The royal family joined in the first scramble for Africa – gold and slaves – with the founding by James, Duke of York (the King's brother), of the Royal African Company in 1660.[25] With the marriage of Charles II to Catherine of Braganza in 1661, England gained possessions in North Africa and India.

After the revolution of 1688–89, Britain became even more of a composite kingdom with overseas attachments. A foreign Protestant monarch, drawn initially from the Dutch Orange republic and then from the electorate of Hanover in north Germany, ruled over European territory: the Netherlands (1688–1702), and then Hanover (1712–1837), to which were later joined Scotland (1707) and Ireland (1801).[26] Both William III and George II proved active defenders of Britain's colonial interests.[27] The Protestant succession in Britain was maintained through royal marriage into other dynasties with colonial possessions, thus George III wedded Charlotte (Princess of Mecklenburg-Strelitz, herself descended from a branch of the Portuguese royal family). Not surprisingly, towards the end of the reign of George II, the term 'empire' was being used to describe both the British Isles and its overseas territories, and, just as significant, they were identified as 'dominions subject to the king of Great Britain'.[28] By the early eighteenth century, the British monarch was seen as the nominal head of the empire. Iroquois and Cherokee delegations came from North America to London appealing for redress from Queen Anne and George II, as Kate Fullagar describes,[29] and later in the century, from India the Mughal ruler, Shah Alam II and the Nawab of Arcot attempted their own personal diplomacy with George III, by sending gifts, much to the alarm of the East India Company, which, since the revolution of 1688, had developed its own sovereign rule in India.[30]

The association of the Crown with the colonies grew under George III. Although famous for losing one empire (the American colonies), his long reign saw the accumulation of another. Canada and swathes of Indian territory came under British control in the first decades of George III's rule, and by the end of the wars with Napoleon in 1815, the colonial empire had expanded exponentially to include former French, Dutch and Spanish colonies and allies in the Indian subcontinent, in the Indian Ocean, Caribbean and Mediterranean and at the Cape of Good Hope. George III remained a 'king'. The title of 'Emperor of Britain and Hanover' was considered but rejected on the occasion of the Act of Union with Ireland, on the grounds that Britain was not an absolutist state like some of the other European powers.[31] However, the form of government chosen by British politicians to administer the growing colonial empire after 1800 was royal, i.e. the system of crown colonies. The executive powers of the governors of crown colonies were granted in the name of the monarch, and, over time, colonial governors acquired the forms and ceremony of royalty.[32] And although governors reported directly to parliament via the Secretary of State for War and Colonies (the two branches were not separated until 1854), it was the Privy Council of the King and his ministers that oversaw any legislation that applied to all colonies and was also the final court of judicial appeal for the Empire. In this way, the acts of the Privy Council, chaired by the monarch – the so-called orders-in-council – were the principal instrument of government for all conquered territories from the 1790s onwards. And they had some force.

Orders-in-council were applied to the slave colonies of the Caribbean to impose amelioration policies.[33] The Privy Council was also part of the information revolution of the early nineteenth century. As Lisa Ford demonstrates, it was the colonial commissions of inquiry instigated by the Privy Council that until the 1840s furnished the information for a new 'colonial jurisprudence' across the British world.[34] Moreover, until the creation of the separate Judicial Committee of the Privy Council in 1833, it was the full Privy Council, presided over by the monarch, that heard all colonial legal appeals – sometimes taking up thirty days of sittings per year in the period between 1814 and 1826.[35] Some measure of the overall importance of the King's Council to the management of Empire in the Hanoverian era is indicated by the unprecedented appointment to the Privy Council in 1827 of the minor member of the government responsible for colonial administration: Robert Wilmot Horton, the Under-Secretary of State at the War and Colonial Office.[36] There may be little reason to associate the Hanoverian monarchs with the spectacle of Empire. After all, George IV only made it as far as Scotland on a famous visit in 1822. However, in constitutional terms, they occupied a more significant role in the governance of the colonies than is usually appreciated.

Queen Victoria and Britain's colonies

Following her accession in 1837, Queen Victoria quickly became caught up in the growing might of Britain's global power. She adorned coins and postage stamps across the colonial empire and in British India.[37] Her name was lent to British territorial claims from the Antarctic (James Ross in 1839) to the Arctic (John Franklin in 1846), from the furthest reaches of the western hemisphere (Victoria Island, Canada, 1839) to the eastern (the Colony of Victoria in Australia, 1851). And as explorers and missionaries penetrated the interior of Africa, so she followed as talisman (Victoria Falls, named by David Livingstone in 1855, and Lake Victoria, put on the map by John Speke in 1858). There was even a new asteroid named after her by John Russell Hind in 1851. Back on planet Earth, however, her constitutional powers were more limited. The first new monarch of the reform era, she was seen and not heard, she was consulted but did not command.

Arguably, the royal prerogative expanded rather than contracted in relation to imperial affairs after 1837. This can be seen in three ways. First, as 'Defender of the Faith', Queen Victoria was head of the Anglican Church during a period of diocesan revival and expansion overseas. Between 1837 and 1863, thirty-five new bishoprics were created in the colonies and in India (both new sees and sub-divisions).[38] The Queen formally approved each appointment. Her own local bishop, Charles Blomfield, the Bishop of London – a frequent preacher at Buckingham Palace – was the chief mover behind the 'Colonial Bishoprics Fund' set up by the Society for the Propagation of the Gospel (SPG) in 1841, to campaign for new overseas outposts for the Church of England. Queen Victoria's consort, Prince Albert, championed the work of the SPG, speaking at its 150th anniversary meeting in 1851 of how the Society was helping to carry Christianity 'to the vast territories of India and Australasia, which at last are again to be peopled by the Anglo-Saxon race'.[39] And the Queen herself showed a particular interest in the work of individual bishops. She supported Daniel Wilson, Bishop of Calcutta (1832–58), in his fundraising for a new cathedral in the city. George Augustus Selwyn, Bishop of New Zealand (1856–67), was another favourite. In 1867, she persuaded him to abandon his ministry in the South Pacific and return to the see of Lichfield in the 'Black Country' and apply his missionary skills there. The Queen also sided with the most controversial colonial primate of the time, John Colenso, Bishop of Natal (1853–83), as he broke away from the metropolitan control of

Cape Town and lent his support to the amaZulu kings.[40] While there is no evidence that Queen Victoria vetoed the appointment of any colonial bishop, she made her frequently strong views well known, especially in India, where, after the rebellion of 1857, she took particular opposition to missionary proselytising. In 1876, she reminded the Secretary of State for India that 'it is so important to have people of very moderate & conciliatory opinions appointed to the highest offices in the Church there'.[41] And, while she quietly conceded to the disestablishment of the Anglican Church across the Empire between 1869 and 1871, only protesting at the removal of the state church in Ireland, the rise and fall of missionary enthusiasm in the colonies and at home owed much to her own personal journey from evangelicalism to toleration.[42]

Second, in the Victorian era, the monarch also remained closely connected to the Army and, hence, close to the military affairs of the Empire. For the colonial theatre of war was where the British Army spent most of its time between 1815 and 1914. Two of the Queen's favourites, the Duke of Wellington and then Henry Hardinge, were Commanders-in-Chief of the armed forces in the early part of her reign. Then her cousin, George, the Duke of Cambridge, took over, holding the position for thirty-nine years (1856–95), the longest tenure of the office since another royal, the Duke of York (1795–1809 and 1811–27) held the post. One of the original mutton-chops whiskered military men of the era, the Duke of Cambridge never had a good press, then or since.[43] The wings of his office were clipped by the army reforms of Edward Cardwell in William Gladstone's first ministry (1868–74), and he was later blamed for the ill-prepared state of the defences in the Edwardian arms race. But throughout his long period in charge, the Duke of Cambridge looked to strengthen Britain's colonial armies and not leave them wholly reliant on reserve forces or dependent on penny-pinching local assemblies. He backed the amalgamation of the European and native armies in India in 1861 and supported a traditional regimental structure as best fitted for mobility, loyalty and tactical acumen. Under his general command, the Army was consistently successful at fighting small colonial wars, at least until the confrontation with the Boers in 1899–1902, and by then he had been finally shuffled out of post. The Duke of Cambridge's staunchest ally throughout was the Queen. While Prince Albert was alive, he and the Duke of Cambridge were her main military advisers. After 1861, Queen Victoria and her cousin corresponded frequently and together staved off reforms to the Army demanded by Parliament.

Royal patronage of the armed forces remained in place across the Queen's reign. In the 1880s, even after streamlining, more than one-third of the army's 146 regiments had a royal connection.[44] There were serving royals, too. The Queen's third son, Arthur, Duke of Connaught, saw action in Cyprus (1878) and Egypt (1882) and was Commander-in-Chief of the Bombay Presidency Army (1886–90).[45] One grandson and one son-in-law lost their lives during colonial campaigns (Prince Christian in the South African War and Prince Henry of Battenberg in the Ashanti War, both from malaria), and military men (and their wives and widows) were prominent at her court. Several senior officers were plucked from the barracks to join the retinue of the Queen and her family; for example, Captain Sam Browne, who served as aide-de-camp to the Prince of Wales during his tour of India in 1875–76, and Colonel Charles Brownlow, aide-de-camp to the Queen in 1869. And in her later years, she adopted Colonel (later Major-General) Redvers Henry Buller, awarded the Victoria Cross in the amaZulu wars, as a favourite and backed him to succeed the Duke of Cambridge as Commander-in-Chief.

From this pool of military experience, the Queen drew much expert knowledge about colonial warfare, leaving her less dependent on the politicians' digest of what was going on. On occasion, she used her own private channels of information to intervene in Cabinet policy, for example, during the early stages of the suppression of the Indian mutiny in 1857 and during the second Afghan war (1879–80). Queen Victoria deserves therefore her reputation as a 'warrior queen'.[46] Hindsight may suggest that she chose poor military counsel, but her letters and journals reveal how much of what she knew about her colonial realm was filtered through the campaigns of her armies, over which she retained a significant degree of patronage.

A third area of the colonial system that extended the reach of royalty in the nineteenth century was government. Crown colonies continued to be created in the Victorian era, and, in 1858, the Crown formally took over the government of India from the East India Company. Courtiers filled the top posts accordingly. This was most evident in India, where the run of governors-general and viceroys included former palace insiders: the Marquess of Dalhousie (1848–56), Viscount Charles Canning (1856–62) and the Earl of Dufferin (1884–88).[47] The network ran beyond India: to Ceylon (7th Viscount Torrington, 1847–50), New South Wales (Lord Carrington, 1885–90), Nova Scotia, Queensland, New Zealand and Victoria (2nd Marquess of Normanby, 1858–84) and the new Commonwealth of Australia (Lord Linlithgow, 1900–2).[48] As with the Army, the Queen's own family were pressed into colonial duties. Early in her reign, Queen Victoria was told of Prime Minister Lord Melbourne's failed attempt to make her uncle, Augustus, the Duke of Sussex, Lord Lieutenant of Ireland.[49]

But that setback may have sowed the seed of an idea that passed to the next generation. As she recalled after his death, Prince Albert 'had often thought of the Colonies for our sons'.[50] The Queen mooted the idea of making Prince Arthur Duke of Canada in 1865, and again in 1876, when she also thought of making Prince Alfred Duke of Australia. Neither title eventuated, but the 9th Duke of Argyll, Governor-General of Canada from 1878 to 1883, with his wife Princess Louise, formed perhaps one of the most successful viceregal couples of the time. Later, two generations of Connaughts (son Arthur and grandson, also Arthur) became Governors-General (respectively in Canada, 1911–16, and South Africa, 1920–23). Such royal colonial appointments were not simply ceremonial offices. This was a working colonial monarchy. The royal princes were groomed for their imperial responsibilities through tours of the Empire: the Prince of Wales as the heir-apparent or *Shahzadah* in India in 1875–76; the naval officer Alfred in 1867–71 on a world cruise (discussed in part by Cindy McCreery in her chapter); the soldier, Arthur, in the Mediterranean and India in the 1870s and 1880s; and the future princes of Wales, Albert Victor, to India in 1889–90, shortly before his premature death, and George (later George V), also to India in 1905–6.[51] Princely tours point to an older tradition dating from the wars of the late eighteenth century of male members of the royal family cutting their military teeth on the colonies. But these tours are also a reminder that the Empire was as important a field of national service for the royals as welfare and philanthropy at home.

Queen Victoria and indigenous peoples

The British monarch also served as a figurehead for Empire by offering subject peoples the opportunity for redress. George III may have sullied the ideal of a 'patriot king' in his handling of the American colonies, but elsewhere the belief endured that the monarch was a disinterested sovereign, detached from politicians and colonial officials and able to dispense justice.[52] As the Empire expanded through the nineteenth century, so too did direct appeals to the Crown. Monster petitions critical of the local governors-general were sent to George IV from Canadian settlers in 1828 and to William IV from New South Wales residents in 1831. Petitions came not only from Europeans. The Maori Chief Hongi Hika visited George IV in 1820, and Maori tribes (*iwi*) also sent a petition in 1831 calling for the King's protection of the islands of New Zealand from French naval incursions. William IV was sent petitions from Sudan and Sierra Leone shortly before his death in 1837. And from India there were a succession of royal visitors to London from the early 1830s through to the eve of the Indian rebellion of 1857 protesting at mistreatment of the princely states and kingdoms by the government of India.[53] Two parts of the Victorian empire – New Zealand and India – offer particularly useful evidence of how appeals to the monarch could combine the language of loyalty with agendas of reform.

New Zealand was the first new colony of Queen Victoria's reign and the only one to be annexed by treaty (the Treaty of Waitangi of 1840) with the Crown as signatory. A royal seal was hurriedly dispatched. It styled Queen Victoria as 'fidei defensor' and represented the Maori chiefs as elderly, Caucasian and wise Corinthians (or ancient Britons perhaps), their heads bedecked with laurels, their spears laid to rest (see Figure 4).

Clause 61 of the Treaty stated that the governor of the new colony must 'prevent and restrain all violence and injustice which may in any manner be practised or attempted' against Maori. Some Maori leaders compared New Zealand to a ship, with the new governor as captain, but the passage of the vessel determined by the laws of God and made safe by the naval supremacy of the Queen.[54] The promise of protection by the Queen's representative was taken seriously enough by Maori leaders for them to look to the Crown for aid during the drawn-out wars that dominated the first three decades of the new colony. Between 1852 and 1863, four sets of Maori chiefs came to London and were given personal audiences with Queen Victoria: Te Tamihana Te Rauparaha from Taranaki in 1852; Te Hipango from Wanganui in September 1855; the Waikato chiefs Toetoe and Te Rerehau in June 1860, as part of a tour that took them to Vienna as well; and Hare Pomare from Northland in July 1863.[55] Although choreographed by missionaries, the four delegations had a wider significance. First, Victoria accorded Maori special treatment. On the arrival of Hipango in 1855, her court actually overrode the Colonial Office, insisting on the meeting. In 1863, Victoria's meeting with the Hare Pomare party was the first occasion since Prince Albert's death at the end of 1861 when she had broken her mourning to receive any visitors. Singling out Maori may have been connected to the poem (*hangi*) that Maori chiefs sent to Victoria after Albert's death. The signatories to the *hangi* included Te Rauparaha, who had met the Queen in 1852. And the poem, with its moving references to the 'crash of the huge headed tree' and the demise of the leader who stood 'in the prow of the canoe', was reprinted in *The Times*.[56] Second, for Maori, the deputations fitted into a sequence of contacts with the British monarch. Hipango travelled to London in 1855 knowledgeable of Te Rauparaha's visit in 1852. All four delegations looked back to the tradition of contact with the British sovereign begun by Hongi Hika back in 1820. Perhaps most important of all, the visits of Maori to Windsor galvanised the united movement of Maori *iwi*, which Vincent O'Malley

4. The Great Seal of New Zealand, from *The Illustrated London News*, 21 June 1845. Source: Private Collection, Look and Learn/ Illustrated Papers Collection/Bridgeman Images, LIP1095609. Reproduced with permission

discusses in his chapter. Te Rauparaha returned to New Zealand after his audience with the Queen in 1852 to make a tour of the North Island, calling for unity behind a king figure. The duly chosen chief, Te Wherowhero, was crowned in 1858, his status as king symbolised by two sticks in the ground, one representing the Governor, the other the Maori King, with a third stick placed on top of both to represent the law of God, with a circle drawn around the sticks to represent the protection of the Queen.[57]

In British India, Victoria herself took the initiative in assuming the role of patriot queen.[58] When the government of India was transferred from the East India Company to the Crown in 1858, she and Prince Albert intervened in an unprecedented fashion to turn the proclamation of the transfer of power into a document of tolerance and clemency. Not only did queen and consort write into the document the clauses that promised toleration for all religions in post-mutiny India and pledges to uphold the rights of succession of the loyal Indian princes, they also insisted on the clause that stated that the people of India would enjoy the same protection as all subjects of Britain. Over time, this royal intervention led to the Proclamation of 1858 becoming known in the Indian subcontinent as 'the Magna Carta of Indian liberties', a phrase which Indian nationalists such as Gandhi later took up as they sought to test equality under imperial law.[59] The 1858 Proclamation also encouraged Queen Victoria's reputation as a benign ruler. For the remaining decades of her life, British officials in India tried in vain to stem the petitions, protestations – and gifts – sent to her directly. Her gender helped, too. The world's most famous widow after 1861, and one known to oppose widows remarrying, she was frequently depicted in vernacular biographies as a devoted wife and then equally devoted widow. Small tokens of kindness shown by Victoria towards India became invested with wider significance, as when she made a personal donation to the famine relief funds of the 1870s or knitted blankets for Indian troops sent to the Egyptian campaign in 1882. By then she had become a figurehead as much for reform movements in India, as of the British Raj – for extending municipal government and for opening up the magistracy to Indian judges, for improving women's health and for the training of native nurses. Victoria's reputation in India peaked in 1882, when her survival of an assassination attempt in London produced an unprecedented volume of addresses from India expressing relief at her escape. Five years later, at the time of her golden jubilee, addresses, presents and memorials of all shapes and sizes were sent from India to Britain, as they were ten years later in 1897. In 1887 there were almost 1,100 addressees from India, double the combined total from the rest of the colonial empire and almost 50 per cent more than were generated back in Britain.[60] Victoria was celebrated as the mother protector of India, its princes and its people. Some of this was orchestrated by the Indian government, mostly it was not. Many of these jubilee addresses contained pleas for constitutional, financial and administrative reform alongside statements of loyalty. Even the Indian National Congress made warm references to the Queen on its formation in 1885.[61] Loyalism to the Crown and Indian nationalism were not creeds apart, at least in Queen Victoria's lifetime.

Other examples of Queen Victoria stepping in as colonial counsellor might be added; for instance, her meeting with the amaZulu King, Cetshwayo, in 1881, to hear his complaints over the loss of his kingdom,[62] or the royal audience granted in 1887 to Princess Lili'uokalani

[39]

and Queen Kapi'olani, of the royal family of Hawai'i, as their kingdom faced conspiracies from within and a covetous USA from without.[63] Historians are drawn to the exotic spectacle of these encounters. Yet that misses the wider point. Queen Victoria, like her predecessors, strengthened the legitimacy of indigenous rulers by offering them protection. Sometimes this seemed to have the force of law, as the afterlives of the Treaty of Waitangi and the Indian Proclamation of 1858 demonstrate.[64] She could empower minor female monarchs by treating them as part of a royal global sisterhood, as she did not only with the Queen of Hawai'i but also with the Begums of Bhopal in India.[65] And, as the titular head of the British Empire, she represented a court of appeal beyond the colonial authorities. For all these reasons, historians need to look more carefully at those moments of 'popular imperialism', such as the jubilees of 1887 and 1897, and be as attentive to the demands being made by colonial subjects as they are to the displays of patriotism.[66]

Federating the colonial empire under the British Crown

Putting the Crown back into the history of British colonialism also places the new imperialism of the 1870s in a different perspective from that of the prevailing historiography. From the 1848 revolutions onwards, Victoria and Albert came to champion a colonial empire based on a union of sovereign states. Albert had in mind the German confederation or Bund (1815–48), whereby the smaller duchies and princely states of Germany retained their independence under the Prussian Crown. In the 1860s and 1870s, Queen Victoria grew alarmed as Bismarck's Prussia swallowed up the smaller German states, and she was similarly concerned by King Vittorio Emanuele's subjugation of the independent Italian states during the unification of Italy. In her own empire, she wanted things done differently. As she explained to her daughter, Vicky, now married into the Prussian imperial family, in 1873, British imperial rule was characterised by 'one head, one army and one diplomacy, but not for dethroning other Princes'.[67] Queen Victoria was referring to India; however, the principle had a wider application. She returned to Albert's confederation model. The British North America Act of 1867, which turned Canada into a federation of provinces, but with dominion status within the Empire to reflect Canadian loyalty to the Crown, is a good example of this federal scheme, not unlike 'Home Rule' for Ireland.[68] And in Ireland itself, most schemes advocated for 'home rule' between the 1850s and the 1900s included the British Crown in a conciliatory role: republican overtones were conspicuously absent.[69] A federal scheme was also considered for India. In 1876, Edward Bulwer-Lytton, the Viceroy, proposed a privy council of Indian princes to accompany the introduction of the new title of Empress of India.[70] A few years later, federation under the Crown was attempted in southern Africa, when the Colonial Secretary, Lord Carnarvon, dispatched the veteran imperial troubleshooter, Bartle Frere, to reconcile the differences between the breakaway republics of the Orange Free State and the Transvaal, the British colonists at the Cape and the amaZulu and other tribal kingdoms. In 1880, Frere suggested to the Queen that a royal prince be sent to southern Africa, to appease everyone.[71] In the event, of these schemes, only Canadian federation under the Crown was successful. In India, it became common to depict the Empress as a sovereign power to whom Indian princes owed allegiance – as the collective portrait of monarch and maharajahs from 1897 suggests (see Figure 5), but it never took an institutional form. Nonetheless, it is surely significant that just as the empires of continental Europe were taking shape in the 1860s and 1870s, Queen Victoria and her advisers were imagining new schemes for federating the colonial empire under the British Crown, sometimes with her own progeny as her representatives. In the late nineteenth century, as in the sixteenth century, visions of imperial dominion were unworkable without the Crown.

For too long historians have consigned monarchy to the margins of the history of Empire. When royalty has been the object of study, as recently, past and present have collided in an unhealthy way, with the current limited ceremonial functions of the monarchy in relation to the Commonwealth taken as the template for understanding the relationship between Crown and colonies over a longer period. This Whiggish approach has left historians focusing on the one aspect of the subject with contemporary resonance: royal tours. And it has encouraged a search for the earliest possible sightings of republican and anti-monarchical sentiment in the colonies. Yet, the Commonwealth monarchy of the twentieth century is perhaps an unhelpful place to start thinking about Crown and colonies more generally. As Philip Murphy has shown recently, between 1914 and the 1950s, successive British governments sought to minimise the involvement of the Crown in colonial politics.[72] The distinct place now occupied by the Crown in the diplomacy of the Commonwealth grew out of a drawn-out debate between Whitehall and Buckingham Palace in the years after the Second World War. In many ways, the current modus operandi is fundamentally different from what transpired between Crown and colonies before 1914. This chapter has argued that the British Crown has been part of the history of Empire since the sixteenth century, and, in this respect, the history of British colonialism merits comparison with the empires of the continental European powers. The rival merits of republics and monarchies in relation to colonial possessions was one

5. Portrait of Queen Victoria and Maharajahs. Reproduced with permission of Maharana of Mewar Charitable Foundation, Mewar Palace, Udaipur, Rajasthan, India

of the great set-piece debates of the Enlightenment. From it, Britain emerged, albeit without the American colonies, as a colonial empire under royal sovereignty. As the powers of the monarchy were reduced at home, in many ways they increased overseas across the nineteenth century, not least because the new colonial empire contained so many cultures and peoples that understood the conventions of kingship. By the time of the new imperialism of the 1870s, the British monarchy was already woven into the fabric of Empire: a tradition, to be sure, but not an invented one.

Notes

1 Jane Holley Connors, 'The Glittering Thread: The 1954 Royal Tour of Australia', unpublished Ph.D. thesis, University of Technology, Sydney, 1996.
2 For the opinion poll, see www.abc.net.au/radionational/programs/latenightlive/republic/5403696 (accessed 23 January 2016). For Boyer's remarks, see *Guardian*, 22 November 2013, http://www.theguardian.com/world/2013/nov/22/governor-general-quentin-bryce-australian-republic (accessed 11 February 2016). And for Key's comments, see *The Daily Express*, 7 April 2014.
3 *Sydney Morning Herald*, 10 May 1901; *Australasian*, 20 October 1934. For a recent account of the 1987 'gift' of the statue, see Mark McKenna, 'The Republic of Australia: A Forgotten Ideal', in Gwenda Tavan (ed.), *State of the Nation: Essays for Robert Manne* (Collingwood: Black Inc., 2013).
4 Hilary Sapire, 'African Loyalism and Its Discontents: The Royal Tour of South Africa, 1947', *Historical Journal*, 54:1 (2011), 215–40; 'Ambiguities of Loyalism: The Prince of Wales in India and Africa, 1921–22 and 25', *History Workshop Journal*, 73 (2012), 37–65; Charles V. Reed, 'Respectable Subjects of the Queen: The Royal Tour of 1901 and Imperial Citizenship in South Africa', in Catherine McGlynn, Andrew Mycock and James Mcauley (eds), *Britishness, Identity and Citizenship: The View from Abroad* (Oxford: Peter Lang, 2011), pp. 11–30; Roger S. Levine, 'Prince Alfred in King William's Town, South Africa: 13 August 1860', *Rethinking History*, 14:1 (2010), 137–44. See also Philip Buckner, 'The Royal Tour of 1901 and the Construction of an Imperial Identity in South Africa', *South African Historical Journal*, 41 (1999), 324–48.
5 Wade A. Henry, 'Imagining the Great White Mother and the Great King: Aboriginal Tradition and Royal Representation at the "Great Pow-Wow" of 1901', *Journal of the Canadian Historical Association*, 11 (2000), 87–108; Colin Coates (ed.), *Majesty in Canada: Essays on the Role of Royalty* (Toronto: Dundurn, 2006); Ian Radforth, *Royal Spectacle: The 1860 Visit of the Prince of Wales to Canada and the United States* (Toronto: University of Toronto Press, 2004); Philip Buckner, 'The Creation of the Dominion of Canada, 1860–1901', in Philip Buckner (ed.), *Canada and the British Empire* (Oxford: Oxford University Press, 2008), pp. 66–86.
6 Cindy McCreery, '"Long May He Float on the Ocean of Life": The First Royal Visit to Tasmania, 1868', *Tasmanian Historical Studies*, 12 (2007), 19–42; Mark McKenna, 'Monarchy: From Reverence to Indifference', in Deryck Schreuder and Stuart Ward (eds), *Australia's Empire* (Oxford: Oxford University Press, 2008), pp. 261–87; Richard P. Davis, 'The Prince and the Fenians, Australasia 1868–9: Republican Conspiracy or Orange Opportunity?', in Fearghal McGarry and James Richard Redmond McConnel (eds), *The Black Hand of Republicanism: Fenianism in Modern Ireland* (Dublin: Irish Academic Press, 2009), pp. 121–34; Jessie Mitchell, '"It Will Enlarge the Ideas of the Natives"': Indigenous Australians and the Tour of Prince Alfred, Duke of Edinburgh', *Aboriginal History*, 34 (2010), 197–216; Gordon Pentland, 'The Indignant Nation: Australian Responses to the Attempted Assassination of the Duke of Edinburgh in 1868', *English Historical Review*, 130: 542 (2015), 57–88. See also Kevin Fewster, 'Politics, Pageantry and Purpose: The 1920 Tour of Australia by the Prince of Wales', *Labour History*, 38 (1980), 59–66.
7 Chandrika Kaul, 'Monarchical Display and the Politics of Empire: Princes of Wales and India, 1870–1920s', *Twentieth-Century British History*, 17:4 (2006), 464–88; Julie F. Codell, 'Introduction', in Julie F. Codell (ed.), *Power and Resistance: The Delhi Coronation Durbars* (New Delhi: Mapin, 2012), pp. 16–43; Julie F. Codell, 'On the Delhi Coronation Durbars, 1877, 1903, 1911', available online at www.branchcollective.org/?ps_articles=julie-codell-on-the-delhi-coronation-durbars-1877-1903-1911 (accessed 23 January 2016).

8 Stephen Constantine, 'Monarchy and Constructing Identity in "British" Gibraltar, c. 1800 to the Present', *Journal of Imperial and Commonwealth History*, 34:1 (2006), 23–44; Klaus Dodds, David Lambert and Bridget Robison, 'Loyalty and Royalty: Gibraltar, the 1953–54 Royal Tour and the Geopolitics of the Iberian Peninsula', *Twentieth Century British History*, 18:3 (2007), 365–90.
9 Paul McHugh, *The Maori Magna Carta: New Zealand Law and the Treaty of Waitangi* (Oxford: Oxford University Press, 1991). For an older study, see Judith Bassett, '"A Thousand Miles of Loyalty": The Royal Tour of 1901', *New Zealand Journal of History*, 21 (1987), 125–38.
10 Ann Spry Rush, *Bonds of Empire: West Indians and Britishness from Victoria to Decolonization* (Oxford: Oxford University Press, 2011), Chapter 2 is a good place to start.
11 Paul Ward, 'Beefeaters, British History and the Empire in Asia and Australasia Since 1826', *Britain and the World*, 5:2 (2012), 240–58.
12 James H. Murphy, *Abject Loyalty: Nationalism and Monarchy in Ireland during the Reign of Queen Victoria* (Cork: Cork University Press, 2001); James Loughlin, *The British Monarchy and Ireland: 1800 to the Present* (Cambridge: Cambridge University Press, 2007).
13 Eric Hobsbawm and Terence Ranger (eds), *The Invention of Tradition* (Cambridge: Cambridge University Press, 1983), especially the chapters by Hobsbawm and by David Cannadine. See also Andrzej Olechnowicz (ed.), *The Monarchy and the British Nation, 1780 to the Present* (Cambridge: Cambridge University Press, 2007).
14 John Mackenzie, *Propaganda and Empire: The Manipulation of British Public Opinion, 1880–1960* (Manchester: Manchester University Press, 1984). See also John Mackenzie (ed.), *Imperialism and Popular Culture* (Manchester: Manchester University Press, 1986); William Kuhn, *Democratic Royalism: The Transformation of the British Monarchy, 1861–1914* (Basingstoke: Macmillan, 1996); and Paul Ward, *Britishness since 1870* (London and New York: Routledge, 2004), Chapter 1.
15 David Cannadine, *Ornamentalism: How the British Saw Their Empire* (London: Allen Lane, 2001); Bruce Knox, 'Democracy, Aristocracy and Empire: The Provision of Colonial Honours, 1818–1870', *Australian Historical Studies*, 25:99 (1992), 244–64.
16 Peter Hoffenberg, *An Empire on Display: English, Indian, and Australian Exhibitions from the Crystal Palace to the Great War* (Berkeley, Calif.: University of California Press, 2001); William Golant, *Image of Empire: The Early History of the Imperial Institute, 1887–1925* (Exeter: University of Exeter, 1984).
17 Eliza Riedi, 'Women, Gender and the Promotion of Empire: The Victoria League, 1901–1914', *Historical Journal*, 45:3 (2002), 569–99; Katie Pickles, 'A Link in "The Great Chain of Empire Friendship": The Victoria League in New Zealand', *Journal of Imperial and Commonwealth History*, 33:1 (2005), 29–50; Alan Blackstock and Frank O'Gorman (eds), *Loyalism and the Formation of the British World* (Woodbridge: Boydell and Brewer, 2014).
18 John Crawford and Ian C. McGibbon (eds), *One Flag, One Queen, One Tongue: New Zealand, the British Empire and the South African War, 1899–1902* (Auckland: Auckland University Press, 2003); Donal Lowry (eds), *The South African War Reappraised* (Manchester: Manchester University Press, 2000), especially the chapters by Lowry and Balasubramanyam Chandramohan; Richard Smith, *Jamaican Volunteers in the First World War: Race, Masculinity and the Development of National Consciousness* (Manchester: Manchester University Press, 2004), p. 39; Timothy Winegard, *Indigenous Peoples of the British Dominions and the First World War* (Cambridge: Cambridge University Press, 2012); Santanu Das, *1914–1918: Indian Troops in Europe* (Ahmedabad: Mapin, 2015).
19 John Robertson (ed.), *A Union for Empire: Political Thought and the British Union of 1707* (Cambridge: Cambridge University Press, 1995), especially the chapter by J. G. A. Pocock; J. G. A. Pocock, 'Monarchy in the Name of Britain: The Case of George III', in Hans Blom, John Laursen and Luisa Simonutti (eds), *Monarchisms in the Age of Enlightenment: Liberty, Patriotism and the Common Good* (Toronto: University of Toronto Press, 2007), pp. 285–302; Peter Miller, *Defining the Common Good: Empire,*

Religion and Philosophy in Eighteenth-Century Britain (Cambridge: Cambridge University Press, 1994); David Armitage, *Greater Britain, 1516–1778: Essays in Atlantic History* (Aldershot: Ashgate Variorum, 2004), esp. pp. 34–63, 91–107, 427–55; Sankar Muthu (ed.), *Empire and Modern Political Thought* (Cambridge: Cambridge University Press, 2012), see the chapters by Michael Mosher, Sankar Muthu and Jennifer Pitts.

20 The European dynamics behind colonial expansion before the 1880s remains a neglected field. For some helpful perspectives, see, variously, Stephen Conway, *Britain, Ireland and Continental Europe in the Eighteenth Century: Similarities, Connections, Identities* (Oxford: Oxford University Press, 2011), Chapter 10; Dominic Lieven, *Empire: The Russian Empire and Its Rivals* (London: John Murray, 2000); Jan Rüger, 'Britain, Empire, Europe: Re-reading Eric Hobsbawm', *Journal of Modern European History*, 11:4 (2013), 417–23.

21 For the Church of England, see Rowan Strong, *Anglicanism and the British Empire, 1700–1850* (Oxford: Oxford University Press, 2007). For viceregal Ireland, see Peter Gray and Olwen Purdue (eds), *The Irish Lord Lieutenancy, c. 1541–1922* (Dublin: University College Dublin Press, 2012). For viceregal India, see David Gilmour, *The Ruling Caste: Imperial Lives in the Victorian Raj* (London: John Murray, 2005); and Hugh Tinker, *Viceroy: Curzon to Mountbatten* (Oxford: Oxford University Press, 1997). For governors-general, see Mark Francis, *Governors and Settlers: Images of Authority in the British Colonies, 1820–1860* (Basingstoke: Macmillan, 1992); and David Lambert and Alan Lester (eds), *Colonial Lives across the British Empire: Imperial Careering in the Long Nineteenth Century* (Cambridge: Cambridge University Press, 2006), especially the chapters by Dale, Howell and Lambert, McLeish and Thomas. For the army and empire, the best place to start is Hew Strachan, *The Politics of the British Army* (Oxford: Oxford University Press, 1997); and Ian Beckett, *The Victorians at War* (London: Hambledon, 2003).

22 Linda Colley, 'The Apotheosis of George III: Loyalty, Royalty and the British Nation, 1760–1820', *Past and Present*, 102 (1984), 94–129; Marilyn Morris, *The British Monarchy and the French Revolution* (New Haven, Conn.: Yale University Press, 1998), pp. 151, 158; Paul Pickering, '"The Hearts of the Millions": Chartism and Popular Monarchism in the 1840s', *History*, 88:290 (2003), 227–48. Dr James Gregory of Plymouth University is currently completing a study of the uses of 'mercy' in the eighteenth and nineteenth centuries, which includes a discussion of royal clemency.

23 Anthony Pagden, *Lords of All the World: Ideologies of Empire in Spain, Britain and France c. 1500–c.1800* (New Haven, Conn.: Yale University Press, 1995); Tonio Andrade and William Reger (eds), *The Limits of Empire: European Imperial Formations in Early Modern World History. Essays in Honour of Geoffrey Parker* (Farnham: Ashgate, 2012). For specific European empires, see Neville Hall, *Slave Society in the Danish West Indies: St. Thomas, St. John, and St. Croix*, ed. B. W. Higman (Mona: University of West Indies Press, 1992), Chapter 1; Magdalena Naum and Jonas M. Nordin (eds), *Scandinavian Colonialism and the Rise of Modernity: Small Time Agents in a Global Arena* (New York: Springer, 2013); A. R. Disney, *A History of Portugal and the Portuguese Empire: From Beginnings to 1807*, vol. I: *Portugal* (Cambridge: Cambridge University Press, 2009), Chapters 10–12; J. H. Elliott, *Imperial Spain, 1469–1716* (London: Edward Arnold, 1963); J. H. Elliott, *Empires of the Atlantic World: Britain and Spain in America, 1492–1830* (New Haven, Conn.: Yale University Press, 2006); John Lynch, *Spain under the Habsburgs: Empire and Absolutism, 1516–98* (Oxford: Oxford University Press, 1964).

24 David Armitage, 'The Elizabethan Idea of Empire', *Transactions of the Royal Historical Society*, 6th series, 14 (2004), 269–77; David Armitage, 'The Cromwellian Protectorate and the Languages of Empire', in *Greater Britain, 1516–1778: Essays in Atlantic History* (Aldershot: Ashgate Variorum, 2004), pp. 531–55; Glyndwr Parry, 'John Dee and the Elizabethan British Empire in Its European Context', *Historical Journal*, 49:3 (2006), 643–75; Ken Macmillan, *Sovereignty and Possession in the English New World: The Legal Foundations of Empire, 1576–1640* (Cambridge: Cambridge University Press, 2006); Ken Macmillan, *The Atlantic Imperial Constitution: Centre*

and Periphery in the English Atlantic World (Basingstoke: Palgrave Macmillan, 2011); Thomas James Dandelet, *The Renaissance of Empire in Early Modern Europe* (Cambridge: Cambridge University Press, 2014), Chapter 5; K. A. Stanbridge, 'England, France and Their North American Colonies: An Analysis of Absolutist State Power in Europe and in the New World', *Journal of Historical Sociology*, 10:1 (1997), 27–55.

25 William A. Pettigrew, *Freedom's Debt: The Royal African Company and the Politics of the Atlantic Slave Trade, 1672–1752* (Chapel Hill, NC: University of North Carolina Press, 2013), p. 25.

26 Nick Harding, *Hanover and the British Empire, 1700–1837* (Woodbridge: Boydell, 2007), especially the Introduction; Brendan Simms and Torsten Riotte (eds), *The Hanoverian Dimension in British History, 1714–1837* (Cambridge: Cambridge University Press, 2007). For a contemporary description of the new united kingdom as a European empire, see Jean Louis de Lolme, *The British Empire in Europe: Part the First, Containing an Account of the Connection Between ... England and Ireland, Previous to the Year 1780. to Which Is Prefixed an Historical Sketch of the State of Rivalry Between ... England and Scotland in Former Times* (London: B. White, 1787).

27 G. H. Guttridge, *The Colonial Policy of William III in America and the West Indies* (Cambridge: Cambridge University Press, 1922); Esther Mijers and David Onnekink (eds), *Redefining William III: The Impact of the King-Stadholder in International Context* (Aldershot: Ashgate, 2007); Brendan McConville, *The King's Three Faces: The Rise and Fall of Royal America, 1688–1776* (Chapel Hill, NC: University of North Carolina Press, 2006).

28 George Bickham, *The British Monarchy; or, A New Chorographical Description of All the Dominions Subject to the King of Great Britain Comprehending the British Isles, the American Colonies, the Electoral State, the African and Indian Settlements* (London: George Bickham, 1748). For similar uses early in George III's reign, see John Entick, *The Present State of the British Empire Containing a Description of the Kingdoms, Principalities, Conquests, and of the Military and Commercial Establishments, under the British Crown, in Europe, Asia, Africa and America*, 4 vols. (London: B. Law, 1774).

29 See also Kate Fullagar, *The Savage Visit: New World People and Popular Imperial Culture in Britain, 1710–1795* (Berkeley, Calif.: University of California Press, 2012); Eric Hinderaker, 'Diplomacy between Britons and Native Americans, c. 1600–1830', in H. V. Bowen, Elizabeth Mancke and John G. Reid (eds), *Britain's Oceanic Empire: Atlantic and Indian Ocean Worlds, c. 1550–1850* (Cambridge: Cambridge University Press, 2012), p. 239; Jenny Hale Pulsipher, ' "Subjects ... unto the Same King": New England Indians and the Use of Royal Political Power', *Massachusetts Historical Review*, 5 (2003), 29–58.

30 On Shah Alam II and George III, see Michael H. Fisher, 'Diplomacy in India, 1526–1858', in Elizabeth Mancke Bowen and John G. Reid (eds), *Britain's Oceanic Empire: Atlantic and Indian Ocean Worlds, c. 1550–1850* (Cambridge: Cambridge University Press, 2012), pp. 276–7. On the Nawab of Arcot and George III, see Peter Marshall, *The Making and Unmaking of Empires: Britain, India, and America c. 1750–1783* (Oxford: Oxford University Press, 2005), pp. 145, 235; Natasha Eaton, 'Between Mimesis and Alterity: Art, Gift and Diplomacy in Colonial India, 1770–1800', *Comparative Studies in Society and History*, 46:4 (2004), 816–44. On the East India Company's claims as a sovereign state, see Philip Stern, *The Company State: Corporate Sovereignty and the Early Modern Foundations of the British Empire in India* (Oxford: Oxford University Press, 2011).

31 Duke of Portland to the King, 31 October 1800; Archbishop of Canterbury to the King, 26 December 1800, in *The Later Correspondence of George III*, ed. A. Aspinall, 5 vols. (Cambridge: Cambridge University Press, 1964), vol. III, pp. 435n, 458.

32 Francis, *Governors and Settlers*; Stephanie Williams, *Running the Show: Governors of the British Empire, 1857–1912* (London: Viking, 2011); Bruce M. Hicks, 'The Crown's "Democratic" Reserve Powers', *Journal of Canadian Studies/Revue d'Études*

Canadiennes, 44:2 (2010), 5–31; Anne Twomey, *The Chameleon Crown: The Queen and Her Australian Governors* (Annandale: Federation Press, 2006).

33 For a list of colonies administered by orders in council, see 'Return of the date at which each colony or foreign possession of the British Crown was captured, ceded or settled; the number of population, and whether having legislative assemblies, or governed by orders of the Queen in council, etc.', *Parliamentary Papers*, vol. XXXI (1845), p. 2. On amelioration, see J. R. Ward, *British West Indian Slavery, 1750–1834: The Process of Amelioration* (Oxford: Clarendon Press, 1988); and Robert Luster, *The Amelioration of the Slaves in the British Empire, 1790–1833* (Frankfurt: Peter Lang, 1995). A contemporary survey of the royal prerogative and colonial law described the king as the 'supreme head of the empire': Charles Clark, *A Summary of Colonial Law: The Practice of the Court of Appeals from the Plantations and of the Laws and Their Administration in All the Colonies; with Charters of Justice, Orders in Council, etc.* (London: Sweet, Maxwell & Stevens, 1834), p. 47.

34 Lisa Ford, 'The King's Peace: Britain's Counterrevolutionary Global Order', unpublished paper, Crowns and Colonies: Monarchies and Colonial Empires conference, University of Sydney, June 2014; see also Zoe Laidlaw, *Colonial Connections, 1815–45: Patronage, the Information Revolution and Colonial Government* (Manchester: Manchester University Press, 2005).

35 'Papers relating to appeals from the colonies to Privy Council, 1814–26', *Parliamentary Papers*, vol. XXII (1826), pp. 29–30.

36 George Canning to George IV, 19 May 1827, in A. Aspinall (ed.), *The Letters of King George IV, 1812–1830*, 3 vols. (Cambridge: Cambridge University Press, 1938), vol. III, p. 1331.

37 Robert Chalmers, *A History of Currency in the British Colonies* (London: HMSO, 1893); Sanjay Garg, 'Sikka and the Crown: Genesis of the Native Coinage Act, 1876', *Indian Economic and Social History Review*, 35 (1998), 359–80; Mount Brown, *Catalogue of British, Colonial, and Foreign Postage Stamps* (London: F. Passmore, 1862).

38 For a contemporary summary, see *Work in the Colonies: Some Account of the Missionary Operations of the Church of England in Connexion with the Society for the Propagation of the Gospel in Foreign Parts* (London: Griffith & Farran, 1865). In the same period, only one new bishopric was created in Britain – Manchester, in 1847 – although there were several transfers across dioceses.

39 See my 'Prince Albert and the British Empire', in Franz Bosbach and John R. Davis (eds), *Ein Wettiner in Großbritannien* (Munich: K. G. Saur, 2004), p. 77. On the 'Colonial Bishoprics Fund', see Rowan Strong, 'The Resurgence of Colonial Anglicanism: The Colonial Bishoprics Fund, 1840–1', *Studies in Church History*, 44 (2008), 196–213.

40 Josiah Bateman, *The Life of the Right Rev. Daniel Wilson, DD, Late Lord Bishop of Calcutta, etc.* (London: John Murray, 1860), pp. 271–2, 279. Selwyn's return elicited a curious entry by Queen Victoria in her journal: 'I do indeed pity him, for the exchange to the Black Country, where there will be no romance, no primitive races, but the worst kind of uncivilised civilisation, will be most trying': 1 December 1867, *The Letters of Queen Victoria, Second Series: A Selection from Her Majesty's Correspondence and Journal between the Years 1862 and 1878*, 3 vols. (London: John Murray, 1926–8), vol. I, p. 471. For Colenso, see Dean Stanley to Queen Victoria, 21 December 1874, in *Letters of Queen Victoria, Second Series*, vol. II, pp. 360–1.

41 Queen Victoria to Lord Salisbury, 1 February 1876, Salisbury papers, Hatfield House, 3M/F.

42 Royal Archives (RA) VIC/MAIN/QVJ (W) 22 March 1865 (Princess Beatrice's copies); J. C. Beckett, 'Gladstone, Queen Victoria, and the Disestablishment of the Irish Church, 1868–9', *Irish Historical Studies*, 13:49 (1962), 38–47.

43 A modern biography is Giles St. Aubyn, *The Royal George, 1819–1904: The Life of HRH Prince George, Duke of Cambridge* (London: Constable, 1963); cf. Strachan, *Politics of the British Army*, pp. 63–5.

44 Walter Richards, *Her Majesty's Army: A Descriptive Account of the Various Regiments, etc.*, 3 vols. (London: H. Virtue, 1888–91).
45 Noble Frankland, 'Arthur, Prince, First Duke of Connaught and Strathearn (1850–1942)', *Oxford Dictionary of National Biography* (Oxford: Oxford University Press, 2004).
46 Walter Arnstein, 'The Warrior Queen: Reflections on Victoria and Her World', *Albion*, 30 (1998), 1–28.
47 Dalhousie masterminded Queen Victoria's first visit to Scotland in 1842, and his wife was a Lady of the Bedchamber. Canning's wife, Charlotte, had also been a Lady of the Bedchamber. Dufferin had been a Lord-in-Waiting.
48 Torrington returned from an unpopular stint in Ceylon to be a Lord-in-Waiting to Albert, and, later, to Queen Victoria. Carrington accompanied the Prince of Wales on his Indian tour in 1875–76. Normanby had been Comptroller and then Treasurer of the Royal Household. Linlithgow had been a Lord-in-Waiting and later became Lord Chamberlain.
49 Lord Melbourne to Queen Victoria, 25 October 1838, 21 December 1838, *The Letters of Queen Victoria: A Selection from Her Majesty's Correspondence between the Years 1837 and 1861*, ed. A. C. Benson and Vct. Esher, 3 vols. (London: J. Murray, 1907), vol. I, pp. 164–5, 175–6.
50 RA VIC/MAIN/QVJ (W) 12 February 1865, 20 February 1876 (Princess Beatrice's copies).
51 John Fabb, *Royal Tours of the British Empire, 1860–1927* (London: Batsford, 1989); Charles Reed, *Royal Tourists, Colonial Subjects and the Making of a British World, 1860–1911* (Manchester: Manchester University Press, 2016).
52 W. D. Liddle, '"A Patriot King, or None": Lord Bolingbroke and the American Renunciation of George III', *Journal of American History*, 65 (1979), 951–70; David Armitage, 'A Patriot for Whom? The Afterlives of Bolingbroke's Patriot King', in *Greater Britain, 1516–1776*, pp. 397–418. For a slightly different argument about the salience of the patriot king ideal in the context of the late nineteenth-century imperial federation movement, see Duncan Bell, 'The Idea of a Patriot Queen? The Monarchy, the Constitution, and the Iconographic Order of Greater Britain, 1860–1900', *Journal of Imperial and Commonwealth History*, 34:1 (2006), 3–22.
53 For the Canadian petition, see John McLaren, 'The Rule of Law and Irish Whig Constitutionalism in Upper Canada', in Jim Philips, R. Roy McMurtry and John T. Saywell (eds), *Essays in the History of Canadian Law: A Tribute to Peter N. Oliver* (Toronto: University of Toronto Press, 2008), p. 337. For the one from New South Wales: *A Petition to the King, for the Repeal of the Existing Land Regulations, from His Majesty's Loyal and Dutiful Subjects, the Landholders, Merchants, and Free Inhabitants of New South Wales, on Behalf of Themselves and Others Interested in the Colony* (Sydney: Stephens & Stokes, 1831). For the 1820 Maori visit, see Timothy Yates, *The Conversion of the Maori: Years of Religious and Social Change, 1814–1842* (Grand Rapids, Mich.: Eerdmans, 2013), p. 27. And for the 1831 Maori petition, see Peter Adams, *Fatal Necessity: British Intervention in New Zealand, 1830–1847* (Oxford: Oxford University Press, 1977), pp. 50–1. For the African petitions, see *Addresses, Petitions, &c from the Kings and Chiefs of Sudan (Africa) and the Inhabitants of Sierra Leone, to His Late Majesty, King William the Fourth, and His Excellency, H. D. Campbell, Late Lieutenant-Governor of That Colony* (London: Gilbert & Rivington, 1838). And for Indian delegations of the era, see Michael H. Fisher, *Counterflows to Colonialism: Indian Travellers and Settlers in Britain, 1600–1857* (Delhi: Permanent Black, 2004), Chapter 7.
54 In a large secondary literature, I have found the following histories of the treaty most useful: Claudia Orange, *The Treaty of Waitangi* (Wellington: Allen & Unwin, 1987); Lindsay Head, 'The Pursuit of Modernity: The Conceptual Bases of Citizenship in the Early Colonial Period', in Andrew Sharp and Paul McHugh (eds), *Histories, Power and Loss: Uses of the Past, A New Zealand Commentary* (Wellington: Bridget Williams, 2001), pp. 97–233.
55 For the 1852 visit, see Tamihana Te Rauparaha to Sir D. McLean [n.d., c. 1852], National Library of New Zealand, Wellington, MS-Papers-11899; and Steven Oliver,

'Te Rauparaha, Tamihana', *Te Ara: The Encyclopedia of New Zealand*. Available online at www.TeAra.govt.nz/en/biographies/1t75/te-rauparaha-tamihana (accessed 23 January 2016). For the 1855 visit, see Richard Taylor, *Te Ika a Maui; or, New Zealand and Its Inhabitants: Illustrating the Origin, Manners, Customs, Mythology, Religion ... of the Natives Together with the Geology, Natural History, Productions, and Climate of the Country* (London: Wertheim & Macintosh, 1855), pp. 473–5; and J. M. R. Owens, *The Mediator: A Life of Richard Taylor, 1805–1873* (Wellington: Victoria University Press, 2004), pp. 206–8. For 1860, see Helen M. Hogan, *Bravo, Neu Zeeland: Two Maori in Vienna, 1859–1860* (Christchurch: Clerestory Press, 2003). And for the 1863 visit, see Brian Mackrell, *Hariru Wikitoria!: An Illustrated History of the Maori Tour of England, 1863* (Oxford: Oxford University Press, 1985).

56 *The Times*, 15 November 1862, p. 9. The original of the poem is in the Grey Collection of Maori MSS, Auckland Public Library, GNZ MMSS 26.
57 Evelyn Stokes, *Wiremu Tamihana Tarapipipi Te Waharoa: A Study of His Life and Times* (Hamilton: University of Waikato, 1999), Chapter 6; Richard Boast, 'Vanished Theocracies: Christianity, War and Politics in Colonial New Zealand, 1830–80', in Lisa Ford and Tim Rowse (eds), *Between Indigenous and Settler Governance* (London and New York: Routledge, 2013), pp. 73–5.
58 This paragraph draws on my 'Queen Victoria and India, 1837–61', *Victorian Studies*, 46:2 (2004), 264–74, and my forthcoming book, *Empress: Queen Victoria and India*.
59 Mahatma Gandhi, *Hind Swaraj and Other Writings*, ed. Anthony Parel (Cambridge: Cambridge University Press, 1997), pp. 79–80; Ramachandra Guha, *Gandhi before India* (London: Allen Lane, 2013), Chapter 6.
60 'List of Addresses and Presents, Queen Victoria's Golden Jubilee', National Archives, Kew, LC 2/115.
61 Proceedings of the 3rd day, 30 December 1885, in Mushirul Hasan (ed.), *Proceedings of the Indian National Congress*, vol. I: *1885–1889* (New Delhi: Nyogi, 2012), pp. 104, 132–3, 139.
62 Bridget Theron, 'King Cetshwayo in Victorian England: A Cameo of Imperial Interaction', *South African Historical Journal*, 56 (2006), 60–87; Catherine Anderson, 'A Zulu King in Victorian London: Race, Royalty and Imperialist Aesthetics in Late Nineteenth-Century Britain', *Visual Resources*, 24:3 (2008), 299–319.
63 Merze Tate, 'Great Britain and the Sovereignty of Hawaii', *Pacific Historical Review*, 31 (1962), 327–48; Christopher Smith, *A Pacific Queen in the East: Kapiolani's Visit in the Year of the Golden Jubilee* (Norwich: C. Smith, 2008).
64 For a later example of the British royal signature on a treaty validating indigenous monarchy, see Constance Turnbull, 'British Colonialism and the Making of the Modern Johor Monarchy', *Indonesia and the Malay World*, 36:109 (2009), 227–48.
65 Caroline Keen, *Princely India and the British: Political Development and the Operation of Empire* (London: I. B. Tauris, 2012), Chapters 3, 5; Barbara Metcalf, 'Islam and Power in Colonial India: The Making and Unmaking of a Muslim Princess', *American Historical Review*, 116:1 (2011), 1–30.
66 Victoria's two jubilees await a comprehensive study. For now, see E. W. Ellsworth, 'Victoria's Diamond Jubilee and the British Press: The Triumph of Popular Imperialism', *Social Studies*, 56 (1965), 173–80; Jan Morris, *Pax Britannica: The Climax of an Empire* (London: Faber, 1968), Chapter 1; John Fabb, *Victoria's Golden Jubilee* (London: Seaby, 1987); Tori Smith, '"Almost Pathetic ... but Also Very Glorious": The Consumer Spectacle of the Diamond Jubilee', *Histoire Sociale/Social History*, 29:58 (1996), 333–56.
67 Queen Victoria to Crown Princess Victoria (her eldest daughter), 1 October 1873, *Letters of Queen Victoria, Second Series*, vol. II, p. 283. See Taylor, 'Prince Albert and the British Empire', pp. 78–9, for Albert's ideas on royal federation.
68 Deryck Schreuder, 'Locality and Metropolis in the British Empire: A Note on Some Connections between the British North America Act (1867) and Gladstone's First Irish Home Rule Bill', in J. A. Benyon, C. W. Cook, T. R. H. Davenport and K. S. Hunt (eds), *Studies in Local History: Essays in Honour of Professor Winifred Maxwell* (Oxford: Oxford University Press 1976), pp. 48–58.

69 William Smith O'Brien, *Principles of Government; or, Meditations in Exile*, 2 vols. (Dublin: James Duffy, 1856), vol. I, pp. 21–9; Matthew Kelly, 'Irish Nationalist Opinion and the British Empire in the 1850s and 1860s', *Past and Present*, 204 (2009), 127–54; Colin Reid, ' "An Experiment in Constructive Unionism": Isaac Butt, Home Rule and Federalist Political Thought during the 1870s', *English Historical Review*, 129:537 (2014), 332–61; Elaine A. Byrne, 'Irish Home Rule: Stepping-Stone to Imperial Federation?', *History Ireland*, 20:1 (2012), 25–7.
70 Lytton, 'Memorandum' (11 May 1876), India Office Records L/PS/20/MEMO33/19, British Library, London.
71 RA VIC/MAIN/QVJ (W) 10 October 1880 (Princess Beatrice's copies); Earl of Carnarvon to Queen Victoria, 29 April 1875, *Letters of Queen Victoria, Second Series*, vol. II, pp. 387–8. For the background, see C. F. Goodfellow, *Great Britain and South African Confederation, 1870–81* (Oxford: Oxford University Press, 1966); Bruce Knox, 'The Earl of Carnarvon, Empire, and Imperialism, 1855–90', *Journal of Imperial and Commonwealth History*, 26:2 (1998), 48–66.
72 Philip Murphy, *Monarchy and the End of Empire: The House of Windsor, the British Government, and the Postwar Commonwealth* (Oxford: Oxford University Press, 2013).

CHAPTER THREE

Two Victorias? Prince Alfred, Queen Victoria and Melbourne, 1867–68

Cindy McCreery

The first British royal tour to Australia drew attention to two Victorias: the Queen and the colony.[1] While the colony of Victoria in Australia was only one of several 'Victorias' created during the august queen's reign, by the 1860s residents could be forgiven for thinking it was the most important.[2] The association between Victoria and the Queen was relatively recent and reflected the opportunism of early British settlers. Unlike the colonies of New South Wales (1788) and Van Diemen's Land (1825; Tasmania from 1856), which were formally established by the British government as penal colonies, Victoria gained its separate colonial status largely through the actions of private individuals. While the government did establish a military outpost at Sullivan's Bay (located due south of modern Melbourne near the entrance to Port Phillip Bay) in 1803 in order to pre-empt the French, Aboriginal resistance plus the apparent unsuitability of the land encouraged the British government to move on to Tasmania. 'Victoria' remained a backwater of the New South Wales colony but still largely under Aboriginal control until pastoralists from Tasmania arrived in 1835 eager to find new grazing areas for their sheep. Gold discoveries from mid-century built upon the expanding agricultural and pastoral sector to attract a massive wave of European settlers and investors, which led to the formal separation of the colony of Victoria from New South Wales in 1851. By 1867, its capital, Melbourne (named after Queen Victoria's favourite prime minister, William Lamb, 2nd Viscount Melbourne), with a population approaching 200,000, was the largest city in the southern hemisphere and probably the most showy. If not yet 'marvellous', Melbourne was well on the way.[3]

So the announcement in 1867 of a visit by Queen Victoria's second son, the twenty-three-year-old Prince Alfred, offered a perfect opportunity for colonists to demonstrate how their society was worthy of its namesake. Like the other Australian colonies, Victoria busied itself with planning an appropriate reception despite the relatively short notice, recent political turmoil and the government's ongoing struggle to access sufficient funds.[4] Victoria was determined that its royal welcome would be bigger and better than that of its neighbours South Australia, Tasmania, New South Wales and Queensland. Throughout his five-week visit to Victoria from 23 November 1867 to 4 January 1868, public festivities frequently reminded Prince Alfred of the links between the two Victorias.

Victoria's main attraction was Melbourne, which best displayed the colony's progress and boasted appropriate facilities for the royal guest. While Alfred did visit briefly the important regional centres of Ballarat, Bendigo and Geelong, and spent some time hunting in the rural Western District, for the most part he remained in Melbourne. Officially Alfred lodged at the Governor's residence in the leafy south-eastern suburb of Toorak, but in practice he spent much time in the exclusive Melbourne Club downtown, as well as making regular visits back to HMS *Galatea*, anchored off Williamstown, south-west of the city. Throughout his visit, Alfred was kept busy laying foundation stones of new buildings, watching street processions, attending formal receptions, balls and banquets, musical and dramatic concerts, picnics, cricket matches and horse races, as well as making and receiving numerous addresses of welcome.

If Alfred's Victorian tour was thus more lavish than his visits to other Australian colonies, it also left an especially rich set of records. These allow us to look beyond the mostly triumphal colonial press accounts as well as the largely deferential official tour volumes to track the responses of both individual colonists and groups.[5] Indeed, we know much more about private responses to Alfred in Victoria than perhaps anywhere else he visited on his global tour.

This chapter explores a range of accounts to provide a fuller understanding of local responses to the royal tour.[6] It considers public sources such as the official published tour volumes, articles in three Melbourne newspapers (the *Australasian*, the *Argus* and the *Age*), articles and cartoons in *Melbourne Punch*, loyal addresses (the testimonials presented by local organisations, whose texts were frequently reprinted in newspapers), as well as the transparencies and illuminations affixed to major public and private buildings.[7] But it also considers private sources such as the diaries of the colonists Curtis Candler and Frederick Standish, which in turn allude to private correspondence and conversations. The chapter concludes by examining three individual petitions presented to Alfred.[8]

Two Victorias?

In fact, there were never just two 'Victorias'. This was true both of the Queen and the colony. Numerous scholars have demonstrated the complexity of Queen Victoria's personality, political and cultural influence, and have traced how these shifted over time.[9] Especially important were the variety of contemporary representations of the Queen: as devoted wife and mother, as grief-stricken widow and as conscientious, caring and/or selfish sovereign. So, too, colonial Victoria was a heterogeneous and rapidly changing society, which encompassed a range of moral attitudes. It was also represented in different ways – as both rough and civilised, for example – by different observers for varying purposes.[10]

Alfred's visit highlighted the often superficial links between monarch and colony, as well as the ways in which individual images of the Queen were employed to make particular arguments about the colony. Beyond her malleability as a symbol, the most important thing about Queen Victoria in Victoria was her absence. The Queen never visited Victoria nor indeed any of her other overseas colonies. Alfred was the first (and, for over a decade afterwards, the only major) member of the British royal family to visit Britain's settler colonies in the southern hemisphere – and much else besides. Without the constraining presence of the Queen, the colony and Prince Alfred were free to reinvent themselves as independent, progressive entities.

Alfred's mother remained behind at Windsor throughout his Australian tour of 1867–68.[11] Yet the monarch was of course remembered, and nowhere more warmly, according to locals, than in colonial Victoria. The Church of England clergy, for example, boasted to Alfred that

> there is no name so beloved and respected among all classes of men in our highly independent-minded community as that of your Royal mother – a name which she has graciously permitted this country to bear.[12]

While Victoria the colony here recognised the worth of Victoria the Queen, the reference to 'our highly independent-minded community' told Prince Alfred that this was no land of sycophantic toadies: Victorians thought for themselves. This insistence on local agency is consistent with the current scholarship on British royal tours, which finds that while Queen Victoria remained mostly ambivalent about her family's travels around the Empire, her name was often manipulated by colonial figures for their own purposes.[13]

Certainly, throughout his Australian tour, Alfred was reminded of his parent in numerous expressions of colonial loyalty.[14] 'I knew your blessed mother when she was a child; I wish she had fifty like you', one elderly woman told the prince in Tasmania, his next stop after Victoria.[15] In Victoria itself, the loyal address from the Primitive Methodist Churches acknowledged 'the great kindness of Her Majesty, also that of your Royal Highness in foregoing [sic] the endearments of home to visit so distant a part of the British Empire.'[16] This served to highlight the significance of Alfred's visit and the great honour Queen Victoria thereby bestowed upon the colony. Yet accompanying this deference, and the acknowledgement of the great distance which Alfred had travelled, was a palpable confidence that he would find the colonial Victoria worthy of the mother country.

Melbourne was the jewel in this Victoria's crown, the place where Alfred accordingly spent most of his time and the site of the most elaborate festivities, dutifully recorded and celebrated in the colonial press. When Alfred laid the foundation stone of the new town hall on 29 November, for example, the *Age* newspaper noted proudly that 'already there are in Melbourne several public buildings that would do credit to a city centuries in age and very much larger than the capital of Victoria'.[17]

Like Melbourne's buildings, local ladies enhanced the city's visual appeal. The *Age* continued:

> The scene was one of a very pleasing and gay appearance. ... [Ladies] dressed in the light and bright-coloured fabrics suitable to the [southern hemisphere's summer] season, and looking altogether as well as might have been expected, they were fitting accessories to a ceremony in which one of the sons of her Most Gracious Majesty took the most prominent part.[18]

This description of colonial ladies as 'fitting accessories' was symptomatic of the entire royal tour – and indeed of colonial society's aspirations to gentility in general.[19] In Melbourne, perhaps more than any other Australian city, female figures, including Queen Victoria, were prominently displayed in the city's public decorations.

Representing Queen Victoria and Prince Alfred

Queen Victoria was most often depicted via transparencies (pictures lit from behind) and illuminations (gas piping 'wrought into motifs and mottoes and then set alight') placed at or near the top of public and major private buildings. These images were designed to be seen at night, and, as Anita Callaway notes, the city thus became a canvas on which its self-confidence and rising status in the world were displayed to advantage.[20] The Queen was frequently represented via her initials 'QV' or 'VR'

(Victoria Regina). This was both simple and relatively inexpensive and could be produced more easily at short notice than portraits. Moreover, her initials functioned as a powerful and immediately recognisable symbol of monarchy for colonists.[21] Victoria was also represented as a female figure in several transparencies.[22] Yet here again the trappings of the Queen's monarchical status (e.g., crown and robes of state) took precedence over her personal physical features.[23] A good example is the wood engraving depicting the fireworks display in Yarra Park (see Figure 6). Here illuminated transparency portraits of the Queen in robes of state (left) and Prince Alfred in naval uniform (right) appear below and beside various symbols including a crown and the initials 'VR'.[24]

This formulaic depiction of Queen Victoria as monarch, which most knowledgeable British visitors agreed bore very little resemblance to

6. 'Fireworks in the Yarra Park, in celebration of the visit of HRH the Duke of Edinburgh', engraved by Samuel Calvert, wood engraving, *Illustrated Melbourne Post*, 27 December 1867. State Library of Victoria, IMP27/12/67/177

her actual features (for example, in the wood engraving in Figure 6, she appears much younger than she was in 1867), was certainly not unique to the colony of Victoria.[25] To save money and time, decorations moved from one Australian colony to another.[26] Even new decorations were often copied from other 'copies', so that any original resemblance to the subject was likely to be lost in translation.

The limitations of colonial craftsmanship, cost-cutting, lack of preparation time and the Queen's absence help explain why locally made images were often poor likenesses and rarely directly depicted her as Alfred's mother. Yet Queen Victoria's likeness was already well established in *British* images (albeit not necessarily up-to-date or high-quality ones) circulating throughout the Empire.

Printed images served to introduce royalty to their far-off subjects. During Alfred's visit to Sierra Leone in 1860, for example, a local newspaper noted that the teenage prince 'has a striking resemblance especially in the upper part of the face to the engravings of the Queen'. Appropriately, during his visit, Alfred 'presented Governor Hill with a fine engraving of the Queen and Prince Consort'.[27] By filling in the visual gaps for colonists who would never lay their own eyes on their monarch, engravings reassured them that they knew what their sovereign looked like. In turn, the circulation of images of the monarch's sons and daughters promoted the idea of the British Empire as an affectionate family.

By the time of Alfred's tour of Victoria in 1867, photographs, as well as engravings (the latter published both separately and as part of illustrated periodicals), showed off the royal family to distant colonists as well as British audiences. From c. 1860, photographs of the Queen and her family began to circulate widely throughout the Empire as part of the worldwide craze for the small photographic portraits known as cartes-de-visite. J. E. Mayall's 1859 carte-de-visite set of members of the royal family created a sensation. The series sold untold copies, making the photographer a fortune and Queen Victoria's family 'household faces' around the world. Indeed, as John Plunkett points out, Queen Victoria and her husband Prince Albert were early adopters of photography and recognised the value of making images of themselves and their family available to their subjects as well as within their own family.[28] The 1863 wedding of the Prince and Princess of Wales (Alfred's elder brother and sister-in-law) increased colonial demand for recent images of Queen Victoria's family.[29] By 1867, there appears to have been a widespread feeling among Australian colonists that they knew what members of the royal family looked like and that in Alfred they recognised something of the Queen.

Certainly, Melbourne newspapers such as the *Argus* felt confident enough in their knowledge of the recently arrived Alfred to complain that many local representations did not resemble the prince in the least:

His Royal Highness was made to assume such an immense variety of absurd, grotesque, and improbable aspects, that his royal mother would certainly have failed to recognize her offspring in the majority of them ... so stiff, and wooden, and glaring were the attitudes and colours in which the authors had chosen to embody their ideas of the British naval commander.[30]

It is significant that here Alfred is represented as a professional naval officer (he was then a captain in the Royal Navy). While this might be explained by local artists' uncertainty about how to represent him as a prince, it is more likely a reflection of the fact that his naval career was essential to colonists' vision of their own progress. By embracing a career as a professional sailor, Alfred demonstrated his pursuit of the same values of self-reliance, industry and lack of pretence that had made Britain a great nation and which the modern Australian colonies prided themselves on.[31] Indeed, public representations of Alfred as a naval officer far outnumbered those of him as a potential king of Australia.[32] For example, the wood engraving depicting the illuminations at the Union Bank of Australia in Melbourne shows Alfred in naval uniform in an oval pendant, with a large image of his ship HMS *Galatea* to the right (see Figure 7).[33]

7. 'Union Bank of Australia', wood engraving, *Illustrated Australian News for Home Readers*, 26 November 1867. State Library of Victoria, IAN26/11/67/SUPP/4

For his part, Alfred seems to have been genuinely proud of his naval career, and he wore naval dress uniform, adorned with royal honours such as the Star of the Order of the Garter, at many of the most important colonial ceremonies.[34]

The familial connection between Victoria and Alfred (as well as Alfred's own princely status) was thus underplayed in public visual representations produced within the colony. For all the respectful mention of the Queen and reminders to Alfred of the importance of this family relationship in speeches, loyal addresses and newspaper articles, very few images created in Victoria depicted the Queen directly as Alfred's mother.

For colonists had another priority when fashioning their images: advancing their own colony's reputation. Local images naturally focused on the colony of Victoria, not the Queen. So, too, ignoring Victoria's status as Alfred's mother further heightened his own significance. As a young man who had recently passed the age of majority, had been created Duke of Edinburgh and had assumed command of his first warship, Alfred was a worthy subject in his own right. Indeed, he was seen as a personification of qualities associated with the colony: youth, modernity, expertise.[35] By depicting Alfred as a responsible adult, Victoria heightened the prestige of his visit, and, in turn, the importance of the colony.

Representing the colony

Both the London and Australian editions of *Punch* played on the notion of Alfred as a would-be suitor to female allegorical representations of 'New South Wales', 'Victoria', etc.[36] But the colony of Victoria could also be represented as a young male companion for Alfred. As *Melbourne Punch* put it, in an analogy that flattered both Prince and colony (and conveniently excused in advance any colonial faux pas): 'The country you are now visiting is young as yourself. You and it were in the cradle together. Both growing to lusty manhood; both showing fair promise of future greatness. Young yourself, you will the more readily forgive the follies of youth.'[37]

In such a narrative, the role of the mother queen took a back seat to that of the would-be colonial daughter-in-law or male companion. Victoria the colony was the focus here; Victoria the Queen (and, by extension, Prince Alfred) merely the frame. A good example is the illuminated picture displayed on the Melbourne premises of the stationers and printers Sands & McDougall (see Figure 8).[38]

8. 'Illuminations in Melbourne: Messrs. Sands and M'Dougall, Collins Street', wood engraving, *Illustrated Melbourne Post*, 27 November 1867. State Library of Victoria, IMP27/11/67/5

Here Alfred is welcomed by an allegorical female figure representing the colony. Other than via her initials above, Queen Victoria is nowhere to be seen.

Yet representations of the colony itself were far from consistent. Sometimes Victoria was effectively reduced to its capital, Melbourne, while at other times it seemed indistinguishable from other allegorical representations of Britannia or New South Wales as young eligible women in classical drapery. As the *Australasian* astutely predicted:

> We may expect to find the crowd of sight-seers gazing in hopeless perplexity at inscrutable pictorial allegories, in which BRITTANIA [sic] and VICTORIA, NEPTUNE and numerous disreputable gods and goddesses will be represented. ... Everything will be fragmentary and incongruous – a star here, a crown there, an anchor in one place, and a gaudy picture in another; the total effect being multiplicity and confusion of detail.[39]

This anxiety about how the colony of Victoria would depict itself (and distinguish itself from its colonial neighbours) was representative of a wider concern about how to represent Australia. Allegorical female figures were frequently used in Australia, as elsewhere, to depict the state. As Penny Russell and Marilyn Lake note, the late nineteenth-century symbol 'Miss Australia' lacked consistent representation, which, in turn, reflects wider uncertainty about the identity of the nation and of women's role within it.[40] Representing women and states as female figures, whether it be Queen Victoria, colonial Victoria, Australia, or actual colonial women in Victoria, continued to prove awkward during Alfred's 1867–68 visit. All too often both visual artists and writers fell back on female stereotypes.

Masculine culture

If representing actual women and colonies via female symbols proved tricky, representing men and masculine behaviour often proved less controversial. In addition to formal and respectful representations of Alfred as a naval officer and as a male companion or potential suitor of colonial Victoria, which presented both him and the colony as loyal, civilised and mature, there was another strain of colonial representation. Satirical journalism formed part of a rich British masculine comic tradition, which was exported and then adapted in individual settler-colonies via such publications as London *Punch* and its colonial namesakes in Sydney and Melbourne. In the 1860s, issues often featured stories or poems purportedly written by working-class correspondents. Much of the joke revolved around locals' use of slang and their numerous spelling and grammatical errors. Thus, a humorous poem in *Melbourne Punch*, 'The Vizzit of Prints Halfred', by 'A. Nidiot. Nowhere', imagines a seasick Alfred aboard the *Galatea* en route to Australia:

> And ees wishin with is muthar,
> Like a good boy, 'e ad stayd;

But it aint no use regrettin',
Four ees bound for Addeylayd.

Here both the British prince and his colonial destination of Adelaide, in the rival colony of South Australia, are ridiculed. But this image of Alfred as a seasick mother's boy and the predictable Victorian put-down of the South Australian capital city is then (partly) redressed once Alfred is welcomed ashore. The Mayor orders the gaslights be turned on to start the illumination:

> Then the Prints replys, 'That's jolly' –
> Now let's go and 'likker up.'
> Then hinto the nearest grog shop
> Kwikli 'ies the kompanee,
> 'Drinks awl round', ses nobul Halfred,
> 'And score 'em up to Misses V.'[41]

According to the poem, Alfred was now acting like a red-blooded man at ease in Australia, a metaphor, perhaps, for the enlivening and egalitarian qualities of hard-drinking colonial life. This sketch, which depicts Alfred as cheerfully charging the Adelaide pub bill to his mother, is typical of *Melbourne Punch*'s irreverent masculine humour. The attribution to 'A. Nidiot. Nowhere' enabled *Melbourne Punch* to distance itself from the poem's more risqué elements while still entertaining its readers.

This light-hearted poem also hints at the benefits of such relaxed masculine behaviour. Alcohol, male companionship – and, indeed, that of unrespectable women – would form a large part of Prince Alfred's actual stay in Melbourne. Such behaviour on Alfred's part, the sketch suggests, would be understood and even admired by *Melbourne Punch*'s male readers, who enjoyed ridiculing the pretensions of genteel colonial society. Even in its more conventional address of welcome to Prince Alfred, *Melbourne Punch* described itself as a 'chartered libertine'. This tells us that there was more than one definition of appropriate 'entertainment' for Prince Alfred in colonial Victoria.

In turn, this perspective forms part of a wider debate between those who stressed the importance of developing Victoria's social and cultural maturity through respectable entertainments open to men, women and, where appropriate, children, and those who urged that male colonists be allowed to continue to indulge in pleasures like smoking, drinking and gambling with other men – as well as dalliances with unrespectable women. The two were not mutually exclusive, however, and Alfred's itinerary encompassed a wide range of both respectable and unrespectable activities.[42]

Respectable society

While Alfred may well have preferred *Melbourne Punch*'s informal masculine hospitality, duty required his attendance at official functions. Here actual women, not just illuminated transparencies, were employed to demonstrate the colony's progress. Two of the planned highlights of the Prince's tour of Victoria – the Free Banquet and the Fancy Dress Ball – were highly dependent on women's participation and, indeed, visible enjoyment. It seemed essential for the colony's reputation as a civilised society that local women shone before the Prince.

The Free Banquet was chosen, in part, as a particularly appropriate way to demonstrate the colony's loyalty to the Prince, and, by extension, Queen Victoria. As the wealthy Melbourne medical entrepreneur Louis L. Smith, the colonist who came up with the idea, explained to his fellow colonists:

> In old times, he said, it was always the custom, when a king or other great personage visited one of the cities of the kingdom, to take care that the visit should be a joyful occasion to the poor of the place, to whom, with that view a public feast was given.[43]

The banquet would thus enable the city of Melbourne to demonstrate its place as 'one of the cities of the kingdom' to its monarch through her visiting son. At the same time, the banquet was intended to display the skills and generosity of local elites, including colonial ladies.

Sadly, the Free Banquet demonstrated none of its organisers' hopes and all of its detractors' fears about colonial behaviour. A very hot, windy day, a huge crowd of up to 100,000 people in the Richmond Paddock, plus the Prince's long-delayed arrival, led to tired, hungry, thirsty and increasingly restless guests.[44] Then, when the Chief of Police cancelled Alfred's appearance because of safety concerns, order collapsed, leading to a drunken free-for-all. Subsequent press discussion focused less on the disappointment of the crowd than on how the fiasco would affect the colony's reputation.[45]

Still, while the working-class guests were blamed, so too were the elite organisers and, indeed, Alfred himself. The editorial in the *Age* went so far as to declare 'It would be wrong to conceal from his Royal Highness the fact that there exists a great deal of soreness in many quarters in consequence of his apparent breach of good manners in not keeping his appointment.'[46]

Frederick Standish, Chief of Police, the Prince's chaperon and the target of much of the criticism for cancelling Alfred's attendance, couched his defence in terms of chivalric concern. According to his friend Curtis Candler, Standish 'said that had he [Prince Alfred] gone, he is sure that great loss of life must have ensued. Women and children must have been crushed by the crowd pressing forward to any point the prince may have gone.'[47]

Chivalry was also cited by Louis L. Smith, but in order to criticise Standish's behaviour rather than to excuse it. Smith wrote to the *Age*:

> Sir, I demand justice to these ladies and gentlemen who had made adequate arrangements to entertain all. ... The noble Prince is the commander of a noble ship filled with brave men, and said to have brave officers. 50 ladies, the wives and daughters of some of our most reputable citizens, were waiting elegantly and uniformly dressed to receive him to his appointment, and present him with a flag of their own design and partial working.[48]

Smith held the Prince and the ladies to a higher standard of personal responsibility than the banquet's working-class guests. He emphasises the gap between two contemporary modes of elite manners: the polite, responsible and chivalrous one associated with the ladies and gentlemen of the banquet committee, while the irresponsible and selfish behaviour is associated with the Prince and his male advisers. Although most contemporary press reports debated whether ordinary colonists could ever be expected to behave properly at a 'free feed', a sizeable minority explored the selfishness of elite male behaviour.[49] The most important victim of this behaviour was not colonial women, however, but the colony's own reputation.

Just as the Free Banquet was intended to display colonial hospitality at its most generous, the emphasis of the Fancy Dress Ball was on inclusion rather than exclusion. Expectations ran high, especially among colonial women:

> Knowing that they had the spacious Exhibition Building at their entire disposal for the evening, the Corporation of Melbourne resolved to be bounteous in their invitations, and accordingly sent them out far and wide. As a consequence the ladies have been at a flutter.[50]

Unlike the disastrous Free Banquet, which was open to all and held outdoors on a blisteringly hot day, the evening Fancy Dress Ball was invitation only and held in a prestigious structure that reminded colonists of the recent success of the 1866–67 Intercolonial Exhibition.[51] It was the preferred venue for grand colonial occasions, and Alfred visited it several times for official receptions, banquets and balls. The Fancy Dress Ball succeeded where the Free Banquet had failed. Local newspapers listed and attempted to describe the dazzling array of both female and male costumes, and wood engravings depicted the ladies conversing on equal terms with the gentlemen.[52] Prince Alfred appeared here, as at many official functions, wearing his naval dress uniform. But the public splendour belied the private deception. Unbeknownst to almost all who attended, the clandestine reappearance of Prince Alfred and his friend Lord Newry in monks' costumes allowed them to gaze freely at the other guests and to eavesdrop on their private conversations.[53] For all the newspapers' emphasis on female influence, the Fancy Dress Ball was still controlled by men and privileged the male gaze. Once again, elite males outmanoeuvred colonial ladies.

The diaries of Curtis Candler and Frederick Standish

The Governor's Ball, also held in the Exhibition Building, further highlighted colonial women's disadvantage. While newspapers were predictably complimentary, and the *Illustrated Melbourne Post* published a decorous scene of 'the royal party dancing the scotch reel', the diarist Curtis Candler painted a different picture:

> The accounts of the Governor's Ball last night I find are various. The women folk do not seem to have enjoyed themselves as much as they expected. F... had to give up his partner, Mrs Panton, to the Duke for the Scotch Reel. He says he shouted just like any other wild Scotchman. ... Amit told me the Duke tried to Waltz with Miss Mabel M Sutton, but directly as has started half a dozen couples followed in full sail and he was cannoned from one to another so that he was compelled to bow to his partner and retire – though whether because of the [crush?] of the crowd, or that the lady was rather 'dewy in hand' does not appear.[54]

While Miss Mabel Manners-Sutton, daughter of the Governor of Victoria, may well have been embarrassed by her dancing partner's early departure, it gave Alfred the perfect opportunity to move on to the next phase of his evening entertainment. Once his official duties at balls and banquets ended (and Alfred himself often determined this), the Prince was free to spend time with whomever he pleased, wherever he wished. As both Curtis Candler's and Frederick Standish's diaries make clear, this often involved visits to actresses at the Variety Theatre and Mrs Fraser's upmarket brothel. But, above all, it meant that Alfred was free to relax with like-minded gentlemen at the exclusive Melbourne Club.

Alfred visited Melbourne with both a private companion (Francis Needham, known by his aristocratic title Lord Newry) and friends with an official role, such as the Hon. Eliot Yorke (equerry) and Adolphus Fitzgeorge (Lieutenant on HMS *Galatea*). These men, along with the other senior or aristocratic officers aboard HMS *Galatea*, were warmly welcomed by the Melbourne Club as honorary members.[55] According to British novelist Anthony Trollope, who visited Melbourne in 1871–72, local gentlemen's clubs (but he was thinking specifically of the Melbourne Club) offered the best of both worlds: 'all the comforts of London clubs' with 'great hospitality' shown to strangers.[56] An essential element of the Melbourne Club was its privacy. Alfred and his friends could enjoy evenings here dining, drinking and playing billiards and cards, often for money, with like-minded members, without fear that their activities would be reported in the press. Yet even here, a curious observer watched their every move, and then often elaborated on it in his diary.

Samuel Curtis Candler, the forty-year-old coroner, diarist and long-term resident member of the Melbourne Club, appeared perfectly positioned to view both the public and private aspects of Alfred's tour.[57] Candler specialised in exposing what he saw as the moral hypocrisy of elite colonial society, particularly its female component. Prior to Alfred's arrival, Candler wrote in the salacious manner typical of his diary:

> There is a great flutter in the Bosom of Society. ... From the last account by this Mail, it would seem Prince Alfred has many of his family's tendencies as regards the sex. Our dames, therefore, are eager to show him they do not forget the Scriptural behest about a stranger. There will be rare food for scandal for many aday [sic] after his departure, I suspect.[58]

But for all Candler's predictions of scandalous behaviour involving Prince Alfred and elite Melbourne women, what he actually recorded were fairly (and perhaps deliberately) vague accounts of the Prince and his companions Newry and Yorke relaxing with women who ranged from notorious to merely not quite respectable. This often involved private meetings and alcohol, but evidence of sexual intercourse is scant. In one of several similar entries, for example, Candler recorded that

> Standish told me this morning that the Prince and Yorke and he went behind the scenes at the Haymarket last night, and had great fun with Miss Celeste. Between the Acts they had cigars & brandy & water with her and she made herself very agreeable.[59]

This is an enthralling entry. Yet it suggests more than it proves. Standish's own diary entry (which Candler would have known well as he transcribed it) noted: 'To the Haymarket where the Prince & Governor's family went. Smoked in Mme Celeste's room with the Royal party.'[60]

'Mme Celeste' was the fifty-something French actress and former dancer Céline Céleste, who was completing an extended tour of Australia.[61] As Standish's entry and her age suggests, Alfred's interest focused on her acting abilities. He even telegraphed from Adelaide to request she delay her departure from Melbourne in order that he might see her perform. As a famous (if ageing) actress, it was unsurprising to find Madame Céleste serving drinks and cigars to a young bachelor prince and his theatre-mad friends backstage. Her popularity was only heightened by such royal patronage, and the Prince's reputation, and indeed the Governor's, was not sullied by such company.[62]

Perhaps more surprising was that visits to Sarah Fraser's upmarket brothel also created no apparent problems for Alfred's reputation. Once again, Alfred had the services of the ultimate tour guide to unrespectable as well as respectable Melbourne, the Commissioner of Police, Frederick Standish. As Paul de Serville notes, Standish led an extraordinary life that spanned a privileged European upbringing as the son of an English Whig MP and, following his ruin by gambling debts, a new life of hard graft on the Victorian goldfields before securing a civil-service post. As Chief of Police and a gentlemanly migrant, he was seen as an appropriate chaperon for Prince Alfred. Standish not only looked after Alfred's safety but also provided him with discreet entrée to the Melbourne brothels, which, it was alleged, he personally supervised on the Paris model.[63] While certainly unusual in its extremes, Standish's double life of outward respectability and inward 'immorality' – gambling, drinking and consorting with prostitutes – in fact mirrored that of other elite men, including fellow members of the Melbourne Club Sir Redmond Barry (Judge and Chancellor of the University of Melbourne) and Curtis Candler.[64]

Upper-class colonial women had much less flexibility to lead double lives while preserving their good reputations. Throughout Candler's diary of the Prince's visit, Alice Knight appears as a woman who was, at best, controversial. Married to J. G. Knight, the chief designer of Melbourne's celebrations and the author of the official Victorian tour volume, Mrs Knight's own family associations compromised her reputation. Candler recorded in his diary on 20 December 1867:

> There was a great deal of astonishment among the womenfolk at Mrs Knight's having been presented to H.R.H. and some rather strong observations were made about the fact that her brother (Bertrand) was in Sydney gaol – a prisoner for life for murder. However, the Duke and Yorke, who presented her, could not be supposed to know this, and that finding her a guest at Government House was sufficient for them. Lord Newry, however, was very savage with Yorke for doing it and told him it was damned bad taste – when there were so many charming and unexceptionable women present.

But more than just her disgraced brother, Mrs Knight's own bold behaviour distinguished her from other ladies. A few days later, Prince Alfred (incognito) chatted extensively with Mrs Knight at the Fancy Dress Ball. She appears to have been the only woman who penetrated his disguise, and she displayed delight at her familiarity with the Prince.[65]

Scandalous behaviour was most at risk of upsetting the rules of colonial social engagement in semi-public surroundings, in the daytime, where the divisions between elite and non-elite society appeared more porous and identity could not be easily hidden. At the New Year's Day horse races at Flemington, for example, social classes clustered in separate yet adjacent groups. All eyes, and ears, were on the Prince – and he knew it. According to Candler:

> H.R.H. lent over and whispered to me: 'don't you think if I were to take Mrs. K. [Mrs. Knight] up into the Vice-Royal box, place her beside her Ladyship, smoke this pipe in view of the whole stand and then shout out to Joe Thompson [a notorious bookie] below th[a]t I would take his five to one on the next event, I should be effectually settled?' I laughed outright at the fearful picture he had drawn and said 'Well Sir I think that would fill up H.E.'s cup of bitterness to the brim.' He was greatly tickled at the thought of this horrible outrage on the proprieties.[66]

Alfred did not proceed with his far-fetched plan, of course, and so the Governor, as well as broader society, was spared the 'horrible outrage on the proprieties'. But while Alfred was joking, his proposal indicates the tensions caused in colonial society when respectable people were brought face to face with disreputable people and behaviour (Mrs Knight, public pipe-smoking, shouting out a bet). So, too, it reflects Alfred's awkward relationship with the Governor and his family, whom Alfred apparently found too formal and officious for his liking.[67] Judging by Candler's response, Alfred had here adroitly judged the line between acceptable and unacceptable behaviour in 1860s Melbourne.

Melbourne society continued to view Prince Alfred and his entourage as gentlemen who (at least generally) observed the public rules of genteel society. There were certainly several references to Alfred's apparent boredom with public engagements and his diffidence in the face of curious crowds.[68] More fundamental criticism was mostly limited to newspapers like the *Freeman's Journal*, whose Irish Catholic editorial focus made it naturally sceptical of British royalty. The *Age*, too, published some critiques, notably after Alfred left the colony, with the emphasis predictably on the Prince's need for a 'sage and mature mentor' who could help the monarch's second son find an appropriate path in what was acknowledged as a difficult role. These critiques were more about what Alfred didn't do in Victoria than what he did:

> He might have done his work in a more business-like way, he might have visited our charitable institutions as well as our theatres, he might have extended his patronage beyond the makers of bon-bons and the workers in upholstery. Although not privileged 'to touch for king's "evil,"' yet he might have lightened some sorrowful hearts. It was not his fault that he did not do these things, or any of them.[69]

'To touch for king's "evil"' was the traditional practice of monarchs 'curing' their subjects' illness through the touch of their hands.[70] Its mention during Alfred's visit suggests the ongoing fascination with royal power as well as the way in which people in Victoria continued to view Alfred as an influential royal figure who served as a proxy for the monarch herself. This in turn suggests that colonists maintained high expectations that the visit of the royal prince would closely resemble that of the monarch herself, a comparison which we saw earlier in Louis L. Smith's discussion of the tradition of cities hosting free banquets for the poor during royal visits. Hence locals' disappointment was all the greater when Alfred failed to live up to their expectations.

Despite this criticism of Alfred's limited public role, his private affairs remained off limits, and Alfred and his companions continued their nocturnal adventures.[71] According to Standish's diary, Alfred's schedule involved sometimes dramatic alternations between respectable public and unrespectable private behaviour. So, while the Prince spent the 1867 Christmas Day morning with the Governor and his family at the viceregal residence in Toorak, including the obligatory church service, he dined with Standish and Candler at the Melbourne Club and then engaged in some gambling on their card game. On Boxing Day evening, Standish took him back to Mrs Fraser's brothel.[72] Within the narrow confines of elite Melbourne society, 'two Victorias' were thus apparent. While Alfred and like-minded elite men could move between the two, more strait-laced upper-class males, as well as their womenfolk, defined themselves as full-time members of respectable society.

Masculine and naval bonds

Alfred's behaviour suggests not only his desire to escape from the proprieties of viceregal society but also his preference for the company of other elite men. Gambling, drinking and even visits to brothels appear to have been not entirely an end in themselves for Alfred but rather a means to relax with like-minded gentlemen. Throughout his diary,

Candler noted Alfred's increasingly relaxed and confident manner in the Melbourne Club, which became his Victorian home away from home. Male friendship was Alfred's ultimate, if perhaps most elusive, goal. In Victoria, the Prince appears to have tried hard to extend his masculine 'family'.[73]

This sense of community with other elite men was unique neither to Alfred nor to the members of the Melbourne Club. It was particularly strong in the contemporary Royal Navy, and officers' loyalty to past and present members of the service was considerable.[74] So, when individual colonists petitioned Alfred for assistance, much mention was made of his family's tradition of rewarding loyal service as well as his own experience in the Royal Navy. Three examples are worth considering for what they tell us about Melbourne society and its relationship with both Queen Victoria and the Navy.

The first was from Mrs Ann Hennessy, who, according to the notes that accompanied her petition: 'Applies for an interview, to solicit assistance in education and maintenance of her grandson, an orphan and a cripple. Served the royal family for 30 years, with fruit and flowers and refers to Lady Palmerston, Lady De Graf and Madame Celeste. Brass badge of Covent Garden enclosed.'

Mrs Hennessy was both persistent and well organised. In her cover letter to Alfred's equerry Eliot Yorke, she introduced herself as 'the aged Widow who sent the Memorial from New Zealand to the Ship Galatea for his Royal Highness also a letter and parcel' and noted that she left her 'Meddle' (presumably the brass badge listed above, which apparently identified her as a licensed trader in London's Covent Garden fruit and flower market, perhaps with official royal patronage) 'at the Club on Tuesday night when I had the Honour of speaking to his Royal Highness I am still waiting in Melbourne thinking I could see his Royal Highness personally again'. As Hennessy now realised that this was impossible, she requested the 'return of the Meddle as I set great value on it, I only send [sic] it to let his Royal Highness know I am the proper person also it was the wish of Madam Celeste.'[75]

The second was from Mrs Ann Hicks, Old Hut Beach, Schnapper Point, Mornington, an address on a then rural peninsula near Melbourne. Like Mrs Hennessy, Mrs Hicks claimed a long-established connection with the royal family. The notes that accompanied her petition describe her as:

> Formerly occupant of a cottage in Hyde Park of which the occupancy was originally granted to her grandfather in 1751, for saving the life of George II when run away with by a horse. ... [A]rrived in the colony with but a shilling in her pocket – is nearly blind, more than 52 years of age and

likely to be turned out of the hut she now occupies – entreats that her destitution may be made known to the Queen.[76]

Lady Palmerston (the wife of the former British Prime Minister), Lady De Graf and the celebrated actress Madame Céleste were certainly influential patrons for Mrs Hennessy to invoke, trumped only by that of the former king, George II, cited by Mrs Hicks. Mrs Hicks also had the advantage, perhaps, of press attention. An annotation on her petition read: 'There has been some correspondence in the papers about this case – H.R.H. may have some knowledge of it and it may? suit to let him read the précis above? LT.'

Yet to obtain current royal approval was tricky. Members of the royal family from Queen Victoria down (and their secretaries) remained cautious about dispensing charity to cases not personally known to them or recommended by intimates.[77] When Mrs Hicks pleaded that her circumstances be communicated to Queen Victoria, she signalled her faith (like so many other petitioners across the Empire as well as in Britain) in the Queen as a magnanimous mother figure who cared for all of her subjects around the world.[78] Mrs Hicks may have been aware that attracting the Queen's personal attention was her best chance for success. Yet it seems unlikely that the Queen was ever informed of Mrs Hicks's situation. Mrs Hicks was only one among many petitioners and distance precluded a timely response.[79]

And while Mrs Hennessy apparently succeeded in gaining a personal interview one evening with Prince Alfred, this may have hurt rather than helped her cause. If the 'Club' she mentions was in fact the Melbourne Club, her presence in this private masculine space was certainly unorthodox (women were not permitted entry) and most likely unwelcome. Club members could of course meet women in a range of nearby venues, from respectable balls at the Exhibition Building to the private pleasures of Sarah Fraser's brothel around the corner on Stephen (now Exhibition) Street. But the club itself remained an exclusively male preserve.

Prince Alfred's responses to both women, as conveyed (and probably determined) by his equerries in conjunction with colonial officials, were polite yet impersonal rejections: 'Circular sent 31.12.67. L[?icence] Badge sent'; 'Circular sent 3.1.68.'[80]

A third petition came from a naval veteran. Whereas Mrs Hicks and Mrs Hennessy apparently wrote cover letters themselves or with the assistance of a Ballarat barrister, James Wilson benefited from not only a cover letter from an 'MP', James McKean, but an accompanying list of ten prominent local colonists, including justices of the peace, a member of the Legislative Council, an army captain and a surgeon, who jointly 'feel great pleasure in bringing under your notice James Wilson, Aged 77 an Old Man of War's man, as an honest hard working, and well conducted man we having known him for years'.

Such recommendations counted. An annotation noted, 'This Petition is supported by several persons who would not dare to if Wilson had not been worthy of assistance H.R.H. may perhaps think it fit to look at the petition – if not Circular.?SW.' In turn, another annotation indicated a successful outcome: 'Cheque for £5 enclosed. 3.1.68.?SJ.'[81]

While having friends in the right places certainly helped, James Wilson's petition probably also succeeded in part because it was from one naval man to another. The petition, which was handsomely written in neat copperplate writing, perhaps by a professional calligrapher, focused not on Wilson's current hardship but rather on his long and colourful naval career, beginning with his first service aboard 'H.M.S. "Windsor Castle", Captain Dashwood, on the Mediterranean Station' and including wartime service, shipwreck, kidnap, etc.

By supporting Wilson, Alfred was acting not only as a prince, demonstrating the royal family's commitment to charity, but also as a naval officer keen to support fellow members of his naval 'family' and their role in bolstering the British nation and empire. Although Wilson, a humble sailor, probably never entered the Melbourne Club nor went aboard HMS *Galatea*, his distinguished naval service gave him access to Alfred's private as well as public sympathy. Here, claims on Alfred's relationship with his naval rather than royal family paid dividends: the respectable sum of five pounds' worth, to be precise.

Epilogue

In 1869, Alfred returned to Melbourne in very different circumstances from his high-profile visit the year before. In April 1868, he had survived an assassination attempt in Sydney, and concerns remained for his safety. Moreover, this was purely a naval visit, and there were thus no public engagements.[82] Instead, Alfred and his companions returned briefly to their favourite haunts, including the Melbourne Club and Sarah Fraser's brothel, accompanied once again by Frederick Standish.

But if the shooting made Alfred cling to trusted male friends in Victoria all the more tightly (and perhaps enjoy disreputable women's attention all the more vibrantly), it made colonists remember his mother all the more fondly. Standish noted that a condolence meeting held in Melbourne's Exhibition Building the day after the shooting had 'wound up with "God Save the Queen" admirably sung by the large assemblage; 6 or 7000 people there'.[83] Now Australians forgot their colonial rivalries and any disappointment with Alfred and sought to demonstrate their shared loyalty to the Queen. The *Sydney Morning Herald* anticipated the reunion between Alfred and Victoria:

> Mothers who have such a son can alone imagine the joy of the QUEEN as she will catch the first sound of his chariot. The fatigues and perils of the voyage will be forgotten, and all the sorrows of home in that moment of gladness.[84]

Here, Queen Victoria resembled respectable colonial mothers and Prince Alfred virtuous colonial sons.[85]

Conclusion

Before the shooting, Prince Alfred's first royal British tour of Australia appeared the perfect opportunity to link two Victorias: the Queen and the colony. In practice, however, Alfred's visit focused greater attention on divisions within colonial society than on its resemblance to the monarch. In particular, Alfred's tour of Victoria revealed the conflict between those, such as the members of the Free Banquet Committee, who argued that the colony showcased respectable, middle-class values associated with 'mixed' society and those, like the editors of *Melbourne Punch* and the members of the Melbourne Club, who stressed the need to allow the Prince, and others, to continue the traditional male pastimes of drinking, gambling and whoring. As well as highlighting the awkward position of colonial women, who were viewed more as adornments than active members, Alfred's itinerary demonstrated the power wielded by privileged male society. Tucked away in the Melbourne Club or within a range of night-time venues, Alfred and his male companions could and did regularly ignore the restrictions and expectations of public respectable society. Indeed, Alfred's reception in Victoria demonstrates not only conventional loyalty to the British Crown but also the strength of local support for private masculine behaviour as well as for male institutions such as the Royal Navy. But, above all, Victorians expressed pride in their colony. The *Argus* reflected:

> while we were proud of his presence; we were also proud of ourselves. ... [W]e are convinced we have given him a prince's welcome, as worthy of the colony as of him. ... [Alfred] wore his naval uniform with the broad blue ribbon of the Garter; and his excellent figure, his face stamped with his mother's likeness, and a sufficiently noble bearing, added to the effect of his presence.[86]

Here Alfred played his part to perfection. So did Queen Victoria. Ultimately, the first royal British tour was all about the other Victoria, the colony.

Notes

1. Prince Alfred's visit to Australia comprised an early stage of his world voyages aboard HMS *Galatea* (1867–71). Alfred also visited South Africa, New Zealand, India, Ceylon, Hong Kong, China and Japan, as well as a range of major port cities and islands. These voyages constituted the first global tour by a member of the British royal family, the subject of my current book project.
2. Other places named or renamed after Queen Victoria include Victoria, British Columbia; Victoria (now Limbe), Cameroon; Victoria, Seychelles; Victoria Harbour, Hong Kong; Lake Victoria, Kenya, Tanzania and Uganda; Victoria Falls, Zambia and Zimbabwe; as well as Queensland, Australia; Queenstown, South Africa and Queenstown (now Cobh), Ireland.
3. This term properly applies to the boom and bust years of the 1880s; see Graeme Davison, *The Rise and Fall of Marvellous Melbourne*, 2nd edn (Carlton: Melbourne University Press, 2004); Miles Lewis, *Melbourne: The City's History and Development* (Melbourne: City of Melbourne, 1995), p. 59.
4. A series of constitutional crises in Victoria included the Appropriation Bill being rejected and, in 1866, the recall of Governor Charles Darling, who was succeeded later that year by John Manners-Sutton.
5. Revd John Milner and O. W. Brierly, *The Cruise of HMS Galatea* (London: W. H. Allen, 1869).
6. See also Brian McKinlay, *The First Royal Tour* (Adelaide: Rigby, 1970); Paul de Serville, *Pounds and Pedigrees: The Upper Class in Victoria, 1850–80* (Oxford: Oxford University Press, 1991); and Anita Callaway, *Visual Ephemera: Theatrical Art in Nineteenth-Century Australia* (Sydney: UNSW Press, 2000).
7. J. G. Knight, *Narrative of the Visit of His Royal Highness the Duke of Edinburgh to the Colony of Victoria* (Melbourne: Mason, Firth, 1868).
8. The Candler and Standish diaries are transcribed in Curtis Candler, 'Notes about Melbourne, and Diaries', 1848–19–, State Library of Victoria, MS 9502.
9. See, for example, Margaret Homans and Adrienne Munich (eds), *Remaking Queen Victoria* (Cambridge: Cambridge University Press, 1997); and A. N. Wilson, *Victoria: A Life* (London: Penguin, 2014).
10. See Knight, *Narrative*; de Serville, *Pounds and Pedigrees*; Penny Russell, *A Wish of Distinction: Colonial Gentility and Femininity* (Melbourne: Melbourne University Press, 1994); and Penny Russell, *Savage or Civilised? Manners in Colonial Australia* (Sydney: NewSouth Press, 2010).
11. Alfred visited Victoria following a short visit to South Australia and before visiting Tasmania, New South Wales and Queensland.
12. Loyal address from 'The Bishop and Clergy of the United Church of England and Ireland in Victoria', reprinted in the *Argus*, 27 November 1867, p. 6.
13. Charles Reed, *Royal Tourists, Colonial Subjects, and the Making of a British World* (Manchester: Manchester University Press, 2015), which the author kindly sent me in manuscript prior to publication.
14. Alfred's late father Prince Albert was also mentioned during the Victorian visit, particularly in relation to colonial projects aimed at improving the conditions of the working classes, a cause close to Albert's heart.
15. *Launceston Examiner*, 16 January 1868, p. 3. See my '"Long May He Float on the Ocean of Life": The First Royal Visit to Tasmania in 1868', *Tasmanian Historical Studies*, 12 (2007), 19–42.
16. Address from 'The Ministers And Lay Representatives Of The Primitive Methodist Churches In Victoria', published in the *Argus*, 27 November 1867, p. 6. Primitive Methodist churches sought to infuse Methodism with the revival spirit pioneered by John Wesley in the eighteenth century.
17. *Age*, 30 November 1867, p. 5.
18. *Age*, 30 November 1867, p. 5.
19. The title of Penny Russell's 1994 history of colonial ladies in Victoria is telling: *A Wish of Distinction*.

20 Callaway, *Visual Ephemera*, pp. 29, 23, 27.
21 See a travelling minister's response to seeing 'VR' inscribed on a hut in the Australian bush; recorded by Ken Inglis, cited in Mark McKenna, 'Monarchy: From Reverence to Indifference', in Deryck M. Schreuder and Stuart Ward (eds), *Australia's Empire* (Oxford: Oxford University Press, 2008), pp. 261–87, p. 262.
22 See, for example, 'Illumination of the Post Office', wood engraving, *Illustrated Melbourne Post*, 27 November 1867, State Library of Victoria.
23 For example, 'Collins St ... Alston and Brown, Drapers – Transparencies of the Queen and Prince, Britannia and Neptune', in *Narrative of the Visit of His Royal Highness the Duke of Edinburgh*, p. 79. As no transparencies survive, our evidence is limited to press descriptions and engraved woodcuts; Callaway, *Visual Ephemera*, p. 27.
24 The other symbols in the image are the rose, the shamrock and the thistle (representing England, Ireland and Scotland) and an outline of HMS *Galatea*. Unusually, this image depicts the Queen and Alfred together. Moreover, the fireworks display included a message (not recorded in the wood engraving): 'Victoria welcomes Victoria's son', which, again unusually, directly acknowledges Victoria's maternal role; 'Early Melbourne: The Duke of Edinburgh's Visit' by "Old Chum", *Truth*, 24 March 1917, p. 3.
25 *Cruise of HMS Galatea*, p. 48.
26 Callaway, *Visual Ephemera*, p. 41.
27 *The African and Sierra Leone Weekly Advertiser*, 19 October 1860.
28 John Plunkett, *Queen Victoria: First Media Monarch* (Oxford: Oxford University Press, 2003), pp. 144–6. Alfred became a keen amateur photographer.
29 Callaway notes that the wedding inspired local artists to copy British representations of the royal family. Callaway, *Visual Ephemera*, p. 31.
30 *Argus*, 27 November 1867, p. 5, quoted in Callaway, *Visual Ephemera*, pp. 42–3.
31 *Sydney Morning Herald*, 22 January 1868, pp. 4–5.
32 Callaway notes that some Melbourne decorations represented Alfred as King of Australia, but newspaper descriptions indicate that far more depicted him as a naval officer. Callaway, *Visual Ephemera*, p. 38.
33 Other naval emblems include two furled anchors.
34 Alfred did occasionally wear other military uniforms, and, especially when off duty, civilian dress.
35 Callaway, *Visual Ephemera*, p. 37.
36 See my 'Rude Interruption: Colonial Manners, Gender and Prince Alfred's Visit to New South Wales, 1868', *Forum for Modern Language Studies*, 49:4 (October 2013), 437–56.
37 *Melbourne Punch*, 28 November 1867.
38 'Illuminations in Melbourne, Messrs. Sands and M'Dougall, Collins Street', wood engraving, *Illustrated Melbourne Post*, 27 November 1867, State Library of Victoria (Fig. 8).
39 *Australasian*, 3 November 1867, p. 563.
40 Penny Russell and Marilyn Lake, 'Miss Australia', in Melissa Harper and Richard White (eds), *Symbols of Australia: Uncovering the Stories behind the Myths* (Sydney: UNSW Press, 2010), pp. 91–5.
41 *Melbourne Punch*, undated clipping, *Record of the Visit of HRH the Duke of Edinburgh to Australia ... Compiled for the Trustees of the Melbourne Public Library*, by A. H. Tulk, Librarian, vol. I (Melbourne, 1868), State Library of Victoria.
42 Prominent colonists such as Sir Redmond Barry frequently combined anxiety about public morality with private immorality; see Ann Galbally, *Redmond Barry: An Anglo-Irish Australian* (Melbourne: Melbourne University Press, 1995).
43 *Australasian*, 12 October 1867, p. 467. For more on Louis Smith's career promoting Melbourne culture, see David Dunstan, 'The Exhibitionary Complex Personified: Melbourne's Nineteenth Century Displays and the Mercurial Dr L. L. Smith', in Kate Darian-Smith, Richard Gillespie, Caroline Jordan and Elizabeth Willis (eds), *Seize the Day: Exhibitions, Australia and the World* (Clayton: Monash University Press, 2008), Chapter 9.

44 Candler recorded 'some unfortunate mismanagement' of the time of Alfred's arrival, 28 November 1867, p. 298.
45 *Age*, 29 November 1867, p. 5.
46 *Age*, 30 November 1867, p. 4.
47 Candler diary, 38 November 1867, p. 298.
48 *Age*, 30 November 1867, p. 4.
49 See, in particular, the *Age*'s editorial comments in the days following Alfred's departure from Victoria in early January 1868.
50 *Age*, 24 December 1867, p. 5.
51 Emily Harris, 'Race and Australian National Identity at the 1866–67 Intercolonial Exhibition', in Darian-Smith et al. (eds), *Seize the Day*, Chapter 3. This building on William Street predates the more famous Royal Exhibition Building in Carlton Gardens (built for the 1880–81 Melbourne International Exhibition), which is now a UNESCO World Heritage site.
52 *Age*, 24 December 1867, p. 6; Samuel Calvert, 'The Fancy Dress Ball in the Exhibition Building', wood engraving, *Illustrated Melbourne Post*, 27 December 1867.
53 Candler diary, 23 December 1867, p. 336. See also Callaway, *Visual Ephemera*, pp. 102–20.
54 Samuel Calvert, 'The Governor's Ball at the Exhibition Buildings, the Royal Party Dancing the Scotch Reel', wood engraving, *Illustrated Melbourne Post*, 27 December 1867; Candler diary, 28 November 1867, p. 298.
55 Alfred was accompanied by a variety of men aboard HMS *Galatea* beyond the official crew. Others included the marine artist Oswald Brierly and, later, the painter Nicholas Chevalier, whom Alfred first met in Melbourne.
56 Anthony Trollope, *Australia*, ed. P. D. Edwards and R. B. Joyce (St Lucia: University of Queensland Press, 1967), p. 385. The editors note that Trollope's manuscript refers to 'club' in the singular and that the Melbourne was the main club Trollope used there.
57 Candler's remarkable double diary, namely his own and his transcription of Frederick Standish's diary, is discussed in Paul de Serville's insightful 'The Double Diary Keeper', *La Trobe Journal*, 80: spring (2007), 109–23.
58 Candler diary, 15 September 1867, p. 98. It remains unclear to what extent Alfred shared the reputation of his elder brother and especially his great uncles for sexual intrigue. But Standish's diary entry recording that he took Newry and Yorke to Mrs Fraser's brothel the day after the *Galatea* arrived suggests possible foreknowledge of this group's interests; Standish diary, 24 November 1867.
59 Candler diary, 29 November 1867, p. 300.
60 Standish diary, 28 November 1867.
61 Jane Moody, 'Céleste, Céline (1810/11–1882)', *Oxford Dictionary of National Biography* (Oxford: Oxford University Press, 2004).
62 Harold Love, *The Golden Age of Australian Opera* (Sydney: Currency Press, 1981), p. 159.
63 De Serville, 'The Double Diary Keeper', pp. 119–20. In France and other Continental European states, brothels were often regulated and inspected regularly by the local police.
64 Certainly Candler's diary suggests that other members of the Melbourne Club indulged in similar pursuits. Following Alfred's visit, Candler and Standish both record numerous visits to Sarah Fraser's, where they enjoyed a 'yarn'.
65 Callaway, *Visual Ephemera*, pp. 102–20.
66 Candler diary, 1 January 1868, p. 352.
67 Candler diary, 2 December 1867, p. 314.
68 For example, *Maitland Mercury and Hunter River General Advertiser*, 3 December 1867, p. 2.
69 *Age*, 6 January 1868, p. 4.
70 Queen Anne (r. 1701–14) was the last British monarch to practise this; Marc Bloch, *The Royal Touch: Sacred Monarchy and Scrofula in England and France*, trans. J. E. Anderson (London, 1973), p. 220.

71 According to Candler, Alfred invited a local courtesan, 'The Psyche', to follow him to Sydney; 15 December 1867, p. 328. Lord Newry and Lieutenant Fitzgeorge also continued their romantic adventures. See, for example, Candler diary, 14 January 1868, pp. 350–1, 354–5.
72 Standish, 25–6 December 1867.
73 Alfred invited select colonists to Christmas dinner at the Melbourne Club, and some of the same guests had accompanied him on an earlier hunting expedition to the Western District. Candler diary, 16 December 1867, pp. 330–1 and 24 December 1867, pp. 337–8.
74 My future research project investigates these bonds of intimacy on naval stations around the world during the latter half of the nineteenth century.
75 398 Ann Hennessy, Melbourne Bittgesuch [petition] an Herzog Alfred gerichtet an Mr. E. Yorke, Gotha Staatsarchiv.
76 418 Bittgesuch Mrs Ann Hicks, Gotha Staatsarchiv (Gotha, Germany).
77 John Lahey suggests that Sarah Fraser wanted to display the royal coat of arms outside her premises but was dissuaded. While this seems far-fetched, Alfred did dispense patronage to Victorian businesses such as photographic studios. John Lahey, *Damn You, John Christie! The Public Life of Australia's Sherlock Holmes* (Melbourne: State Library of Victoria, 1993), p. 21.
78 Queen Victoria's reputation as a champion of her overseas subjects, especially indigenous people, is discussed in Sarah Carter and Maria Nugent (eds), *Mistress of Everything: Queen Victoria in Indigenous History and Politics* (Manchester: Manchester University Press, 2016).
79 There is no record of the Victorian government providing financial assistance either, and, indeed, these were only two of many cases of impoverished British migrants in the colony at the time.
80 Numerous annotations and cover-sheets indicate that individuals from several offices reviewed Mrs Hennessy's request. Likewise, Mrs Hicks's petition contains several annotations in different hands. 'Circular' here refers to a standard rejection letter.
81 423 James Wilson, 43 Little George Street, Fitzroy, Gotha Staatsarchiv.
82 Following the visit to Victoria, Alfred was shot by Henry James O'Farrell in Sydney in March 1868. He made a swift recovery and returned to Australia as part of his naval voyages on HMS *Galatea* in 1869 and again in 1870.
83 Standish diary, 13 March 1868.
84 *Sydney Morning Herald*, 7 April 1868, p. 4.
85 Long after Alfred's Australian visit and the attempted assassination attempt, Queen Victoria continued to wield symbolic power in Melbourne. In 1975, a statue of 'Her Most Gracious Majesty Who Wrought Her People Lasting Good', which also included allegorical female figures representing Wisdom, Justice, History and Progress, was blown up as part of ongoing sectarian division between Irish Protestants and Catholics. In the decade of 'The Troubles', Alfred's mother still excited strong reactions in some Melbourne viewers; Carmel Bird, 'Queen Victoria', in Andrew Brown-May and Shurlee Swain (eds), *The Encyclopedia of Melbourne* (Cambridge: Cambridge University Press, 2005), p. 205.
86 *Argus*, 27 November 1867, pp. 5–7.

CHAPTER FOUR

Kaiser Wilhelm II and the limits of the royal prerogative in German South-West Africa

Matthew P. Fitzpatrick

In the second half of the nineteenth century, Germany was a newly unified state, the King of Prussia having been proclaimed Emperor of the new *Reich* in 1871 in the aftermath of the Franco-Prussian War. Building on decades of pro-imperial agitation and activity, the German Empire also formally added to its territory several colonial possessions in Africa and Oceania during the 1880s. Among these new territories was German South-West Africa (present-day Namibia), which, in 1904, was the site of a genocidal colonial war. This war, and the legal and military role of Kaiser Wilhelm II in its prosecution, has been the object of heated debate as scholars have attempted to ascertain precisely how involved the Kaiser was in colonial affairs. This chapter demonstrates that despite the Kaiser's predilection towards bombastic proclamations of militarist zeal, Wilhelm II's notable lack of involvement in the management of the war in South-West Africa was indicative of his marginal role in German imperialism.

The Kaiser's prerogative power in the colonies

The so-called *Hunnenrede* ('Hun Speech') of 1900 was the most infamous of Kaiser Wilhelm II's pronouncements on colonial warfare. It was singled out by German Chancellor Bernhard von Bülow as 'perhaps the most damaging speech Wilhelm II ever gave'.[1] In it the Kaiser seemed to exhort his troops to radical violence against the Chinese in the Boxer Rebellion:

> Pardon will not be given! Prisoners will not be taken! Those who should fall into your hands will be lost! Just as a thousand years ago the Huns under their King Attila made a name for themselves that is still renowned in tales and fables, so may the name 'German' be established by you in China for a thousand years, so that never again should a Chinese look askance at a German.[2]

As it turned out, what looked like an outrageous imperial order for the application of unlimited violence was in fact an unscripted flourish meant to inspire the martial spirit of departing troops who would miss the war by some weeks and who would be left to conduct mopping up operations in occupied Peking.[3] Yet, once another colonial war was under way in Africa four years later, Bülow was moved to warn the Kaiser that unless he used his prerogative power to intervene, the radical violence being visited upon German South-West Africa would see the crude sentiments of the Hun Speech look like formal colonial policy.[4]

With more than 100 German settlers and soldiers massacred in the initial stages of the Herero War,[5] the conflict in South-West Africa seemed to jeopardise the very existence of Germany's only real settler colony.[6] The German outpost was still shifting from its beginnings in the mid-1880s as a chartered mining company colony on the Anglo-Dutch model (augmented by the 'civilising' efforts of the Rhenish Mission) towards wholesale settler colonialism. This process of creating space for German settlers had placed intense pressure upon the lands and herds of indigenous pastoralists such as the Herero. Having staged an armed insurrection in January 1904 aimed at reversing their dispossession and immiseration, the Herero ultimately paid an exceedingly high price for their resort to armed struggle. Not only was their plight greatly accelerated by the brutal nature of their defeat, the genocidal conduct of the war saw their numbers plummet from as high as 80,000 before the war to 15,000 after it. The conditions placed upon their post-war reintegration into the colony also saw the remnant population reduced to a semi-free workforce suffering enormous mortality rates.[7]

It was precisely because of the unfolding genocide that the Chancellor had sought to engage the Kaiser with the events of the war and indeed to warn him that the German commander in the field, Lothar von Trotha, was waging the war in a manner that was incompatible with both Germany's material interests and its international reputation. As Bülow's intervention suggests, the Kaiser technically possessed the sovereign power to unilaterally recast the contours of German colonial warfare. As will be shown, the silences on colonial matters in the German constitution were filled by laws that inserted what appeared to be a dictatorial role for the Kaiser. Nevertheless the fact that Bülow had to ask the Kaiser to turn his attention to Germany's vicious war in South-West Africa illustrates that the powers granted to the crown by these laws were not always exercised.

Two questions then arise. How far did Kaiser Wilhelm II's prerogative power over the German colonies actually extend, and to what extent did he seek to exert this power to its limits? Focusing on the use of prerogative power in German South-West Africa during the crisis of the Herero War, this chapter shows how the Kaiser, as the organ of the state notionally possessing prerogative power that approached the unbounded, was remarkably absent from decision-making. Despite his apparent enthusiasm for military affairs, beyond the unavoidable choices foisted upon him by the Chancellor,[8] and the Chief of the German Army's General Staff, Alfred von Schlieffen, the Kaiser avoided almost all comment on and responsibility for the colonial war. The seemingly unconstrained royal prerogative, it seems, was limited by the Kaiser's own unwillingness to become involved unless explicitly called upon. It was not, however, only the Kaiser's lack of interest in colonial matters that diminished his capacity to control the waging of colonial warfare. The legal peculiarities of the colonies as juridical spaces also made it difficult for the royal prerogative to extend over all colonial affairs.

Despite Wilhelm II's declaration during a visit to Munich that 'the King's will is the highest law',[9] the constitutional parameters of the Kaiser's metropolitan authority were firmly spelt out in Articles 11–19 of the Constitution in the section entitled 'Executive'. Here it was stipulated that in terms of foreign policy the Kaiser was granted the power to declare war and to announce peace, to sign treaties and to commission ambassadors. He was the chief commander of the navy, and all German army troops (including those of the independent Bavarian army) were to obey his orders during times of war. Domestically, the Kaiser could call, open and dissolve the popularly elected Reichstag and the upper chamber 'states' house', the Bundesrat. He was the final signatory to newly promulgated laws and appointed state secretaries, the German equivalent of ministers, who were answerable to the Chancellor.[10]

Properly contextualised, the Kaiser's constitutional role extended to those aspects of statecraft where a single figurative head of the state was required: war and peace, and the formal promulgation of laws already passed by the two parliamentary chambers. Although significant military power was available to him, in most domestic matters the Kaiser was only one (and often the last) of several authorities who comprised a network of bodies that authorised decisions, ordinarily coming behind the Chancellor, the Bundesrat and the Reichstag.[11]

While historians of Imperial Germany essentially agree that the first two Kaisers did not carve out strong roles as interventionist monarchs, the exact extent of Kaiser Wilhelm II's power, as expressed in Germany's constitution and in practice, has been the subject of debate for more than a century. Despite the longevity and intensity of the debate over the Kaiser's power in Germany, little research on the degree of his personal power over colonial sites has been undertaken, a surprising situation given the significantly enhanced sovereignty he enjoyed in that domain.

To be sure, firm views have been proffered regarding the Kaiser's role in what has been misunderstood as a 'sudden' shift to a new *Weltpolitik* under Kaiser Wilhelm II. Entering an already well-formed controversy in 1985, Geoff Eley famously pronounced that the Kaiser was 'uninterested and uninvolved in the practice of governing in anything but the most sporadic, arbitrary and whimsical of ways' after 1897.[12] For his part, the structuralist Hans-Ulrich Wehler described late Wilhelmine Germany as being characterised by an increasingly irrelevant 'shadow Kaiser' whose anxious and haphazard gestures towards preserving his authority hid the more central reality of a state devoid of a centre.[13] Wehler also argued that the Kaiser's role in colonial affairs was minimal:

> Did the Kaiser himself direct the China, Pacific or Africa policies of German imperialism, or the unsuccessful informal expansion in the Near East with the help of the Baghdad railway? Or was he not simply one actor amongst many others, who embodied the thoroughly different forces, each pursuing different ends and able to claim varying degrees of agency in decision-making?[14]

On the other side of the debate, historians such as John C. G. Röhl, Isabel V. Hull and Annika Mombauer have focused on what they have seen as the Kaiser's 'personal rule' or the 'kingship mechanism.'[15] On the general question of Germany's imperial ambitions, Röhl, for example, has argued that global empire was the personal project of the Kaiser. For Röhl, it was 'the almost overwhelming personal power of Kaiser Wilhelm, who was able to determine the Reich's policy down to the smallest detail', which was at the root of 'the global dimensions of German aims'.[16] For her part, Mombauer has charted the Kaiser's clumsy role in garnering European support behind Alfred von Waldersee, his candidate for 'commander-in-chief' of the multinational force operating in China during the Boxer Rebellion.[17] Correctly, she pointed out that, as Commander-in-Chief, the Kaiser theoretically had enormous latitude in military affairs.[18] Still, for Mombauer, the Kaiser's role essentially amounted to eroding Germany's standing abroad by dabbling in symbolic politics and precipitating a foreign-policy crisis from which he then had to retreat.

In the accounts of those stressing the Kaiser's power, the effects of this power were often fraught. Yet it is possible to go further than arguing that the Kaiser was an imperial activist by looking beyond his own sense of his importance to events and paying attention to the judgements of those who surrounded him. Despite Wilhelm II's own sense of himself as a seriously engaged global military figure, the Kaiser was often shielded from the full weight of his constitutional powers by others who understood his limitations only too well. As the Kaiser's long-time confidant Prince Philipp of Eulenburg-Hertefeld understood it, assisting the Kaiser during a colonial war consisted of prompting all those surrounding the Kaiser 'to regale the Kaiser with harmless stories and to avoid politics' while praying that 'nothing complicated approaches His Majesty'.[19] When the Kaiser insisted that, as Chief Commander of the armed forces, he should receive the correspondence of Waldersee in China and not the Foreign Office, the Kaiser's delusion that he alone was competent to deal with military matters was quietly circumvented by those, such as Eulenburg, Bülow and Schlieffen, who knew that 'this standpoint is neither *politically nor militarily* feasible and *must* inevitably lead to a catastrophe'.[20]

His colonial secretary, Wilhelm Solf, was similarly blunt about the Kaiser's role in colonial affairs, recalling later that 'the Kaiser was extraordinarily uninterested in our colonies and colonial politics'.[21] He participated in it more as a curiosity, and, unlike liberal imperialists such as Solf, he never considered colonies to be an essential part of his goal for Germany's global prestige. This picture of the Kaiser's imperial rule being marked by an absence of overarching royal power has also been borne out by decades of work on the theatrical but politically unimportant public colonial utterances of the Kaiser – the 'Hun speech', the Krüger telegram and the *Daily Telegraph* interview – which points to a sporadically enthusiastic Kaiser who was consistently managed, corrected and at times disowned by the Chancellor, the Reichstag and the bureaucracy, who all ensured that a more predictable form of *Weltpolitik* did not unduly unsettle the other European powers.[22]

The formal extent of the royal prerogative in the German colonies was quite clear.[23] Articles 1 and 2 of the German Constitution made clear precisely to which German territories the Constitution pertained. The German colonies in Africa, the Pacific, China and, indeed, Alsace-Lorraine, were not among them.[24] Strictly speaking, all constitutional provisions were therefore redundant in the colonies.[25] As territories 'not incorporated into the Reich' which were 'foreign lands in the sense of the imperial constitution and imperial law',[26] the colonies (or more correctly German dependencies, *Schutzgebiete*) were areas outside the guarantees of the Constitution and the concomitant regulatory role of German law. Although sometimes unsuccessfully contested,[27] the operative legal position was that the German colonies were sites external to the constitutional *Rechtsstaat* and subject to the prerogative power of the Kaiser,[28] whose authority in the colonies was 'objectively unrestricted'.²⁹ In addition, Paragraph 1 of the 1886 Protectorate Law made it clear that in South-West Africa, 'sovereign power is exercised by the Kaiser in the name of the Reich'.³⁰

Given the apparent lack of legal restraints on the Kaiser's power over the colonies, one contemporary jurist noted that the qualitative differences in the nature of imperial power exercised by the Kaiser amounted to two separate forms of imperial rule: domestic constitutional monarchy and the prerogative colonial state.³¹ Yet this strict dichotomy between a metropolitan sphere of law and an excised colonial zone of exception oversimplifies the unevenness of the application of imperial sovereignty outside the metropole.³² As Ignacio Czeguhn has remarked, 'with constitutional provisions unclear ... the question of which organ of the Reich and on what grounds had the competence to regulate colonisation remained contested.'³³ With the Constitution silent and the pertinent colonial laws still to be thoroughly tested through their application, the balance of sovereign power in German South-West Africa was more complex than the apparent zone of meta-juridical royal prerogative suggested.

Utilising power: the Kaiser and the Herero War

Without doubt, the Kaiser's seemingly untrammelled power found some concrete limits. In 1886, the Protectorate Law applied a modified version of the 1879 Consular Jurisdiction Act to the colonies, effectively insinuating important elements of the civil-law code of Germany into South-West Africa.³⁴ It delineated the extent and limits of the Kaiser's power and the role of colonial officials, including the degree of their subordination to the Chancellor.³⁵ Here, four clear limitations to the Kaiser's exceptional colonial sovereignty were created. First, judicial affairs for German settlers were placed under the purview of the Colonial Department, which was a branch of the Foreign Office, whose secretary was ultimately answerable to the Chancellor.³⁶ Second, the power to offer citizenship to foreigners and indigenous people living in the colony also resided with the Chancellor.³⁷ Third, the Chancellor became the legal co-signatory of the 'Kaiser's' colonial decrees and could technically decide to refuse to sign. This never happened, because these decrees originated not with the Kaiser but from the Colonial Department.³⁸ Finally, and most importantly, through the combination of its power as a prominent bully pulpit and its constitutional power to refuse to pass the colonial budget, the Reichstag could seek to temper flagrant abuses of power in the colonies, albeit generally *ex post facto*, as the example of the 'Hottentot Election' of 1907 discussed below illustrates.

This balance of sovereign power in German South-West Africa was, however, tested by the events of the 1904 Herero War. For the first half of 1904, a successful military outcome for the Germans was far from certain. Yet, despite the increasingly acute military crisis and its potential broader ramifications for Germany's *Weltpolitik*, the Kaiser intervened only twice in the conflict, once to choose a commander from a list of options already decided by others and once to ratify a decision made by every other arm of the state.

Contradictory pressures influenced the first decision in regard to the command of the force that would fight the Herero. Those wishing to keep the conflict as a problem of colonial law and order to be managed by the existing colonial protection force (*Schutztruppe*) under the continued command of Governor Theodor Leutwein on behalf of the Colonial Department were opposed by those seeking to redefine the conflict as a formal war to be managed by the German Army's general staff and its chief, Schlieffen.[39] Initially, beyond assenting to the hastily assembled relief force of 500 men, the Kaiser had steadfastly refused to intervene in the conflict, to the point that his inaction had distressed some of his advisers. Despite technically being the chief of the armed forces, the Kaiser avoided taking an active role as the Commander-in-Chief of the German Army 'because there was no glory or fame associated with it',[40] preferring instead to let the war drift while he remained silent and absent aboard his royal yacht.

Four months into the war, when the fate of the colony seemed to hang in the balance,[41] the Kaiser's man in the Foreign Office, Friedrich von Holstein, kept an anxious watch on the Kaiser's approach to military matters, worried that if he actually decided to direct the African war (much less any European war), it would lead to a 'terrible catastrophe' because of his 'military ineptitude'.[42] He understood that, confronted with an acute military crisis in Africa, the Kaiser preferred to spend his time obsessing about Russia's war with Japan instead, badgering Bülow with fantastic warnings that the Japanese could conquer Moscow in twenty years.[43] With the Kaiser remaining at sea on his royal yacht, Holstein came to suspect that this absence was a deliberate shirking of the Kaiser's responsibilities:

> I regret that the Kaiser has remained away for so long. It is increasingly suspected of him that it is because of the Herero uprising. He's quite content with the blandishments offered on the subject. But the political rumour disseminated from here that the Kaiser is leading operations in South Africa from the *Hohenzollern* is a sham. He is directing nothing of the sort. It might not have been a bad thing, if more troops had been sent over right at the beginning under the command of General von Trotha who can be trusted with colonial situations, as the Kaiser had wanted.[44]

Instead of actively and personally directing the war according to his initial inclinations, the Kaiser had accepted the diminishment of his responsibility as commander-in-chief and left others to direct the colonial war. Observers were ambivalent about whether this lack of royal engagement was a blessing or a curse. The German courtly diarist Baroness Hildegard von Spitzemberg noted that some at court were complaining of the Kaiser's 'constant overestimation of his political worth'. Others fretted, however, that 'the indifference that he shows towards the Herero uprising is dreadful.'[45]

Eventually, in a May 1904 crisis meeting, where military officials and civil authorities met with the Kaiser to discuss Leutwein's offer to resign his military command after what from Berlin appeared to be a series of military reversals, the Kaiser was informed that he had to nominate which senior military figure would lead the much larger military force about to leave for the colony.[46] Apart from his deficiencies in the eyes of military planners, it was suggested by some that Leutwein, as an *Oberst* (colonel), was not of sufficient rank to lead a major campaign of the German military undertaken by a force that could potentially include others of equal or higher rank.[47] In the context of the Herero War, the Kaiser's first major use of his imperial prerogative and his command as head of the armed forces was to comply with this request to make a choice of commander,[48] notwithstanding the protests of the Colonial Department, who wished to maintain civilian (that is to say, their) control over the war.

As Röhl has argued, Lothar von Trotha was an unpopular choice among representatives of the civilian colonial bureaucracy who wished to maintain control of the war,[49] yet on precisely whose advice the Kaiser chose Trotha over other military colonial specialists is still the subject of some disagreement. Hull suggests that the press had reported to this effect and that Trotha was strongly supported by the military's Chief of the General Staff Schlieffen and the Chief of the Military Cabinet, Dietrich von Hülsen-Häseler.[50] Bley argued, however, that while the Director of the Colonial Department of the Foreign Office, Oscar Wilhelm Stübel, and other civilian officials such as Heinrich Schnee, wished to keep Leutwein in command, the military was split between the Prussian Minister for War, Karl von Einem, who suggested Waldersee's subordinate in the Boxer Rebellion, Georg von Gayl, and Schlieffen, who suggested to the Kaiser that he choose Trotha.[51] For Christopher Clark and Susanne Kuß, however, Trotha's appointment was against the advice of Chancellor Bülow, Stübel and, importantly, the military's Schlieffen.[52] Katharine Anne Lerman has further argued that, in addition to Schlieffen, the Kaiser's own military adviser, the Chief of the Military Cabinet, Hülsen-Häseler, also opposed Trotha's appointment.[53]

According to two sources from May 1904, having been called upon, the Kaiser chose Trotha from the shortlist of three candidates against not merely the advice of civilian authorities but indeed against everyone's advice. At the end of his report to the Bavarian War Ministry on 10 May 1904 detailing plans for the reinforcement of the colonial troops, Nikolaus Endres commented, 'the naming of Lieutenant-General von Trotha as the leader of the Expedition Corps was done by His Majesty against the objections of the Imperial Chancellor, the War Minister, the Chief of the General Staff and the Colonial Director.'[54] Two days later, Bavaria's representative in Berlin, Hugo Lerchenfeld-Köfering, also reported to Munich:

> The transfer of the leadership of the troops in Southwest Africa to Lieutenant-General von Trotha has sprung utterly from the initiative of His Majesty the Kaiser. In the opinion of the responsible departments, the Colonial Division of the Foreign Office, the Prussian Ministry of War and the General Staff, there were no grounds for relieving Leutwein of command. That there were losses and failures at the beginning of the operation against the Herero, which regularly occur elsewhere at the beginning of such operations, [and] were, according to the departments, due to the hitherto lack of available troops and horses, not because of the mistakes of the commander. It is commonly thought that with the coming reinforcements Leutwein would fulfil his mission at least as successfully as his successor, who is inexperienced in Southwest African relations. It is also presumed that the change in commander will be seen in an unfavourable light abroad. The Chancellor shares this view, even if he has defended the change in command in the Reichstag.[55]

Yet, despite being an unpopular choice, Trotha's selection was not a total surprise. Trotha had extensive military experience dating back to Prussia's campaigns against Austria in 1866 and against France in 1870–71. More pertinently, he had led the campaign against the Wahehe in German East Africa in 1896 and had also served against the Chinese in the Boxer Rebellion. Given the options of three experienced colonial commanders presented to him, the Kaiser arguably chose the best known. Holstein, the Kaiser's Foreign Office 'grey eminence', was certainly under the impression that Trotha had been the Kaiser's preferred candidate since the beginning of the war.[56] Interestingly, however, although he had seemingly favoured Trotha for more than four months prior to this meeting, the Kaiser had hitherto left the prosecution of the war in the hands of the Colonial Office, to the extent that he had been accused of allowing the war to drift out of control. Notwithstanding the legal opportunities for direct intervention, he did not formally offer his view until it became clear that it was his direct and unavoidable responsibility to decide on who would lead the expeditionary force. It was only once the law demanding that the Kaiser, as head of the armed forces, name the new military leader that he chose the general he had long preferred over the other two candidates, Gayl and Leutwein. As a prominent veteran of both the Wahehe Uprising in German East Africa and the Boxer Rebellion in China, Trotha had made a name for himself as an uncompromising colonial-war specialist.[57] The Kaiser's choice confirms that he agreed with the military that what was occurring in South-West Africa was 'no longer the defeat of a "native revolt" but a veritable war'.[58] Where they differed was on the question of who was best-suited to prosecute that war.

There was a marked difference between Leutwein's strategy and the military track record of Trotha, and, given Trotha's unflinching use of violence in the past, the Kaiser would have been aware that he had chosen the option of a full-scale military crackdown rather than Leutwein's business-as-usual approach of a negotiated settlement. Contrary to Jeremy Sarkin's assertion, however, the awarding of command to Trotha does nothing to indicate that the Kaiser had gone beyond seeking a military solution to demanding a genocidal one,[59] as the genesis of the genocide demonstrates. While Leutwein had sought victory followed by a negotiated settlement as soon as the Herero could be brought to favourable terms that would allow him to preserve the Herero polity as a future workforce,[60] Trotha was committed to destroying the independent national existence of the Herero through an overwhelming military victory. This strategy of the decisive military blow was not, however, predicated upon the physical extermination of the Herero *in toto*. Rather, it was only upon the utter failure of the strategy of the 'battle of annihilation' that the war was radicalised to become an all-encompassing attempt to eradicate all Herero from the colony, to destroy the Herero 'as such'.

Trotha's inability to defeat the Herero in the kind of decisive battle favoured by Schlieffen was laid bare at the battle at Waterberg on 11 August 1904.[61] In the wake of this inconclusive encounter, Trotha mounted a chase through the Omaheke desert in an attempt to bring about yet another 'decisive' battle. Failing to achieve this,[62] he then shifted to a radicalised campaign of attrition characterised by denying the enemy access to waterholes, effectively ensuring that the Herero – including Herero women, children and non-combatants – would die in the desert of hunger and thirst.[63] It was here, with Trotha's tactical innovation rather than a royal order, that the shift to a military cordon ensuring widespread and indiscriminate starvation occurred.[64] Formal acknowledgement of this strategic shift came with Trotha's decree of 2 October – almost two months after the battle of Waterberg – which made clear that any Herero found returning to settled areas would be shot.[65] As he explained to Schlieffen two days later in his report, given his failure with orthodox military tactics he had come to believe that 'the nation as such must be destroyed, or if this is not possible on tactical grounds ... expelled from the territory'.[66]

Unsurprisingly, Leutwein explicitly distanced himself from the expulsion order, arguing that the Herero had sent letters of surrender and that the military campaign to all intents and purposes had been won.[67] Trotha's response to Leutwein's attempt to appeal above his head to Berlin so as to end the war was blunt: 'In such situations there is no parliamentarising. I am happy to listen to your advice, but I cannot allow you an independent role in decision-making as long as the Kaiser retains me in my position, given the foundational differences in our views.'[68] On this point, Trotha was technically correct. As the Kaiser had given Trotha military command over an extra-constitutional German colonial territory, only the Kaiser had the power to force Trotha to rescind his order.

The Chancellor and the Kaiser

Notwithstanding the fact that Trotha had been the Kaiser's personal choice, this is precisely what happened. The rescinding of Trotha's genocidal expulsion proclamation in November 1904 was the Kaiser's second significant use of prerogative power during the conflict. Yet, once again, this deployment of sovereign power was far from an example of the Kaiser's broader commitment to playing the active leadership role offered him by the Protectorate Law. Rather, Trotha's *Vernichtungsbefehl* (order of annihilation) was first rejected by all of the organs of the German *Rechtsstaat* before being presented to the Kaiser for final ratification.

As early as mid-March 1904, the Social Democrat August Bebel had protested in the Reichstag against what he claimed was Germany's 'bestial' policy under Leutwein of hanging or shooting Herero prisoners of war and attacking women and children.[69] Such views had then shocked the governing parties and had been vigorously denied by Colonial Director Stübel and Chancellor von Bülow.[70] As Trotha's command wore on, however, pressure was applied by Pastor Haußleiter of the Rhenish Mission, Governor Leutwein, the Colonial Office and elements of the Reichstag to rein him in. By November 1904, Trotha's tactical radicalisation was anathematised by all arms of the state. Recognising that the military campaign had effectively achieved everything it could, Schlieffen accepted the ineffectiveness of Trotha's attrition tactics in a letter to the Chancellor on 23 November 1904, arguing that despite his sympathy for Trotha's thoroughness Herero prisoners must be accepted and that the Herero should be approached for a negotiated surrender, conceding that this had been made difficult by Trotha's proclamation.[71] Bülow also informed the Kaiser that Trotha's order was 'inconsistent with the principles of Christianity and humanity' and, paraphrasing ex-governor Leutwein, undermined the economic basis of the colony which relied on Herero labour.

Bülow is often presented in the literature as a Kaiser loyalist, anxious to abide by the Kaiser's decisions and to shield the faltering prestige of the Crown, battered by a monarch who 'was driven to greet the most conventional occasions with rodomontade'.[72] For many, Bülow remained that which he declared himself to be in 1896 when he was ingratiating himself with the court's inner circle, namely 'the executive tool of His Majesty'.[73] Such obsequiousness was, however, long gone by 1904. In the interim, Bülow had repeatedly demonstrated his independence on a number of foreign-policy and domestic issues, all the while carefully managing the Kaiser's awareness of his growing marginality.[74]

Thus, it was not unusual for Bülow to have to manage Wilhelm II's understanding of events, even if it was occasionally marked by a display of royal petulance. Upon broaching the matter of Trotha's radical violence, Bülow later recalled, the Kaiser's 'eyes widened and he became greatly agitated', declaring that Christian values did not extend to 'heathens and barbarians'. Bülow parried this by arguing that he was not interested in a theological discussion but merely wished to point out that Trotha's conduct was 'was worse than a crime, it was a mistake ... Wars cannot be conducted purely militarily; politics requires a voice too.' The Kaiser left Bülow in a huff, but within hours, Bülow reported, he had received word from the Kaiser to the effect that the monarch would submit to the Chancellor's judgement on the issue.[75] In accordance with the constitutional chain of command, Chancellor Bülow had formally requested the Kaiser on 23 November 1904 to countermand Trotha's order. In deference to the Chancellor, the Kaiser complied with this request on 29 November, ordering that 'yielding Herero be granted mercy'. Thereafter, he left it to Bülow and Schlieffen to negotiate precisely how this new policy would be carried out.[76] At the same time, Bülow entered the Reichstag and boldly announced a drastic revamp of colonial rule, all of which aimed at reducing the prerogatives of the Kaiser.[77]

Jeremy Sarkin has asserted that the Kaiser's initial hesitation in agreeing to countermand Trotha stemmed from his desire to see through the genocide he had secretly ordered.[78] More coyly, Jan-Bart Gewald has argued that 'the personal involvement of the German Kaiser, Wilhelm II, in deciding how the war was to be fought in German South-West

Africa, signalled the highest authorisation and endorsement for acts committed in the name of Imperial Germany'.[79] So, too, David Olusoga and Casper W Erichsen's book *The Kaiser's Holocaust* suggests a direct congruence between the monarch and Trotha's genocidal command.[80] Not only is there simply no evidence for any 'secret' royal order, as Hull makes clear,[81] it misunderstands the cumulative radicalisation of the colonial war from a military 'battle of annihilation' to a clearly enunciated policy of shooting and starving an entire nation. The Kaiser could not have known that this radicalisation would occur, much less ordered it. Certainly it is true that while Bülow, Leutwein and the Rhenish mission all raised questions about the inhumane nature of the October expulsion order and its consequences, the Kaiser professed to being moved only by questions of strategy. What is crucial, however, is that the Kaiser's views were sidelined in favour of those of the Chancellor. As almost all eyewitnesses from the time concur, the Kaiser was not in active command and contributed precisely nothing to the military campaign beyond what he was explicitly required to do by Schlieffen and Bülow, namely to empower a military leader of the expedition in May 1904 and rescind Trotha's genocidal October order in November 1904. The only sign of an independent line from the Kaiser was the deeply unpopular naming of his favoured colonial war expert, Trotha, as the commander of the *Schutztruppe*, a decision he was forced to reverse.

With his declaration that no mercy would be shown the Herero having been overturned by metropolitan powers, Trotha still managed to hold on to his overall command for a further nine months, despite his now publicly acknowledged incompetence. For many, the Kaiser's own prestige was too closely intertwined with Trotha, given that he was hand-picked. With this bond in mind, Lerchenfeld glumly reported back to Munich on 6 August 1905:

> Including amongst official circles, the view is established that the choice of General Trotha as commander was not a good one. Even upon his announcement significant doubts about his ability had been raised but since military victory eludes him and a number of poor decisions in civilian administration have been reported, he has been adjudged as sorely wanting. As he was appointed by His Majesty the Kaiser, no change in command can be expected soon. For the moment the loss of lives continues and the financial losses continue to grow. Already the costs of the uprising are in the vicinity of five hundred million [marks].[82]

Such considerations bore little weight with Bülow, who, by the end of the same month, had convinced the Kaiser to recall Trotha from South-West Africa.[83]

Upon arriving back in Germany, Trotha was invited to a late December dinner with the Kaiser in Potsdam, ostensibly to honour him for his military deeds in South-West Africa. However, both Bülow and the Kaiser pointedly snubbed Trotha and remained virtually mute on the subject of the war, with the sum total of the Kaiser's comments to Trotha amounting to a loose diatribe on Russia, hunting and art, which ended with the words 'anyway the war is over now', at which point the Kaiser abruptly left, to the embarrassment of everyone else in the room.[84] Shortly thereafter, Trotha was quietly retired from active military service. Despite Lerchenfeld's sense that the Kaiser's decision in favour of Trotha had stood no prospect of being reversed, the royal prerogative had again been subjected to critique and ultimately reversal, via the chain of command established by the Protectorate Law. Even in the exceptional circumstances of a state of genocidal colonial warfare, the Kaiser acceded to the demands of his Chancellor, though at the cost of a public loss of face.[85]

Beyond these elite representatives of the various arms of the German state, the entire voting population of Germany, too, was eventually able to adjudicate on the war in German South-West Africa. The so-called 'Hottentot election' of 1907 was triggered after Social Democratic and Centre Party deputies expressed their discontent with the war and the Empire's prevailing *Kolonialpolitik* by utilising the Reichstag's power of fiscal review to block military spending in German South-West Africa. In doing so, they deliberately challenged the Kaiser's role in colonial and military affairs. With the parliament reaching an impasse, Chancellor von Bülow was forced to seek the dissolution of the Reichstag so as to seek a popular mandate for colonial spending.[86] As Erik Grimmer-Solem has argued, the election highlighted the participatory dimension of German colonial rule via 'a national referendum on the entire German colonial endeavour', wherein Reichstag deputies and candidates, civil-society organisations and voters took part in a public debate on the legitimacy of German colonial rule.[87] Had the electorate voted for strongly anti-colonial parties, Germany's overseas empire and the Kaiser's ostensible 'sole rule' over the colonies would have foundered for want of popular support and, subsequently, fiscal backing in the Reichstag. Far from hamstringing colonial endeavours, however, the German electorate spoke out strongly in support of the war in German South-West Africa, convinced that the anti-colonial, Social Democratic position was tantamount to agreeing that the murdered German settlers in South-West Africa deserved their fate.[88] Instead of endorsing parties sceptical of the direction taken by Germany's colonial enterprise, power was firmly handed back to those advocating the continuation of Germany's *Kolonialpolitik*, irrespective of the price.

As a result, the relative strengths of the German electorate and the monarchy were never directly tested.

Conclusion

The order for colonial genocide in South-West Africa was not issued by anyone above Trotha. The Kaiser's decision to empower Trotha as the commander in the field was perhaps a necessary but certainly not sufficient precondition for the genocide accomplished by Trotha's shift to a war of attrition on the fringe of the Omaheke desert. This shift was neither discussed with nor condoned by the Kaiser and was, albeit belatedly, disowned and rescinded by the pillars of the German *Rechtsstaat*: civil society and missionary organisations, the bureaucracy, the Reichstag, the Chancellor, the military general staff and the Kaiser.[89] The genocide was not a direct consequence of the royal prerogative, as Sarkin suggests, and was certainly not a consequence of the military leadership of the only sporadically involved Kaiser.

While the viceregal power delegated to 'men on the spot' by the Kaiser made political or juridical oversight more difficult, it did not extinguish it. On the strong advice of those actually actively involved in the prosecution of the war, the Kaiser disavowed the kind of warfare he had seemingly endorsed in 1900 in his Hun Speech when it was tried by Trotha in 1904. Thereafter, the German Empire moved to other, more accepted forms of colonial oppression in South-West Africa: wholesale territorial dispossession, a murderous detention regime and the forced-labour programmes of the post-1904 period.[90] Ultimately, all of this was endorsed in 1907 by those who held the bluntest, most sluggish share of sovereign power: the German electorate, which decided who had the right to make budgetary decisions for the Empire. The role of the electorate, as well as that of the Chancellor, the Reichstag, the colonial bureaucracy and the Army, illustrates that rather than a zone of legal exception where the Kaiser's anomic, metajuridical sovereignty could not be reduced to legally prescribed norms, German South-West Africa was a carefully codified zone of legal specificity, a bespoke legal site situated squarely within the edifice of a functioning *Rechtsstaat*.

Notes

1 Bernhard von Bülow, *Denkwürdigkeiten*, 4 vols. (Berlin: Ullstein Verlag, 1930) vol. II, pp. 20–1.
2 Manfred Görtemaker, *Deutschland im 19 Jahrhundert Entwicklungslinien* (Opladen: Leske & Budrich Verlag, 1996), p. 357.
3 Sabine Dabringhaus, 'An Army on Vacation? The German War in China, 1900–1901', in Manfred Boemeke, Roger Chickering and Stig Förster (eds), *Anticipating Total*

War: The German and American Experiences (Cambridge: Cambridge University Press, 1999), pp. 459–76, at pp. 459–60.
4 Bülow, *Denkwürdigkeiten*, vol. II, pp. 20–1.
5 Helmut Bley, *Namibia under German Rule* (Hamburg: Lit Verlag, 1996), p. 149.
6 Germany's colonies included South-West Africa (today's Namibia), Togo, Cameroon, German East Africa (straddling today's Tanzania, Burundi and Rwanda), Samoa, New Guinea and a large number of islands in the Pacific including some in the Solomon, Marshall and Caroline Islands groups. It also possessed a small concession in China (Qingdao). Despite some wishing to transform Samoa into a settler colony, only South-West Africa received large numbers of colonists.
7 On the history of the Herero, see Jan-Bart Gewald, *Herero Heroes: A Socio-political History of the Herero of Namibia, 1890–1923* (Athens, Ohio: Ohio University Press, 1995). For the effects of the Herero War on the Herero polity and people, see Jürgen Zimmerer, *Deutsche Herrschaft über Afrikaner: Staatlicher Machtanspruch und Wirklichkeit im kolonialen Namibia* (Münster: Lit Verlag, 2002); George Steinmetz, *The Devil's Handwriting: Precoloniality and the German Colonial State in Qingdao, Samoa, and Southwest Africa* (Chicago, Ill.: Chicago University Press, 2007), pp. 179–216. Military actions had not begun in the colony in 1904, however, because military action against indigenous peoples had taken place under Curt von François in the early 1890s. His 1894 replacement, Theodor Leutwein, also resorted to violent forms of pacification to facilitate the settlement of the colony by European pastoralist farmers. By 1913, 15,000 European colonists had settled in the colony (of whom only 1,220 were adult German males). On the course of settler colonialism in German South-West Africa, see Dörte Lerp, 'Farmers to the Frontier: Settler Colonialism in the Eastern Prussian Provinces and German Southwest Africa', *Journal of Imperial and Commonwealth History*, 41:4 (2013), 567–83; Bley, *Namibia under German Rule*, pp. 3–57; Zimmerer, *Deutsche Herrshaft über Afrikaner*, pp. 13–21; Ulrich van der Heyden, 'Christian Missionary Societies in the German Colonies, 1884/1885–1914/1915', in Volker Max Langbehn and Mohammad Salama (eds), *German Colonialism: Race, the Holocaust, and Postwar Germany* (New York: Columbia University Press, 2011), pp. 215–52.
8 In colonial affairs, the chancellor carried what Ernst Rudolf Huber called the 'parliamentary accountability for countersigned actions of the colonial government'. See Ernst Rudolf Huber, *Deutsche Verfassungsgeschichte seit 1789*, vol. IV: *Struktur und Krisen des Kaiserreichs* (Stuttgart: Kohlhammer Verlag, 1982), p. 630.
9 In the City of Munich's visitors' book, the Kaiser wrote '*Suprema lex regis voluntas*' (the will of the king is the highest law), scandalising not only German public opinion but also that of his (dowager empress) mother. See Robert K. Massie, *Dreadnought: Britain, Germany and the Coming of the Great War* (London: Vintage, 2007), pp. 108–9.
10 Ernst Rudolf Huber (ed.), *Dokumente zur deutschen Verfassungsgeschichte*, vol. II: *Deutsche Verfassungsdokumente, 1851–1900*, 3rd edn (Stuttgart: Kohlhammer Verlag, 1986).
11 Alexander König, *Wie mächtig war der Kaiser? Kaiser Wilhelm II zwischen Königsmechanismus und Polykratie von 1908 bis 1914* (Stuttgart: Franz Steiner Verlag, 2009), pp. 267–75.
12 Geoff Eley, 'The View from the Throne: The Personal Rule of Kaiser Wilhelm II', *The Historical Journal*, 28:2 (1985), 469–85, at p. 481.
13 Hans-Ulrich Wehler, *Deutsche Gesellschaftsgeschichte*, vol. III: *1849–1914* (Munich: C. H. Beck, 2006), pp. 999–1020.
14 Wehler, *Deutsche Gesellschaftsgeschichte*, p. 1019.
15 John C. G. Röhl, *The Kaiser's Personal Monarchy, 1888–1900* (Cambridge: Cambridge University Press, 2004); John C. G. Röhl, *Kaiser, Hof und Staat: Wilhelm II und die deutsche Politik* (Munich: C. H. Beck, 1988), pp. 116–40; John C. G. Röhl, 'Introduction', in John C. G. Röhl and N. Sombart, *Kaiser Wilhelm II: New Interpretations* (Cambridge: Cambridge University Press, 1982), pp. 1–22. On the inner circle of the Kaiser, see Isabel V. Hull, *The Entourage of Kaiser Wilhelm II, 1888–1918* (Cambridge: Cambridge University Press, 1982). For work reiterating

Röhl's position, see Annika Mombauer and Wilhelm Deist (eds), *The Kaiser: New Research on Wilhelm's Role in Imperial Germany* (Cambridge: Cambridge University Press, 2003).
16 John C. G. Röhl, *Wilhelm II: Into the Abyss of War and Exile, 1900–1941* (Cambridge: Cambridge University Press, 2014), p. 73.
17 Annika Mombauer, 'Wilhelm, Waldersee and the Boxer Rebellion', in Annika Mombauer and Wilhelm Deist (eds), *The Kaiser: New Research on Wilhelm's Role in Imperial Germany* (Cambridge: Cambridge University Press, 2003), pp. 91–119.
18 Mombauer, 'Wilhelm, Waldersee and the Boxer Rebellion', p. 116.
19 Eulenburg to Bülow, 14 July 1900, in John C. G. Röhl, *Philipp Eulenburgs politische Korrespondenz*, vol. II: *Krisen, Krieg und Katastrophen, 1895–1921* (Boppard: Harald Boldt Verlag, 1983), pp. 1983–4. See, too, Mombauer, 'Wilhelm, Waldersee and the Boxer Rebellion', p. 101. Emphasis in the original.
20 Eulenburg to Bülow, 3 October 1900, in Röhl, *Philipp Eulenburgs politische Korrespondenz*, p. 2006.
21 Solf to Geheimrat Eltester, 28 March 1930, Bundesarchiv Koblenz, N1053/81 Nachlaß Solf Amtliches und Politisches. Im Ruhestande Bd 4, January–June 1930, pp. 88–9.
22 On the 'Hunnenrede', see Bernd Sösemann, 'Die sog. Hunnenrede Wilhelms II Textkritische und interpretatorische Bemerkungen zur Ansprache des Kaisers vom 27 Juli 1900 in Bremerhaven', *Historische Zeitschrift*, 222:2 (1976), 342–58. See also Bülow, *Denkwürdigkeiten*, vol. I, pp. 358–61. On the Krüger telegram, see Paul Hoser, 'Die Krügerdepesche (1896)', in Jürgen Zimmerer (ed.), *Kein Platz an der Sonne: Erinnerungsorte der deutschen Kolonialgeschichte* (Frankfurt: Campus Verlag, 2013), pp. 150–63. On the *Daily Telegraph* affair, see Peter Winzen, *Das Kaiserreich am Abgrund: Die Daily-Telegraph-Affäre und das Hale-Interview von 1908* (Stuttgart: Franz Steiner Verlag, 2002); Terence F. Cole, 'The Daily Telegraph Affair and Its Aftermath: The Kaiser, Bülow and the Reichstag, 1908–1909', in John C. G. Röhl and Nicolaus Sombart (eds), *Kaiser Wilhelm II: New Interpretations – The Corfu Papers* (Cambridge: Cambridge University Press, 1982), pp. 249–68.
23 For a detailed theoretical discussion of the constitutional balance of powers and colonial affairs, see Marc Grohmann, *Exotische Verfassung: Die Kompetenzen des Reichstags für die deutschen Kolonien in Gesetzgebung und Staatsrechtswissenschaft des Kaiserreichs (1884–1914)* (Tübingen: Mohr Siebeck, 2001); Ignacio Czeguhn, 'Die Mitwirkung von Bundesrat und Reichstag bei der Kolonialgesetzgebung', *Jahrbuch der Juristischen Zeitgeschichte*, 8 (2006–7), 174–202. See also Ernst Rudolf Huber, *Deutsche Verfassungsgeschichte seit 1789*, 8 vols. (Stuttgart: Kohlhammer Verlag, 1982), vol. IV, pp. 604–34.
24 Huber, *Dokumente zur deutschen Verfassungsgeschichte*, vol. II, pp. 64–5.
25 For Wilhelmine attempts to argue for the jurisdiction of the Reichstag and the domestic constitution, see Friedrich Giese, 'Zur Geltung der Reichsverfassung in den deutschen Kolonien', in *Festgabe Bonner juristischen Fakultät für Paul Krüger zum Doktor Jubiläum* (Berlin: Weidmann Verlag, 1911), pp. 417–46.
26 Paul Laband, *Das Staatsrecht des Deutschen Reiches*, 3rd edn (Tübingen: J. C. B. Mohr, 1902), p. 146. On whether the colonies should be designated as 'Inland', 'Ausland', 'Reichsnebenland', 'Nebenstaat' or 'Außerdeutsche Reichslande', see Simon Reimer, *Die Freizügigkeit in den deutschen Schutzgebieten inbesondere die Ausweisung von Reichsangehörigen* (Münster: Verlag der Universitäts-Buchhandlung Franz Coppenrath, 1911), pp. 8–12.
27 Victor von Poser und Gross-Naedlitz, *Die rechtliche Stellung der deutschen Schutzgebiete* (Breslau: M&H Marcus, 1903), p. 45. On comparisons with Alsace-Lorraine, see Schreiber, 'Die rechtliche Stellung der Bewohner der deutschen Schutzgebiete', *Zeitschrift für Kolonialpolitik, Kolonialrecht und Kolonialwirtschaft*, 6 (1904), 760–75, at p. 761; Herbert Hauschild, *Die Staatsangehörigkeit in den Kolonien* (Tübingen: J. C. B. Mohr, 1906), p. 27.

28 Karl von Stengel, *Die Rechtsverhältnisse der deutschen Schutzgebiete* (Tübingen: J. C. B. Mohr, 1901), pp. 33, 38ff.
29 Laband, *Das Staatsrecht des Deutschen Reiches*, p. 147.
30 'Gesetz betreffend der Rechtsverhältnisse der deutschen Schutzgebieten', *Reichs-Gesetzblatt*, 17 April 1886.
31 Giese, 'Zur Geltung der Reichsverfassung', p. 436.
32 On this question, see Lauren Benton, *A Search for Sovereignty: Law and Geography in European Empires, 1400–1900* (Cambridge: Cambridge University Press, 2009), pp. 279–99; Lauren Benton, 'Empires of Exception: History, Law, and the Problem of Imperial Sovereignty', *Quaderni di Relazioni Internazionali*, 6 (2007), 54–67.
33 Czeguhn, 'Die Mitwirkung von Bundesrat und Reichstag', p. 175.
34 'Gesetz über die Konsulargerichtsbarkeit', *Reichs-Gesetzblatt*, 19 July 1879, pp. 197–206. This was strengthened in 1900. See Laband, *Das Staatsrecht des Deutschen Reiches*, p. 148.
35 'Gesetz betreffend der Rechtsverhältnisse der deutschen Schutzgebieten', §§2–3.
36 The exception to this was in the instance of legal cases regarding administrative disputes in the colonies, which would be referred to the Bundesrat. Egon Kruckow, *Ausweisungen aus den deutschen Schutzgebieten*, p. 28. Laband, *Das Staatsrecht des Deutschen Reiches*, pp. 147–9.
37 Poser und Gross-Naedlitz, *Die rechtliche Stellung der deutschen Schutzgebiete*, p. 61.
38 Laband, *Das Staatsrecht des Deutschen Reiches*, p. 148.
39 As per the law establishing the colonial armed forces of 9 June 1895. This law was supplemented by a series of provisions for the colonial armed forces, which codified the role of the governor. Laband, *Das Staatsrecht des Deutschen Reiches*, p. 149.
40 Rudolf Vierhaus (ed.), *Das Tagebuch der Baronin Spitzemberg* (Göttingen: Vandenhoeck & Ruprecht, 1963), p. 442.
41 Isabel V. Hull, *Absolute Destruction: Military Culture and the Practices of War in Imperial Germany* (Ithaca, NY: Cornell University Press, 2005), p. 22.
42 Vierhaus, *Das Tagebuch der Baronin Spitzemberg*, pp. 440–1.
43 Bülow, *Denkwürdigkeiten*, vol. II, p. 64.
44 Holstein to Stülpnagel, 23 April 1904, in Helmuth Rogge (ed.), *Friedrich von Holstein Lebensbekenntnis in Briefen an eine Frau* (Berlin: Ullstein Verlag, 1932), p. 232.
45 Vierhaus, *Das Tagebuch der Baronin Spitzemberg*, p. 442.
46 Hull, *Absolute Destruction*, p. 22.
47 Bülow in *Verhandlungen des Reichstags*, 9 May 1904, p. 2788; 5 December 1904, pp. 3374–7. This was a lesson learned by the forced resignation of Hermann Wissmann as Governor of German East Africa during the Wahehe uprising in 1896, when Trotha, leading the campaign, outranked him and was therefore beyond the Governor's control.
48 Bley, *Namibia under German Rule*, pp. 155–60.
49 Röhl, *Wilhelm II: Into the Abyss of War and Exile*, p. 298. Röhl argued that the Kaiser chose Trotha, 'overruling civilian objections' (p. 298).
50 Hull, *Absolute Destruction*, pp. 24–5.
51 Bley, *Namibia under German Rule*, pp. 158–9.
52 Christopher Clark, *Kaiser Wilhelm II* (London and New York: Routledge, 2000), p. 103. Susanne Kuß, *Deutsche Militär auf kolonialen Kriegsschauplätzen: Eskalation von Gewalt zu Beginn des 20 Jahrhunderts* (Berlin: CH Links Verlag, 2010), p. 83.
53 Katharine Anne Lerman, *The Chancellor as Courtier: Bernhard von Bülow and the Governance of Germany, 1900–1909* (Cambridge: Cambridge University Press, 2002), p. 96.
54 'Endres, Berlin, 10 May 1904, Betreff: Verstärkung für die südwestafrikanischen Schutztruppen' in BHStA München, Abt IV Kriegsarchiv MKr2657 Herero-Aufstand in Deutsch-SüdwestAfrika.
55 Lerchenfeld to Ministerium des Außern, 12 May 1904, in BHStA München Abt II MA 2682.
56 Holstein to Stülpnagel, 23 April 1904, in Rogge, *Friedrich von Holstein Lebensbekenntnis*.

57 For Trotha's military experience prior to 1904, see Christoph Kamissek, '"Ich kenne genug Stämme in Afrika" Lothar von Trotha: eine imperiale Biographie im Offizierkorps des deutschen Kaiserreiches', *Geschichte und Gesellschaft*, 40:1 (2014), 67–93.
58 Kuß, *Deutsche Militär auf kolonialen Kriegsschauplätzen*, p. 83.
59 Jeremy Sarkin, *Germany's Genocide of the Herero: Kaiser Wilhelm II, His Generals, His Settlers, His Soldiers* (Cape Town: UCT Press, 2011), p. 191.
60 Theodor Leutwein, *Elf Jahre in Deutsch-Südwestafrika* (Berlin: Ernst Siegfried Mittler und Sohn, 1907), pp. 541–2.
61 Kriegsgeschichtliche Abteilung I des Großen Generalstabes, *Die Kämpfe der deutsche Truppen in Südwestafrika* (Berlin: Ernst Siegfried Mittler, 1906), pp. 156–91, especially p. 189.
62 Kriegsgeschichtliche Abteilung I des Großen Generalstabes, *Die Kämpfe der deutsche Truppen in Südwestafrika*, pp. 193–9.
63 Kriegsgeschichtliche Abteilung I des Großen Generalstabes, *Die Kämpfe der deutsche Truppen in Südwestafrika*, p. 207. On the genocidal intent of the order, see Jan-Bart Gewald, 'The Great General of the Kaiser', *Botswana Notes and Records*, 26 (1994), 67–76.
64 Kuß, *Deutsche Militär auf kolonialen Kriegsschauplätzen*, p. 88.
65 BA Berlin, R1001, No. 2089, p. 7.
66 Trotha to Schlieffen, 4 October 1904, BA Berlin R1001/2089 Differenzen zwischen Generalleuntnant v Trotha und Gouverneur Leutwein bezgl. der Aufstande in DSWA im Jahre 1904, pp. 5–6.
67 BA Berlin R1001/2089, p. 46. Jörg Schildknecht, *Bismarck, Südwestafrika und die Kongokonferenz: die völkerrechtlichen Grundlagen der effektiven Okkupation und ihre Nebenpflichten am Beispiel des Erwerbs der ersten deutschen Kolonie* (Hamburg: Lit Verlag, 2000), p. 260.
68 Trotha to Leutwein, 5 November 1904, as cited in Jörg Schildknecht, *Bismarck, Südwestafrika und die Kongokonferenz*, p. 260.
69 *Verhandlungen des Reichstages*, 17 March 1904, pp. 1891–3.
70 *Verhandlungen des Reichstages*, 87 Sitzung, 9 May 1904, pp. 2787–9. On the claims and counterclaims of German atrocities during the early phases of the war, see Hull, *Absolute Destruction*, pp. 13–21.
71 Schlieffen to Bülow, 23 November 1904, in BA Berlin R1001/2089 Differenzen zwischen Generalleuntnant v Trotha und Gouverneur Leutwein bezgl. der Aufstande in DSWA im Jahre 1904, pp. 3–4.
72 Margaret L. Anderson, *Practicing Democracy: Elections and Political Culture in Imperial Germany* (Princeton, NJ: Princeton University Press, 2000), p. 181.
73 John C. G. Röhl, *The Kaiser and His Court: Wilhelm II and the Government of Germany* (Cambridge: Cambridge University Press, 1996), p. 4.
74 Clark, *Kaiser Wilhelm II*, pp. 94–8.
75 Bülow, *Denkwürdigkeiten*, vol. II, pp. 20–1.
76 Schoen to Bülow, 29 November 1904, BA Berlin R1001/2089, p. 13. The General Staff took until 8 December to send the order, which was received in Windhoek the following day. General Staff to General Trotha, 8 December 1904, in BA Berlin R1001/2089, p. 48.
77 *Verhandlungen des Reichstages*, 5 December 1904, pp. 3376–8.
78 Sarkin, *Germany's Genocide of the Herero*.
79 Jan-Bart Gewald, 'Imperial Germany and the Herero of Southern Africa: Genocide and the Quest for Recompense', in A. Jones (ed.), *Genocide, War Crimes and the West: Ending the Culture of Impunity* (London: Zed Books, 2003), p. 60.
80 Casper Erichsen and David Olusoga, *The Kaiser's Holocaust: Germany's Forgotten Genocide and the Colonial Roots of Nazism* (London: Faber & Faber, 2010), pp. 138, 157–8.
81 Hull, *Absolute Destruction*, pp. 28–30.
82 Lerchenfeld to Staatsministerium des Außerns, 6 August 1905, in BHStA München Abt II, MA2683.

83 Lerman, *The Chancellor as Courtier*, p. 136.
84 Vierhaus, *Das Tagebuch der Baronin Spitzemberg*, pp. 452–3.
85 For another example of the Chancellor intervening to ensure that the will of the Reichstag prevailed over that of the Kaiser in the colonies, see the Kubub-Keetmanshoop railway controversy, briefly discussed by John S. Lowry, 'African Resistance and Center Party Recalcitrance in the Reichstag Colonial Debates of 1905/06', *Central European History*, 39:2 (2006), 244–69, at p. 262.
86 G. D. Crothers, *The German Elections of 1907* (New York: Columbia University Press, 1941).
87 Erik Grimmer-Solem, 'The Professors' Africa: Economists, the Elections of 1907, and the Legitimation of German Imperialism', *German History*, 25:3 (2007), 313–47, at p. 322. Crucially, Lowry has pointed to the fact that 'African actions' precipitated this colonial crisis within Germany, thereby reversing the usual causal chain from African agency to metropolitan crisis. See Lowry, 'African Resistance and Center Party Recalcitrance'.
88 John Phillip Short, 'Colonialism, War, and the German Working Class: Popular Mobilization in the 1907 Reichstag Election', in Bradley Naranch and Geoff Eley (eds), *German Colonialism in a Global Age* (Durham, NC: Duke University Press, 2014), pp. 210–27, at p. 211.
89 Bley, *Namibia under German Rule*, pp. 164–5.
90 Jan-Bart Gewald, 'The Issue of Forced Labour in the Onjembo: German South West Africa 1904–1908', *Itinerario*, 19:1 (1995), 97–104.

CHAPTER FIVE

Orangists in a red empire: salutations from a Dutch queen's supporters in a British South Africa

Susie Protschky

In 1909, Queen Wilhelmina of the Netherlands received a spectacular letter from the Women's Committee of the Netherlanders of Johannesburg in Transvaal, then a British colony. It was an *oorkonde*, a formal salutation handwritten in calligraphic script and richly illustrated with symbols of the Netherlands' Royal House of Orange: a coat of arms, the Dutch tricolour crossed with an orange flag and a trailing border of orange blossoms bearing, significantly, one fruit (see Figure 9). Indeed, the letter heralded the arrival of a royal baby and accompanied a gift, a child's 'porridge bowl with saucer and spoon of Transvaal gold, offered as a tribute on the occasion of the happy event of 30 April 1909, the birth of PRINCESS JULIANA'. After eleven years on the throne, eight years of marriage, two miscarriages and a stillbirth, the Dutch Queen had at last produced an heir.

In the European context, *oorkonden* originated in the medieval period as charters serving a wide range of administrative purposes for individuals and institutions: for instance, as deeds of property ownership and transfer, diplomatic correspondence, guarantees, contracts, agreements and writs to officials.[1] In the Dutch context, over time the term *oorkonde* came to include any formal written salutation. By the nineteenth century, Dutch monarchs were receiving hundreds of ceremoniously worded, illuminated greetings that incorporated the term *oorkonde* in their text from subjects in the Netherlands and around the world.[2] Other European monarchs with empires received similar missives from their supporters. The medium was favoured by groups of people to collectively present themselves to and congratulate a member of the royal family on a regnal or personal milestone such as a birthday, jubilee, wedding or inauguration. The collective often took an enduring, official form (an arm of government, for example, or a women's organisation). Signatories to an *oorkonde* also came together temporarily for a royal celebration, usually under the direction of a special

9. *Oorkonde* for Queen Wilhelmina from the Johannesburg Women's Committee, July 1909. Koninklijk Huisarchief, The Hague, A50 VIIIe 11. Reproduced with permission

committee, to plan a public festival, offer a gift and send a salutation. The *oorkonde* was, thus, part of a larger, organised and often public engagement of groups and individuals with the monarch *in absentia*, especially in the case of the colonies, which were rarely graced by the presence of Dutch royalty. Indeed, unlike their British counterparts, for example, Dutch royals in the nineteenth and twentieth centuries showed little predilection for touring their overseas possessions.[3]

During her half century as Queen of the Netherlands and its colonies – the East Indies (now Indonesia), West Indies (Aruba, Bonaire, Curaçao, Sint Maarten, Saba and Sint Eustatius), and Suriname – Wilhelmina never visited any of her colonies, nor those of other European powers. Perhaps because of her physical remove from her non-European subjects, she received scores of *oorkonden* from her supporters around the world, especially at the milestones of her reign. These included her investiture in 1898, marriage in 1901, the birth of her daughter in 1909, her silver jubilee (twenty-five years as queen) in 1923 and her golden jubilee (fifty years on the throne) and abdication in 1948. Predictably, most of the *oorkonden* Wilhelmina received came from formal Dutch colonies. The largest number – twenty in total – came from the East Indies, then the most important, extensive and populous overseas possession of the Netherlands.[4] More surprisingly, Wilhelmina received a similar number of *oorkonden* – seventeen altogether – from South Africa. These were less varied in their authorship than those the Queen received from the East Indies, where a wide range of indigenous, Asian and European commoners and elites sent or put their names to felicitations.

The *oorkonden* Wilhelmina received from South Africa came from European settlers, many with Dutch names and who identified themselves as belonging to a community of Dutch heritage. Most were sent on behalf of organisations whose members exceeded the signatories on the letters themselves. Importantly, the salutations came from a territory that was marked on contemporary world maps in red, the colour of the British Empire, for most of Wilhelmina's reign. Indeed, throughout the history of the Dutch monarchy the Netherlands had held no claim to territory in South Africa. By 1815, the year that the House of Oranje-Nassau was created a monarchy, Britain had acquired a spate of possessions formerly held by the then defunct Vereinigde Oostindische Compagnie (VOC, Dutch East Indies Company). Among the spoils was the Cape Colony, a settlement founded in 1652 to service ships en route to the East Indies.[5]

The *oorkonden* Queen Wilhelmina received from South Africa have escaped scholarly attention perhaps because they seem an ornamental sideshow to the hefty matters of state that historians trace in the (unadorned) documents of official archives.[6] However, viewed as visual and textual sources that speak to particular modes of social and cultural encounter – between collectives of mostly Dutch-descended people in South Africa on the one hand and a remote royal figure invested with potent symbolic significance by her followers – the *oorkonden* offer provocative insights into the histories of early twentieth-century South Africa, modern Dutch imperialism, and the role of the House of Orange in both spheres.

Wilhelmina's long reign (1898–1948) coincided with a turbulent period of South African history, beginning within a year of the onset of the South African War (1899–1902) and ending only months before the National Party was elected the government of South Africa and Apartheid was implemented as state policy. The fate of Transvaal, from which the 1909 *oorkonde* was sent, aptly illustrates the conflicts of the preceding century and sets the context for Wilhelmina's special meaning for white settlers who claimed Dutch ancestry. Transvaal was named the South African Republic (SAR) in 1852, following the Great Trek of Boers (literally, 'farmers' or 'peasants') in the 1830s and 1840s from the British-claimed Cape into the interior. The SAR was annexed by the British in 1877, reclaimed by Boers following the Transvaal War (1880–81), then fell to the British again in 1900. The year the Johannesburg *oorkonde* was sent, Transvaal – along with the Orange Free State, Natal and the Cape Colony – was a self-governing colony within the British Empire. These lands were combined in 1910 to form the Union of South Africa, a British dominion.

Rather than herald themselves as Orangists, the signatories to the 1909 Johannesburg Women's Committee *oorkonde* ought to have been declaring fealty to the British King Edward VII (r. 1901–10). For residents of Johannesburg to send an *oorkonde* to a Dutch monarch in this context, then, was a political statement, one that was particularly meaningful for a key group of her supporters: women. The *oorkonden* from Wilhelmina's female supporters in South Africa reveal how the Dutch queen, in this part of the world as elsewhere, served as an exemplar for contemporary women's movements. As a female king, Wilhelmina drew attention both to the gendered inequities among colonial populations *and* the transnational solidarities that were emerging among women across the Dutch colonial world in the early twentieth century.

More broadly, this chapter uses Wilhelmina's *oorkonden* from South Africa to investigate her importance as a figure of acclaim and appeal in a global context of competing European empires, not just among her colonial subjects in formal Dutch possessions but also among Dutch-descended peoples in the contested imperium of South Africa. Conflict between British and Afrikaner settlers continued for decades after the battle for territorial sovereignty was determined in favour of the British in 1902. Analysing the text and images of *oorkonden* to Wilhelmina reveals how narratives of struggle for cultural and political supremacy between white settlers imbued even the stylised, relatively innocuous genre of the *oorkonde*. For many people who traced their ancestry, language and religion to the Dutch who settled at the Cape of Good Hope in the seventeenth century, loyalty to Wilhelmina was a protest against co-optation into a British empire and a way of maintaining a Dutch cultural orientation.

Enduring queen of an oneiric empire: Wilhelmina and the dream of South Africa

In one of the few works of modern Dutch colonial history that examines part of the 'lost' VOC empire contiguously with the Netherlands' key crown colony of the modern era, the East Indies, historian Martin Bossenbroek outlines a notional Dutch world that still, in the late nineteenth and early twentieth centuries, included southern Africa as a 'dream colony' (*droomkolonie*).[7] Throughout the South African War, the Dutch government remained officially neutral for fear of British reprisal in South-East Asia, where the two countries were close colonial neighbours (the Dutch East Indies being adjacent to British Singapore, Malaya and Borneo).[8] However, sections of Dutch society had strongly supported the Boers since their first ventures to establish settlements after the Great Trek inward from the Cape Colony in the 1830s and 1840s and later, during the Transvaal War. Public enthusiasm in the Netherlands peaked feverishly at the onset of the South African War, when the former Boer republics of Transvaal and the Orange Free State took up arms against British incursion. In the Netherlands, the press printed propaganda for the Boers' campaign, organisations were founded comprising a who's who of the country's political and intellectual elite, and there was almost unanimous partisan and confessional support for the Boers' efforts.[9]

Wilhelmina emerged in the Netherlands at that time as an important figure for the articulation of extra-parliamentary assistance to the Boers. As head of state, she was officially constrained by the government policy of neutrality. Privately, however, she exercised her influence wherever possible, personally appealing to her relatives, Kaiser Wilhelm II and Queen Victoria, for Prussian and British support in favour of the Boer republics – to no avail. However, in May 1900, when the former president of the defeated SAR, Paul Kruger, fled his country, and the Dutch government, under enormous pressure to do something, sent a warship to pluck him from his voyage of exile, Wilhelmina supported the action and formally received him in the Netherlands.[10] The incident was frequently mentioned in the commemorative books (*gedenkboeken*) published at subsequent milestones of the Queen's reign, which referred to Kruger as a family member – *Oom* (Uncle) Paul – of the Dutch nation.[11]

To date, scholars have focused on how the Queen's gestures towards South Africa were received in the Netherlands. Less attention has been paid to how the Dutch monarchy was conceived as meaningful for South Africans. The *oorkonden* to Wilhelmina from here suggest that for many Dutch-descended South Africans the interest was reciprocal. Two still mentioned her intervention on behalf of 'Oom Paul' at the end of her reign, in 1948.[12] As well as *gedenkboeken* published in the Netherlands, then, *oorkonden* from South Africa suggest that, in some quarters, the Queen persisted as the figurehead of an oneiric Dutch empire well beyond the end of the South African War. Indeed, the number of *oorkonden* Wilhelmina received from South Africa remained steady throughout the half century of her reign.[13]

The notable change over this period was in the collective identity of some of the letters' senders. In the Netherlands, membership of the key organisations that supported the Boer effort during the wars of the late nineteenth century waned after 1902, particularly the NZAV (Nederlandsch Zuid-Afkrikaansche Vereniging, Dutch South-African Society), which fostered linguistic, cultural and intellectual connections between the Netherlands and South Africa.[14] This decline has been key for most scholars in dating the end of Dutch dreams of retaining a foothold in Africa.[15] However, Wilhelmina's *oorkonden* from South Africa reflect a sporadic but enduring loyalty from local chapters of the NZAV and similar organisations well into the 1940s.[16] Indeed, it was among the educated elite in South Africa that connections with the Netherlands had been most strongly cultivated before the South African War. In the late nineteenth century, a significant proportion of civil servants and schoolteachers in the Boer republics (especially the SAR) were of Dutch birth, and for promising students a scholarship programme sponsored by the NZAV enabled an education in the Netherlands.[17] Importantly, from 1923 onwards, Afrikaner organisations also began sending salutations to Wilhelmina.[18] This suggests the Queen's persistent cultural and political significance for some Dutch-descended South Africans living in a British empire, most particularly in Transvaal. Here, Pretoria hosted its first festivals for the young princess Wilhelmina in 1893 and continued celebrating the Queen until the end of her reign.[19]

Land, language and Stamverwantschap: *heritage and settler identities in text and image*

The South African War, which commenced not long after the advent of Wilhelmina's reign, ended in 1902 with British victory but continued to shape strained relations between British and Dutch-descended settlers for decades afterwards. International observers were shocked by what was arguably the first 'total war' of the modern era, one that developed into a guerrilla conflict and drew a large civilian population into its ambit, leaving bitter memories in its wake.[20] On the Afrikaner side, the internment of Boers in British camps, where more than 22,000 children and 4,000 women died, was for many an unforgettable (and unforgivable) aspect of the war.[21] Further, while emigration schemes designed to encourage settlers from Britain were largely unsuccessful and Afrikaners remained numerically dominant in many parts of South Africa in the early decades of the twentieth century, Afrikaners were economically marginalised and politically divided and thus in a tenuous position in the emerging South African state.[22]

For the duration of her reign, the *oorkonden* that Wilhelmina received from Dutch-descended supporters in South Africa were indelibly formed by the conflict and aftershocks of the only war between white settlers in the whole ignominious European 'scramble for Africa'.[23] These missives frequently articulated a heritage and loyalty distinct from that of British settlers and thereby protested the British policy of Anglicisation in South Africa that officially commenced in 1902.[24] Wilhelmina's *oorkonden* reveal some of the ways that the contest for supremacy between white settlers in southern Africa was articulated to an external audience – a head of state, no less – as a rhetorical jostling for recognition on an international stage by way of appeal to a venerable institution with significant purchase in a world then dominated by monarchies and empires. The texts of the *oorkonden* frequently develop links between Orangists in South Africa and Queen Wilhelmina through a discourse of Dutch heritage centring on two elements that reveal not only points of Afrikaner difference from English settlers but also divisions *between* Afrikaners as to their collective identity. The first was language and the second was the notion of *stamverwantschap* (descent from a common ancestor).

From its very inception, the free farming burgher population that grew out of the Company settlement of soldiers and sailors at the Cape had at best an ambivalent and often a hostile relationship with authorities outside their own communities, churches and, in the frontier settlements that developed in the nineteenth century, even families. Successive administrations – the VOC, the British colonial government, even the republican authorities of the late nineteenth century – failed to capture their united loyalties, nor did a stable sense of nationality define them. Instead, for centuries it was European descent, a sense of European superiority, adherence to Christianity, burger (free citizen) status and the Dutch language that held together those people proclaiming themselves to be 'Afrikaners'.[25] Elements of that loosely held identity increasingly divided the ethno-nationalist Afrikaner movement that developed in the twentieth century. In the early part of Wilhelmina's reign, for instance, the status and use of Afrikaans was deeply contested among the cultural, intellectual and political elites of South Africa, particularly among nationalists who disputed whether it or High Dutch should be adopted to resist Anglicisation programmes in schools, the press and public institutions.

These arguments continued long after 1925, when Afrikaans joined English and Dutch as official languages of South Africa and became established in high as well as popular culture.[26] Tellingly, of the seventeen *oorkonden* Wilhelmina received from South Africa, twelve were partly or entirely written in High Dutch, which suggests an elite orientation.[27] Indeed, many were sent by collectives that self-identified variously as 'Netherlanders' (meaning they were Dutch expatriates) or, conspicuously, governing officials (among whom 'Hollanders' comprised a significant proportion in South Africa, especially in senior positions).[28] An *oorkonde* from 'exiles in Amsterdam' represented some of the thousands of Dutch-speakers who fled South Africa (or who were forcibly repatriated, in the case of the SAR) for the Netherlands during the South African War. These particular émigrés attracted the Queen's attention. Both she and Kruger visited their lodgings on the Nieuwe Herengracht (Amsterdam) in 1900.[29] Other *oorkonden* in High Dutch came from South African organisations that were officially pro-Dutch, namely, the NZAV and the NV (Nederlandsch Verbond).

The NZAV was founded in the Netherlands in May 1881, during the Transvaal War, to promote closer ties with South Africa through Dutch delegations to the governments of the Boer republics, to raise money for war veterans and their families and to sponsor Dutch language and education in southern Africa. At the organisation's height in 1899, the NZAV had thirty-five offices across the Netherlands and the Boer republics. The organisation sent *oorkonden* to Wilhelmina from South Africa only during the South African War and then ceased (even if the organisation itself did not – in fact, it continues to this day).[30] The ANV (Algemeen Nederlandsch Verbond, General Dutch Alliance), whose South African arm was the NV, was more internationally oriented than the NZAV, although the two organisations cooperated during the war. Founded in 1896 after the Jameson Raid, a botched British attack on Transvaal, the (A)NV aimed to promote a Greater Netherlands, mainly through language. 'Uncle' Paul Kruger was Honorary President of the Transvaal branch,[31] and it was the office in the capital, Pretoria, that sent Wilhelmina an *oorkonde* in 1941, in solidarity over the German occupation of the Netherlands.[32]

Significantly, while Wilhelmina continued to receive *oorkonden* from South Africa in High Dutch throughout her reign, from 1923 onwards most of them addressed her in Afrikaans, a language close enough to that from which it originated (the Dutch spoken by VOC merchants and free burghers) that Wilhelmina would have been able to read it, certainly in the brief and formal salutations she received. Around the same time (1924), the Afrikaner Nationalist Party, led by J. B. M. Hertzog, first came to power in a coalition government. While Hertzog was not in favour of ethnic separatism among whites, he did support the adoption of Afrikaans as an official language, although this was by no means a unanimous position among nationalists.[33] Wilhelmina emerges in *oorkonden* from South Africa during this period as a point of unity between Afrikaners who otherwise disagreed on the language in which they ought to express their notion of heritage and ethnic solidarity. The use of Afrikaans also distinguished Wilhelmina's correspondents in South Africa from her supporters in other parts of the Dutch imperium, including the *patria*. Doing so asserted a distinctive settler identity that acknowledged Dutch roots while celebrating a distinctive evolution in an African environment.

A similar notion of settler identity informed many of the letters Wilhelmina received that made explicit use of *stamverwantschap*. The term's flexible meanings, which ranged from recognition of shared cultural traits (language, religion and customs) to 'racial kinship', made it attractive for users in the Netherlands as well as South Africa and encompassed a spectrum of political agendas.[34] Evoking the Queen as an embodiment of *stamverwantschap* worked because she led an institution whose entire legitimacy rested on lineage, a notion that was also the basis of Afrikaner claims to territory and pre-eminence in South Africa. However, the term was not used in addresses to the Queen early in her reign. Its first explicit use in an *oorkonde* was in 1923, in a letter from the Afrikaner-Dutch Reading Union of Pretoria. Despite being written in Afrikaans, the letter gave vent to 'the feeling that we belong to the ancient Dutch race, here in South Africa, [and] speak the beloved language of our fathers', before professing, 'We shall remain true to our national character [*volksaard*] and hold sacred and protect the love of a Dutch way of life and Dutch striving among our racial kin [*stamverwanten*] of Dutch origin.'[35]

Significantly, in 1948, the year of the National Party victory, all three *oorkonden* that Wilhelmina received from South Africa used the term *stamverwantschap*. The 'Residents of South Africa' mentioned their *afstamming* (descent) from the *stigters-land* (land of [our] founders),[36] while the Afrikaner Culture Council compared Pretoria to the Netherlands as 'a small and racially-related nation'.[37] Most tellingly, the elaborate letter from the Government of the Union of South Africa expounded twice on the importance of *stamverwantschap* in binding Afrikaners with the Netherlands. The success of the National Party was met with consternation in the Netherlands because (among other reasons) of its Apartheid policy agenda, so the correspondence of the government with the Dutch head of state was controversial.[38] The salutation came as a parchment wrapped around a wooden rod and presented in a velvet-lined wooden box. It was signed by the first Apartheid Prime Minister, D. F. Malan (1874–1959), who had studied at the University of Utrecht, which perhaps explains why the letter was written in High Dutch.[39] The text brushed over a long history of settler contests with first VOC and then colonial authorities to commemorate 'the many bonds of an historic and cultural nature that had existed between the Netherlands and South Africa over the last three centuries'.[40] It honoured Johan van Riebeeck (1619–77), founder of the VOC station ('our *Volksplanting*' – the 'sowing' of our people) at the Cape of Good Hope, and gave short shrift to the British colonial period: 'while the Netherlands was forced to give up the prize of the Cape of Good Hope after one and a half centuries of successful colonisation, the bonds of racial and language kinship with the former motherland had not been entirely broken'.[41]

The letter also mentioned the Dutch language as progenitor of the 'daughter language' of Afrikaans and the *Statenbijbel* (the authorised bible of the Dutch Reformed Church, dating from the mid-seventeenth century) as influential in the formation of an Afrikaner community. It hailed Dutch support for the 'freedom fight of the racially and linguistically related Boer kin' and, particularly, 'the princely gesture of Your Majesty, then as Youthful Sovereign the only one among the crowned heads of Europe' to extend asylum to Paul Kruger.[42] Finally, the letter gave thanks for the last President of the Orange Free State, Marthinus Steyn (1858–1916), having been accommodated in the Netherlands during a serious illness early in Wilhelmina's reign. It was in fact Steyn's widow, named in the document as the nation's *'Volksmoeder'*, who delivered the *oorkonde* in person at Wilhelmina's golden jubilee.[43]

Most importantly, the letter from the government of South Africa connected the founding histories of the Afrikaner people with the origins of the House of Orange through their vague mutual location in the seventeenth century, a so-called Dutch golden age (and the era of early VOC expansion), a temporal linkage that cannot in fact withstand scrutiny. The founder of Wilhelmina's dynasty, Willem I (the Silent) (1533–84), established the princely House of Orange in 1544, more than a century *before* the VOC settled the Cape of Good Hope. Further, the VOC station was founded during the First Stadhouderless Period (1650–72), when the Prince of Orange was excluded from power in the Dutch Republic. To the South African composers of this and other *oorkonden* for Wilhelmina, it was Willem I's resistance to and victory over Spain and his establishment of the Dutch Republic that resonated with narratives of Boer defiance against British expansion in southern Africa.⁴⁴ A similar rhetoric had fired the bellies of those intellectuals and politicians in the late-nineteenth-century Netherlands, who compared the Boers to the feisty Protestant *geuzen* (sea-beggars) in revolt against the Catholic Spanish.⁴⁵ That the analogy was alive and well seventy years later, and among the leaders of the government of South Africa, addresses Vincent Kuitenbrouwer's and Bernard Slaa's compelling arguments for the longevity of Dutch ties to South Africa with evidence of a reciprocal affection from South Africa for the House of Orange.⁴⁶

Landscapes of the settler-colonial imagination: an Orange South Africa?

Most of the ornamental components in the *oorkonden* Wilhelmina received from South Africa derived chiefly from the calligraphic text and, in several instances, stock decorations of orange blossoms and heraldry (see, for example, Figure 9). A few, however, stand out for their elaborate illustrations, which include painted landscapes, city views and botanical specimens, all from local environments. The Queen was a keen artist herself, with landscape a favourite genre. Commencing in the 1930s, her paintings toured the Netherlands and its colonies several times, but they never made it to South Africa.⁴⁷ Significantly, while the texts of South African *oorkonden* celebrate the Dutch queen and often proclaim historical connections to the Netherlands, the visual content serves to acquaint Wilhelmina with the land of her South African supporters. Afrikaner claims to territory are uniformly presented as outcomes uncontested in these scenes either by rival British settlers or by black Africans, despite the significant presence particularly of the latter in landscapes settled by Boers.⁴⁸

For example, the *oorkonde* Wilhelmina received from the NZAV in the South African Republic for her inauguration in 1898 was bordered along its lower edge with a watercolour of an archetypal *veld* – the landscape of the Boer's Great Trek – replete with cattle in the foreground and a Boer farm in the distance (see Figure 10). A column of three medallions forms the left border: beneath the crowning royal coat of arms the two great cities of the SAR, Pretoria and Johannesburg, are shown as modern, bustling metropolises, with imposing buildings, telegraph poles and trams. In the top right-hand corner are the arms of the SAR: a lion, an armed Boer and an ox wagon with the motto *Eendragt maakt magt* (unity makes strength). Together, the images celebrate the ostensive success of a white settler colonialism (since no Africans are visible) with a distinctive Afrikaner character. The SAR's vulnerability is given no expression here, yet its annexation by the British in 1877 had triggered the Transvaal War, and in less than two years of Wilhelmina's inauguration, it would fall definitively to the British.

The strongest outpouring of artistic energy came a decade later, in the tributes Wilhelmina received in 1909 for the birth of her heir. The 'Dutch and former Dutch and Interested Parties [*belangstellenden*] of Transvaal' included two watercolour paintings in their *oorkonde*. The landscapes resonated with those of the NZAV's offering: one was of an unpopulated *veld*, the other of a rudimentary Boer encampment.[49] Ironically, it was in the elaborate, oversized greeting card made by the Cape Town Women's Committee – residents of a colony that had been British for more than a century – that a Boer-settled landscape most clearly emerged. Its cover page was decorated with botanical drawings of local wildflowers (see Figure 11). The second page led with relics of VOC settlement, 'The Old Slave Market' (right) and the 'Entrance

10. *Oorkonde* from the Nederlandsch Zuid-Afkrikaansche Vereniging (Dutch South-African Society) for Queen Wilhelmina's inauguration, 1898. Koninklijk Huisarchief, The Hague, A50 XIVb 91.
Reproduced with permission

11. Cover page of the *oorkonde* from the Cape Town Women's Committee for Juliana's birth, 1909. Koninklijk Huisarchief, The Hague, A50 VIIIe 12. Reproduced with permission

to the Old Dutch Fort' (left) (see Figure 12). A pendant between these images showed a woman encircled by a protective tendril of orange blossom and the motto 'The Good Hope will not be shamed'. The Cape thus appeared as a woman whose honour had to be protected from marauders – the seafaring kind, if the anchors at the base of the medal have any meaning. Given the pro-Dutch sentiments suggested in the visual content of the *oorkonde*, and the freshness of the South

CROWNS AND COLONIES

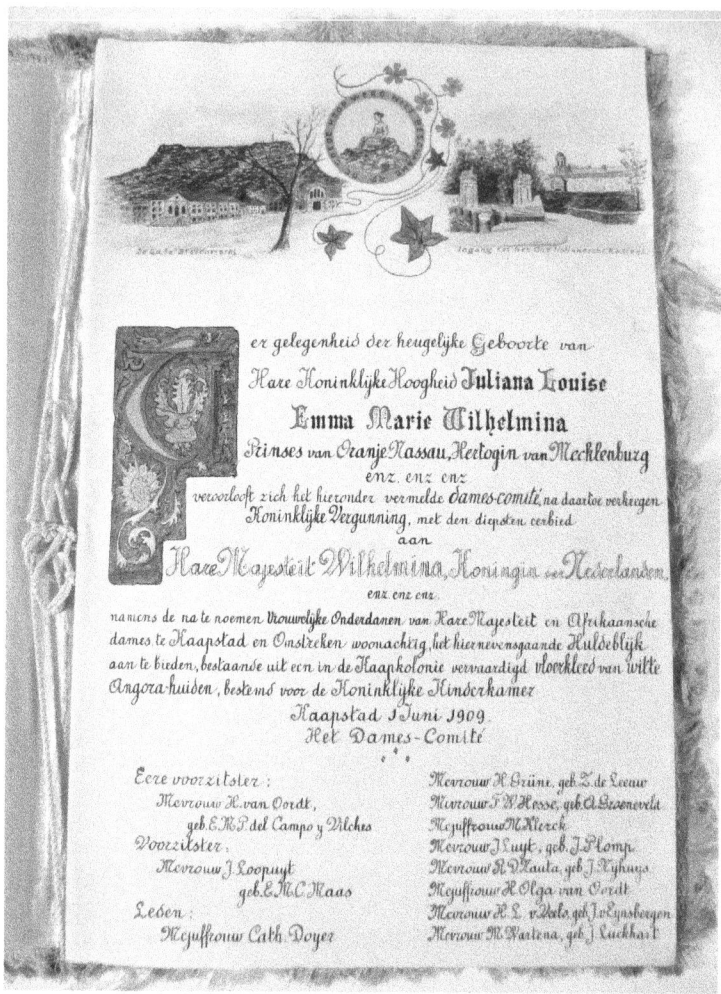

12. Second page of the 1909 Cape Town Women's Committee *oorkonde*. Koninklijk Huisarchief, The Hague, A50 VIIIe 12. Reproduced with permission

African War, Britain is not excluded from the danger implicated to the maiden.

A painting on the third page of the *oorkonde*, which lists the 'names of the Dutch contributors' to the gift for Juliana, deepens this ambiguity and its insubordinate connotations (see Figure 13). A view of Table Mountain and Table Bay is flanked by a map of southern Africa on one side and the Netherlands on the other. Any suggestion of British sovereignty – a

13. Detail from the third page of the 1909 Cape Town Women's Committee *oorkonde*. Koninklijk Huisarchief, The Hague, 50 VIIIe 12. Reproduced with permission

political fact since 1902 – is completely occluded by the evocation of Cape Town as a place with an unbroken connection to the Netherlands.

This was the first of the *oorkonden* sent to Wilhelmina to use Afrikaans, more than fifteen years before it became an official language. A banner at the base of the third page, addressed to the Crown Princess Juliana, read *'Dat sy mag opgroei froom en rein om Holland's volk tot heilte syn'* (That she may grow up pious and pure to ensure the good of Holland's people). That the dynastic heir to the House of Orange, the future hope of 'Holland' (in fact a province of the Netherlands), should be addressed in the fledgling language of a recently defeated but defiant settler group, by members of a women's committee, illustrates the special appeal of a female monarchy to Dutch-descended women in South Africa.

Crafty subjects: aspirations and agency in women's oorkonden *for a female king*

The woman's lot of childbearing (and, in Wilhelmina's case, of losing children in the process) did not distinguish between queens and commoners, a factor that many historians have overlooked in recognising Wilhelmina as an unusually popular Dutch monarch.[50] Instead, scholars have gone to some lengths to explain her appeal, particularly as a virginal princess, to her *male* subjects.[51] As an adult, however, Wilhelmina was endearing to women who might identify with the travails of wifehood and motherhood and who might take inspiration from the unusual power that came from these positions being combined with kingship. That a female king – the Dutch *koningin* renders this gender-qualified political concept more clearly than the English 'queen' – reigned in the Netherlands and would continue to do so in the next generation, given the sex of the long-awaited heir, resonated with many of Wilhelmina's women admirers around the world. Powerful by virtue of her royalty and rank as head of state but legally constrained by parliament (an entirely male institution in the Netherlands up to 1946), the queen exercised influence by legally confirming governments that came and went while maintaining her dynasty through a single act of reproduction.[52] The female king was thus supreme *and* subordinate, exemplary yet exceptional.[53] She was a model of good womanhood and a template for subversive possibilities.

The elaborate, handcrafted *oorkonden* that Wilhelmina received upon the birth of her daughter in 1909 from the Women's Committees of Cape Town and Johannesburg were the result of South African women organising into collectives, donating money and commissioning gifts (Figures 9, 11, 12 and 13). To this end, the letters provide novel examples of the forms of organisation that preceded the establishment of Afrikaner women's political parties in 1914 and the extension of the vote to white women in 1930. Indeed, the *oorkonden* from 1909 can be regarded as political acts within the limits of Afrikaner women's aspirations to power. Extant studies show that from the time of the South African War to the formation of the Union in 1910, Afrikaner women had become self-consciously political and were increasingly active in charity and welfare organisations, where their social roles as carers were given legitimate community expression. Boer women's collective experience of itinerancy or incarceration in British concentration camps during the South African War, and of organised resistance and charitable interventions to alleviate this suffering, provided both the will and the skills for later political organisation.[54] After 1914, women became a formidable force in the Afrikaner nationalist movement in their sanctioned roles as *volksmoeders*, bearers of children who would populate the nation and be reared according to Afrikaner custom.[55] Indeed, women formed the critical mass to bring about a nationalist electoral victory in the 1940s (after which, as Louise Vincent explains, they receded from public life for several decades while their male colleagues returned to dominating politics).[56]

The *oorkonden* from South African women's committees in 1909 were but two in a raft of international salutations for Wilhelmina when she became a mother. She also received *oorkonden* from her female subjects in Dutch overseas possessions, the East Indies, West Indies and Suriname.[57] Women from these disparate locales shared three important conditions: first, all were disenfranchised. Women in the Netherlands were the first to gain the vote, in 1920. White South African women followed in 1930, and women gained voting rights in the East Indies in 1941 (although they had no opportunity to exercise their powers before the Japanese occupation in 1942).[58] Second, these rights were the culmination of women's movements that gained strength in the first decade of Wilhelmina's reign, when she was a young queen and became a new mother.[59] Third, women in the Dutch (colonial) world could look to a royal female head of state in the Netherlands as an example of power and leadership. Indeed, Wilhelmina was frequently represented (often against her will) as a precedent for female political agency, particularly by Dutch feminists.[60]

Research on the development of feminism and women's political rights in South Africa has to date focused on the co-optation of Afrikaner feminists into British dominion politics and outlines a local women's movement led by British settlers.[61] The *oorkonden* presented here suggest a new line of inquiry for following the development of a political consciousness and rhetoric among Afrikaner women, one that pursues transnational connections in the Dutch imperium in the early twentieth century.

Conclusion

Queen Wilhelmina's South African *oorkonden* reveal the flexible symbolic appeal of a parliamentary monarchy in an imperial context. By virtue of the Queen's subjects being mostly 'commoners' rather than 'citizens' (a privilege confined to the people of the Netherlands for most of Wilhelmina's reign), colonial supporters were able to conceive of themselves as equal with their metropolitan counterparts in ways that colonial politics did not enable. This was particularly so since monarchs were popularly thought to be 'above' both European and colonial governments, at least in so far as crowns persisted while administrations came and went.[62] That the Crown could be addressed directly and mobilised rhetorically by those who claimed allegiance to it gave some voice to those groups – women, colonial subjects – to whom formal political rights were denied. To this end, monarchs fostered important allegiances and encouraged unity within their empires, as David Cannadine has rightly pointed out.[63]

However, Wilhelmina's South African *oorkonden* also reveal how monarchies heightened rivalries *between* empires as well as ethno-national groups in contested colonies. Letters to Queen Wilhelmina speak to aspects of the conflict between Afrikaner and British settler colonial aspirations that have to date been neglected in histories of the Dutch monarchy and early twentieth-century South Africa. They provide new evidence of the persistence of a broader, notional Dutch world that exceeded the formal bounds of the Empire and highlight the importance of the Dutch Crown for connecting colonies actual and oneiric. Wilhelmina emerges in this analysis as a figure to whom Afrikaners in a British dominion particularly appealed, a focus for a dissenting settler identity based on Dutch cultural, linguistic and historical affiliations.

Further, for women caught between the oft-competing aims of settler nationalism and a nascent feminism, Queen Wilhelmina personified a dynastic form of political power that authorised public roles for women without radically destabilising contemporary gender hierarchies. In this regard, Wilhelmina's *oorkonden* reveal further differences: between metropole and colony, between colonies, between the enfranchised and the unenfranchised. Women situated in different parts of the Dutch world – the Netherlands, South Africa, the East Indies – were united in their struggle to gain political rights given first to their male counterparts and brought together in admiration of a female king who reigned in a world still largely ruled by men.

Acknowledgement

The research for this essay was funded by the Australian Research Council. I would like to thank the Koninklijk Huisarchief in The Hague for granting access to the primary sources. I would also like to thank Robert Aldrich, Cindy McCreery, Kirsten McKenzie and Nigel Worden for feedback on improvements to the essay in an earlier form, as well as my colleagues at Monash University, Megan Cassidy-Welch, Noah Shenker, Al Thomson, and Charlotte Greenhalgh for the same.

Notes

1. M. T. Clanchy, *From Memory to Written Record: England 1066–1307* (Oxford: Blackwell, 1993), pp. 45, 52–6. For Dutch examples, see the compendium of A. C. F. Koch, *Oorkondenboek van Holland en Zeeland tot 1299* (The Hague: Martinus Nijhoff, 1970).
2. See *oorkonden* held at the KHA, The Hague.
3. The notable exception in this regard was Prince Hendrik 'The Navigator' (*de Zeevaarder*) (1820–79), a brother of King Willem III. Hendrik sailed to the West Indies in 1835, the East Indies in 1837 and the Cape of Good Hope in 1838. It was more than a century later that a Dutch royal set foot on colonial soil again; Juliana visited the West Indies as Queen in 1955. Gert Oostindie, *De Parels en de Kroon: Het Koningshuis en de Koloniën* (Amsterdam: De Bezige Bij, 2006), pp. 102, 108–9.
4. All *oorkonden* to Wilhelmina referred to here are held at the KHA, The Hague.
5. Sovereignty over all the Verenigde Oostindische Compagnie (VOC, Dutch East Indies Company) possessions – including the East Indies, Ceylon and Melaka, as well as the Cape Colony – passed back and forth between Dutch, French and British authorities after the French invasion of the Dutch Republic in 1795. It was, in fact, an ancestor of Wilhelmina's – Willem V, Prince of Orange (1748–1806) – who, fleeing the Batavian Republic for London in 1795, asked the British government to occupy the Cape and other Dutch possessions. In 1799, the VOC was dissolved, and of its former colonies only the East Indies became a Dutch crown colony (in 1816). The fate of the Cape Colony was a brief return to Dutch rule in 1803 before falling again to the British in 1806. British control over the territory was ratified in 1814.
6. Assuming these are accessible: the transactions of the Queen's Cabinet (*Kabinet der Koningin*) are publicly available at the National Archives in The Hague. The Queen's dealings outside the Cabinet are held at the KHA (consulted for this essay), which is private. Here it is currently difficult to obtain access to most correspondence from South Africa after 1914, with some exceptions.
7. Martin Bossenbroek, *Holland op zijn breedst: Indië en Zuid-Afrika in de Nederlandse cultuur omstreeks 1900* (Amsterdam: Bert Bakker, 1996), pp. 87–90, 95, 105, 163, 200, 255, 260–1, 307.
8. Maarten Kuitenbrouwer, *The Netherlands and the Rise of Modern Imperialism: Colonies and Foreign Policy, 1870–1902*, trans. Hugh Beyer (New York and Oxford: Berg and St Martin's Press, 1991), pp. 27, 82, 311.
9. Kuitenbrouwer, *The Netherlands*, pp. 26–7, 189–91, 202, 219, 365; Henk te Velde, *Gemeenschapszin en plichtsbesef: Liberalisme en nationalisme in Nederland, 1870–1918* (The Hague: SDU, 1992), pp. 164, 181; Bossenbroek, *Holland op zijn breedst*; Vincent Kuitenbrouwer, *War of Words: Dutch Pro-Boer Propaganda and the South African War (1899–1902)* (Amsterdam: Amsterdam University Press, 2012).
10. Kuitenbrouwer, *The Netherlands*, pp. 221, 294, 301, 303–6; Cees Fasseur, *Wilhelmina: De jonge koningin* (Amsterdam: Uitgeverij Balans, 1998), pp. 245–6, 404–7.
11. J. W. Pont, 'De banden tusschen Nederland en Zuid-Africa (1898–1923)', in W. G. Bas (ed.), *25 jaar geschiedenis van Nederland 1898–1923* (Amsterdam: Dalmeijer's Volksuniversiteit, 1923), pp. 686–9; H. C. M. Fourie, '"n stem uit Suid-Afrika', in *Na vijf en twintig jaren* (Zwolle: La Rivière & Voorhoere, 1923), pp. 381–4; 'Wilhelmina en Oom Paul', in *De gouden kroon* (Haarlem: Spaarnestad, 1948), pp. 95–7.
12. *Oorkonde* from the Afrikaner Culture Council of Pretoria (1948), KHA A50 XIVf 104; *Oorkonde* from the 'Residents of South Africa' (1948), KHA A50 XIVf 82i.
13. Wilhelmina received three or four *oorkonden* from South Africa at every milestone, in 1898, 1901, 1909, 1923 and 1948, which is comparable to the numbers received from the East Indies.
14. Kuitenbrouwer, *War of Words*, 288.
15. Excepting the important studies by Kuitenbrouwer, *War of Words*, pp. 42–3, 287–8, 300; Vincent Kuitenbrouwer, 'De geografie van stamverwantschap: Op zoek naar

Nederlandse plaatsen van herinneringen in Zuid-Afrika', *Tijdschrift voor Geschiedenis*, 124 (2011), 334–49; and Bernard Slaa, 'Revitalising *Stamverwantschap*: The Role of the *Nederlands Zuid-Afrikaanse Werkgemeenschap* on Dutch-Afrikaner Relations in the Twentieth Century', *South African Historical Journal*, 65:4 (2013), 504–25.

16 Wilhelmina received two *oorkonden* from the NZAV in South Africa during the South African War: one in 1898 and another in 1901 (KHA A50, XIVb 91 and IIc 39 respectively). She also received two *oorkonden* from the Pretoria *Nederlandsch Verbond*, or Dutch Alliance: one in 1923 and another in 1941 (KHA A50, VIXc 4b and VIIIc 21n, respectively).

17 Hermann Giliomee, *The Afrikaners: Biography of a People*, 2nd edn (Charlottesville, Va.: University of Virginia Press, 2009), pp. 365–6; Kuitenbrouwer, *War of Words*, pp. 43, 56; Kuitenbrouwer, *The Netherlands*, p. 286.

18 Wilhelmina received *oorkonden* from the Pretoria chapter of the Afrikaner-Dutch Reading Union (*Afrikaner-Hollandse Leesunir*) in 1923 and from the Afrikaner Culture Council of Pretoria in 1948 (KHA A50 XIVc 47 and XIVf 104 respectively).

19 A high proportion of Wilhelmina's *oorkonden* from South Africa – seven of the seventeen – came from organisations in Transvaal. Publications commemorating celebrations for Wilhelmina were issued here even after her death. See, for example, J. J. Plenaar, *Huldiging van H. M. Koningin Wilhelmina in Transvaal* (Johannesburg, 1940); *Nederlandsche Vereeniging van Pretoria, 1898–1948: programma* (Pretoria, 1948); Cornelis de Jong, *'Ek sal handhaaf': (je maintiendrai): verslag van die herdenking van Koningin Wilhelmina se geboortedag 31 Augustus 1880 te Pretoria in 1980* (Pretoria, 1980). On celebrations for Wilhelmina in Pretoria, see Cornelis de Jong, *Koningin Wilhelmina en Suid-Afrika* (Pretoria: Nasionale Kultuurhistoriese en Opelugmuseum, 1980), pp. 3, 19, 21, 25.

20 Donal Lowry, 'The Play of Forces World-Wide in Their Scope and Revolutionary in Their Operation [J. A. Hobson]: The South African War as an International Event', *South African Historical Journal*, 41 (1999), 83–105; Martin Bossenbroek, *De Boeren oorlog* (Amsterdam: Athenaeum, 2014), pp. 21–2.

21 Women and children formed the majority of the 115,000 civilians interned by the British, ostensibly to remove them from combat zones but only to place them in miserable conditions. Almost a quarter of all internees died, around 10 per cent of the entire population of the two Boer Republics. Bossenbroek, *De Boeren oorlog*, p. 12. The 1904 census showed the decimation of a generation of mostly children (in the age group of five to twenty years). Elizabeth van Heyningen, *The Concentration Camps of the Anglo-Boer War: A Social History* (Sunnyside: Jacana, 2013), p. 309.

22 Giliomee, *The Afrikaners*, pp. 201, 211, 356, 433.

23 Bossenbroek, *De Boeren oorlog*, p. 20.

24 Giliomee, *The Afrikaners*, pp. 197–8, 227, 400, 428.

25 Giliomee, *The Afrikaners*, pp. xiv, xix, 1–2, 6–7, 21, 26, 50, 55, 58, 88, 144, 150, 189, 190–1, 196, 223.

26 Isabel Hofmeyr, 'Building a Nation from Words: Afrikaans Language, Literature and Ethnic Identity, 1902–1924', in Shula Marks and Stanley Trapido (eds), *The Politics of Race, Class and Nationalism in Twentieth Century South Africa* (London and New York: Longman, 1987), pp. 95–123; Giliomee, *The Afrikaners*, pp. 358, 365–6, 369, 429.

27 Hofmeyr, 'Building a Nation from Words', pp. 46–7.

28 Kuitenbrouwer, *The Netherlands*, pp. 204, 286.

29 Kuitenbrouwer, *War of Words*, pp. 119–20, 126. The *oorkonde* in question is from 1901, KHA A50 IIc 84.

30 See www.zuidafrikahuis.nl/# (accessed 11 May 2015).

31 Kuitenbrouwer, *War of Words*, pp. 58–9.

32 KHA A50 VIIIc 21n.

33 Nigel Worden, *The Making of Modern South Africa*, 3rd edn (Oxford: Blackwell, 2000), p. 102.

34 Kuitenbrouwer, *The Netherlands*, pp. 125, 196; Kuitenbrouwer, *War of Words*, pp. 36, 63.

35 KHA A50 XIVc 47.
36 KHA A50 XIVf 82i.
37 KHA A50 XIVf 104.
38 Slaa, 'Revitalising *Stamverwantschap*', p. 511.
39 The inscription on the brass plate labelling the box, however, was in Afrikaans.
40 KHA A50 XIVf 106.
41 KHA A50 XIVf 106.
42 KHA A50 XIVf 106.
43 KHA A50 XIVf 106.
44 Wilhelmina's direct descent from Willem the Silent and his fight against Spain were also mentioned in the *oorkonde* from the exiles in Amsterdam in 1901: KHA A50 IIc 84. It was also a favourite analogy among Dutch intellectuals. See, for example, the essay of J. W. Pont, a professor at the University of Utrecht, 'De banden tusschen Nederland en Zuid-Afrika (1898–1923)', p. 688.
45 Kuitenbrouwer, *The Netherlands*, pp. 191–2, 201, 296.
46 Kuitenbrouwer, *War of Words*; Slaa, 'Revitalising *Stamverwantschap*'.
47 Emerentia van Heuven-van Nes, '"Een aandachtige bezichting ten volle waard": De tentoonstellingen van het werk van koningin Wilhelmina', in Marieke E. Spliethoff, Emerentia van Heuven-van Nes, Mieke Jansen and Paul Rem, *Koningin Wilhelmina; Schilderijen en tekeningen* (Zwolle: Waanders, 2006), pp. 37–56.
48 The significant numbers not simply of black Africans but also of prosperous black farmers in the Boer republics at the onset of the South African War are noted in Van Heyningen, *The Concentration Camps of the Anglo-Boer War*, pp. 24–6.
49 KHA 50 VIIIe 33.
50 The exception here is Maria Grever, who briefly mentions this factor in the appeal of the Queen to Dutch women in 'Koningin Wilhelmina en het feminisme of de ogenschijnlijke onverenigbaarheid van karakters', *Tijdschrift voor Genderstudies*, 2:3 (1999), 4–19, at p. 13.
51 Siep Stuurman, *Wacht op onze daden; het liberalisme en de vernieuwing van de Nederlandse staat* (Amsterdam: Bert Bakker, 1992), pp. 151, 153, 159–60; Bossenbroek, *Holland op zijn breedst*, p. 235; Te Velde, *Gemeenschapszin en plichtsbesef*, pp. 151–2, 159–60; Maria Grever, 'Colonial Queens: Imperialism, Gender and the Body Politic during the Reign of Victoria and Wilhelmina', *Dutch Crossing: A Journal of Low Countries Studies*, 26:1 (2002), 99–114, at pp. 106–7.
52 Hans Dijkhuis, *Monarchia: Het fenomeen van het koningschap* (Amsterdam: Boom, 2010), pp. 245–6; Grever, 'Colonial Queens', p. 103.
53 William Monter, *The Rise of Female Kings in Europe, 1300–1800* (New Haven, Conn.: Yale University Press, 2012).
54 Van Heyningen, *The Concentration Camps of the Anglo-Boer War*, pp. 128, 275.
55 Louise Vincent, 'The Power behind the Scenes: The Afrikaner Nationalist Women's Parties, 1915 to 1931', *South African Historical Journal*, 40:1 (1999), 51–73, at pp. 55–7; Marijke Du Toit, 'The Domesticity of Afrikaner Nationalism: *Volksmoeders* and the ACVV, 1904–1929', *Journal of Southern African Studies*, 29:1 (2003), 155–76; Charl Blignaut, 'Untold History of a Historiography: A Review of Scholarship on Afrikaner Women in South African History', *South African Historical Journal*, 65:4 (2013), 596–617, at pp. 604, 605–7, 610.
56 Vincent, 'The Power behind the Scenes', pp. 54, 71.
57 For the East Indies, see KHA A50 VIIIe 22, also gifts and *oorkonden* from the West Indies in A50. A Suriname example is discussed in Fred Oudschans Dentz, 'Het geschenk van Suriname's vrouwen en meisjes aan Hare Majesteit de Koninging ter gelegenheid van de geboorte van Princes Juliana', *Nieuwe West-Indisch Gids*, 29:1 (1948), 279–81.
58 Susan Blackburn, 'Winning the Vote for Women in Indonesia', *Australian Feminist Studies*, 14:29 (1999), 207–18.
59 See note 55 for the political activities of Afrikaner women during this period. For the rise of feminism in the Netherlands and its colonies in the early 1900s, see L.

H. Gallois and M. G. Schenk (eds), *Vrouwen van Nederland 1898–1948: De vrouw tijdens de regering van Koningin Wilhelmina* (Amsterdam: Scheltens & Giltay, 1948); Maria Grever and Berteke Waaldijk, *Transforming the Public Sphere: The Dutch National Exhibition of Women's Labor in 1898* (Durham, NC: Duke University Press, 2004); Maria Grever and Berteke Waaldijk, 'Women's Labor at Display: Feminist Claims to Dutch Citizenship and Colonial Politics Around 1901', *Journal of Women's History*, 15:4 (2004), 11–18; Elsbeth Locher-Scholten, 'Morals, Harmony, and National Identity: "Companionate Feminism" in Colonial Indonesia in the 1930s', *Journal of Women's History*, 14:4 (2003), 38–58, at pp. 40–1.
60 Grever, 'Koningin Wilhelmina en het feminisme', pp. 5, 13–16.
61 See, for example, Deborah Gaitskell, 'The Imperial Tie: Obstacle or Asset for South Africa's Women Suffragists before 1930?', *South African Historical Journal*, 47:1 (2002), 1–23.
62 Dijkhuis, *Monarchia*, p. 246.
63 David Cannadine, *Ornamentalism: How the British Saw Their Empire* (London: Penguin, 2001).

CHAPTER SIX

Sultans and the House of Orange-Nassau: Indonesian perceptions of power relationships with the Dutch

Jean Gelman Taylor

Introduction

In 1601, in Aceh, Sultan Alauddin Shah placed his seal on a letter, dated 11 December 1600, that had been presented to him by Dutch merchant-envoys on behalf of Holland's Maurits of Orange-Nassau.[1] Alauddin's envoys carried their sultan's letters (wrapped in silk) and gifts across the seas to Maurits. This embassy of 1601–3 was to institute a long history of links between Indonesia's sultanates, the Dutch Republic and its successor, the Kingdom of the Netherlands.

All human encounters are two-way. In the historiography of Europe's colonies in Asia and in Africa the European side of this cross-cultural encounter has received most attention. This perspective gives us European history, for it presents colonies as chapters in the history of Europe overseas. We can account for this imbalance by referring to the voluminous information in colonial archives and to the personal interests of individual scholars.

Shifting our focus to the Asian or African partner in the relationship has the potential to give us a history of peoples, not in the single dimension of colonised subjects but as star performers of their own, longer history, into which there were periodic foreign intrusions. We fit Europeans and their colonialism into a different, indigenous historical sequence.

This other side of the equation is more elusive. My attempt to discover how rulers in states across the Indonesian archipelago viewed the Dutch lacks the equivalent of colonial archives. So we have to turn to other kinds of sources. There is also the problem of place. Indonesia's 17,000 islands, 300-plus ethnic groups, sultanates and statelets merged piecemeal into a single political entity through actions of the Dutch over three centuries. Today's Republic of Indonesia is the successor state to the colony known as the Netherlands East Indies and has the same boundaries.

Older history books narrated Indonesian history as a series of broken sequences. Opening chapters began within the archipelago, describing early communities and the rise of Hindu, Buddhist and then Muslim monarchies. With the arrival of Dutch ships in Indonesian ports (in 1597 in West Java), the narrative left its bases in the archipelago to anchor itself in Amsterdam and The Hague and focus on the spread of Dutch power across the archipelago. Local Indonesian histories moved into a Dutch history of governors-general, commercial plantation agriculture, colonial policies on education, the rise of independence movements and the like. In short, Indonesia's history lost Indonesians as its central actors.[2]

In the first two centuries of contact, sultans dealt with Dutch merchant-envoys who represented the directors of the United East Indies Company (Verenigde Oostindische Compagnie, VOC, 1602–1799), and they sent letters and gifts to members of the House of Orange-Nassau.[3] In this period Maurits and his successors were not crowned monarchs but monopolisers of the office of governor (*stadhouder*) and were major shareholders in the VOC.[4] Over two centuries in the Indonesian archipelago the VOC did business in harbour towns and inland cities ruled by sultans and established its own fortified trading settlements.

The Company dissolved in bankruptcy in 1799, career government officials replacing its merchant-administrators. The archipelago's many sultanates were incorporated into the colony of the Netherlands East Indies that Dutch military and economic power was creating over the course of the nineteenth century. Alternatively, the Dutch dissolved sultanates if sultans refused to enter contractual alliances that made them grand pensioners of the colonial state. Sultans now dealt with officials who were responsible to a minister of colonies in the Netherlands, and they maintained relationships with the House of Orange-Nassau, which had transformed itself in 1813 into the hereditary monarchy of the Kingdom of the Netherlands.

Gifts flowed from Indonesian to Dutch royals until the Japanese invasion in 1942 brought an end to the Netherlands' eastern empire.[5] These artefacts of material culture, such as ceremonial and ritual objects fashioned from costly materials and exhibiting a high degree of artistry, embody statements about power, sacredness and projection of the royal self. Paintings and photographs of the gifts and surviving documents from the royal givers explaining the significance of the items are indicators for how sultans perceived their relations with Dutch royals. Visual records of processions and pageants in colony and metropole also offer evidence of presentation of the royal self to Dutch monarchy and Indonesian home audience alike.

Sultans and their world

Indonesia's islands lie along the sea highways that connect China and Japan to India, the Middle East and Europe. Communities living along the coasts came into contact with variants of Hinduism and Buddhism. There emerged kings who claimed descent from Hindu gods and a concentration within their own person and capital of spiritual-magical powers. They accumulated regalia that acquired great significance through association with royalty, especially ceremonial daggers (*kris*), lances and pennants. These magically charged objects continued to be part of royal regalia in Muslim courts of the archipelago in the long history of foreign rulers becoming indigenised. Dutch merchants sailed into states and societies that were Islamising. There they were one more variety of foreign traders alongside South-East Asians, Indians, Chinese, Arabs, Spanish and Portuguese.

European written accounts and drawings of Indonesian Muslim courts deliver important information for a period when there is a dearth of material from indigenous sources.[6] But clues to sultans' perceptions of the distant *stadhouders* and of their merchant-envoys may be found in the urban layout of their cities, court procedure and etiquette, as well as in royal parades, letters and gifts. A brief sampling provides background to Indonesian perceptions in the nineteenth and twentieth centuries, for which there is more evidence.

In the seventeenth century, port cities in the archipelago were walled. Muslims lived within the walls. Living and work quarters assigned to non-Muslim traders were outside.[7] Such spatial arrangements convey an indigenous view of non-Muslims as polluting. Court etiquette was designed to impress a sense of inferiority on newcomers. Merchants were kept waiting for days before being granted audience with the local sultan. Alauddin looked down on Maurits' envoys, Gerard de Roy and Laurens Bicker, from a luxuriously fitted *howdah* (canopied platform) atop a white elephant as they presented Maurits' letter. Visitors to Muslim courts were given sets of clothes in the local style to wear, thereby assigning them to the ranks of the sultans' subjects. Jobs could be offered at court to men who were willing to convert. New Muslims received new names and a girl from the sultan's establishment. (Royal polygamy redistributed women for the purpose of securing men's loyalty.)

Indonesian sultans saw themselves as part of an international company of rulers. They sent envoys to other Muslim courts, to Mecca, to kingdoms in South-East Asia and, from 1601, to Europe. They replicated marks of Islamic kingship that were common across the Muslim world, such as royal seals and weekly procession to the Friday or chief mosque where the sultan was hailed as Protector of Islam. Seals were modelled on those of Mughal emperors in India. The oldest known seal, that of Sultan Alauddin of Aceh, has his name engraved in the centre. The formula circling the seal's border reads: 'The Sultan Alauddin, son of Firman Shah / he who trusts in the King [Allah], who has chosen him to possess kingdoms and is pleased with him; may God perpetuate his glory and grant victory to his banner.'[8]

English merchant Peter Mundy was in Aceh in 1637. His drawing of a royal procession to the chief mosque shows Sultan Iskandar Thani at the head of many nobles on elephants and horses, with pennants flying and lances aloft, amidst a great crowd of male onlookers on foot.[9] This public display of piety kept minor princes and nobles busy in the royal capital and directed their incomes to shoring up royal power while broadcasting statements about the characteristics of royalty to locals and the transient foreign merchant-envoys. We find these personal qualities spelt out in the opening lines of the letter Sultan Alauddin sent to Maurits:

> A King, shining like the sun at midday, and like the full moon; a King perfect as the North Star; a King who, when standing erect, gave shelter in his shadow to all his slaves; a King whose eyes sparkle like the morning star; a King who possesses a toothed elephant, red, coloured, black, white and speckled elephants; a King who, God-Almighty-like, gives clothing for the elephants, decorated with gold and precious stones, plus a great number of war elephants with iron houses on their back, whose toes are covered with iron sheathes and have copper shoes; a King who, God-Almighty-like, has horses with gold coverings with precious stones and emeralds, plus hundreds of war horses, splendidly equipped from Arabia, Turkey, Cati and Balakki; a King who can show everything that God has created; a king whom Almighty God has placed to reign over everything on the throne of Aceh.[10]

Few royal letters from this period have been preserved. They are works of art, written in coloured inks, with elaborate headings and borders in gold embellished with repeated floral motifs.

Sultan Alauddin addressed Maurits as 'Captain'. The term was more than a royal slight. Maurits was military commander of Holland's forces in the war against Spain, and Indonesian sultans were interested in the Dutch as potential allies and mercenaries. Dutch troops introduced new arms and fighting techniques. They built cannon-proof earthworks for forts when they helped sultans put down rebellions by rival claimants to their thrones and challenges from charismatic Muslim preachers who headed their own militias. Some sultans saw the Dutch as a convenience. Java's kings had the Dutch remove troublesome princes and Muslim leaders to other parts of the archipelago or ship them to the VOC's far-off trading settlements in Ceylon and the Cape of Good Hope.

Few of the gifts sent by sultans to successive members of the House of Orange-Nassau in the first two centuries of contact have survived time, fires, dispersal of collections or loss at sea. From documents in the Netherlands General State and Royal Archives we know these gifts were of three kinds: ornamental weapons, precious objects and 'exotica'. Sultan Alauddin, for instance, sent Maurits a *kris* in a gold sheath ornamented with rubies, a silver-gilt beaker in a wooden case, the equivalent of 380 Dutch pounds of spices, and two red, Malay-speaking parrots attached to silver chains. Gifts from Sultan Iskander Thani (r. 1636–41) to Maurits' successor included four highly prized bezoar stones.[11]

In 1890, looking back on this first period of contact, an unknown Javanese artist showed another understanding of how Indonesian rulers viewed the Dutch. In two beautiful watercolours, Dutch military officers are incorporated as decorative elements, bystanders and witnesses to events of great significance in Java's history. Both are set in the court of Amangkurat II (r. 1677–1703). In the first, the sultan is shown personally stabbing the rebel prince, Trunajaya. Here Amangkurat is centre stage. Female attendants on Trunajaya weep. Various court officials witness the execution, including two Dutchmen in uniforms with swords. A Javanese attendant holds the Dutch flag above them. In the second painting, the sultan sits on high as one of his wives and her lover are executed. The witnesses again include Dutch officers.[12]

It is worth stressing the date of composition of these paintings of traumatic events in Amangkurat's reign. In Western historiography of Indonesia, 1890 marks the beginning of 'high colonialism', when Dutch power was reaching into every part of the archipelago. And yet the artist, a subject of this colonial state, presents the Dutch as decorative bystanders. By the 1890s, the world Indonesia's sultans actually inhabited was bounded. Their wide-ranging contacts with Asia and the Islamic heartland were confined, for the Dutch determined the colony's foreign policy. At home it was the Dutch who administered the territories beyond their mini-palace states.

Preservation of the archipelago's monarchs was part of this Dutch strategy for controlling their vast colony. Blandishments presented the Dutch as guardians of indigenous traditions and cultures, and preservers of the ancient sacred bonds between kings and populace. Colonial officials paid outward respect and honours to the indigenous rulers whose budgets, daily affairs and foreign relations they controlled. From the point of view of Indonesian monarchs, their thrones, privileges, pomp and public deference were upheld. The colonial state's stipends allowed them to spend lavishly. Sultans patronised visual and performing artists and literati at their courts. The gifts they sent to Dutch royals in the nineteenth and twentieth centuries showcase this renaissance in traditional arts and also new trends in artistic concept and design.

Gifts and giving, nineteenth and twentieth centuries

A sample of these royal gifts reveals continuity in choice of items: weapons, precious objects and exotica. We also find new categories of gifts. Alongside objects for public display, sultans now commissioned items for private use by individual Dutch royals. Examples are furniture pieces, such as a writing desk, chairs and carved screens. They also selected personal items for pleasure and refreshment: accessories such as fans, jewellery and walking sticks, betel and tea sets. And, as a sign of the times, the royal self was represented by proxy through the commissioned photograph. Two queens, Emma and Wilhelmina, occupied the Dutch throne between 1890 and 1948.[13] It is in these years that Java's royal women sent gifts in their own name and their own photo-portraits.

The method of conveying gifts also changed. They were presented in person. Junior members of Indonesia's royal houses – the younger brothers, sons, daughters and daughters-in-law of the sultans – travelled to the Netherlands, where, in formal audience with the Dutch monarch, they presented the gifts. An important characteristic of gifts from this period is their educative function. Sultans spoke to Emma and Wilhelmina through letters accompanying the gifts. They explained what these precious gifts were, their names in Indonesian languages, the occasions when they were used and by whom. They pointed out the significance and symbolism of the objects. In this regard, gifts were not just gorgeous examples of Indonesia's goldsmithing and woodcarving. They had an instructive intent.

In 1901, Wilhelmina's speech from the throne to the Netherlands States-General (national legislature) reformulated the Dutch colonial mission in the Indies. It was to be guided by 'ethical policy' whose animating principle would be uplift of the natives from their ignorance. Among the colonised, including the sultans, there prevailed the view that the Dutch had much to learn too. The sultans' gifts were a subtle expression of this sense of a two-way partnership. Dutch-educated contemporaries of the sultans expressed this concept explicitly in writing. An example is a document prepared for the States-General in that same year, 1901, by Raden Ajeng Kartini (1879–1904):

Popular knowledge about the Indies and its people should be spread among the Dutch; they should be taught to understand the Javanese from a proper point of view through which prejudice will dwindle and in the future not only the exceptional, but also the ordinary Netherlanders will regard the Javanese as fellow human beings who, through no fault of their own, are intellectually their inferior and not because they are brown-skinned.[14]

Photographs and personal gifts suggest that Indonesia's royals were clearly visualising their Dutch counterparts as actual people and not just as generic rulers of remote, unknown places. In this sense, the sultans were asserting relationships with the House of Orange-Nassau as fellow royals with common interests and predilections. They were projecting themselves to audiences in the Netherlands and the Netherlands Indies, and, beyond this, they were staking a place for themselves within a worldwide context. A sampling of gifts from Indonesian royals illustrates these general observations.[15] It is followed by a closer focus on one gift-giver, Paku Buwono X (r. 1893–1939), *susuhunan* and Sultan of the Independent Principality of Surakarta in Central Java.[16]

Gifts: objects in motion

The oldest known gift in the possession of the House of Orange-Nassau is a gold ceremonial *kris* and sheath of chased gold, set with small gemstones (for a similar *kris* see Figure 14). The dagger's hilt is in the form of a *wayang* figure.[17] The *kris* is a stabbing weapon found across Indonesia. On Java, Madura and Bali, *krises* formed part of the royal regalia of the sultans and were honoured as sacred heirlooms. These *krises* were given titles and personal names. They could be sent to ceremonies in place of the ruler himself. Smiths forged together many fine layers of metal into a wavy blade and treated the iron with chemicals to bring out a pattern of spiritual potency on the blade that was transmitted to the possessor. Smiths prepared themselves for forging special *krises* by fasting, prayer and meditation.

Krises form the majority of gifts sent to the Netherlands. In commissioning the making of *krises* with richly ornamented sheaths, Indonesia's sultans can be seen to convey several messages. The *kris* was a symbol of royalty; its function as gift confirmed the status of both giver and receiver. As a magically charged object, the donated *kris* created a mystical bond between the monarchs. It served also to display Java's wealth in precious materials and in artisanship. Examples of magnificent *krises* sent to Dutch royals include a Balinese-style, straight-bladed *kris*, with a gold sheath incised with plant designs and birds, and studded with diamonds, sent to King Willem I by Cakra

[125]

14. Dagger and sheath (*kris*), Javanese, late nineteenth century, iron, wood, brass (a–b) 48.8 × 14.6 × 2.8 cm (overall), National Gallery of Victoria, Melbourne, Purchased, 1974, image code 53033.
Reproduced with permission

Adiningrat VIII, Sultan of Madura, in 1835;[18] a Javanese *kris* with wavy blade and sheath of sandalwood elaborately set with diamonds and rubies, presented to King Willem III in 1851 by Paku Buwono VII, King of the Sultanate of Surakarta;[19] and a *kris* with an ivory hilt and a gold sheath embossed with peacock motifs, coloured with green enamel and set with diamonds, presented by Sultan Hamengku Buwono VIII of Yogyakarta to Queen Wilhelmina.[20]

This latter gift of a ceremonial dagger, which represented a male sovereign, was presented to a female ruler in the Netherlands to mark the silver jubilee of her reign in 1923. The choice of gift suggests a concept of the relationship between royals that transcended gender. By contrast, the betel set was a ceremonial item of royal regalia associated with both male and female royals in Indonesian courts. It consists of a receptacle within which are compartments or small containers to hold ingredients for preparing the betel that was ceremonially offered to welcome guests and had a role in wedding rituals between bride and groom. The offering of betel symbolised the purity of intent of the giver and betokened desire for smooth and lasting relationships. Betel sets were carried in public processions and were set near the throne in public audiences. The betel set figures prominently in photographs taken of sultans and their queens (see

Figure 15).²¹ Examples of gifts of betel sets to Dutch monarchs include a gold bowl with small gold lidded boxes and a gold cuspidor, presented by Paku Buwono X to Queen Wilhelmina in 1901;²² and a golden betel bowl bearing the coat of arms of the Sultan of Yogyakarta, Hamengku Buwono VIII, in diamonds, presented to Princess Juliana in 1937.²³

15. Sultan Hamengku Buwono VII of Yogyakarta (r. 1877–1921) with gold betel set from his royal regalia. Photographer Kassian Cephas, restored by Durova, Tropenmuseum, part of the National Museum of World Cultures, image code: 60001455. Wikimedia Commons, licensed under CC BY-SA 3.0

Sultans sometimes commissioned European artists to make the gifts they presented. For example, the Sultan of Siak (East Sumatra) sent an elephant tusk in 1898 to silversmiths in the Netherlands, who decorated it with silver flowers and plants native to Indonesia and set it on a base ornamented with deer, trees and plants.[24] This gift marked the investiture of Queen Wilhelmina. But mostly sultans showcased Indonesian craftsmanship and distinctive Indonesian elements, even when they made gifts of familiar European objects, such as the walking stick. We see this in the walking stick presented to Queen Wilhelmina by Sultan Hamengku Buwono VIII.[25] Its gold handle is shaped in the form of a *naga* (snake) bearing a crown of diamonds. The *naga* motif, carried over from Java's ancient Hindu and Buddhist traditions, is associated with water, fertility, protection and royalty. In 1923, when this gift was made, Wilhelmina was celebrating the silver jubilee of her investiture. The gift shows how an item from a European repertoire could be construed to make a statement about royal power and the cultural heritage of Java. The tight connection between walking stick and royalty is also apparent in the gift Hamengku Buwono made to Queen Emma (then Queen Mother) in 1929. This one is in ivory. A gold band below the handle combines a crown and the initials HB VIII in relief, inlaid with diamonds.[26]

Queen Emma was seventy-one years old when she received this walking stick from Yogyakarta. The choice of a utilitarian accessory suggests the sultan's solicitous consideration for the age and health of a senior Dutch royal. As such, the walking stick belongs to a cluster of goods sent to individual members of the House of Orange-Nassau that were age-appropriate. Other examples include a golden rattle made in the shape of a three-tiered *payung* (sunshade), each tier decorated with bells and the whole topped with a crown set with diamonds.[27] The *payung* is a traditional symbol of royalty in Indonesia, part of the ruler's regalia, connoting authority and protection. The humble baby's rattle was transformed into a statement of alliance between royal houses in the grand gift of the Sultan of Deli (East Sumatra) to the newborn Princess Beatrix in 1938.

Princess Juliana received a costly toy for her second birthday from Paku Alam VII in 1911. It was a little two-wheeled gold cart made in the shape of a Garuda bird, painted in red, gold, green and blue.[28] The design chosen by this Javanese prince for a Dutch royal child's plaything draws on the Hindu tradition in which Garuda carried the god Vishnu on his back. In its Java context, Garuda represents loyalty, bravery and preservation of order. It is today the national symbol of Indonesia. The gift suggests an educative motive from Paku Alam to the new heir to the Dutch throne. And this characteristic in giving is also evident in the present of dolls made to Juliana's mother, Wilhelmina, by Hamengku Buwono VII in 1894.[29] The dolls were made in Germany but sent to Yogyakarta, where eighteen tiny sets of clothes were made in the costumes of various members of Javanese society from the crown prince, consort and court attendant down to lower-ranking individuals. All were made with the materials, jewellery and headdress appropriate to each social status. The letters HB, the initials of the sultan's reign name, were engraved on the silver buttons of the crown prince's costume. The intent of the sultan in giving these dolls to the fourteen-year-old Wilhelmina was, perhaps, to develop her understanding of Javanese hierarchy and associated customs.

An exhortatory intent may be seen in the gift of a writing desk to Queen Wilhelmina in 1923 from Paku Buwono X of Surakarta.[30] Five different Javanese woods are in the ornate desk and its central panel brings together the Dutch crown and the Sultan's coat of arms. Paku Buwono explained to the Queen in an accompanying letter that the shape of the desk was based on the pulpit in Surakarta's principal mosque. He added that when the imam spoke from the pulpit, his whole attention was given to his sermon. Paku Buwono went on to commend to the Queen: 'May Her Majesty marshal Her thoughts with the same power on the matter which claims her exalted attention, as She sits at this desk.'[31]

Scholars often note that the act of placing objects originating in Asia and elsewhere in Europe's curiosity cabinets and museums alters their meaning. Glass cases isolate ritual objects from their original sacred context and strip them of their intended associations. Indonesia's sultans knew this. They were aware that the act of giving and sending precious items across the seas produced change in function and meaning. Paku Buwono seems to indicate such understanding when he directs Wilhelmina to put his gift to a new use and to emulate the devotion of Muslim religious leaders to their congregants.

The art of giving changed over time. Royal women of Java's courts emerged from the seclusion of the palace to offer gifts jointly with their husbands and also in their own name. Women's gifts were costly personal items for female members of the Dutch royal family. For example, the golden cart shaped as a Garuda presented to the young Princess Juliana was expressly given in the names of both Paku Alam VII and his consort, Retno Puwoso, who was a daughter of Paku Buwono X of Surakarta.[32] The Ratu Kencana, widow of Hamengku Buwono VII, chose a golden fan in the shape of a peacock with wings and tail outstretched for Wilhelmina in 1923.[33] The fan has peculiarly female as well as royal connotations. It suggests Hamengku Buwono's queen had given thought to what would be an appropriate luxury gift from one woman to another in choosing the fan over a *kris*.

Royal women also made themselves knowable through sending photographs of themselves to the Netherlands. A photograph of Paku Buwono X's consort, known by the title Ratu Hemas or Golden Queen, was presented to Queen Wilhelmina in 1898.[34] The year marked the Dutch Queen's investiture and as such was a gesture from one reigning queen to another. Public display of photographs of royals and reproduction of their images in posters, newspapers and magazines was long a controversial issue in Indonesia. Members of the royal houses would be insulted if a photograph of a sultan and a common labourer appeared on the same page or, worse, a royal image could be trampled upon when these ephemeral media were discarded. Paku Buwono X also took the controversial step of imposing on Queen Wilhelmina a consciousness of royal polygamy and of the hierarchies of women in his palace by sending her photo-portraits of himself, his chief and junior consorts in three-quarter length in large elaborately carved wooden frames.[35] Photo-portraits were formal stagings of the royal self and could be understood as a modern form or updating of the custom of sending a *kris*.

Other royal gifts included jewellery, woven and batikked cloths, gold and silver tea services, desk sets of pen and ink and small models of Indonesian house styles and boats from the sultans of Asahan, Langkat, Pontianak, Bulungan and Sumbawa. Distinctive gifts from rulers of Bali included incense boxes, palm-leaf manuscripts, statues of Hindu gods and prayer mats. Many lesser-ranking rajas and hereditary chieftains also sent gifts, including chieftains in Aceh whose sultan had been deposed by the Dutch and the sultanate abolished. Their gifts included betel sets, such as the one sent to Juliana and Bernhard on their marriage by the acting *datu* of Paloppo, Sulawesi, and the betel set presented as a wedding gift by Teuku Umar of Aceh.[36] It is noteworthy that some gifts from the lesser ranks of hereditary rulers included explicitly Islamic symbols and calligraphy. An example is a silk cloth for wrapping the Quran in which is woven in Arabic letters the names of Allah and Muhammad and the Muslim confession of faith presented by the Sultan of Sumbawa to Wilhelmina on the twenty-fifth anniversary of her reign.[37]

Giving as performance

In the twentieth century, royal gifts from Indonesia's sultans were borne to Holland's monarchs by junior members of Indonesian royal families. While young princes travelled to the Netherlands for study in Dutch universities or to train as officers in the kingdom's army, they did not leave the Indies once they had themselves succeeded to the throne. Junior relatives who represented Indies' sultans donned palace formal attire when they were received in official audience in the Netherlands and presented the gifts. They joined public celebrations marking milestones in the reigns and personal lives of Dutch monarchs, such as accession to the throne, marriages and births. The newspaper-reading publics in the Netherlands and Netherlands Indies could see these alliances materialised.

For the investiture of Wilhelmina in 1898, the Dutch government sent official invitations to the most prominent royal family of each major island in the colony. This meant that Java was represented by a delegation from Surakarta, for the Dutch recognised Paku Buwono X as 'emperor of Java' and Surakarta as the island's senior sultanate. Sumatra was represented by the Sultan of Siak and Borneo by sons of the Sultan of Kutai. Indonesia's royals took their place alongside royals from Europe's courts in the processions, receptions and festivities marking the investiture and may be seen in the large painting of the coronation made by Mari ten Kate.[38] Prince Ario Mataram, brother of Paku Buwono X, is prominently placed in the front row of dignitaries close to the Queen in this painting. He wears full court dress. The entire delegation posed in formal court or military dress with ceremonial swords of state for a photo-portrait in another staging of the claim to relationships of alliance, not subordination.

Most sultans sided with the Dutch in the 1920s and 1930s when there was a proliferation of study clubs and political parties demanding an independent state that would be constituted as a republic. (Notably, the Sultanate of Yogyakarta, which had not been invited to send representatives to Wilhelmina's investiture, supported Sukarno and the nationalists during the independence struggle of 1945–49.) The climax in the efforts of Indonesia's royals to sustain the perception of an alliance of equals with the Dutch monarchy came in 1936 just five years before Japanese army and naval forces invaded the Indies. The occasion, which promised continuation of the House of Orange-Nassau, was the marriage of Princess Juliana to Prince Bernhard. For the first time in the long history of royal connections, a significant court ceremony of Java was jointly enacted in Java and in Holland, facilitated by the new technology of radio transmission. This was the staging simultaneously in two palaces of the *serimpi* dance. This dance, which dates from the seventeenth century, is performed by four young female dancers from Java's royal houses at state ceremonies, weddings and coronations. On 28 December 1936, Gusti Raden Ajeng Siti Nurul Kusumowardhani, daughter of Mangku Negara VII, danced for the bridal couple in the Noordeinde Palace in The Hague to *gamelan* music broadcast by radio as her three partners performed the same movements in the Mangkunagaran palace in Surakarta (see Figure 16). It was the ultimate statement of how Indonesian royals conceived of their place in the colonial world.

16. Gusti Raden Ajeng Siti Nurul Kusumowardani, daughter of Mangku Negara VII of Surakarta, dances in the Noordeinde Palace, The Hague, as a wedding gift to Princess Juliana and Prince Bernhard, 28 December 1936. Leiden University, KITLV Digital Image Library, image code 53255. Reproduced with permission

SULTANS AND THE HOUSE OF ORANGE-NASSAU

Projection of self: parade and pageantry

Paku Buwono X of Surakarta (r. 1893–1939) is the dominant figure in the work of projecting the royal self in the Dutch empire as a player rather than as its pensioner. He contrived to have his subjects in Surakarta perceive him as king and to impress this status on colonial officials and fellow royals in the Indies. Recognition by Dutch royals was essential to this strategy of dealing with colonial rule. The House of Orange-Nassau was to be seduced into performing a part in sustaining both his throne and prerogatives. Paku Buwono X's long reign coincided with the long reign of Wilhelmina, and it took place in the age of photography, which allows us to see him performing at home to colonial officials and subjects.

Gifts sent in one direction only may be perceived as tribute. But the gift-giving was two-way. Dutch royals regularly sent precious gifts of European workmanship, letters and honours such as medals and titles, to mark important milestones in the reigns of Indonesia's sultans. Paku Buwono X, for instance, received the Grand Cross in the Order of the Netherlands Lion in 1932 on the fortieth anniversary of his installation as sultan. In photographs dating from the middle years of his reign, Paku Buwono X presents himself in a braided jacket laden with the many medals and decorations he had received from the Netherlands.[39]

Photographs also indicate how Paku Buwono X wished to present himself to colonial officials and home audiences. In grand processions, he walks beneath *payungs*, surrounded by retainers bearing his regalia, followed by a retinue so numerous that the colonial official representing the Governor-General is barely distinguishable in the great throng of the Sultan's subjects.[40] He also hosted state dinners for visiting dignitaries. He received King Chulalongkorn of Siam in 1897 and hosted a reception and formal dinner in the palace for the Governor-General of French Indochina in 1939.[41]

A note on modern times

Sultans found no place in independent Indonesia. Sumatra's royal families were massacred in the chaos following the collapse of the colonial state. President Sukarno swept aside the remaining sultans. The Surakarta sultanate of the Paku Buwono dynasty lost its territory and now comprises the site of the palace-city only. Lower ranks of the aristocracy and new middle class sided with the republic. Their descendants run Indonesia today. Histories usually privilege the nationalist movement of the 1920s and 1930s in the narrative of the making of modern Indonesia. If we look at membership numbers, however, royalist parties on Java far outstripped the nationalist parties.⁴²

The Sultanate of Yogyakarta preserved its integrity and was incorporated as a Special Region into the Indonesian Republic in 1949 in recognition of the support its sultan and people gave during the years of fighting for independence against the Dutch. Within the new state, Sultan Hamengku Buwono IX (r. 1940–88) combined the hereditary role of sultan with the appointive role of governor of Yogyakarta Special Region. He became prominent in the nation's political and business life as Minister of Defence and Coordinating Minister for Development in national governments and was elected as Suharto's Vice-President of Indonesia from 1973 to 1978. On his death, the position of sultan passed to his son. Hamengku Buwono X was formally installed as Sultan of Yogyakarta in 1989, but President Suharto did not appoint him as its governor. In constitutional reforms following the fall of Suharto, the position of provincial governor was made elective, so that Hamengku Buwono X had to campaign to gain the governorship. Local sentiment, however, deemed it insulting to the royal house for its sultan to submit to general election in every political cycle and a breach of the convention that had awarded special privileges to Yogyakarta. This sentiment eventually prevailed. In 2012, Indonesia's central government passed legislation that affirms the right of Yogyakarta's sultans to also inherit the office of civil governor. Hereditary rights now supersede rights to vote and stand for public office, rights that are guaranteed in Indonesia's constitution. The long history of Indonesian royals acting to preserve their prerogatives within the colonial empire has entered a new phase within its successor republican state.

Conclusion

In the seventeenth and eighteenth centuries, the world that sultans knew comprised Indonesia's islands, mainland South-East Asia, China, India, Sri Lanka, the Muslim holy cities of Mecca and Medina and the Ottoman sultanate, whose capital they called Rum. It was a slow-motion world of transport by foot and by animal and sea power. Sultans of the Indonesian archipelago were used to receiving foreigners, whether diplomatic envoys, merchants or travelling religious scholars and adventurers. They were accustomed to the formal giving and receiving of letters and gifts. They set the conditions under which foreigners might stay and transact business. Sultans had a sense of personal superiority as Muslims and as descendants of semi-divine ancestors.

In this period, sultans became acquainted with Europeans. They became well aware of the varieties of Europeans and the enmities between them. They sought to exploit rivalries, such as the competition for the spice trade between the Portuguese and the Dutch. Sultans from one end of the archipelago to the other saw Europeans as potential allies and a source of mercenaries. They were alive to the threat Europeans posed to their political and commercial interests. Indonesia's sultans also saw Europeans as possessors of useful items, some novel, others improved versions of what they already had. They wanted the latest in muskets and cannon; they saw the possibilities of cloth sails and maps; they wanted globes and horses. They saw Europeans as a pool of skilled employees. They hired Dutchmen to be their trumpeters, coachmen, building surveyors and interpreters.

In the nineteenth and twentieth centuries, the world the sultans knew now encompassed Europe. They or their relatives and staff had been there. Their world, while wider, was more circumscribed. They found themselves obliged to adapt to a new superpower, the colonial state. Sultans had to make themselves useful to the Dutch, construct a past based on sacred bonds between rulers and ruled to convince the Dutch that colonial power would work best if based on an alliance of interests. They espoused habits of the modern man. They belonged to the faster world of steamship, train, tram, car and telegraph. Surakarta's Paku Buwono X owned the first car in the colony (a one-cylinder Benz Phaeton, acquired in 1894). It was nine years before the Governor-General acquired a car.

Sultans were used to having to accommodate themselves to Europeans, used to playing games to maintain and increase their wealth and status. They relied on colonial officials to keep new men down, that is, the Western-educated Indonesian men who saw them as outdated representatives of a feudal past and the Muslim firebrands who denounced sultans and the Dutch alike. Sultans grew used to greater court pomp. They wanted residents of the Netherlands Indies, coloniser and colonised, to see them as rulers. They perceived members of the House of Orange-Nassau as potential allies to shore up their dynasties.

Such reflections were not confided to diary and memoir. The visual record helps us understand how Indonesian performers of their own history perceived Europeans. Here is the importance of material culture for giving insights into attitudes and power relationships. It reminds us that European monarchs also performed for multiple audiences. In the context of Netherlands imperial history, the attitudes and actions of Indonesia's sultans constituted an exercise in self-aggrandisement that had no material impact on colonial might. Placing this 'exercise' in the context of Indonesian history points us to a different conclusion: colonial rule rested on an alliance of elites.

The Japanese smashed that alliance. Despite Dutch efforts in the immediate post-war years, it could not be revived for former allies were discredited or gone, swept away in the chaotic first months of the struggle for independence. There was no one left who was willing to make colonialism work.

Notes

1 Aceh is located at the northern end of Sumatra. It was incorporated into the Netherlands East Indies in 1903 and has been a province of the Republic of Indonesia since its declaration of independence from the Netherlands in 1945.
2 I use 'Indonesia' and 'Indonesian' as convenient shorthand for the islands and peoples of the Indonesian archipelago in the years before these terms were adopted by nationalist youth in 1928 and formalised with the declaration of Indonesia's independence on 17 August 1945.
3 The United East Indies Company or Vereinigde Oost-Indische Compagnie is mostly referred to here as the VOC, the initials of its Dutch name, or simply as the Company.
4 *Stadhouder* literally means placeholder or lieutenant. The office originated as a non-hereditary, appointive position. *Stadhouders* governed regions of territories held in the Low Countries by the dukes of Brunswick and later the Spanish Crown. By the time of the embassy from Aceh, Maurits had thrown off his Spanish king and was waging war against him for the new Dutch republic.
5 Royal exchanges have continued since Indonesia's independence but are outside the scope of this study.
6 See, for example, Anthony Reid (ed.), *Witnesses to Sumatra: A Travellers' Anthology* (Oxford: Oxford University Press, 1995).
7 J. Kathirithamby-Wells, 'The Islamic City: Melaka to Jogjakarta, c. 1500–1800', *Modern Asian Studies*, 20:2 (1986): 333–51.
8 Annabel Teh Gallop, 'Ottoman Influences in the Seal of Sultan Alauddin Riayat Syah of Aceh (r. 1589–1604)', *Indonesia and the Malay World*, 32:93 (2004), 176–90, at p. 187.
9 See vol. III of *The Travels of Peter Mundy in Europe and Asia, 1608–1667* (London: Hakluyt Society, 1919).
10 The Sultan's letter was composed in Spanish. Dr Wap gives his Dutch translation of these opening lines in *Het gezantschap van den sultaan van Achin 1602 aan Prins Maurits van Nassau en Oud-Nederlandscbe republiek* (Delft: J. H. Molenbroek, 1862), pp. 19–20, which I have translated here into English. I acknowledge the problems posed by the many tongues involved in this communication beginning with the Sultan's original communication in Malay to his translator, but we can still discern contextualising of the Sultan and distill his key qualities as being resplendent, rich, munificent and appointed by Allah.
11 *Bezoars* are masses of undigested material found in the stomach of animals such as goats and porcupines. Arab medical manuscripts from the tenth century classify varieties of bezoars and describe them as an antidote to poison. European merchants sought them for markets at home. See Peter Borschberg, 'The Euro-Asian Trade in Bezoar Stones (approx. 1500–1700)', in Michael North (ed.), *Artistic and Cultural Exchanges between Europe and Asia, 1400–1900* (Surrey: Ashgate, 1988), pp. 29–44.
12 The paintings may be viewed in the KITLV Digital Image Library, image codes 48M-5 and 48M-6 respectively.
13 Emma, widow of Willem III, acted as Queen-Regent from 1890 until her daughter, Wilhelmina, came of age in 1898.
14 Jean Taylor, 'Educate the Javanese!' (My translation of *Geef den Javaan opvoeding!*), *Indonesia*, 17 (April 1974), p. 91. Kartini came from a family of Dutch-speaking Javanese aristocrats who claimed connection to the royal house of Madura and whose

male members administered regions of Java as officials of the colonial government. Family connections brought her to the notice and sponsorship of prominent members of the colonial elite who promoted formation of a Dutch-speaking, Western-educated elite among Java's ranking families. Kartini's personal and public campaigns were for the rights of women to schooling, jobs and choice of marriage partner.

15 The objects discussed here are housed in the Royal Family Archive in the Netherlands and so are not exhibited to the public, but some may be viewed online at https://www.koninklijkhuis.nl/foto-en-video/tentoonstelling-koninklijk-huisarchief/de-indische-zaal-in-paleis-noordeinde/. In 1995, the House of Orange-Nassau Trust authorised publication of *Royal Gifts from Indonesia: Historical Bonds with the House of Orange-Nassau (1600–1938)*. This *catalogue raisonné* was prepared by the anthropologist Rita Wassing-Visser. She selected 200 items from the collection, shown in full colour, from sultanates in Java, Madura, Sumatra, Borneo, Sulawesi, Sumbawa and Ternate. The objects I have selected are identified by figure and page numbers in *Royal Gifts from Indonesia*. Ethnological museums in the Netherlands have many examples of Indonesian arts. The sampling here is restricted to those objects presented by Indonesia's sultans to their Dutch counterparts.

16 *Susuhunan* is the title given to the legendary bringers of Islam to Java. It was also used by kings of the Mataram Sultanate (c. 1570–1755) and by the sultans of Surakarta. In the Dutch colony, the Central Java sultanates of Surakarta and Yogyakarta were accorded the status of Independent Principality.

17 Wassing-Visser, *Royal Gifts from Indonesia*, pp. 44–5, Figs. 16–17. *Wayang* refers to stylised images of heroes of the Javanese versions of the Indian-Sanskrit epics, the *Ramayana* and *Mahabharata*. Characters have standardised features common to their puppet, dance drama, painted and sculpted forms.

18 Wassing-Visser, *Royal Gifts from Indonesia*, p. 61, Fig. 31.
19 Wassing-Visser, *Royal Gifts from Indonesia*, pp. 168–9, Figs. 157–8.
20 Wassing-Visser, *Royal Gifts from Indonesia*, pp. 196–7, Figs. 197–8.
21 Examples from the KITLV Digital Image Library of photographs of royal family members in which a betel set is placed include 'Pangeran Adipati Ario Mangku Bumi in Court Costume at Yogyakarta', image code 4042, 1889, and his wife 'Raden Ayu Mangku Bumi', 1889, image code 4045, and 'Sultan Hamengku Buwono VII of Yogyakarta', image code 20027, c. 1885.
22 Wassing-Visser, *Royal Gifts from Indonesia*, p. 152, Fig. 134.
23 Wassing-Visser, *Royal Gifts from Indonesia*, p. 222, Fig. 240.
24 Wassing-Visser, *Royal Gifts from Indonesia*, p. 108, Fig. 83.
25 Wassing-Visser, *Royal Gifts from Indonesia*, pp. 198–9, Figs. 201, 203.
26 Wassing-Visser, *Royal Gifts from Indonesia*, p. 101, Fig. 69.
27 Wassing-Visser, *Royal Gifts from Indonesia*, p. 233, Fig. 257.
28 Wassing-Visser, *Royal Gifts from Indonesia*, p. 156, Fig. 143.
29 Wassing-Visser, *Royal Gifts from Indonesia*, pp. 96–7, Figs. 59–61.
30 Wassing-Visser, *Royal Gifts from Indonesia*, p. 194, Fig. 194.
31 See Wassing-Visser, *Royal Gifts from Indonesia*, p. 203 for the quotation from Paku Buwono's letter.
32 The Pakualaman was an enclave, similar to a duchy, within the sultanate of Yogyakarta. It was founded in 1812. Its members intermarried with the ruling families of two major sultanates on Java and the Mangkunagaran, the enclave established within the Surakarta Sultanate in 1757.
33 Wassing-Visser, *Royal Gifts from Indonesia*, p. 200, Fig. 204.
34 Wassing-Visser, *Royal Gifts from Indonesia*, p. 106, Fig. 78.
35 Wassing-Visser, *Royal Gifts from Indonesia*, p. 195, Fig. 195.
36 Wassing-Visser, *Royal Gifts from Indonesia*, p. 179, Fig. 173 and p. 212, Fig. 226.
37 Wassing-Visser, *Royal Gifts from Indonesia*, p. 204, Fig. 213.
38 The painting, completed in 1899, is housed in the Royal Family Archive in The Hague. It is reproduced in Wassing-Visser, *Royal Gifts from Indonesia*, p. 105, Fig. 76.
39 Wassing-Visser, *Royal Gifts from Indonesia*, p. 215, Fig. 229. This photograph is also in the KITLV Digital Image Library, image code 49558. Numerous other photographs

of Paku Buwono X may be found in the KITLV archive by entering his name using the Dutch spelling 'Pakoe Boewono'.
40 See 'Installation of Paku Buwono X as Susuhunan of Surakarta, 1893, with the Dutch Resident [senior colonial official] A. A. Burnaby Lautier', KITLV image code 27481.
41 See KITLV image codes 155365 and 155388 of Governor-General H. E. P. Pasquier being received by Paku Buwono X in the Surakarta Palace, May 1929, and 9890 of Chulalongkorn's visit.
42 See Chapter 1 of George McT.Kahin, *Nationalism and Revolution in Indonesia* (Ithaca, NY: Cornell University Press, 1959); and William J. O'Malley, 'Second Thoughts on Indonesian Nationalism', in James J. Fox (ed.), *Indonesia: Australian Perspectives*, 3 vols (Canberra: Australian National University Press, 1980), vol. III, pp. 601–13.

CHAPTER SEVEN

The return of the throne: the repatriation of the Kandyan regalia to Ceylon

Robert Aldrich

The regalia of a monarchy are its most potent symbols. In the Western tradition, they include a throne, crown, sceptre and sword, objects made of precious metals and gemstones and richly decorated with heraldic and symbolic motifs.[1] Often they are of considerable age and historical significance and invested with a quasi-religious aura. They figure in coronation ceremonies and other state occasions such as the opening of Parliament.[2] Exhibited to the public, they provide glittering reminders of reigning monarchs (the British crown jewels at the Tower of London) or extinct dynasties (for instance, the Habsburg regalia at Hofburg Palace in Vienna).

Few greater blows befall a monarch, other than loss of the throne itself, than capture or destruction of regalia by conquerors, revolutionaries or iconoclasts. In establishing their overlordship, triumphant colonial powers often did capture the regalia of defeated leaders. Soldiers pillaged palaces for booty, and the treasures of a king or queen offered prize lots. Symbols of displaced potentates and regimes held special value: taking the regalia away in a very real sense epitomised the taking away of the sovereignty of indigenous rulers. The fate of such objects varied: presented as trophies, sold at auction, entered into museum collections, occasionally repatriated. Even today demands are regularly voiced for restitution of heritage objects, regalia among them.

This chapter will consider the regalia of the kingdom of Kandy, the last independent realm on the island known in colonial times as Ceylon and now as Sri Lanka, which was fully annexed by the British in 1815.[3] The 'biographies' of such treasures, their peregrinations from colony to metropole, and the issues aroused about their possession, significance and use shed light on the complex and dynamic relationship between European monarchies, on the one hand, and pre-colonial polities, colonial states and independent successor states on the other. After some background on colonialism in Ceylon, the chapter will examine the circumstances in which the regalia were taken in the early 1800s and the way in which the British monarchy tried to assume the mantle of the pre-colonial monarchy in Ceylon. It then moves forward to look at the repatriation of objects in the 1930s, and, finally, the place of the regalia in ceremonies marking the independence of Ceylon in 1948.

Colonialism and the conflict of monarchies in Ceylon

The Portuguese in the late 1500s made the initial European incursions into Ceylon, valued for its spices (such as cinnamon), precious stones and prime geostrategic location in the Indian Ocean. In the 1600s, the Dutch displaced the Portuguese and by the 1760s controlled the entire littoral of the island, leaving the kingdom of Kandy as the last (and landlocked) independent state, heir to over 2,000 years of Sinhalese kingship. Next to the royal palace in Kandy stood Sri Dalada Maligawa, the temple housing a reputed tooth of the Buddha, one of the most sacred relics for the largely Buddhist Sinhalese population and the palladium of the kingdom, a relic providing protection and safety to ruler and people.

Searching for geopolitical advantage and fearful that their wartime enemies, the French, might take over the island, the British invaded Ceylon in 1796 and occupied the Dutch possessions there. Over the next years, they negotiated trade and resources with King Sri Vikrama Rajasinha, who had ruled since 1798 as the fourth king in the Nayakkar dynasty, established in 1739. The first king of the line was a Tamil, from southern India, who succeeded his heirless brother-in-law; the Kandy kings had customarily married Kshatriya-caste wives from southern India. However, the dynasty, as Michael Roberts has argued, was largely 'indigenised', and the king served as protector of Buddhism and absolute monarch, though occasionally facing opposition from Sinhalese noblemen.[4]

In 1803, in an attempt to consolidate their hold over Ceylon, the British waged war against Vikrama Rajasinha, even lending support to a rival pretender to the throne. The rebellion, pretender and war failed, and an uneasy standoff between British and Kandyans prevailed until, in 1815, under the new and expansionist governor, Sir Robert Brownrigg, the British again invaded Kandyan territory. The British accused Vikrama Rajasinha of a catalogue of misdeeds, portraying him as a cruel despot whose subjects cried out for emancipation. They also took advantage of a plot against the King fomented by several Kandyan chiefs, led by a nobleman named Ehelepola, who nursed grievances ranging from changes in taxation policies, which reduced their rent revenues, to fears that the King practised inappropriate Savaite rituals. This time, the British, allied with the conspirators, successfully occupied the royal capital. They tracked down Vikrama Rajasinha, who had fled to a village hideout, and took the King and his wives into custody. After months in detention in Colombo, in early 1816, they were exiled to Vellore in India, where the King would spend the rest of his life. Meanwhile, the British had extracted a convention in which the Kandyan chiefs ceded the realm to the British in return for retention of their rights and privileges and for British protection of Buddhism. Ehelepola probably hoped to become king under the British, but the colonisers proved uninterested in sponsoring a new dynasty or maintaining the Kandy monarchy. Discontent with British rule soon sparked an insurrection in 1817 and 1818, although it was finally quelled; several key leaders were executed, and Ehelepola, who had been indirectly implicated, was exiled to Mauritius.[5] Over the next three decades, less potent revolts broke out, often with the appearance of a pretender to the throne, though men with increasingly less credible claims to the crown.[6]

The British, as Sujit Sivasundaram has argued, meanwhile effectively assumed the mantle of the abolished Kandyan monarchy, setting in place law codes, administration and taxation. The first British Resident in Kandy, John D'Oyly, respectfully took part in Buddhist processions and made temple offerings, just as the kings had done. Governor Brownrigg, created a baronet in March 1816, later incorporated a representation of the Kandy crown and sceptre into his personal coat of arms. Governors represented the British monarch with pomp and pageantry, touring the island to receive expressions of obeisance from their subjects. The British took on the old royal role of builder, constructing a botanical garden on the site of an old royal garden, erecting grand viceregal residences in Colombo and Kandy, and developing roads and, later, railways. They maintained the old system of *corvée* labour (*rajakariya*) until 1831 and then instituted a new system of labour conscription. They explored and valorised the archaeological sites at Anuradhapura and Pollonaruwa and the pilgrimage site of Sri Pada (Adam's Peak), just as the rulers of the *ancien régime* had done. By the late nineteenth century, the British monarch created Ceylonese knights and awarded other imperial honours. From 1870, with the Duke of Edinburgh, a series of royal tours took place; there were eleven visits of members of the royal family before 1948. The British sovereign was the new royal power in Ceylon, presenting itself as the inheritor of the Kandyan crown. Ceylonese culture, Sivasundaram suggests, was indeed capable of encompassing British rule into the islanders' purview, as evidenced, for instance, by a poem in honour of King George IV cast in the idiom of the glorification of Kandyan kings.[7]

The celebration of Queen Victoria's jubilees provided a notable occasion for loyalist sentiments. A poem composed (by a settler) for the 1897 Diamond Jubilee, 'Ave Victoria Imperatrix', enjoined:

> Sons of Ceylon, whatever your nation,
> Your creed or your caste, your race or your name,
> Rise up to-day with the old salutation ...
> God save the Queen.

The second stanza provided a history lesson:

> Some may talk of past annals when Lanka, beholden
> For palace of brass and for temple of stone
> To Monarchs despotic, believed that age golden;
> But say if those centuries ever had known
> Such a Queen of the years that are famous in story
> Whose rule pure and perfect in lustre is seen
> As the Diamond – our symbol to-day of Her glory
> Whom all the world honours with
> God save the Queen.[8]

The British colonial state put down roots in Ceylon, though new currents – principles of constitutionalism and democracy which gained traction in 1848 and Buddhist revivalism later in the century, alongside ideas of nationalism and anti-colonialism which filtered in from Europe and India – gradually began to undermine British authority. The image of the Kandyan monarchy as a symbol was effaced, though never fully so. In the early twentieth century, Indian-style annual durbars (receptions) brought together Kandyan and Jaffna chiefs attired in traditional clothing; a painting of the visiting Duke of Cornwall and York (later George V) at a durbar in 1901 shows Kandyan chiefs bowing before the King's son, and newspapers as far away as Tasmania reported on the royals' visit to 'the old castle of the Kandyan Kings'.[9] The British were still trying to harness the culture of the *ancien régime* to colonial rule.[10]

However, John De Silva, a reformist and pioneer of a Ceylonese theatre movement, in 1906 wrote a Sinhalese-language play about Vikrama Rajasinha. The year 1915 marked the centenary of his deposition, and the March issue of *Sinhala Tarunnaya (Young Sinhalese)* included a picture of the King and the Sinhalese flag.[11] *The Buddhist* newspaper reminded readers that the date marked the anniversary of the end of Ceylonese independence. Nineteen-fifteen was indeed tumultuous, as bloody riots, fuelled by religious conflicts and economic rivalries, pitted Sinhalese against Muslims, rumours circulated about a possible German plot in Ceylon, and the British executed by firing squad

Captain D. E. Pedris of the Colombo Town Guard, scion of one of the country's wealthiest families, who was wrongfully accused of instigating anti-British insurrection. Prominent figures counted among the thousands arrested and briefly imprisoned, including George E. De Silva and Don Baron Jayatilaka, both later to play a role in the return of the Kandyan regalia.

As communal tensions exploded and nationalist campaigns gained strength, often with reference to the heritage of the Sinhalese dynasties, a contingent of settler volunteers who had gone to serve in British forces fighting for 'King and Country' perished in late 1915 when their ship was sunk by Germans. A hundred years after the exile of the King of Kandy, memories thus competed, and dynasties – pre-colonial and colonial – could stand as rallying points for allegiance. Over the next decades, as the British tried to calm the winds of nationalism in their empire, the regalia of the Sinhalese monarchy would make an appearance in the struggle between old and new orders.

The capture of the Ceylonese regalia: 1815

Although Kandyan monarchs lacked the immense fortunes of the Indian princes, the King of Kandy possessed an imposing palace and a grand audience hall, ornate clothing and the regalia of office.[12] Along with a jewelled sword and sword-belt, the most imposing of the regalia were the crown and throne (see Figure 17). The throne, given by the Dutch Governor, Thomas Van Rhee, to King Vimaladharmasuriya II as a token of amity in 1692 or 1693, stood five foot high and was carved of wood, covered in gold plate and decorated with amethysts and other precious stones. Two lions – symbol of the Sinhalese people – fronted the armrests of the throne, while a sun, representing the dynasty, adorned the back; other decorations included female deities and floral motifs. There was a matching footstool.[13] Nira Wickramasinghe rightly remarks that 'the throne was, in many ways, a hybrid object, modelled in the Dutch style, sculpted possibly by South Indian craftsmen for a Kandyan king'.[14] The crown, dating from 1737, was also of gold, a circlet with several out-facing points, studded with precious stones and topped by a symbolic small tree emblem.

The British came into possession of the throne and possibly the crown during the overthrow of Vikrama Rajasinha; Ehelepola, hoping one day to don the crown himself, appears to have been instrumental in their acquisition. Soldiers confiscated the King's sword and sword-belt when he was captured, and several tore earrings off the queens. With the pillage of the royal palace, the British procured more of the King's treasury. Some items no doubt remained in private

17. The regalia of the King of Kandy in the National Museum, Colombo. Photograph by Robert Aldrich

possession, but a large horde arrived in Britain – under what conditions remains unknown – and were sold at public auction in London in 1820, the items detailed in a 'catalogue of a splendid and valuable collection of jewelry, forming the regalia of the King of Kandy, the whole of the purest massive gold'. Among the items were armour, armlets and bracelets, gemstones, a dagger, gold buttons, rings, shells, boxes, chains, a jewelled chair and other objects, which, the catalogue said, euphemistically, had been 'presented by His Majesty to the captors for whose benefit they will be sold'.[15]

The Kandyan throne had been packed up and taken to Britain in the care of Governor Brownrigg's son. The exact details are fuzzy, but it seems that the throne was offered to the Prince Regent, and in 1821 the returning governor had personally presented the crown (which may or may not have been the headdress sold in the 1820 auction) and sword to King George IV, as the Prince Regent had become, at Carlton House. The objects were there until Carlton House was pulled down in 1828. The Kandyan regalia were then moved to Windsor Castle as part of the Royal Collection; the throne ended up in the Garter Throne Room, venue for investitures to the Order of the Garter, Britain's most noble order of chivalry.

Taking the regalia away from Ceylon meant that the British now held the symbols of the deposed king and the abolished dynasty. In the words of J. B. Disanayaka: 'Removing the throne from the Palace in Kandy prevented anyone from ascending it either as a mark of protest or as an attempt to regain political power.'[16] The throne was now enshrined in the sanctum of the British imperial monarchy, and, for over a century, it inspired no real concern.

The return of the regalia, 1934

The fate of captured treasures is a conflicted issue: for those who took them, they represent the spoils of war or cessions by defeated rulers, while for those from whom they are taken, what has occurred is both theft and a violation of cultural patrimony. The restitution of objects seized in war or colonial conquest continues to exercise public opinion. Countries that claimed colonies have generally shown little eagerness to return heritage objects, though some signal cases of repatriation have occurred.[17] The British saw the return of the Kandyan regalia as a benevolent royal gesture in recognition of the loyalty of the King's Ceylonese subjects. Not surprisingly, however, the restoration of the regalia was somewhat more complex.

In early 1924, Frederick Grubb, a London-based journalist for the *Ceylon Daily News*, published in Colombo, became aware that the Kandyan throne had at some time in the recent past been removed from the Garter Throne Room to another position in Windsor Castle. Rumour had it, he reported, that the throne had been shifted because it was considered a Buddhist seat inappropriate for a Christian king. Grubb wrote that although he was personally unaware of how the throne had arrived in London, 'it will be admitted on all hands that there could be no more appropriate setting for it than was graciously granted to it by the British Sovereign'. That it was 'occupied on solemn occasions by no less a person that the King-Emperor' brought honour to the Ceylonese and 'also constituted a bond between the people of Ceylon and the British Sovereign'. Manifesting clearly loyalist sentiments, he continued:

> Though the minion and the lizard keep the court of many a petty king of a former age and though King George is by right of conquest the lawful occupant of their deserted thrones, of the numerous trophies won from Eastern nations, very few are actually used by the British Sovereign. The Throne of Ceylon however took a prominent place among the few thus honoured. ... If as it is maintained the Sinhalese people by common

consent [in the convention of 1815] substituted in place of the tyrant from Malabar the Constitutional Sovereign of the British Throne, there is sound ground for the contention that the King of England is also the 'King of Ceylon'.

He concluded: 'Just as he took his place on it by his Sovereign right, so it was but right that the Throne should have become the seat of one who is in a special manner King of Ceylon', and the Ceylonese would now greet with 'genuine regret' its removal from the Garter Throne Room.[18]

The journalist wrote to the King's private secretary about the displacement of the throne. A reply informed him that the Kandyan throne had in fact been placed on the dais in the Garter Room only during the reign of King Edward VII in place of an ivory chair from India. The Kandyan throne had only been formally used by the King three times, for the installation of the kings of Norway and Portugal and the Prince of Wales as Knights of the Garter. It was removed because the current view was simply that it did not fit in with the general decor of the room. The official told Grubb: 'Now the Chair of the Kings of Kandy occupies a place which is not only more appropriate, but in which it will be more visible.' In the Grand Vestibule, it had been set at the top of a staircase in front of a statue of Queen Victoria 'amongst Indian relics and other Oriental trophies'.[19]

This, it seemed, was the end of the story. Nine years later, however, the question of the throne arose again, this time in the State Council of Ceylon. On 30 November 1933, a resolution was moved by George E. De Silva, a successful lawyer and member of the Kandy City Council before being elected to the State Council in 1931, despite implication in the disturbances of 1915. (In the 1940s, De Silva would hold several ministerial portfolios, and he also served as president of the Ceylon National Congress.[20]) The proposed motion stated: 'This Council respectfully requests His Majesty's Government in England that the Crown and Throne that were removed from Ceylon and which are now at the Windsor Castle be restored to this Government to be kept as a national possession.'[21] On 15 February 1934, the resolution was passed by the State Council and approved by the Governor.

The Council of State, created in 1931, included sixty members, forty-two of them elected on the basis of universal suffrage. (Ceylon was one of the first colonies to grant the vote to women.) The Council had substantial powers but considerable areas of competence, including defence, foreign affairs, justice and finance, were 'reserved' for the British government, and the Governor retained a right of veto on decisions. Many elected members of the Council were well-educated upper-class men who espoused greater reform and aimed for self-government. The Ceylon National Congress, founded in 1919, the largest if most moderate reformist group, regularly pressed for revision of the constitution and full responsible government. Since the withdrawal of Tamils from the Congress in 1921 – with incipient fears about domination by the Sinhalese Buddhists – Sinhalese had dominated the Congress, with several of their leaders key members of the State Council. On the political scene were also more radical nationalists, including members of Young Ceylon, and their remonstrances against the British were becoming ever stronger.[22] With the Sinhalese in the ascendency, and with the expression of a more affirmed nationalism and moves for responsible government, the request for the Kandyan regalia was not devoid of political or communal inflection, though not articulated in those terms. It also served as what Wickramasinghe calls one of the 'identity markers' for which nationalists were searching, though she adds that 'nationalists chose to forget about the origin of the throne, a gift from the colonisers and a product of non-Kandyan artisans'.[23]

The resolution of the Council predictably sparked interest in the Colombo press, and Frederick Grubb again took up the case, noting in the *Ceylon Daily News* that the British repatriation of heritage items to Boers in South Africa provided a precedent for restitution of the regalia. Returning the regalia, he argued, 'might at least gratify a well-founded patriotic feeling', adding that there was no reason for the objects to be kept in England and they naturally belonged in Ceylon. The only objection he had heard was that the 'Royal palaces and museums will be denuded of a considerable number of their possessions', a view that provided no justification 'to hold spoils of war and conquest if they can in these days be put to the far nobler purpose of establishing kindlier relations with other people'.[24] There thus existed a complex context for the issue that had been raised: not only ethnic Sinhalese nationalism, demands for self-government for Ceylon and resentment at British possession of 'spoils of war' but also sentiments of loyalty for the King-Emperor.

Grubb took it upon himself to contact the King's private secretary, now Colonel Sir Clive (later Baron) Wigram, about the regalia, but Wigram put him off, on the grounds that the Colonial Office had not yet officially forwarded the State Council motion to the palace. Over the next few months there followed a small flurry of communications between Wigram at Buckingham Palace and E. C. Boyd at the Colonial Office, Sir Philip Cunliffe-Lister (later 1st Earl of Swinton, the Secretary of State for the Colonies in Ramsay MacDonald's national government), the office of Governor Sir Reginald Stubbs in Colombo (who had just taken up his appointment in December 1933), and curators of the Royal Collection at Windsor.[25] Grubb persisted with his inquiries, leading one official to note testily that the journalist was really just after a scoop and could become a nuisance.

With little apparent controversy, however, the Secretary of State for the Colonies advised the Palace that he and the Governor thought it would be good for the throne to be handed over.[26] This would be a goodwill gesture to what was now considered a near model colony (despite the budding nationalism) and a gesture in favour of the moderate and loyalist sentiments of a local elite still considered Anglophile, possibly in hopes of defusing more radical anti-colonialism. The decision about the future of the regalia went right up to the King, who inspected the items during a sojourn at Windsor in June 1934, and within six months of the Ceylon State Council's resolution, King George V agreed to repatriate the throne and crown. The forthcoming visit to Ceylon of Prince Henry, the Duke of Gloucester, the King's third son, provided an opportune moment to do so.

Buckingham Palace informed the Colonial Office that on 5 June the King had approved a telegram to the Governor in Colombo:

> His Majesty the King is anxious that the visit to Ceylon of his son the Duke of Gloucester should be marked by some expression of his personal favour towards his Ceylonese subjects. He has accordingly decided to restore to Ceylon the ancient throne of the King of Kandy which has been preserved at Windsor Castle for over a hundred years. His Majesty believes return of this historic monument of Ceylon will be agreeable to sentiments widely entertained by all sections of [the] Ceylon community.[27]

The wording was judicious, leaving aside the circumstances of the arrival of the regalia in London. ('We do not want to reopen the question of to whom the Throne was given', remarked one memorandum from the Colonial Office.) Speaking of the throne, rather curiously, as 'a historic monument' emphasised its status as a relic of the past rather than a symbol of current sovereignty. The reference to 'all sections' of the community was perhaps synonymous with the 'national' of the State Council petition, though without using the word – there was perhaps no wish to acknowledge nascent nationalism – and recognition of the multicultural nature of the island's population, which included the majority Sinhalese, indigenous and migrant Tamils, Malays and other Muslims, mixed-race Burghers and British settlers. There was, pointedly, no mention of the State Council resolution. At this stage, it was still uncertain whether the crown, which the resolution had requested along with the throne, was indeed in the Royal Collection, but, more importantly, as officials explicitly said in their correspondence, the

King and government did not want to make the repatriation appear to be a response to such a request, no matter how loyally it had been made. Royal and colonial officials thus cast the repatriation not as return of captured objects or 'spoils of war', or as an agreement to the demands of a colonial council but as a munificent personal gesture by the British monarch towards his faithful subjects.[28]

Everything went according to plan except for one glitch: the announcement of the restitution. The Colonial Office had wanted the announcement to be made simultaneously in London and in the *Government Gazette* in Colombo shortly after the Governor verbally informed the Ceylon State Council, but the news was leaked to the BBC, which included it in an evening broadcast, in time for a Colombo newspaper to feature a report in their morning edition, which appeared before the State Council assembled. The announcement in the *Government Gazette* later in the day thus seemed a bit 'silly' (in Governor Stubbs' words), and he was forced to smooth over the ruffled sentiments of the Kandyan chiefs and council members who had learnt the news over their morning tea. Exchanges of notes back at the Colonial Office show authorities fussing about whether 'we can control the BBC'.

In late September 1934, the Duke of Gloucester landed in Ceylon.[29] He banqueted at King's House, laid a wreath at the war memorial, enjoyed a game of polo and called at the colonial club before taking a train up-country to the hill station of Nuwara Eliya, where he spent the night before proceeding to Kandy. A telegram to London from the Governor's Office reported: 'To Kandy 8 a.m. Sunday. Divine service. Received Chiefs and High Priest King's Pavilion. Presentation of the Throne 9.15. Then Perahera[30] and display of fireworks. Most successful. Crowds at Kandy indescribable. His staff informs me that there is no doubt H.R.H. is really enjoying his visit.'

The Duke's busy day had begun with the trip from Nuwara Eliya to Kandy (with a stop at Peradinya to don his uniform). Kandyan dancers led his procession to the Planters' Hall and the Queen's Hotel in the centre of Kandy, where he inspected a guard of honour and was introduced to the Kandy City Council and local members of the State Council before proceeding to St Paul's Church for a prayer service, after which he retired to the King's Pavilion (the Governor's Kandy residence) to meet the Kandyan chiefs, to lunch, to have an afternoon rest and to dine. Among the Duke's duties and diversions – he found time for tennis on another day – the 'presentation of the throne' was the very heart of the tour.[31] The handover ceremony began only after 9 p.m., taking advantage of the cool evening. Around 1,500 people gathered in the audience hall, next to Sri Dalada Maligawa, and after the band played 'God Save the King', the Duke delivered a short speech, prepared by the Colonial Office and approved by George V. It recapitulated the earlier announcement of the return of the regalia:

> It is a matter of great gratification to me that I have been expressly charged by the King as a mark of his personal favour to his Ceylonese subjects, to restore to Ceylon the ancient Throne and Crown of the Kings of Kandy. The Throne and Crown, after their capture by the British in 1815, were sent to England by Sir Robert Brownrigg and have been preserved at Windsor Castle for over a hundred years. His Majesty believes that the return of these historic treasures to Ceylon will be warmly welcomed by all sections of the community in the Island. It affords me special pleasure to be able to make the presentation in such historic surroundings and in the actual Audience Hall of the Kandyan Kings.[32]

The wording was careful and neutral; though the word 'capture' was used, there was no mention of the circumstances of British takeover, nor of the Sinhalese character of the Kandyan monarchy. The Duke added that he would convey to the King 'the demonstrations of Loyalty of which my visit has been the occasion'. He then unveiled the throne and the crown, in the glare of floodlights, to what one newspaper called 'tumultuous cheering'. After the ceremony, participants enjoyed a *perahera* and a fireworks show.

Not surprisingly, the Duke's visit sparked much attention in the Ceylonese press. In an era fascinated with royal events, the *Times of Ceylon* – an English-language publication whose main readership would have been English settlers and the Ceylonese elite – gave a wealth of detail, including information that during his visit to the Governor's residence the Duke seated himself on a chair given to Kirti Sri Rajasinha, Vikrama Rajasinha's predecessor, previously used by the future George V and Edward VIII on their visits to Ceylon. The paper headlined a 'rapturous welcome for royal visitor' on the 'gala day' of his arrival when 'country folk flock to city'. The 'crowds and scenes in Colombo ... were unquestionably the largest and most exuberant [there have] ever been in the metropolis of the Island', and there were 'extraordinary demonstrations of loyalty'. The newspaper rightly noted of the regalia that 'Whilst the return of these treasures to this island is a matter of interest to every section of the community it is of course especially so to the Kandyans from whose country they were originally taken away.' It added, however, that the Ceylonese 'are united in their devoted loyalty to His Majesty's Throne and Person', a fine segue from the Kandyan to the British monarchy. The *Times of Ceylon*, in an issue with a full page of pictures, characterised the handover as an 'epoch-making ceremony occupying the space of a few magnetic moments' and stated that 'tonight's ceremony will go down in history as one of the most striking events in the Island'.[33]

THE RETURN OF THE THRONE

The handover, and the Duke's visit, indeed passed smoothly, though newspapers reported one note of dissent: a petition by Buddhists against the decoration of the octagon tower at Sri Dalada Maligawa with a crown surmounted by a cross. The British, according to the *Times of Ceylon*, stated that the octagon, which had been constructed by Vikrama Rajasinha, was crown property because it was part of the pre-colonial kings' domain, but Buddhists countered that it formed part of a religious edifice and that use of a cross was inappropriate. Several other questions nevertheless arose around the regalia, drawing in figures including members of the State Council, Kandyan chiefs, a Buddhist priest, an assembly of villagers and an irate letter-writer, the response suggestive of the public attention given to the regalia in Ceylon but revelatory about some concerns in London.

First of all, in Britain, it had initially been unclear exactly what items would be returned; the State Council had explicitly mentioned the throne and crown. The Colonial Office, in internal memoranda, remarked on the sale of Kandyan royal jewels at auction – a fate that merited an exclamation point in one official's minute. At first, it was thought that the crown had been sold to a private individual, but then the aptly titled Inspector of Trophies at Windsor Castle discovered that the crown as well as the throne was in the Royal Collection, as was the footstool for the throne, sceptre, sword and sword-belt. In 1934, it was decided that the crown should accompany the throne, as E. C. Boyd thought that 'otherwise there might be an agitation raised in Ceylon about the Crown'.[34] The King's Private Secretary personally thought that all of the items might be returned but cautioned to the Colonial Office that 'the King and Queen do not much like the idea, because the removal of all the trophies will make a sad gap in the room at Windsor where the trophies are exhibited'. An official replied, 'I do not think that the Sinhalese, who are a polite people, will dispute His Majesty's liberty to decide' on the selection of objects to be sent back.

The items presented something of a mystery for the staff at Windsor; one detailed memorandum described the lions on the throne as 'dragons'. (The inventory of Carlton House, where the regalia were originally stored, spoke of the 'barbaric splendour, though hardly in good taste' of the throne.) It was decided that only the throne, footstool and crown would be returned to Ceylon, though the reasons are not clarified. This rather less than magnanimous decision thus fulfilled the express request of the State Council but left part of the regalia at Windsor. Some Ceylonese hoped that the sceptre, sword and belt would be returned to Ceylon for King George VI's twenty-fifth anniversary on the throne, but only after his death were they repatriated, under King Edward VIII, in 1936.[35]

A second issue was *to whom* the regalia were being returned, even if there was no question that the Governor would officially receive the items on behalf of the colony. Who would be their custodian? When he was overthrown, Vikrama Rajasinha had reigned over only part of Ceylon, and the Kandyan dynasty had historically only very seldom ruled over the whole of the island. The regalia held different resonances for Kandyans and for low-country Sinhalese, and for the other communities. The State Council's resolution had asked that the regalia 'be restored to this Government to be kept as a national possession', and the King's telegram had carefully made reference to all of the communities on the island, with officials no doubt eager to avoid sectarian claims or inter-ethnic conflict.

However, some in Kandy felt that the traditional noblemen had an exclusive right to the regalia. F. B. Nugawela, Vice-President of the Kandyan Chiefs' Union, one A. Ratnayake, described as 'Elected Member Kandyan People State Council [sic]', and the Most Ven. Pahamune Nayaka Thero 'of Buddhist hierarchy Ceylon' sent a lengthy telegram directly to the King, claiming the paramount rights of the Sinhalese, and in particular the Kandyans and their chiefs, to the regalia. They argued that presenting the objects to the 'people of Ceylon' would 'create constitutional rights for aliens who are enfranchised under Donoughmore scheme', a reference to the increasing number of Tamils recruited from India who laboured on tea plantations but whose presence and enfranchisement sparked resentment among Sinhalese. The writers reminded the monarch that in the 1815 Convention sovereignty had been relinquished to the British by the Kandyan chiefs in return for explicit promises to protect the rights of the Kandyans and of Buddhism. They also objected to use of the Kandyan royal audience hall for the handover ceremony, presumably seeing this as British appropriation of a hallowed Kandyan space. Giving the throne to 'the people of Ceylon', they added, could even endanger the status of the Buddha Tooth Relic, though they did not explain why. The message closed with a rather odd parallel suggested as a lesson: the return, after the Great War, by German President Paul von Hindenburg of a set of British drums specifically to the regiment that had used them rather than to the 'British public'.[36]

The Governor reported to London that the authors of the telegram represented only a faction of the chiefs (a 'corrupt group' among them) and that the lead writer was 'not very reputable'; Ratnayake, he noted, was not the State Council member for Kandy but for another constituency. The chiefs, Stubbs added, wanted to 'claim rights which they have never possessed and which are incompatible with the present constitution'. Unstated but implicit was the communalist division in

Ceylon and claims to a privileged position advanced by Kandyan chiefs, who had been somewhat sidelined not only by the British but also by coastal Sinhalese and the new middle class. Given the Governor's information, officials in London dismissed the telegram. A note from the Prime Minister's office nevertheless suggested that the 'special interests' of the Kandyans should be honoured, and Stubbs assured him they would be acknowledged: the throne would be officially handed over in the Royal Pavilion in Kandy (which he, if not the protesters, thought a just recognition), and the chieftains would be seated on the dais and formally presented to the Duke of Gloucester. But 'I am not prepared to go further in recognition of the Kandyans as a separate people', he wired.

The regalia went on exhibit in Kandy from 24 to 27 September, with estimates that 40,000 people viewed the treasures. They were then taken to Colombo and kept on display from 1 October until 14 November, where, on several days, attendance topped 30,000 to 40,000, reaching 72,274 on the busiest Sunday. A total of 902,920 Ceylonese viewed the throne and crown, more than one in seven people on the island. Sir Don Baron Jayatilaka – Oxford graduate, barrister, political activist, British prisoner in 1915, Buddhist scholar, President of the Ceylon National Congress and leader of the State Council – remarked in discussing a vote of thanks to the King, 'It may be safely said that within the last 100 years at any rate no event has appealed so strongly to the people of this country and stirred their imagination.'[37]

Jayatilaka's fellow member of the State Council, George De Silva, who had initiated requests for the repatriation, proposed a resolution that 'thank[ed] His Majesty for his gracious act in so generously acceding to this Council's request ... to restore to the people of this Country the Crown and the Throne of the Sinhalese Kings'. Yet he then withdrew the motion, possibly both because of its partisan nature with the reference to 'Sinhalese' and the wording about the King 'acceding' to the request (which had never been acknowledged in London). This was replaced by a motion proposed by Jayatilaka, expressing 'the deep appreciation, shared by every community in the Island, of His Majesty's gracious act in restoring to the people of Ceylon the Throne and Crown of the Kings who reigned in Kandy'.[38] That phrasing was thus more guarded, with only limited reference to kings who had reigned 'in Kandy'. The message of thanks, formally from the Board of Ministers, since the State Council was not in session, was conveyed to Buckingham Palace by the Governor. The King asked what the 'Board of Ministers' was ('as it savours of a commercial Company', in the words of a note from the King's private secretary, who said that the King did not like the phrase); the

King was reminded that an order-in-council in 1931 had indeed instituted a board of ministers.

The King received other messages of thanks, one from a village committee in Talawa, which pointedly mentioned return of the objects 'for the admiration of the Sinhalese nation as a national monument of archaeological interest' (the last words a singular formulation) and another from Mahinda College, a secondary school. Yet another came from Ceylonese in Selangor, in the Malay States, suggestive of interest in the Ceylonese diaspora. These letters received acknowledgements in due course, but another missive did not: an angry communication from a man who claimed to be a descendant of a signatory of the 1815 Convention, who also objected to the return of the throne to the colony of Ceylon rather than to Kandyans. He lambasted the Duke of Gloucester's reference to the 'capture' of the King Sri Vikrama Rajasinha (and a Colonial Office staff member conceded in a minute that the word was 'technically' incorrect). Finally, he demanded that the British strictly adhere to the provisions of the Kandyan Convention or 'the condition of affairs here will become very bad'.[39]

Another issue was where the regalia would be housed. Some Kandyans hoped that they would remain in the royal capital, perhaps in one of the palace buildings. (The palace of the queens became a museum, opened in 1942, which displays various artefacts of the Kandyan monarchy.) However, the objects ended up in the National Museum in Colombo, perhaps underlining that they were both part of the patrimony of 'all communities' rather than just Kandyans and, in a museum, items primarily of historical interest surviving from an extinct dynasty.[40]

The resolution of thanks from the Ceylon Board of Ministers was expressed in terms of loyalty to the monarch and the harmony of the Ceylonese population, with no hint of other grievances or autonomist sentiments. It is impossible to know whether the tens of thousands of people who turned out to view the throne and crown were motivated by simple curiosity, loyal gratitude to the British King, collective reminiscence about the old Kandyan monarchy or incipient nationalist beliefs that fixed upon these 'ancient', 'captured' and now returned symbols of sovereignty. The interest of politicians and the public, however, shows that the regalia were far more than curious relics of a bygone age.

The regalia at Independence, 1948

The regalia made a major ceremonial reappearance in 1948, when Ceylon regained its independence, becoming a dominion in the Commonwealth of Nations. As David Cannadine has shown, rituals surrounding independence days represent signal moments in decolonisation, a time of celebration for newly emancipated nations but times of concern among colonial authorities relinquishing their overlordship. The Colonial Office and Buckingham Palace, from the independence of India and Pakistan in 1947 to the handover of Hong Kong fifty years later, were preoccupied with the pomp and protocol of independence ceremonies. In the best possible scenario, states Cannadine, 'the aim of the "freedom at midnight" ceremonials was to give the impression that independence had always been the intention of the British imperial mission' and that Britain and its former colony (and government) would remain on amicable terms. The programme of events was carefully negotiated between London and the capitals of new states, with close attention to the wording of speeches, the lowering and hoisting of flags and other details. It became customary for members of the royal family (never the monarch) to take part, though a less than amicable transition, questions of security or other circumstances meant this was not always the case.[41] The royal presence, according to Philip Murphy, offered goodwill, 'a powerful symbolic assertion that the transfer of power was a voluntary and calculated decision by a country whose power, dignity and sense of hierarchy were undiminished by the act of granting independence'; it also added glamour and celebrity to the occasion.[42]

Ceylon officially became independent on 4 February 1948, but the major ceremony involved the opening of the second session of the dominion's first parliament – the first session had met before independence – on 10 February. Representing King George VI was none other than his younger brother, the Duke of Gloucester. The Duke took part in a week of celebrations, during which he again journeyed up-country to meet with the Kandyan chiefs and Buddhist dignitaries in Sri Vikrama Rajasinha's audience hall, toured archaeological sites in Pollonaruwa and Anuradhapura and laid the foundation stone for the Convocation Hall at the University of Ceylon.

The Duke presided over the opening of Parliament, held in a disused aircraft hangar in Torrington Square in Colombo – rather uncomfortably hot in the tropical weather, to judge by film footage showing guests fanning themselves. He acknowledged that 'Ceylon has now achieved independence as a fully responsible member of the British Commonwealth of Nations and with the attainment of the status of a Dominion.' He read King George's speech from the throne, in which the monarch stated that 'I know that my people in Ceylon are ready to make a full and rich contribution to the association of free peoples.'[43] The new flag of Ceylon was in evidence; the banner featured as central emblem the lion passant, sword held aloft in its paw, of the Kandyan kings.[44]

On the dais for the ceremony sat the royal duke, Governor-General (the new title of the sovereign's representative) Sir Henry Monck-Mason Moore and the new prime minister, Don Stephen Senanayake, and their spouses.[45] The throne of the kings of Kandy was prominently placed on a platform behind the dais, standing a tier higher than the dignitaries. At the beginning of the ceremony, the guests and the royal party stood as the leader of the House of Representatives, S. W. R. D. Bandaranaike (a future prime minister), and the leader of the Senate, Sir Oliver Goonetilleke (a future governor-general), carried into the hall and placed on either side of the throne the crown and sword of Sri Vikrama Rajasinha.[46] Thus, in the midst of the pomp and pageantry of the British imperial monarchy, did Ceylon become a dominion not just with a royal benediction and hallowed British ritual but with manifest reference to the dynasty of Kandy and the symbols of its antecedence.

The ceremony may have been read, of course, in different ways. As the visit of the Duke of Gloucester was being planned and officials in London learnt that the Kandyan throne would appear, there had been some disquiet. The Duke was opening the Ceylon Parliament, but one memorandum noted that 'as the King is not opening Parliament in person, it would be in accordance with United Kingdom practice to leave [the] Kandyan throne empty and for [the] Duke and Duchess to occupy special seats just below'. The throne, in this perspective, thus represented the British sovereign. However, the Governor of Ceylon expressed concern that 'the ordinary spectator ... may regard the empty throne as something superior to the Duke as King's Representative'.[47] Such reservations did not change the scenography; it would have been a pointed gesture if the representative of the British monarch had seated himself on the throne of the deposed king, even if the British king had previously used the same throne at Windsor Castle. Both reports at the time and later accounts, however, give attention to the throne as the symbol of the Kandyan rather than the British monarchy.

For the British, the inclusion of the Kandyan regalia did agreeably recall the monarchs' restitution of the items to Ceylon. They acknowledged restoration of sovereignty to Ceylon, over which the King still reigned as head of state, under a loyalist government firmly anchored in the Commonwealth. Indeed, as H. Kumarasingham has shown, the transition to independence was markedly amicable in Ceylon, with the British confident that Ceylon would remain a trusted member of the imperial family and glad that such politicians as Senanayake were imbued with respect for the monarchy, the institutions of Westminster and British culture.[48] The British monarch would indeed continue to reign in Ceylon until 1972.[49] For some Ceylonese, the visible presence of the throne in 1948 may have been a symbol not only of the successful restoration of sovereignty but also a marker of the legal and cultural connections between the new government and the pre-colonial history of the island, the sacred and secular potency of the Kandyan kingship, the heritage of the Sinhalese people and the success of the nationalist campaign for independence.

The site of the February 1948 ceremony was subsequently renamed Independence Square, and an open-air hall was erected, the structure inspired by the royal audience hall in Kandy and featuring intricately carved columns and four sculptures of Sinhalese lions. Nearby stands a statue of Senanayake, hailed as 'Father of the Nation'. The ground floor of the monument houses the Independence Memorial Museum, with busts of national heroes, including leaders of the 1817–18 revolt (signposted as the 'first independence struggle against the British'), though not Sri Vikrama Rajasinha. Meanwhile, the bronze statue of Queen Victoria erected for her jubilee in 1897 outside the governor's residence continued to stand there until it was moved in 2006 to a site near the rear entrance to the National Museum, across the road from what had once been Victoria Park, now called Viharamahadevi Park, after a Sinhalese queen. The statue was restored and shifted to a slightly more prominent position for the Commonwealth Heads of Government meeting, held in Colombo in 2013 and presided over by the Prince of Wales. Other traces of the British monarchy remain in nomenclature and monuments, from the prestigious Royal College in Colombo to the veteran Queen's Hotel in Kandy. A journalist in the Colombo *Sunday Times* has remarked: 'Victoria is present in the bones of the city, its roads and railways and extant 19th century structures. She is built into the urban infrastructure. ... Queen Victoria is also in our psyche.'[50]

As in most colonised countries, the imprint and legacy of the colonial period remain strong, after seventy years of independence, as well as the vicissitudes of political change, and in Sri Lanka, the decades of ethnic conflict. The impress of the pre-colonial Kandyan monarchy also remained present through almost a century and a half of British rule, even though the references for nationalists more often were ancient kings rather than the final Kandyan ruler. The regalia were still for some a symbol of the dynasty abolished by the King and the despoliation of the patrimony of the Sinhalese. The 1948 Colombo ceremony serves as a reminder that regalia and other objects of heritage have their itineraries in the colonial age and afterwards, with incidents that chart intertwined histories: the destruction or acquisition of objects by colonisers, dispossession and exile of rulers whose sovereign instruments they were, the continued value of regalia for both colonisers and colonised, requests for their return, their retention or repatriation, their 'museumification'. The peregrinations of the Kandyan throne – from a workshop carrying out a Dutch commission to Kandyan audience hall, and on to Windsor Castle, and back to Kandy and finally to the National Museum in Colombo – trace much of the chronological expanse of colonialism and decolonisation. The repatriation of the regalia reveals the complex nature of colonial relations: the actions of diverse individuals and groups in the colony and the metropole, right up to the monarch in person.

Ensconced in the Colombo museum, the throne is now linked more to the heroic seventeenth-century kings and their predecessors than to the last Kandyan monarch, as Wickramasinghe has pointed out, and is portrayed as a symbol of an authentic and unified Sinhalese identity rather than either an object specific to the Kandyan realm or a hybrid European-Sinhalese artefact.[51] It stands as both a cultural (Sinhalese) and national (Sri Lankan) icon. It is, nevertheless, in a museum, not in the President's House (the former British governor's residence), nor was it installed in Ceylon's 1929 Parliament House or in the new parliament building designed by Geoffrey Bawa and completed in 1982. The new parliament's copper roof is 'an abstraction of the traditional Kandyan roof', the copper recalling the 'brazen palace' of the second-century King Dutugemunu in Anuradhapura, and its interior is festooned with other markers of the country's history and artistic heritage.[52] Since the parliament was built for a republic, not a monarchy, however, the throne would not have its place there, it might be argued, and even in the period 1948–72, when the British monarch reigned over an independent Ceylon, it would have been a somewhat awkward intrusion into the parliament despite its use in the 1948 ceremonies.

The regalia nevertheless underline the importance of symbol and pageantry in the colonial world, the material culture of sovereignty and the crown, and the role of monarchs (and their representatives), both indigenous and colonial. Their return shows the importance of language in imperialism, with the delicate choice of words about the restitution of objects to 'the nation', 'the people of Ceylon' or – as some wished – to a regional or cultural community. The power of the media is also in evidence in the way a colonial newspaper helped to instigate return of the regalia, the eagerness of journalists to break the story, the technology that made it possibility for the news to be broadcast over the airwaves before being printed in the broadsheets and for the independence celebrations to be filmed and shown as newsreels (and now available on the Internet).[53] Messages of support or criticism sent to the King testify to the engagement of diverse groups. The petition from Ceylonese in Selangor suggests connections of expatriate Ceylonese with their homeland. Reports around the empire of the handover – 'Cingalese Throne to Be Restored to Ceylon: The King's Gift', headlined the *Sydney Morning Herald*, the word 'gift' of note[54] – signal the spread of information around the British world and 'imperial family'. The story underscores how colonialists, in taking booty, conquered the signifiers of sovereignty and treasures of national heritage. Restitution of objects taken away could be used to affirm royal generosity and acknowledge the loyalty of colonial subjects, though such actions might echo differently in various circles.

The Kandyan regalia were not the only ones taken by the British during acquisition of colonies, nor the only ones to be returned. The British confiscated a throne of King Thibaw as they completed the conquest of Burma (and deposed and exiled the king) in 1885; it was returned to Burma on the country's independence in 1948 and is a highlight in the national museum in Rangoon (Yangon). In 1925, King George V authorised the return to Ethiopia of a crown taken in 1868,[55] and, in 1964, Queen Elizabeth II, during a state visit to Addis Ababa, personally returned the cap of Emperor Theodore.[56] Yet the Golden Throne of Maharajah Ranjit Singh still stands in London's Victoria and Albert Museum. The history, and fate, of such objects contributes to an understanding of the theory and practice of kingship in the societies from which they originated, the circumstances in which trophies came into European possession and the significance they continued to hold for those who created them, acquired them and curate them. Gazing at the throne and crown in the Colombo museum, Sri Lankans and visitors can see into the complicated encounters of Europeans and Ceylonese, and, in particular, the entangled histories of the Kandyan monarchy and the British Crown, over centuries of contact, colonialism and decolonisation.

Notes

1 This chapter forms part of a larger study of the deposition and exile of indigenous rulers by colonial authorities in the nineteenth and early twentieth centuries. See also Robert Aldrich, 'The Exile of the Last King of Kandy', in Ronit Ricci (ed.), *Exile in Asia* (Honolulu, HI: University of Hawaii Press, 2016). Key general studies of Sri Lanka are K. M. de Silva, *A History of Sri Lanka* (Colombo: Vijitha Yapa Publications, 2005); Nira Wickramasinghe, *Sri Lanka in the Modern Age: A History of Contested Identities* (Honolulu, HI: University of Hawaii Press, 2006); and Sujit Sivasundaram, *Islanded: Britain, Sri Lanka and the Bounds of an Indian Ocean Colony* (Chicago, Ill.: University of Chicago Press, 2013).
2 See, for example, Yves Vadé and Bernard Dupaigne (eds), *Regalia: Emblèmes et rites du pouvoir* (Paris: Harmattan, 2011).
3 To date, the fullest discussion of the symbolism of the throne is in Wickramasinghe, *Sri Lanka in the Modern Age*, pp. 106–11, to whose account I am indebted.
4 Michael Roberts, *Sinhala Consciousness in the Kandyan Period, 1590s to 1815* (Colombo: Vijitha Yapa, 2003), especially Chapter 3.

5 These developments are discussed in detail in Geoffrey Powell, *The Kandyan Wars* (London: Leo Cooper, 1973); and P. E. Pieris, *Tri Sinhala: The Last Phase, 1796–1815* (New Delhi: Asian Educational Services, 2001; first published 1939).
6 See, in particular, Kumari Jayawardena, *Perpetual Ferment: Popular Revolts in Sri Lanka in the 18th and 19th Centuries* (Colombo: Social Scientists' Association, 2010).
7 Sivasundaram, *Islanded*.
8 Dodwell F. Browne, 'Ave Victoria Imperatrix', *Royal Diamond Jubilee Commemoration Programme: Colombo* (Colombo: H. W. Cave & Co., 1897).
9 *The Mercury* (Hobart), 3 July 1901.
10 Sivasundaram, *Islanded*, pp. 298 and 330.
11 Kumari Jayawardena, 'Economic and Political Factors in the 1915 Riots', *Journal of Asian Studies*, 2:2 (1970), 223–33; see also Ameer Ali, 'The 1915 Racial Riots in Ceylon (Sri Lanka): A Reappraisal of Its Causes', *South Asia*, 4:2 (1981), 1–20.
12 In early modern Kandy, five items of regalia were used in a coronation ceremony: sword, umbrella, fan, diadem and footwear. See J. B. Disanayaka, *Lanka: The Land of Kings* (Maharagama: Sumitha, 2007), pp. 56–7. The diadem was superseded by a European-style crown by the 1700s; it is unclear what became of the umbrella, fan or footwear of the last Kandyan sovereign.
13 Joseph Pearson, 'The Throne of the Kings of Kandy', *Journal of the Royal Asiatic Society (Ceylon Branch)*, 31:82 (1929), 380–3. It is unclear where the throne was made. On authenticity, identity and Ceylonese material culture, see Nira Wickramasinghe, 'From Hybridity to Authenticity: The Biography of a Few Kandyan Things', in Neluka Silva (ed.), *The Hybrid Island: Culture of Crossings and the Invention of Identity in Sri Lanka* (London: Zed Books, 2002), pp. 71–92.
14 Wickramasinghe, *Sri Lanka in the Modern Age*, p. 107.
15 *Regalia of the King of Kandy*, catalogue issued by Thomas King, Covent Garden (British National Archives 1394.h.32 1.2). The catalogue also describes, in Lot 76, an item called 'The King of Kandy's Crown', which resembles the one returned to Ceylon in 1934. If it is the same crown, then I have been unable to discover how it came into the possession of the British government after the auction, although it may have been purchased at the time since Governor Brownrigg was able to present it to King George IV the following year.
16 Disanayaka, *Lanka*, p. 55.
17 Jeanette Greenfield, *The Return of Cultural Treasures* (Cambridge: Cambridge University Press, 2007).
18 The Royal Archives, Windsor (hereafter RA) PS/PSO/GV/PS/MAIN/40455: press cuttings, *The Ceylon Daily News*, 12 January, 4 March 1924; *The Times*, 20 March 1924. The permission of Queen Elizabeth II to use material held in the RA is gratefully acknowledged.
19 RA PS/PSO/GV/PS/MAIN/40455: memoranda, 9, 11 February 1924.
20 C. A. Gunawardena, *Encyclopedia of Sri Lanka*, revised edn (Nugegoda: New Dawn Press, 2005), pp. 109–10.
21 RA PS/PSO/GV/PS/MAIN/40455: press cutting, *The Ceylon Daily News*, 1 December 1933.
22 Roberts, *Sinhala Consciousness in the Kandyan Period*, provides the background on Sinhalese national identity.
23 Wickramasinghe, *Sri Lanka in the Modern Age*, p. 110.
24 RA PS/PSO/GV/PS/MAIN/40455: press cutting, *The Ceylon Daily News*, 22 May 1934.
25 Stubbs had been Colonial Secretary of Ceylon (and occasionally Acting Governor) from 1913 to 1919. He served as Governor of Hong Kong (1919–25), Jamaica (1926–32), Cyprus (1932–33) and Ceylon (1933–37). He is, in particular, associated with the 'Bracegirdle Affair', the controversial deportation in 1937 of an Australian planter and trade-union activist accused of being a Communist agitator. See Alan Fewster, *The Bracegirdle Incident* (Melbourne: Arcadia, 2013). Indicative of growing radicalism, the first Marxist Party in Ceylon, the Lanka Sama Samaja Party, had been established in 1935.

THE RETURN OF THE THRONE

26 RA PS/PSO/GV/PS/MAIN/40455: Edmund Boyd to Sir Clive Wigram, 28 May 1934.
27 RA PS/PSO/GV/PS/MAIN/40455: draft telegram, King George V to Sir Reginald Stubbs, enclosed with a note from Sir Clive Wigram to Edmund Boyd, 4 June 1934.
28 The uses of the return of regalia to affirm a view of benevolent colonial power – rather than the power of the pre-colonial monarch – can be seen in one report of the return of other items to Ceylon in 1936. An article in the *Examiner* (Launceston, Tasmania), 'A Tyrant's Regalia High Cost of Credulity', contrasted the old and new regimes: 'Kings of Kandy were despots of an extreme type, with absolute power over the lives of their subjects, that power being based on mystic titles which read to-day as if designed by a humorist.' However, 'The people of Ceylon, who have prospered greatly under wise and benevolent British rule, will look with interest on the regalia of their ancient sovereigns without wishing for a restoration of their line' (1 December 1936).
29 This was not the first royal tour of Ceylon, which had seen Prince Alfred, Duke of Edinburgh, in 1870, the Prince of Wales (the future Edward VII) in 1875, the Duke of Cornwall and York (the future King George V) in 1901, and the Prince of Wales (the future Edward VIII) in 1921. Queen Elizabeth II became the first reigning monarch to visit, in 1954.
30 A *perahera* is a religious procession in which priests, caparisoned elephants, musicians, dancers and drummers take part. Each temple celebrates an annual *perahera*, often lasting several days. The most important is the Esala Perahera at Sri Dalada Maligawa in Kandy. A *perahera* can also be organised for other special occasions.
31 Much of this documentation comes from the National Archives (Kew), CO 54/921/3, from which quotations are taken unless otherwise indicated. I would like to thank William Matthew Kennedy for photographing the entire file for me.
32 RA PS/PSO/GV/PS/MAIN/40455. The speech was printed in various newpapers in Ceylon and conformed with the undated draft contained in the RA.
33 *The Times of Ceylon*, 16, 20, 21, 22 and 24 September 1934. I would like to thank the Department of National Archives (Colombo) for given me access to microfilms of these newspapers.
34 RA PS/PSO/GV/PS/MAIN/40455: Edmund Boyd to Sir Clive Wigram, 6 July 1934.
35 In 1936, there was confusion at Windsor about whether there was a chowry or *chama-raya*, a ceremonial yak-tail fly-whisk. One was found at Windsor, and the King's Private Secretary consulted Dr Paulus Pieris, Ceylon's Trade Commissioner in London, about the object; in a report of 2 November, he said that the chowry was not from Ceylon but from northern India. He noted that on a visit to Windsor he had found three swords and a dagger from the island in the Royal Collection (RA PS/PSO/GVI/PS/MAIN/01006).
36 CO 54/921/3, National Archives (Kew).
37 Gunawardena, *Encyclopedia of Sri Lanka*, pp. 202–3.
38 Extract from Minutes of State Council Meeting, 6 November 1934, RA PS/PSO/GV/PS/MAIN/40455.
39 Seneviratne Bandara Galagoda to King George V, 11 October 1934, RA PS/PSO/GV/PS/MAIN/40455.
40 Displayed alongside the crown, throne and sceptre are a watch given to Sri Vikrama Rajasinha by the Dutch, a ring, ceremonial flutes, fans, swords, scent sprinklers, coffers and an ebony chair used by the last king. There is also a silver-decorated gun from Vikrama Rajasinha's armoury, taken to Britain in 1815, purchased through the Ceylon Trade Commissioner there and returned in 1936. The jacket worn by one of his queens when captured in 1815 – stained with drops of blood from where her earrings had been torn off – as well as a golden-threaded jacket of the King are also in the exhibition. There are several portraits of the King and his queen. Elsewhere in the museum is a brass tray with decorations depicting the gruesome execution of Ehelepola's family.
41 David Cannadine, 'Introduction: Independence Day Ceremonials in Historical Perspective', in Robert Holland, Susan Williams and Terry Barringer (eds), *The Iconography of Independence: 'Freedoms at Midnight'* (London and New York: Routledge, 2010), quotations p. 9.

42 Philip Murphy, 'Independence Day and the Crown', *The Round Table*, 97:398 (2008), 667–75, at pp. 670–1.
43 *Ceylon Celebrates Independence* (Colombo, 1948), a *Times of Ceylon* souvenir publication. (The Sinhalese lions also figure on the mace and on the Speaker's Chair of the Sri Lankan Parliament, both gifts from the British House of Commons in 1949.)
44 The Kandyan crown also ensigned the roundel in Ceylon's seal, replaced by the Buddhist wheel of the law (*dharmachakra*) when Sri Lanka became a republic.
45 The hall also had Nandi flags representing the Tamils and Muslim cultural motifs, though neither so prominent as the Kandyan throne and Sinhalese decorations. The decor of the hall was designed by H. R. Premaratne, from Ceylon's Public Works Department, who did a painting recording the occasion.
46 See *Sunday Times* (Colombo), 11 February 2007 (online), for an article on the 1948 ceremony.
47 Quoted in Murphy, 'Independence Day and the Crown', p. 672. Murphy's article implies, incorrectly, that the throne was returned to Ceylon at this time.
48 H. Kumarasingham, *A Political Legacy of the British Empire: Power and the Parliamentary System in Post-colonial India and Sri Lanka* (London: I. B. Tauris, 2012).
49 Queen Elizabeth II opened a session of the Ceylon Parliament in 1954.
50 *Sunday Times* (Colombo), 10 November 2013.
51 Wickramasinghe, *Sri Lanka in the Modern Age*, p. 110.
52 David Robson, *Geoffrey Bawa: The Complete Works* (London: Thames & Hudson, 2002), pp. 146–55, at p. 150.
53 See www.britishpathe.com/video/ceylon-independence (accessed 16 May 2015).
54 *Sydney Morning Herald*, 11 June 1934.
55 RA PS/PSO/GV/PS/MAIN/40475: Return of King Theodore's crown.
56 RA RC/RLCENT/MAIN/FCO/20, Return of King Theodore's cap.

CHAPTER EIGHT

Kingitanga and Crown: New Zealand's Maori King movement and its relationship with the British monarchy

Vincent O'Malley

Early in 2014, a minor controversy arose in New Zealand when the Maori King, Tuheitia Paki, rejected a proposed visit by the Duke and Duchess of Cambridge to his headquarters at Turangawaewae, Ngaruawahia, as part of the royal couple's tour of the country. There was no shortage of interest in a meeting between the two royal families. The problem was that the ninety minutes allocated for such a visit was seen as a snub. As one Maori leader was quoted as saying, 'Maori royalty "was not some carnival act to be rolled out at the beck and call of anyone".'[1] The King's *mana* or dignity demanded a less rushed meeting. Meanwhile, further north, the Ngapuhi *iwi* (tribe) were said to be angered that Waitangi, where a famous treaty had first been signed between Queen Victoria's representative and the Maori chiefs in 1840, had been left off the itinerary altogether.[2]

Both incidents point to an enduring and profoundly significant relationship between the British royal family and Maori – in one case with a tribe, Ngapuhi, which largely remained aloof from the Maori King movement, and in the other with the movement itself. It is the second of these that is the focus of this chapter. It is easy to see how tribes that remained 'loyal' to the Crown throughout the tumultuous New Zealand Wars conflict over land and sovereignty of the mid-nineteenth century might remain strongly attached to the British monarchy today (even if their supposed 'loyalty' was a much more nuanced stance than is sometimes appreciated).[3] The more intriguing question is why those tribes who fought against Queen Victoria's army, having been accused of setting up a rival monarch to the Queen herself, should share a similar outlook.

There are two aspects to this: first, how did Maori in general view their relationship with the British monarchy; and, second, how did the establishment of the King movement (or, in Maori, the Kingitanga) influence such perceptions? Let us consider each of these matters in turn.

[163]

For Maori, leaders embodied the *mana*, power and prestige of their communities.[4] British monarchs, as the heads of a great nation, were seen as a kind of *ariki*, the most senior (and spiritually significant) rank of chieftain. For all chiefs, their word was considered their bond, and an agreement entered into between powerful *ariki* would assume a kind of spiritual power of its own. From an early date, senior chiefs travelled to Britain in an effort to secure an audience with the British sovereign (and in this way to demonstrate their own *mana*). Only some were successful, among them the great northern chief Hongi Hika, who famously met with King George IV in 1820 (and in Ngapuhi tradition established a bond with the British Crown that endures to this day).[5] In 1831, a number of northern leaders appealed to King George's successor, William IV, for protection from 'the tribe of Marion' (the French), prompting the King to appoint an official British Resident in New Zealand while extending the hand of 'friendship and alliance' to the Maori people.[6]

After sanctioning an 1835 Declaration of Independence, by 1839 the British government had determined to pursue formal annexation of New Zealand. In its English translation, the preamble to the Treaty of Waitangi expressed Queen Victoria's wish to protect and defend the just rights and property of the chiefs and tribes of New Zealand. Although the precise understanding of the three articles that followed has been much debated, especially in light of significant discrepancies with the Maori-language document that most signatories consented to, the whole agreement was framed as one between Queen Victoria and the chiefs.[7] As such, it cemented a deeply personal bond between the Queen and her successors on the one hand (represented locally by the *kawana*, or governor), and the chiefs, their tribes and descendants on the other.[8] There was an additional dimension to this relationship in that by 1840 many Maori, especially in the north of New Zealand, where the Treaty was first signed, had embraced the Christian faith, or were at least familiar with it. Christian missionaries also played a significant role in securing Maori consent, and these factors meant that the Treaty came to be understood as 'a special kind of covenant with the Queen, a bond with all the spiritual connotations of the biblical covenants'.[9] From both customary and Christian perspectives, the relationship with royalty was one that resonated. The Queen's *mana* was dependent on upholding her end of the bargain, and, for this reason, Maori looked to the British monarch to give effect to the Treaty long after all real power had transferred to the colonial government after 1865.

There are various traditions as to the origins of the Kingitanga. Some say it was the visit to England of Pirikawau in the mid-1840s that first sparked the idea.[10] Many others point to Tamihana Te Rauparaha's time there in 1852. The son of a famous warrior chief, Te Rauparaha was young, educated, progressive and Christian. He was received by Queen Victoria at Buckingham Palace and made a favourable impression on the monarch.[11] But Tamihana Te Rauparaha was himself impressed by most things English, and it was his admiration for the British monarchy and a desire to provide better and more unified forms of governance within Maori communities that was to provide a key early driver for the King movement. Te Rauparaha travelled the North Island seeking support for the notion of a Maori king.[12] The kingship was offered to a number of important *rangatira* (chiefs), all of whom rejected the title. It was not until an important gathering held at Pukawa, on the shores of Lake Taupo, in 1856 that momentum for the instalment of a Maori king began to take off. By this time attention had focused on Potatau Te Wherowhero, a powerful Waikato *ariki* whose ancestry was such that it connected him to all the major founding canoes from which Maori traced their descent.[13] Te Wherowhero, like those approached before him, wanted no part of the kingship. He was elderly, had nothing left to prove and was already one of the most senior *ariki* in the land. What could he possibly gain by a meaningless new title?

Despite his own serious misgivings, through a series of important gatherings, support for Potatau Te Wherowhero's instalment gathered steam and in 1858 the chief was formally proclaimed as king. Yet the precise title that would be used was debated right up until the final moment. Fearing possible conflict with the government, some followers urged that a title such as *matua* (which could be translated as either 'parent' or 'father') be adopted.[14] But the counter-argument was that an entirely new title was required, one that had no equivalent in existing Maori custom, and the term 'king' was said to be favoured because of its use in the Bible.[15] That decision prompted some tribes, and especially those from the lower Waikato, to withdraw their backing. Although the Kingitanga could be said to have had nationalist (or proto-nationalist) aspirations, its support was always regionally concentrated, strong backing in the upper Waikato and across many other parts of the central North Island combining with lower rates of adherence, and a more divided response, elsewhere.[16]

Traditional tribal rivalries played an important part in shaping these responses, as did concern over how the government might react to the movement. In this way, a distinctive 'Queen's party' began to emerge. Despite this development, however, key figures within the Kingitanga, including the so-called 'kingmaker' Wiremu Tamihana, had from the outset declared their desire to live in peace alongside Europeans under the mantle of Queen Victoria.[17] What they objected to was what appeared to be their own submission to the settlers and their increasingly powerful provincial and parliamentary assemblies.[18] As Tamihana saw it, the Kingitanga was for Maori. It was not against the Europeans. And as for the Queen, she was, as Tamihana told one visiting official, to be 'a fence for us all', Maori and settler.[19] That sentiment was widely shared, with Kingitanga supporters said to have declared themselves in favour of 'The Queen, the King and the Runanga' (which was a kind of tribal council).[20] Potatau Te Wherowhero had long been a friend to the Europeans in New Zealand, even taking up residence in Auckland in 1845 in order to protect the settlement from other potentially hostile tribes. He affirmed his own bond with Queen Victoria in an 1842 letter that addressed her as 'mother' and urged her to appoint a kind and wise man as the new governor for the colony.[21]

Few Europeans seriously thought that the great chief would lend his name to a movement committed to ending those friendly relations with Europeans or their monarch. But Governor Thomas Gore Browne, having initially dismissed the movement as being of 'no immediate danger',[22] soon came to reverse that view, considering the Kingitanga an affront to the Queen's sovereignty (and an illegal land league that was preventing the peaceful transfer of territory to the settlers).[23] In 1860, British troops attacked Maori in Taranaki who were attempting to block the survey of a disputed land purchase at Waitara. After some Waikato supporters of the Kingitanga intervened later that same year and joined the fight on the side of those defending their Waitara lands, the Governor prepared plans for the invasion of Waikato with a view to dismantling the Maori King movement by force.[24] Potatau Te Wherowhero had died in June and was soon succeeded by his son Matutaera (who later became known as Tawhiao). That succession was by no means a certain thing because the Kingitanga was founded on an elective rather than hereditary basis. The new king's commitment to peaceful relations with the settlers was not enough to assuage the Governor, who demanded that the movement be dismantled or suffer the consequences.[25]

Browne was recalled in 1861 before those plans could be put into effect. But nearly two years later, his successor, Sir George Grey, launched his own invasion of Waikato. Relying upon trumped-up charges of an imminent Kingitanga threat to the settlement of Auckland, in July 1863 Grey ordered imperial troops into the Waikato, while at the same time forcibly evicting large numbers of Maori from their homes north of there.[26] By the end of the fighting in April 1864 some 1.2 million acres of Maori land had been seized and hundreds of Kingitanga followers killed defending their homeland. Crucially, however, the Kingitanga, though sustaining serious damage, had not been destroyed, and most of its Waikato supporters retreated south of the Puniu river into an unconquered area that henceforth became known as the King Country. For the best part of the next two decades this area effectively remained, in the memorable words of James Belich, 'an independent Maori state nearly two-thirds the size of Belgium'.[27]

Throughout this period of turmoil and beyond there remained a firm belief among Kingitanga supporters that if only the Queen knew the real situation in New Zealand she would intervene to secure justice to the Maori people whom she had pledged to protect under the terms of the Treaty of Waitangi. The Queen herself had entered into a solemn and binding compact with the chiefs. It followed from this that her representatives as governors (and, by 1865, the colonial governments which had assumed almost all of their substantive powers) were not acting in accordance with the Queen's wishes. Kingitanga leaders confronted with hostile local political leaders would need to go over their heads in order to obtain justice. They would need to appeal to the Queen herself (an approach with wider precedent among other indigenous peoples of the British Empire).[28] From this notion would eventually emerge the idea of travelling to London in order to directly place the grievances of the Maori people before Queen Victoria and her successors.

Meanwhile, the New Zealand government was not averse to exploiting such sentiments for its own ends. The presence in the colony of Prince Alfred, the Duke of Edinburgh, in 1869 was viewed as a prime opportunity to finally secure Kingitanga submission to the Crown. For their part, senior Kingitanga chiefs made it clear that they were more than willing to meet with the Queen's son. But they were not prepared to do so without an understanding that the confiscated lands should be returned in full and that the Maori King should have his authority over the Waikato recognised by the government. Despite a lengthy period of negotiations that had commenced in October 1867, when Governor Grey wrote to King Tawhiao that 'one of the sons of the Queen' was to visit New Zealand shortly, and if he was 'willing to give up your weapons of war to a great chief, none greater than this chief will ever come near to you', Prince Alfred eventually left the colony without meeting the Maori King.[29]

In 1882, a Ngapuhi deputation travelled to England with a petition addressed directly to Queen Victoria and an avowed aim of gaining an audience with her. The petition set out the familiar grievances of Maori generally, including those relating to the invasion and subsequent confiscation of much of the Waikato district. But the petitioners added their view that

We did not believe the utterances of the Europeans as to the wrongs we suffered, that they were brought about by your queenly authority; but our decision was that such acts were not sanctioned by you, O Queen, whose benevolence towards the Maori people is well known.[30]

In the context of this conviction that the Queen would bring justice to the Maori people if only she knew their real circumstances, it made perfect sense to undertake the long journey to England. And even without such an audience, the presence in London of Maori deputations of this kind could cause considerable embarrassment for the New Zealand government, especially as this first deputation came soon after the controversial sacking of the pacifist Maori settlement of Parihaka by armed constabulary in November 1881. Francis Dillon Bell, a former colonial minister and by this time New Zealand's official representative in London, worked furiously (and successfully) behind the scenes to prevent a meeting with Queen Victoria.[31]

But two years later the Maori King led his own deputation to London. This was of an altogether different magnitude to the earlier mission. Tawhiao, having abandoned his former policy of isolation from Europeans within the King Country in 1881, would travel to Europe to seek recognition of his authority and a return of all lands wrongfully confiscated from the tribes. The Queen had shown her affection for her Maori subjects when securing their rights through the Treaty. She would be sure to intervene if alerted to the fact that those rights had been trampled upon. And, given that the Queen had recently met with the Zulu King Cetshwayo (in 1882), precedent was on King Tawhiao's side.[32] He left New Zealand in a blaze of publicity and soon became a centre of attention in London. Tawhiao and his entourage were freely admitted into high society and received overwhelmingly positive coverage in the London press.[33] Almost no one had a bad word to say about them – except, that is, the New Zealand government agent, who this time redoubled his efforts to prevent the meeting of king and queen.[34] Tawhiao's petition set out eloquently the Maori understanding that Queen Victoria had personally pledged to protect and uphold the rights of her Maori subjects under the Treaty of Waitangi.[35] But such sentiments counted for little in the end, as Tawhiao was also refused a meeting with the Queen. He had to make do with an interview with the Secretary of State for the Colonies, who was informed that 'I am called a king, not for the purpose of separation, but in order that the natives might be united under one race, ever acknowledging the supremacy of the Queen, and claiming her protection.'[36] Lord Derby, as was to become standard practice, simply referred the matter back to the New Zealand government for a response – the very same government whose unwillingness to act on their grievances in the first place had prompted the appeal over their heads.[37] It eventually (and predictably) dismissed the grievances outright, insisting that there had been 'no infraction of the Treaty of Waitangi' since 1865, when full authority had passed to the colonial legislature and cabinet.[38]

A final plea, shortly before the Maori King's deputation was due to return to New Zealand, that 'since the signing of the treaty of Waitangi, the Maori race have looked up to the Queen as our great mother' and that their failure to be allowed to see her was 'as if we were cast away as a race who had nothing to do with the Queen', failed to reverse the original decision.[39] Dillon Bell once more appears to have played a key role in pressuring the British government not to relent to the pleas of the popular Maori visitors and their many influential supporters from the Aborigines' Protection Society and other groups, even going so far as to assert that Tawhiao was not of sufficiently good character to be allowed an audience with the Queen.[40] Ironically, that outcome might have reinforced the idea that, if only they had been allowed to meet with the Queen, things might have been different.

In 1914, King Te Rata and his chief adviser, Tupu Taingakawa, followed in Tawhiao's footsteps with a petition to London. The pair were even presented to King George V and Queen Mary in June 1914 – the first meeting between British and Maori monarchs – though with one crucial condition attached: no grievances were to be raised in the presence of the royal couple.[41] They sailed for New Zealand just days after the British Empire's entry into the First World War, having achieved little in a political sense. Once more the British government referred their grievances back to New Zealand authorities. During their stay, a lawyer who had promised to look into their grievances fleeced the group of £500 in return for a five-page legal opinion on 'Maori rights' that was of no assistance.[42]

In 1924, Tupu Taingakawa returned to England, this time in the company of the prophet Tahupotiki Wiremu Ratana. Taingakawa was able to present a letter to the Prince of Wales during a garden party at St James's Palace that set out the grievances of the Maori people and solicited assistance. It was forwarded to the Colonial Office for the usual disposal. But the prince caused grave cultural offence when his office subsequently returned various gifts that had been presented to him, on the grounds that these had not gone through the proper official channels.[43] It was not the last time that Maori encounters with royalty would leave a sour taste.

By the twentieth century, members of the British royal family increasingly made their way to New Zealand. It became customary for them to receive a Maori welcome at Rotorua, a prominent tourist spot that was also home to the 'loyalist' *iwi* Te Arawa.[44] When the

Duke and Duchess of Cornwall and York (the future King George V and Queen Mary) toured the colony in 1901, the Maori King, Mahuta, was invited to attend the Rotorua ceremony but refused: if he was going to welcome royal visitors then it would be on his own territory, and not that of another *iwi*.[45] And so, when the Prince of Wales (later King Edward VIII) came to New Zealand in 1920, King Te Rata extended a formal invitation to visit Ngaruawahia.[46] The New Zealand government refused the request out of hand, insisting that the King travel to Rotorua if he wished to meet the young prince. But still King Te Rata kept the faith. Perhaps the government might change its mind or the Prince of Wales might hear their story and intervene. As one historian described the ensuing scene:

> And so on the morning of 27 April, as the train carrying the Prince from Auckland to Rotorua was about to pass, Te Rata stood on Ngaruawahia Station with a retinue of elders and a karanga [welcoming] party; the [King's] Parliament House was stocked with food; hundreds of Kingite supporters milled about the entrance to watch Maori royalty re-establish its links with English royalty. The train, of course, passed straight through. There was not even a pause. And Waikato felt humiliated.[47]

Prior to the visit, rumours circulated that some Kingitanga supporters were threatening to lie down on the track if the Prince's train failed to stop at Ngaruawahia.[48] But the only hint of a concession to Kingitanga feeling was that the train slowed as it passed by the welcoming party waiting on the station platform.[49] It was little consolation for Kingitanga supporters.

Further royal visitors in 1927 and 1935 again did not stop at Ngaruawahia. As part of planning for another royal tour of New Zealand in the late 1940s – the first by the reigning monarch – Ngaruawahia was initially included on the itinerary, before being removed by an incoming government after 1949 when the King's illness saw the visit postponed. Following protracted negotiations that went almost up to the final moment, when Queen Elizabeth II and Prince Philip, the Duke of Edinburgh, toured the country in 1953, a scheduled three-minute stopover at Ngaruawahia (which eventually lasted seventeen minutes) was eventually permitted.[50] Prior to this last-minute concession, the intention not to travel to Ngaruawahia had been widely (and unfavourably) reported on as a snub to the Kingitanga, and some observers noted that Waikato elders still smarted from the humiliation they had endured in 1920.[51] King Koroki was this time invited to meet with the Queen at Waitangi instead. He refused, and preparations for a royal visit to Ngaruawahia continued.[52] One of the Maori speakers at Waitangi pleaded with the Queen to go to Ngaruawahia, and at least one report suggested that she had personally overruled the New Zealand government's continuing objections and used her royal prerogative to insist on visiting Ngaruawahia.[53] It was a rare victory for the Kingitanga in the face of continuing official wariness of the movement, and the royal couple received a rapturous welcome on to the Turangawaewae *marae* (meeting place) on 30 December 1953, just two days after the Waitangi gathering.[54]

In the late nineteenth century, the Kingitanga had been viewed by many colonial politicians and officials as a threat to settler hegemony, and its efforts to obtain some kind of legal recognition were rebuffed.[55] Within the Kingitanga itself, supporters were deeply divided over whether to pursue a rapprochement policy with the government. After accepting a seat in the Legislative Council (New Zealand's upper house until later abolished) in 1903, a disillusioned King Mahuta quit when his term ended in 1910, frustrated at the inability to gain any traction on Maori grievances. Critics had feared that his appointment was no more than a cynical government effort to erode and undermine Kingitanga independence.[56] It appears that Mahuta probably shared these concerns, having formally entrusted the kingship in his younger brother at the time of his appointment. He resumed the title of king only upon departing the Legislative Council.[57] More strained relations followed, especially when large numbers of young Waikato tribesmen were arrested for resisting conscription during the final stages of the First World War.[58]

A period of gradually improved relations later developed, particularly under the first Labour government of 1935–49. Nevertheless, by the middle decades of the twentieth century, the Kingitanga was seen by some (especially those on the right of New Zealand politics, including the National government of 1949–57) as at best irrelevant or outmoded. It was regarded as inconsistent with long-standing policies aimed at encouraging Maori assimilation or amalgamation.[59] Separate Maori institutions such as the Kingitanga had no place in this schema. But attitudes were beginning to change. Although the Kingitanga was (and remains) completely unofficial, having no legal or constitutional status, by the 1970s it was becoming more difficult to shun the movement altogether. In February 1974, Queen Elizabeth and Prince Philip again visited Ngaruawahia (this time for several hours and accompanied by the newly wed couple Princess Anne and Mark Phillips).[60] Far from attempting to block the visit, the government was anxious to ensure sufficient time was allowed to follow correct welcoming protocol and custom in full (in contrast with the compromises Kingitanga hosts of the first royal guests had been forced to make).⁶¹ The following year, Queen Elizabeth hosted the Maori Queen, Te Arikinui Dame Te Atairangikaahu (she had been made a Dame Commander of the Order of the British Empire in 1970), in England.⁶²

By this time, the notion that the British monarch could have any real influence on New Zealand's treatment of Maori had been well and truly dispelled. Yet still many Maori (including Kingitanga supporters) clung to the notion of the Treaty as a deeply personal bond with the British royal family. That could sometimes have negative repercussions, as the Queen herself discovered when she was caught up in the highly charged events of February 1990, when the 150th anniversary of the Treaty of Waitangi was marked with angry speeches and a T-shirt hurled in her direction.⁶³ But it also provided the opportunity for a unique act of atonement. The Waikato Raupatu Claims Settlement Act of 1995 was one of the first major settlements of historical Maori land claims in the modern era. Besides monetary compensation of NZ$170 million and the return of a small portion of the lands confiscated that were still in Crown ownership, the settlement also included an apology for the Crown's unjust invasion of Waikato in the 1860s, including the statement that 'The Crown expresses its profound regret and apologises unreservedly for the loss of lives because of the hostilities arising from its invasion, and at the devastation of property and social life which resulted.'⁶⁴ Waikato leaders had wanted the Queen to personally deliver this apology. But that was a bridge too far for local officials (and without constitutional precedent).⁶⁵ And so, agreement was reached that the Queen would herself give royal assent to the Act, including the apology, the first and only time she had personally signed into effect New Zealand legislation. It was not quite the same thing as the Queen 'saying sorry' to the Kingitanga (as some newspapers at the time reported), but it was nevertheless a momentous occasion.⁶⁶ As one government minister noted afterwards, it was the symbolism, rather than actual signing, that counted most.⁶⁷ What really mattered for the Waikato tribe was just who was doing the signing and the message this silently conveyed. The Queen had been under no obligation to sign the apology and could have left it to the Governor-General, as was normal. But Buckingham Palace, understanding the significance of the occasion, had agreed to her participation. It was without precedent.

Even the act of signing the apology, conducted before the Maori Queen and other Waikato representatives during a visit to New Zealand to attend the Commonwealth Heads of Government meeting in Auckland in November 1995 (see Figure 18), was enough to spark calls from descendants of other victims of British imperial expansion around the globe for similar apologies.[68] And yet, for the Kingitanga, and for the Waikato-Tainui people, it was the final fulfilment of the mission that Tawhiao had first set out to achieve when he visited London in 1884. Queen Victoria's heir had personally assented to an apology in the presence of King Tawhiao's heir and in this way made good the special bond between Kingitanga and Crown that had for so long been a central tenet of Waikato Maori belief. Their faith was eventually rewarded. Perhaps the long years of appealing to London for assistance had not been in vain after all. Nevertheless, as the dispute over the recent royal itinerary indicates, even today the relationship is not without its challenges, however much the connection continues to resonate for the people of the Kingitanga.

18. Queen Elizabeth II, the Maori Queen, Te Arikinui Dame Te Atairangikaahu, Prime Minister Jim Bolger and Douglas Graham (Minister in Charge of Treaty of Waitangi Negotiations) at the signing of the Waikato Raupatu Claims Settlement Act, Auckland, 4 November 1995. Source: EP/1995/4375B/33A-F, Alexander Turnbull Library, Wellington, New Zealand. Reproduced with permission

Notes

1 'Maori King Refuses Meeting with British Prince', see www.nzherald.co.nz/world/news/article.cfm?c_id=2&objectid=11214321 (accessed 28 April 2014).
2 'Royal Snub Annoys Kingi Taurua', see www.nzherald.co.nz/northern-advocate/news/article.cfm?c_id=1503450&objectid=11218190 (accessed 28 April 2014).
3 Vincent O'Malley, 'Uncle Toms and Kupapas: Collaboration versus Alliance in a New Zealand Context', unpublished paper, Cooperation and Empire conference, University of Bern, June 2013.
4 Angela Ballara, *Taua: 'Musket Wars', 'Land Wars' or Tikanga? Warfare in Maori Society in the Early Nineteenth Century* (Auckland: Penguin, 2003), p. 80.
5 Manuka A. Henare, 'The Changing Images of Nineteenth Century Maori Society: From Tribes to Nation', Ph.D. thesis, Victoria University of Wellington, 2003, pp. 160–72; Vincent O'Malley, *The Meeting Place: Maori and Pakeha Encounters, 1642–1840* (Auckland: Auckland University Press, 2012), pp. 63–5.
6 Wharerahi and others to King William, n.d., enclosed in William Yate to Church Missionary Society, 16 November 1831, *Great Britain Parliamentary Papers* (GBPP), 1840 (238), p. 7; Lord Viscount Goderich to the Chiefs of New Zealand, 14 June 1832, GBPP, 1840 (238), pp. 7–8.
7 On the Treaty, see Claudia Orange, *The Treaty of Waitangi* (Wellington: Allen & Unwin/Port Nicholson Press, 1987); R. M. Ross, 'Te Tiriti o Waitangi: Text and Translations', *New Zealand Journal of History*, 6:2 (1972), 129–57; Peter Adams, *Fatal Necessity: British Intervention in New Zealand, 1830–1847* (Auckland: Auckland University Press, 1977); Vincent O'Malley, Bruce Stirling and Wally Penetito (eds), *The Treaty of Waitangi Companion: Maori and Pakeha from Tasman to Today* (Auckland: Auckland University Press, 2010).
8 Anne Salmond, 'Brief of Evidence of Distinguished Professor Anne Salmond', Waitangi Tribunal Northland District Inquiry (Wai-1040), Document A22, 2010, pp. 19–22.
9 Orange, *The Treaty of Waitangi*, p. 57.
10 Pei Te Hurinui Jones, 'Maori Kings', in Erik Schwimmer (ed.), *The Maori People in the Nineteen-Sixties: A Symposium* (Auckland: Blackwood & Janet Paul, 1968), pp. 132–73, at p. 132.
11 Brian Mackrell, *Hariru Wikitoria! An Illustrated History of the Maori Tour of England, 1863* (Oxford: Oxford University Press, 1985), p. 12.
12 Thomas Buddle, *The Maori King Movement in New Zealand, with a Full Report of the Native Meetings Held at Waikato, April and May, 1860* (Auckland: New Zealander office, 1860), pp. 3–4.
13 Angela Ballara, 'Introduction: The King Movement's First Hundred Years', in *Te Kingitanga: The People of the Maori King Movement: Essays from the Dictionary of New Zealand Biography* (Auckland: Auckland University Press, 1996), pp. 1–2.
14 *Southern Cross*, 11 June 1858.
15 'Story of the King Movement, Told by a Maori Chief', *New Zealand Herald*, 18 February 1882.
16 B. J. Dalton, *War and Politics in New Zealand, 1855–1870* (Sydney: Sydney University Press, 1967), pp. 72, 83, 110–11.
17 Evelyn Stokes, *Wiremu Tamihana: Rangatira* (Wellington: Huia Publishers, 2002).
18 Alan Ward, *A Show of Justice: Racial 'Amalgamation' in Nineteenth Century New Zealand* (Auckland: Auckland University Press, 1973), pp. 98–101.
19 B. Y. Ashwell to Church Missionary Society, 1 May 1861, Ashwell Letters and Journals, qMS-89, Alexander Turnbull Library (ATL), Wellington.
20 J. Morgan to C. W. Richmond, 21 June 1858, in Guy H. Scholefield (ed.), *The Richmond–Atkinson Papers*, 2 vols. (Wellington: Government Printer, 1960), vol. I, p. 410.
21 Te Wherowhero to Queen Victoria, IA 1/1842/1862, Archives New Zealand (Archives NZ), Wellington.

KINGITANGA AND CROWN

22 Thomas Gore Browne and Henry Labouchere, 23 September 1857, *Appendices to the Journals of the House of Representatives* (AJHR), 1860, F-3, p. 124.
23 Alan Ward, 'A "Savage War of Peace"? Motives for Government Policies towards the Kingitanga, 1857–1863', in Richard Boast and Richard S. Hill (eds), *Raupatu: The Confiscation of Maori Land* (Wellington: Victoria University Press, 2009), pp. 67–109.
24 Vincent O'Malley, 'Te Rohe Potae Political Engagement, 1840–1863', Waitangi Tribunal research report, Wellington, 2010, pp. 355–8.
25 Copy of a Declaration by the Governor to the Natives Assembled at Ngaruawahia, 21 May 1861, GBPP, 1862 [3040], p. 71.
26 Vincent O'Malley, 'Choosing Peace or War: The 1863 Invasion of Waikato', *New Zealand Journal of History*, 47:1 (2013), 39–58.
27 James Belich, *The New Zealand Wars and the Victorian Interpretation of Racial Conflict* (Auckland: Auckland University Press, 1986), p. 306.
28 See Ann Curthoys and Jessie Mitchell, '"Bring This Paper to the Good Governor": Aboriginal Petitioning in Britain's Australian Colonies', in Saliha Belmessous (ed.), *Native Claims: Indigenous Law against Empire, 1500–1920* (Oxford: Oxford University Press, 2012), pp. 182–203; Zoë Laidlaw and Alan Lester (eds), *Indigenous Communities and Settler Colonialism: Land Holding, Loss and Survival in an Interconnected World* (Basingstoke: Palgrave Macmillan, 2015).
29 George Grey to Matutaera, 17 October 1867, Grey New Zealand Maori Letters, GNZMA 260, Auckland City Library; Vincent O'Malley, 'Te Rohe Potae War and Raupatu', Waitangi Tribunal research report, Wellington, 2010, pp. 750–8.
30 AJHR, 1883, A-6, pp. 1–3.
31 Orange, *The Treaty of Waitangi*, pp. 206–7; Vincent O'Malley, *Agents of Autonomy: Maori Committees in the Nineteenth Century* (Wellington: Huia Publishers, 1998), pp. 144–5.
32 See Bridget Theron, 'King Cetshwayo in Victorian England: A Cameo of Imperial Interaction', *South African Historical Journal*, 56:1 (2006), 60–87.
33 *The Times*, 23 July 1884; *Morning Post*, 24 July 1884; *Daily Chronicle*, 23 July 1884; *Globe*, 23 July 1884; *Echo*, 23 July 1884; *St James's Gazette*, 23 July 1884; *Evening News*, 23 July 1884; *Evening Standard*, 23 July 1884; *Daily News*, 24 July 1884; enclosures in F. D. Bell to New Zealand Premier, 24 July 1884, MA 23/4A, Archives New Zealand.
34 Roger Blackley, 'King Tawhiao's Big O. E.', *Turnbull Library Record*, 44 (2012), 36–52; Orange, *The Treaty of Waitangi*, pp. 211–14.
35 Memorial of King Tawhiao and others to Queen Victoria, 15 July 1884, GBPP, 1884–85 (c.4413), pp. 5–8.
36 *The Times*, 23 July 1884.
37 Earl of Derby to Governor William Jervois, 9 August 1884, GBPP, 1884–85 (c.4413), p. 9.
38 Robert Stout (Premier) to Governor William Jervois, 12 March 1885, AJHR, 1885, A-1, p. 32.
39 Te Wheoro to Lord Derby, 13 August 1884, Aborigines Protection Society Papers, Micro-MS-Coll-20-2432, ATL.
40 Ann R. Parsonson, 'Te Mana o te Kingitanga Maori: A Study of Waikato-Ngatimaniapoto Relations during the Struggle for the King Country, 1878–84', MA thesis, University of Canterbury, 1972, p. 182.
41 Michael King, *Te Puea: A Biography* (Auckland: Hodder & Stoughton, 1977), p. 75; Orange, *The Treaty of Waitangi*, p. 228.
42 Jones, 'Maori Kings', p. 147.
43 Angela Ballara, 'Te Waharoa, Tupu Atanatiu Taingakawa', in *The Dictionary of New Zealand Biography*, vol. III: *1901–1920* (Auckland: Auckland University Press, 1996), p. 520.
44 See Vincent O'Malley and David Armstrong, *The Beating Heart: A Political and Socio-economic History of Te Arawa* (Wellington: Huia Publishers, 2008).
45 King, *Te Puea*, p. 106.

46 Although Ngaruawahia had been included in the lands confiscated after 1863, a site was repurchased for the King's residence in the 1920s. Over time it came to feature more of the trappings of a European-style monarchy (with distinctively Maori twists) than earlier, much more modest residencies. However, the King's role was largely symbolic or ceremonial by this time, including annual visits to supporters that provided an opportunity to secure financial and moral support for the Kingitanga.
47 King, *Te Puea*, p. 107.
48 'Local Gossip', *New Zealand Herald*, 15 May 1920.
49 'Prince of Wales Begins Tour of Auckland Country Districts', *Bay of Plenty Times*, 28 April 1920; 'Departure from Auckland', *Colonist*, 28 April 1920.
50 Jock Phillips, *Royal Summer: The Visit of Queen Elizabeth II and Prince Philip to New Zealand 1953–54* (Wellington: Daphne Brasell Associates Press, 1993), p. 37; King, *Te Puea*, pp. 267–71.
51 A. B. Galbraith, Mayor of Ngaruawahia, to the Under Secretary, Department of Internal Affairs, 4 April 1951, IA 1 184/136, Archives NZ; 'A Snub for the Maori King', *Otago Daily Times*, 12 December 1953; 'Maori King May Not Meet the Queen', *Evening Post*, 13 October 1953; '"Sacred Soil" that the Queen Will Not Tread', *Evening Post*, 11 December 1953.
52 'Waikatos Still Prepare Welcome at Turangawaewae', *Evening Post*, 24 December 1953.
53 'Queen Uses Royal Prerogative to Heal 95-Year-Old Grievance', *Taranaki Daily News*, 2 January 1954.
54 'The Queen Greeted at the Court of King Koroki', *The Times*, 31 December 1953; 'The Queen Cheered by King Koroki's Painted Warriors', *Dominion*, 31 December 1953; Phillips, *Royal Summer*, pp. 30–1.
55 John A. Williams, *Politics of the New Zealand Maori: Protest and Cooperation, 1891–1909* (Auckland: Auckland University Press, 1977), pp. 40–7; Richard S. Hill, *State Authority, Indigenous Autonomy: Crown-Maori Relations in New Zealand/ Aotearoa, 1900–1950* (Wellington: Victoria University Press, 2004), pp. 33–5.
56 Ballara, 'Introduction: The King Movement's First Hundred Years', pp. 20–1.
57 David McCan, *Whatiwhatihoe: The Waikato Raupatu Claim* (Wellington: Huia Publishers, 2001), pp. 171–2.
58 P. S. O'Connor, 'The Recruitment of Maori Soldiers, 1914–1918', *Political Science*, 19:2 (1967), 48–83.
59 King, *Te Puea*, pp. 267–71; Richard S. Hill, *Maori and the State: Crown–Maori Relations in New Zealand/Aotearoa, 1950–2000* (Wellington: Victoria University Press, 2009), pp. 42–5.
60 'Royal Visit to Turangawaewae, Ngaruawahia, Friday, 8 February 1974: Procedure', IA 1 210/35/1, Archives NZ; Royal Visit 1974: Itinerary and Programme, IA 31 171/10, Archives NZ.
61 Matiu Rata, Minister of Maori Affairs, to Prime Minister Norman Kirk, 2 July 1973, IA1 210/14, Archives NZ.
62 *Queen Te Atairangikaahu: The First Twenty-Five Years* (Ngaruawahia: Estate of Te Puea Herangi, 1992), pp. 75–81.
63 Claudia Orange, *An Illustrated History of the Treaty of Waitangi* (Wellington: Bridget Williams Books, 2004), pp. 199–203.
64 *New Zealand Statutes*, 1995, No. 58, Part 1.
65 'Queen Apology Improper: Graham', *Dominion*, 3 July 1995.
66 'Queen to Say Sorry to the Maori People', *Independent*, 2 July 1995.
67 'Queen Puts Signature to Historic Land Deal', *Dominion*, 4 November 1995.
68 'Okay, So We're Very Sorry for Being British', *Guardian*, 5 November 1995; 'Famine Apology', *Irish Times*, 13 November 1995; 'Queen Faces Demands for Apology over Treatment of Boers', *Irish Times*, 11 November 1999.

CHAPTER NINE

The Maharani of Kutch and courtly life before and after Indian Independence

Jim Masselos

An obvious major consequence of its success in quelling the great Indian uprising of 1857 was that Britain remained in control of the subcontinent for the next ninety years. It did so by ruling both directly and indirectly. It exercised direct rule over British India through the Indian Civil Service, a bureaucratic structure of mainly British officials who hardly ever numbered more than 1,300 at any time over the period of the British Raj. Though India was never a colony of settlement, the number of Britons on the subcontinent was always bulked up by British soldiers, sailors, police and railway officials, and private merchants, traders, engineers, plantation managers and other occupations. At the apex of the bureaucracy in each presidency or province was a governor and his council of advisers while the governor-general (who was also the viceroy) ruled the Indian Empire in tandem with senior officials. He had the cachet of being the representative of Queen Victoria or of the monarchs who followed her, though he was of course responsible to the British Parliament through the Secretary of State for India.

Paramount control over the princely states was vested in the governor-general, whose powers of superintendence were deployed through a British resident or other political officer stationed in a princely state. As a reward for their loyalty, Queen Victoria had guaranteed in her famous proclamation of 1858 the continuation of whatever privileges the princes had enjoyed under the East India Company. In what was virtually a bill of rights for the surviving princes, the Queen announced that all treaties and engagements that had been in force earlier would be 'scrupulously maintained' just as the same obligation (of observing the *status quo ante*) was expected of the 'native Princes of India' in ruling their territories, albeit under the paramountcy of the British Crown.[1]

Thus, in the aftermath of 1857, the British government directly ruled some two-thirds of the Indian subcontinent (i.e. British India) and indirectly controlled the other third. That third was princely India, territory ostensibly ruled by some 600 to 700 princes known under a range of titles, variously *maharaja, raja, rana, rao, maharao, nizam* and so on, according to family and lineage tradition. The princes had their own bureaucratic structures by which they governed their territories while they ensured the support and loyalty of their subsidiary nobles and notables by requiring attendance at the royal court. Larger kingdoms had extensive powers in exercising administrative functions such as collecting revenue and maintaining law and order. Some even issued coinage and stamps, had token soldiery and operated railway systems within their territories though the government of India by the end of the nineteenth century was beginning to challenge these rights or privileges.[2]

Those royals who had not joined in the 1857 uprising thus managed to hang on to their thrones and territories and ensured the succession of their lineages though at a cost: that of continued subsidiary status in Britain's Indian empire. They continued to enjoy their positions in the aftermath of 1857 until India gained independence in 1947. Thereafter, they would have to come to an understanding with a different set of rulers, elected Indian governments.

Imperial ruler and subsidiary rajas

The relationship, however, was more complex than merely polarised subordination between imperial ruler and subsidiary rajas. There was a degree of interaction between the two. The leading British bureaucrats who ruled India increasingly themselves became a virtual neo-royalty whose quasi-regal ceremonial and social modes influenced and were influenced by the ritual displays of princely pomp and regal position in the royal courts. There was much a foreign ruler could learn from the traditional rulers just as traditional rulers learnt from foreign bureaucrats Western styles of regal status and modes of behaviour.

Viceroys and lesser officials, for instance, were quick to adopt – and then adapt – the ritual ceremonial of formal court levees often known as durbars. In pre-colonial times maharajas had received pledges of allegiance from their tributary nobles at functions in dedicated spaces in their own palaces, and some perforce in turn attended durbars in the Mughal courts. In the later period of different foreign rule, the princes attended on British dignitaries at what were often grand formal occasions where they attested their loyalty to the foreign paramount ruler.[3] The most spectacular of such events were the three Delhi durbars: the first was in 1877, when Queen Victoria was proclaimed Empress of India; the second in 1903 celebrated the coronation of Edward VII; and the third in 1911 had the presence of a British monarch, George V, who used the occasion to announce the important decision to move the capital of Britain's Indian Empire from Calcutta to Delhi.[4] The Delhi durbars drew on Mughal and other precedents to create spectacular variants that nevertheless had a serious underlying political intent. They reaffirmed British paramountcy, fulfilled the objective of impressing Indian audiences and provided an event in which subordinate feudatories were required to assert their loyalty to the British throne. They also of course reflected par excellence a British liking for pomp and circumstance.

While the Delhi durbars provided prime examples of public displays of British imperial power, the Indian princes concurrently continued to hold lesser formal durbars in their own kingdoms and for their own purposes. They were less glamorous, less grandiloquent and far less spectacular than the three grand set pieces mounted by the British Raj. In practice, many of them were somewhat staid gatherings of male nobles exchanging gifts with the monarch and taking sight (*darshan*) of their maharaja in a general assemblage, a sighting from which both, it was thought, would receive mutual benefit.[5] Such durbars were usually held within the space of the royal palaces where the nobles would be seated strictly according to precedence and protocol.

These formal occasions were limited to men, and, with the notable exception of the Muslim Begums of Bhopal who appeared in public usually in purdah (i.e. veiled or unseen behind a curtain), royal women did not attend out of purdah at such public or other semi-public court occasions though they might well be discreetly hidden observers. Princely India was very much a male-dominated world where women were kept separate and apart. In the royal palaces they had their own quarters where other dynamics operated and other customs applied. Their presence, even when unseen, raises issues regarding their place in the structure of the state and generally of just what life in the Indian courts consisted of during and after the British Empire.

An idea of how the kingdoms were constituted, and of the ordered lives within them, may be gleaned less by looking at the big picture of paramount rule and the interactions paramountcy set up and more by examining the particularity of courtly life and the extent of autonomy allowed those who lived in the royal palace. To do so, I shall use the example of Kutch (or, in its present-day official spelling, Kachchh), a large and important kingdom on the western edge of Gujarat, bordering Sind to the west and Rajasthan to the north.[6] The information that follows about life in Kutch in the two decades before Indian independence in 1947 comes from an extended but intermittent series of taped conversations in English with the then Maharani of Kutch (r. 1948–91) recorded between 1988 and 1991.[7] It is her story, as she wanted it heard through what was recorded at our various meetings.

I had first been introduced to the then Maharani through a friend, Mrs Meher Patuck, whose Parsi family in Bombay had had a long connection with her. In the 1980s, I was doing research on Kutch court embroidery about which the Maharani was able to provide much information. We then chatted about her life in Bhuj, and I was invited to meet her again for more reminiscing. During our conversation then and later, she suggested she could tell me much about her life, and the idea grew that I should record our conversations and that I would learn a great deal about India from her. So on my next visit to India I arrived in Bombay at her apartment carrying a small new state-of-the-art tape recorder on which I began recording our conversations, usually free-flowing in format and lasting up to an hour. Each session focused on one aspect or other of the various stages of her life though there was of course some slippage from one idea to another. She became involved in telling her story and between sessions would plan what she would cover when we next met. Occasionally she would tell me to stop the machine and would chat off the record about some sensitive matter or other, but these parts were not recorded and I kept no notes of what had been said. We both enjoyed the conversations and looked forward to them. What she told me for the tapes she did not consider confidential, and she was pleased that their content would be used in research projects.

The discussion that follows introduces another voice to the scant few that appear in the literature on the royal women of princely India. It is not surprising that they hardly figure in histories of the princely states, since no matter how good the quality of the research their authors have different concerns and a different direction to their gaze. The books that do specifically focus on royal women vary in content and approach. Some look at the ranis and maharanis in terms of gossip and scandal, but there are others that take a more considered approach, especially those that are autobiographies and reminiscences.[8] What emerges from these accounts, those that are personal memoirs, is that the experience of being royal varied considerably from kingdom to kingdom though structurally the experience of a new entrant coming to terms with a new household and a court with its own different traditions was similar. That experience, the new wife arriving in the groom's household, was not at all unique to the royal wife though it may well have been more convoluted for a newly wed princess faced with a whole dynasty of accrued custom and tradition to understand. What the wife made of her situation and how she related to all that was new around her becomes the underlying narrative for the royal women after marriage as much as it was for a commoner in the same situation. That overall the culture of the princely kingdoms survived and operated with such confidence and with an élan and spirit at a time when the kingdoms were under the umbrella of the British Empire at the triumphant height of its powers says something about the difference between appearance and reality. Oral history helps fill in some of the gaps as to what was going on in the kingdom, and the material presented in what follows could not have been obtained from any other kind of source, apart possibly from a written memoir. Both enable access to voices and experiences that would otherwise remain unheard, whatever the methodological difficulties inherent in relying on memory for information or in the ambiguity of the spoken word and its transmission. Without such words though we would not have quite the same insights about a person and her environment and in particular of course far less would be known about the central figures of this chapter or the roles they played in the state.

The Maharani of Kutch

Maharani Rajendra Kunverba came from a prestigious Rajput lineage, that of Kishangarh. Though Kishangarh is not the largest or oldest of the royal Rajasthani kingdoms, it is one that has great prestige. It is, among other matters, famous for the paintings that came from its artists' studios.[9] The paintings depict the Maharaja and his consort as Krishna and Radha, as great lovers, both in a secular sense but also in their representing the all-encompassing divine love that the Hindu god Krishna had for Radha. The dreamlike, languorous depiction of their love together, enacted on the lake in front of the palace, has become a stereotype of Indian romance, while the raja's loved one, the Radha of the paintings, with her fish-shaped eyes, elongated nose and delicately delineated features, has become very much the archetype of Indian feminine beauty. However, Kunverba's Kishangarh lineage was through the maharaja, the male line. A sense of her confident assuredness is conveyed in photos I took of her at the time (see Figure 19).

Kunverba's father, the Maharaja of Kishangarh, had three daughters but no sons. He died in January 1926 when she was about five years old (she had been born in 1921 and died in 2000). Since he had no male issue, he was succeeded by a male relative who had little concern for the daughters of the former raja. So, in order to maintain her suitability for marriage, Kunverba was brought up strictly by her mother who was faced with the problem of finding suitable husbands for her daughters. The two elder sisters were found good matches with other kingdoms, and the search went on to find Kunverba a husband. He had of course

19. The late Maharani Kunverba of Kutch.
Photograph by Jim Masselos

to be of suitable Rajput lineage – something that largely eliminated many princely kingdoms outside Rajasthan that did not have compatible pedigrees.

Kunverba was lucky. The Kutch family in south-western Gujarat had been looking for some time for a match for the unmarried twenty-four-year-old grandson of Khengarji III, the Maharao who had ruled since 1884. Kunverba suited their requirements as someone young enough to be moulded into the customs and behaviour of their family. So, at the age of eleven, Kunverba was betrothed into a family of appropriate lineage and one that was entitled to a nineteen-gun local and a seventeen-gun public salute. Kishangarh, on the other hand, was entitled to a lesser fifteen-gun public salute.[10] In the two years before she was formally married, she remained in Kishangarh while she was prepped for her new life, studying, among other things, the unfamiliar language, Gujarati, she would need to speak in her new home. She married two years later in 1933 at the age of thirteen.

Kunverba was delighted with the arrangement even if, as she said, she did not know what marriage meant. Nor did she know what her husband looked like – she was not shown a picture of him before her marriage, though her sisters told her he was a tennis player of some quality. He, on the other hand, was more fortunate, as his sisters did show him a small photograph of Kunverba, so he had some idea what she looked like. Kunverba's immediate reaction had less to do with her husband and more with being free of her mother's discipline, which had irked her. Her first reaction to the news that she would be married was, she said, 'Thank goodness. I'll be out of Mother's clutches.' And out of her mother's clutches she was. It was to be thirteen years after her marriage before it was possible, given her new family's constraints, for Kunverba to meet up with her mother – and this was outside Kutch when she was on a short visit to Bombay.

Part of the reason the Kutch family had selected such a young partner was, according to Kunverba, that the family wanted to ensure their customs and behaviour were continued. That she was so young meant they would be able to make sure she fitted into her new family and its ways of behaving. Because she had no close male relatives, there was no one who could keep an eye out for her and take her away from the family on short holidays or visits. Other possible Rajput princesses from other families were a few years older than Kunverba, around seventeen or eighteen, had brothers to take care of them and were already indoctrinated with the somewhat freer life their families led. They were already too progressive for Kutch.

None of this mattered to Kunverba, who was excited by all that was happening to her. In 1933, when she was ready for marriage, her husband-to-be and other male members of the Kutch family travelled to Kishangarh for a marriage ceremony and then escorted her away from what had been her home. On the journey she was constantly in purdah so that she was always secluded and travelled in enclosed rooms and compartments behind drawn curtains. Although she might perhaps have cautiously peeked through the curtains to get a sense of what was passing by, being in purdah meant she should not be seen publicly at all and certainly not by any men. The journey was extended – Kishangarh being landlocked and in the northern part of Rajasthan while Kutch was in Gujarat on the sea coast to the south-west – and to get her there was a complicated undertaking though it was a journey that excited her. In turn, she travelled by palanquin, train, ship and palanquin again to her new home in Bhuj, the capital of the kingdom and the place of its palaces.[11] Once there, other grand ceremonies and rituals were performed and another marriage ceremony took place. After the ceremonies were over, she moved into her own apartment in the palace *zenana* (the part exclusively for women) alongside other royal women with their own separate apartments. All of them lived away from public gaze and away also from the sight of any male member of the family apart from their own husbands. Looking back on her life in the *zenana* she summarised the experience: 'I never felt trapped ... one got used to it.' The fact that in Kishangarh her own mother had been in purdah, removed from any public or male gaze, and that in Kutch her mother-in-law and grandmother-in-law were also both in purdah beside her meant that she saw it working as 'a sort of system'. And she was always careful in our conversations to point out that the Kutch family were good people and were good to her. As for her experience of the marriage itself and arriving in Kutch, she recalled:

> I was just like a little girl, everything was so new. I couldn't think of anything ... very serious. I was just taking in what was happening. ... Well I was in a way excited and in a way, we were told not to get too much, too excited, we have to take it very calmly, everything that comes to you. You can't just yell, or you can't just show your happiness, We are told from childhood not to laugh loud, not to cry loud, not to do this loud ... I was enjoying everything, everything was new to me which I didn't expect. I didn't expect all this. I had never seen any weddings before. ... My sisters had got married when I was very small. And there was no wedding in the Kishangarh family so I had nothing to learn from.

The Kutch family attitude to tradition and Kunverba's place in it is summed up in an anecdote about her grandmother-in-law:

> She gave me her cup of tea. She had drunk half, and she said, 'Look, this is my tea and I'm giving it to you. You keep up the tradition of the house and the tradition of the Rajput ladies. Don't let me down ever.' So still when there's certain things to do I always think, 'What would she have thought' or 'She wouldn't like me doing this.' And I still put up with many things, and I have put up in life [with] so many things which were not right because of her.

Life in the *zenana* had its particular requirements, both for Kunverba and for her husband. The tradition of the house, as exercised through her mother-in-law and grandmother-in-law, was that proper clothing be worn always in the *zenana*. For Kunverba, that meant wearing a sari instead of the long skirts she had worn as a young girl. On special ceremonial occasions, the saris were so heavy with precious metals woven into them that she needed help to get about. And when there were male members of the family present, she would be completely covered and would need someone to navigate her around the space as she could not see where she was going. Her grandfather-in-law, Maharao Khengarji III, and her father-in-law, Vijayarajji, who was then the *Yuvraj* or Crown

Prince, did not ever see her face, and when she did come out of purdah some decades on, they had already passed away. She, on the other hand, could at least see her male in-laws by peeping through curtains from rooms above the meeting place. Despite her lack of visibility she maintained contact with the men of the family and every day would send her grandfather-in-law, the Maharao, her greetings, and he would, in turn, send a reply to her through her grandmother or mother-in-law. So there was contact of a kind between them, and care and concern for her, even if there were no meetings or conversation as such. The Maharao always knew what was happening in his palace and among his people. Part of his information came from a daily meeting with his wife, Kunverba's grandmother-in-law. Every morning she would visit him for an hour or so, around 6.30. They would not meet again during the day: 'She had her own life, and he had his own. ... So they stopped being together many years before I came.'

The entry to the *zenana* area in the palace compound was signalled by a 'big huge gate with a red curtain'. Beyond it, the three women, Kunverba, her mother-in-law, and her grandmother-in-law each had their own quarters, and therefore they each had a degree of independence. The geography of the space, however, was such that entry to Kunverba's apartments was through her grandmother-in-law's space. To ensure that propriety was observed, a eunuch, Miya Sahib, who Kunverba thought was probably Arabian, guarded the entrance to Kunverba's apartments. He had his own quarters, presumably a small room, beside the entrance and so was always present. At night, Kunverba said, he would get drunk and melancholic.

It was not only Kunverba who had to be dressed appropriately when in or moving around the *zenana*. Similar rules applied to all who had access to it: 'Even the little babies had to have bonnets on their heads', and even her children as toddlers had to wear a cap or a turban when they came into the *zenana*. 'They just couldn't go with their bare head. Bare head was considered not decent. ... Even the doctors when they visited had to wear a turban.'

Though he was second in succession to the throne, the formality even applied to her husband. He would go out to play tennis early in the morning and would then come back through the *zenana* in his tennis shorts. The royal women, his mother and grandmother, objected and demanded he change before he could come into the *zenana*. According to Kunverba, 'Even he had to wear a long coat, a long pant, wear a turban on his head to come in the *zenana*. He just couldn't walk in just like that.' This was sufficiently irksome for her husband that he decided they would move to a smaller palace in the gardens of the palace. There he no longer had to worry about the informality of tennis shorts. However, to maintain contact with her in-laws, Kunverba made it a practice every evening at five o'clock to go and visit her mother-in-law and then separately her grandmother-in-law.

Apart from husbands, who, of course, had access to their wives or children to their mothers, or the male doctor when needed for consultations, only women were allowed into the *zenana* area. Restrictions applied even for women who entered from outside the palace in that they needed to satisfy the standards of propriety expected of the Kutch family. There was no suggestion of the impropriety that was the subject of gossip in regard to one or two of the other princely houses elsewhere in India. And in Kutch only on festive days were women from 'a certain [upper] class of women' in the town allowed in. Strictly excluded from the palace entirely were 'the dancing girls and others [presumably of lesser repute]'.

> The [Kutch] menfolk were very straightforward. They didn't have these kept wives and concubines and all that kind of [thing]. So that way it was very good in those days. Neither my grandfather-in-law had, nor my father-in-law had [such women, and] there was no question about my husband, he was too young.

So those who entered the palace had to be 'respectable people', but they came to satisfy their curiosity.

> Oh, it was a great honour to them, to come and see us and see our jewels and what we were dressed in, how we were sitting and how beautiful we looked or whether we were ugly, or who was fairer than the other. It was a sort of, like present day you know, actors and actresses, how people flock to see them. And that is how these people used to come and flock. They all [said] 'Oh today she is wearing red and last time she wore pink and yellow.'

While such occasions were relatively informal, there were also occasions in the *zenana* which were fully formal and paralleled the male durbar, the formal sighting of the ruler and his relatives by subordinate nobles and lords. The *zenana* could also be the site for a formal gathering, perhaps in honour of a special birthday or other event. As Kunverba described it:

> A lady from the palace would go the day before and invite the women to attend a celebration for His Highness' birthday the next day. The state would send bullock cart vehicles, and the women would come all packed together in those covered carts, so that the women were able to observe purdah. Then we would feed them, they would have their lunch in the palace and in the evening we would have songs and dances.

THE MAHARANI OF KUTCH AND COURTLY LIFE

Despite the singing and the dancing to music provided by women performers, these occasions had serious implications as much for the royal women as for the ladies who were brought in. They asserted the existence of precedence among the royals and reminded those who were not royal of their carefully apportioned places. Kunverba's description of the detail of what went on in these gatherings illustrates the point:

> We ladies used to hold a durbar, and my grandmother[-in-law], senior people used to sit on a thick sort of a mattress, white ... with a cushion at the back. And we, the daughter-in-laws [sic], would sit on carpets, embroidered ... carpets. Each one would have their own square, in line. First my mother-in-law would sit, then myself, then my court, then some other family member, like that, and they all had, we all had our places. And the girls of the family would be sitting on [the mattress] or even a low silver chair ... the daughters used to sit on that ... only the daughters and the senior members of the family. My grandmother used to sit [on it] but not even my mother-in-law [would do so] ... We would all be sitting on those ... carpets. ... We were all sitting in a line ... with our backs to the wall ... and all these people would come and naturally greet my grandmother-in-law, the senior members. They would all greet us. ... And they would be in the front ... and after greeting they would sit down and talk.
>
> People who were senior officers, they were officers' wives who would come and sit just next, just in front of us. ... Others would be at the back. And there was a section where the Mahommedan [Muslim] families used to sit and [others for] our [distant] relations and rich merchants' wives.

This is not much different from the kind of durbar a prince might hold to ensure the loyalty and support of his nobles. The spatial elements present in the *zenana* durbars echoed the kind of spatial separation inherent in the male ceremonial. Central in the *zenana* seating map was the Maharani, the wife of the Maharao and Kunverba's grandmother-in-law. Positioned close to the Rani were princesses of the royal Kutch line. They sat apart from the daughters-in-law who were not, of course, of the Kutch lineage, even though their childbearing role would ensure the continuance of the line. A signal of the difference in standing was that the new wives who came into the Kutch family quickly acquired nicknames derived from their home kingdom, signalling that they were considered not yet fully part of the kingdom of their husbands. Kunverba was thus Kishangarh Walle: the woman from Kishangarh. She had largely lost the name by the time she became Maharani, and any slighting suggestion of her external origins had certainly disappeared when she became Raj Mata (or Queen Mother) in 1991. By then she was, after all, the senior-most royal of the line. While such durbars acknowledged the facts of lineage, they were much more about interacting with various parts of Kutch society, reinforcing loyalty to the kingdom and cohesion between its various sectors. In addition, by providing occasions for the various princesses to interact with other women, the durbars broke down some of the isolation of the *zenana* and seem to have been so enjoyed by them. On some occasions they may have been little more than a relaxed party or social gathering.

For Kunverba, as for the other royal Kutch women, most of their lives were spent inside the *zenana*. Even when they travelled outside their kingdoms, purdah had to be observed. Kunverba's experience on first making the long journey from Bhuj through Gujarat to Bombay was of being in 'strict purdah'. The car she travelled in had 'curtains or black, dark glasses. Even in Bombay I wasn't allowed to go to any shops. Everything was brought to me, whatever I wanted to see.' But, in comparison with the existence she later led in Bombay in the 1980s and perhaps earlier, she would become nostalgic: 'Sometimes when shopping in the city now I think that would be a good thing ... because if I was in purdah everything would have been done for me. ... We didn't have to do anything for ourselves.' And, she added, 'I never felt trapped' in the *zenana*. Yet when her cousins called on her when she was on one of her early visits to Bombay, she found her social life was restricted to meetings and meals in the afternoon and evening but not at night, and there were no late dinners for her. This, of course, gave the young princes the nights in which to enjoy themselves as prudently as they wished. Likewise, there were limitations on her movements when she was in Bombay. If she wanted to watch a movie, for instance, it had to be showing in a cinema that had a curtained purdah area at the back from which she could safely look through the curtain and see the movie and enjoy herself. When it was over, she would wait a while till the audience had dispersed, and then she would walk through a curtained passage out to her waiting car.

Out of purdah

Kunverba travelled overseas to Europe with her husband, who had joined the Indian Foreign Service and had a posting in India's London mission as Honorary Minister from 1953 to 1956.[12] She stayed there for three years, living freely out of purdah, but when she came back to Bombay, she was immediately returned to her assigned place in the customary structures of social behaviour. Her experience on arriving at Bombay airport was a return to the past:

> But as soon as I came back again Miya Sahib [her eunuch door-keeper] would be there with the *zenana* purdah car. And from the plane I would walk straight into the purdah car. The car used to come right up to the plane. And I would just get into it so that nobody sees me.

And there was a simple answer to the question of how she felt when she saw the purdah car: 'Well, I thought it was old, old custom. You just couldn't feel anything much about all these things.'

Old customs, as far as she was concerned, finally went in 1953. It was a time when everything seemed to be changing. India became independent in August 1947, and Kutch acceded to the Indian Union and was one of the first princely states to so accede. Kunverba's husband, Madansinhji, became Maharao on the death of his father in January 1948, and his reign ended on 1 June 1948. Along with it ended the Jadeja dynasty's rule over Kutch. Kutch thereupon came under the direct administration of the government of India in Delhi, as what was known as a Part C chief commissioner's state.[13] This meant that Kutch would be governed by a chief commissioner appointed by the Congress government in Delhi. The second incumbent was Sambhajirao Appasaheb Ghatge, who served from 1952 to 1956. His wife was active in supporting welfare causes in the state, much as the wives of British residents, heads of districts and other important officials had done in the days of British rule. She was popular in Kutch, and Kunverba thought her 'very nice and educated and very capable'. On one occasion in 1953, she buttonholed Kunverba's husband, the Maharao, and told him it was time the Maharani joined in the social work she was doing. He was placed in a situation he could not easily back out of, and

> so my husband couldn't say so, he didn't like it but he couldn't say so. He said, 'Of course, of course, if you think so and if you will take her out I have no objection.' So then there was a function ... and I had to do an opening ceremony of an exhibition of Kutch ... arts and crafts. And I did the opening ceremony and read my first speech on the loudspeaker which I found very funny. But anyway I did it, that and I came out. ... Hundreds of people came to see me, what I looked like, because they hadn't seen me ... the men came ... there were more men [than ladies] to see me ... everybody after that, all the family came out of purdah that day ... my sister-in-laws [sic] and all.

The liberating sweep meant that the women of the court 'all sort of dropped' purdah. But, as for Kunverba, the moment did not last. Her husband insisted that when she went into town she should go in the *zenana* car; in other words, she was again restrained in her movement and actions. What changed the situation happened unexpectedly. It centred on the President of India, Dr S. Radhakrishnan, who had come to Kutch to lay the foundation stone for a medical college in Bhuj and was staying as a guest of the royal family in their palace. Kunverba was waiting in the morning ready to go to the ceremony separately. Radhakrishnan saw her and, assuming she was to travel with him, invited her to enter his car, and she did so, getting in before him, the President. She explained that he said to her:

> 'Madam, you first.' So I looked at my husband to sort of see what shall I do, because I knew he didn't much approve of all these things. So he said, 'Come, get in.' So then I got in. That was the final break of purdah. ... Radhakrishnan ... wasn't at all aware [of what he was doing]. He was a very polite and clever man. ... He just did it naturally. He didn't think I would be in purdah. That is how I got rid of my purdah.

The new freedom was somewhat mixed, and the Maharani admitted on several occasions during our conversations there were times when she regretted what had gone: 'I was much happier living in that world [the world of purdah] than now I am to face my own difficulties. ... I have to take decisions; I have to take much more trouble. At that time everything was done for me.' She was philosophical about the mix of elements in her life: 'happiness and unhappiness are together. ... These are little things in life you know, joy and sorrow, they keep on coming.'

But over the years from the time when she married to when she came out, there had been subtle and not so subtle changes in the way she was perceived in Kutch and with changes to her public role. In purdah, she had had a definite role, a particular place in the life of the kingdom and one that was affirmed once she had children. Her relative position in the family hierarchy also altered over time. Successively she had proceeded from being granddaughter-in-law, daughter-in-law and Crown Princess, Maharani and, in her final years, Queen Mother. Her positioning changed in 1942 when her grandfather-in-law, Khengarji III, passed away after reigning for sixty-eight years, and it changed again when her father-in-law, Vijayarajji, died early in 1948 after a brief reign of six years, and Madansinhji became Maharao and Kunverba Maharani.

Madansinhji handled the state's accession to the Indian Union, and when the state was absorbed into it on 1 June 1948, he formally brought to an end the 400 years of Jadeja rule over Kutch. There was some slight compensation for the Kutch lineage as there equally was for the other princes who throughout India were giving or were about to give up their territories to the new nation in the months after 1947. What the royals received in compensation was an annual privy purse, and they were allowed to retain their status and titles, a right taken from them by Prime Minister Indira Gandhi in 1971. As for Madansinhji, he served as a diplomat in Europe for the new government and died in 1991, and their son assumed the title Maharao Pragmulji III. In consequence, Kunverba became Queen Mother. Her status then was considerably different from what it had been when she had come to Bhuj as a somewhat unpopular outsider, a very young foreigner, whose duty was to provide heirs and ensure the continuation of the lineage. This she had done; giving the royal family three sons and two daughters meant that she had satisfied the requirements of her position and the expectations that went with her marriage.

Not only had she fulfilled her duty, but she had developed a persona – she had become a recognisable figure. This had not been the case in the days of purdah, when, if she had gone driving in the countryside or visited a village, the people who saw her would not know who she was: 'They wouldn't recognise me so much. ... [We] used to be in the flag car and my driver used to be in a *saffar* [a form of headgear] and Miya Sahib would be in the headgear. So they would all know that I was somebody from the royal family.'

They may have realised she was from the royal family on such occasions, and, as such, she symbolised royalty and the royal family. But people did not know who she was, and in those years they had no way of knowing what she looked like. When she moved around the kingdom she did not do so as a known person with her own identity and character, and her face and her features were not familiar. Instead, she was marked and identified as royal only by the kingdom's regalia – and not by her physical presence. She had been accessible in the *zenana*, and some women in those days might come and consult her privately, but that was about it. After she came out, and after the changeover to independence and Kutch's absorption into India, she acquired a visible and tangible persona among many of the state's citizens. As she moved from being Maharani to Rani Mata, how she was perceived had altered. Ironically, she had become much more a public figure as an important part of the ruling family, and she was recognised as such. More women from the villages came to her for advice on all sorts of matters, even on problems like whether they should sell their silver or gold or not, or which doctor they should go to. She became more popular out of purdah and away from the *zenana* durbars than she had been or could have been from within. And the fact that by then she was the oldest surviving senior royal earned her regard and respect.

In her later years, she said,

> even now the people who come to me come with great respect and they treat me like a goddess, they come and do the *aarti* [the waving of a flame] and the *agarbati* [the burning of incense sticks] and all, and I just close my eyes and sit. I am nobody, just why, I don't know why they do it. I tell them not to do it, but if it is their wish I let them do it. They say you are, you are the mother. We want to worship you.

Increasingly, as Ranima or Rani Mata people sought her out for advice, and many came also to take her *darshan*. Many of those who called on her came from Kutch and particularly from the Kutch clan, the Jadeja, but as she got older she became less familiar a personality:

> Now people don't recognise [us], first everybody used to do the greetings and pay respects to us. As soon as our flag car came everybody would stand up if they were sitting and they would fold their hands. But now nobody knows. New people [and] so many of outsiders have come to Kutch they don't know these customs. ... [O]nly people who know us do it.

Late in her life, when I asked her whether she was still Kishangarh Walle, her answer was unambiguous: 'No, no more Kishangarh Walle ... I'm a grandmother now, I belong totally to Kutch.'

Notes

1 See 'Queen Victoria's Proclamation, 1 November 1858', in C. H. Philips with the co-operation of H. L. Singh and B. N. Pandey, *The Evolution of India and Pakistan, 1858 to 1947: Select Documents* (London: Oxford University Press, 1962), p. 10.
2 Ian Copland, *The Princes of India in the Endgame of Empire, 1917–1947* (Cambridge: Cambridge University Press, 2002), pp. 20, 1.
3 See, for instance, Douglas E. Haynes, 'Imperial Ritual in a Local Setting: The Ceremonial Order in Surat, 1890–1939', *Modern Asian Studies*, 24:3 (1990), 493–527.
4 J. Masselos, 'The Great Durbar Crowds: The Participant Audience', in Julie F. Codell (ed.), *Power and Resistance: The Delhi Coronation Durbars, 1877, 1903, 1911* (Delhi: Alkazi Collection of Photography and Mapin Publishing, 2012), pp. 176–203, and see also the other essays in the volume.
5 From the original religious usage of *darshan* as 'auspicious viewing' of a deity or religious teacher, the term has expanded its applicability to the social and political spheres where it has extended connotations apart from the religious. See the *Encyclopaedia Britannica* definition of *darshan*: 'in Hindu worship, the beholding of a deity (especially in image form), revered person, or sacred object. The experience is often conceived to be reciprocal and results in the human viewer's receiving a blessing.' See www.britannica.com/EBchecked/topic/151828/darshan (accessed 10 May 2015).
6 For a survey of the history of the kingdom, see Azhar Tyabji, *Bhuj: Art, Architecture, History* (Ahmedabad: Mapin, 2006), pp. 19–72. For basic statistics about the state at the end of the 1940s and early 1950s, see S. H. Steinberg (ed.), *The Statesman's Year-Book* (London: Macmillan, 1955), p. 195.
7 The tapes have been digitised; one set is with the royal family and another is with the author. It is proposed to make them the basis for a fuller account of her life and attitudes than is possible in this chapter.
8 See, for instance, Elaine Williams, *Maharani: Memoirs of a Rebellious Princess* (Delhi: Rupa, 2003); Lucy Moore, *Maharanis: The Lives and Times of Three Generations of Indian Princesses* (London: Viking, 2004); Gayatri Devi and Santha Rama Rau, *A Princess Remembers: The Memoirs of the Maharani of Jaipur* (Philadelphia, Pa.: Lippincott, 1976); Jarmani Dass and Rakesh Bhan Dass, *Maharani: Love Adventures of Indian Maharanis and Princesses* (Delhi: S. Chand, 1972); and Coralie Younger, *Wicked Women of the Raj* (Delhi: Harper Collins, 2005).
9 The classic account of these paintings is one of the earliest: Eric Dickinson and Karl Khandalavala, *Kishangarh Painting* (New Delhi: Lalit Kalā Akademi, 1959).

10 The number of guns in a salute provided a way for the British government to rank the princely states. It used the system to recognise particularly helpful rajas and reward them by increasing their entitlement to gun salutes. Kutch had a hereditary external salute of seventeen guns and a local salute of nineteen. As Kishangarh's hereditary salute was fifteen guns, what was indicated was that Kutch was higher in ranking and that Kunverba had moved up in princely familial status rating.
11 For a visual record of the journey of the marriage party and external parts of the wedding, see the film by V. C. Steer-Webster, *Wedding of Maharaj Kumar Shri Meghrajji Shaeb of Kutch and Maharaj Shri of Kishangarh, 1933* (UK, 1933). This is a 32-minute documentary held by the British Film Institute (BFI) Archives in London at ID61289. See http://explore.bfi.org.uk/4ce2b9fc48d3a (accessed 6 May 2015). The BFI synopsis describes the film as 'Amateur footage of the wedding scenes, including, arrival of the Indian princes by yacht and train; the Dandia Ras [Gujarati dance with sticks], ritual sword dance; fuleka [or phuleka] procession of Princes [and bridegroom proceeding ceremonially to his marriage]; state katchery [office of administration]; garden parties and fireworks and the ceremonies of the wedding'.
12 See L. F. Rushbrook Williams, 'A Glimpse of Princely India', in *The Spectator Archive*, 22 March 1957, p. 5.
13 For genealogical details of the dynasty, see, among other websites, 'Cutch5: The Jadeja dynasty. Genealogy'. Available online at www.royalark.net/India/cutch5.htm (accessed 10 May 2015).

CHAPTER TEN

Colonies, monarchy, empire and the French *ancien régime*

François-Joseph Ruggiu

In 1765, the instructions given by the Secrétaire d'État de la Marine to the Comte d'Ennery and Président de Peynier, respectively governor and *intendant* of the island of Martinique, asserted: 'One would be strangely misled in considering our colonies as provinces of France simply separated by the sea from the homeland.' And the instructions continued: 'They differ from the provinces as much as the means does from the end. They are only commercial outposts.'[1] This declaration, which bluntly acknowledged the problem of territorial continuity or discontinuity for an early modern state, points to a complex and, at the time, growing debate: were the French colonies a part of the Kingdom of France and, if not, what were they? At the heart of this question, which was repeated at different moments of the early modern period, lies the problem of the constitutional and political relations between the French Crown and the French colonies. Was every overseas territory automatically a colony? Did the existence of overseas territories automatically make an empire?

To answer these questions, three working hypotheses have been advanced. The first is that the imperial framework of the nineteenth and twentieth centuries must not be projected onto the overseas expansion of France during the seventeenth and eighteenth centuries. Historiography about the French colonial empire of the early modern period is split into two rather distinct views. In present-day French historiography, the term 'empire' is commonly used in order to refer to all the French colonial possessions during the early modern era.[2] The continuity between the colonial territories of the seventeenth and eighteenth centuries and the empire of the nineteenth and twentieth centuries is postulated rather than explained. Conversely, anglophone historians have discussed the nature of the French Empire, and they tend to call into question the very idea of a coherent French empire.[3] They express doubts about a constant interest and a real involvement of the French Crown in its overseas possessions. And they also tend to minimise the coherence and the consistency of the policy inaugurated by Colbert and developed by his successors. Indeed, nothing is obvious about the overused notion of a 'first French colonial empire', neither its extent or composition, nor its origins or imperial nature.

The second working hypothesis follows the Canadian historian Helen Dewar, who has recently reminded us that the formation of the Bourbon state during the seventeenth century and the expansion of the French overseas territories were parallel and not successive phenomena.[4] The establishment of the French colonial domination was not the result of the projection of a fully constituted royal power beyond the seas but was part of a wider political and social process that included, among other things, the enforcement of royal authority on the kingdom, the evolution of the relations between Crown and grandees and the clarification of the place of Protestants in the kingdom. This is all the more important in that the historiography of the period has evolved significantly over the past forty years with a reassessment of the practical enforcement of absolutism by the Bourbon kings and, consequently, of the political struggles and the military revolts of the first half of the seventeenth century.[5] These are no longer seen as the last struggles of a declining feudal aristocracy against the endeavours of a rising bureaucratic and a modern state but rather as a common rebuilding of the respective roles of the Crown and of the noble and urban elites.

The third hypothesis is that it is important to consider together all the overseas enterprises of the French during the early modern period and especially during the seventeenth century. Scholars' attention has traditionally focused on America and, more exactly, on New France or on the French West Indies, which were at the heart of the French colonial domain and the main sources of its wealth during the eighteenth century.[6] But French colonisation during the seventeenth century was multifaceted and included besides New France numerous enterprises in Brazil (Fort Coligny-Guanabara Bay, Maragnan-Maranhão), Florida, Guiana, West Africa, Madagascar and India. It is important not to concentrate on the 'successful' stories of French colonisation but to observe what the 'failed' ones might tell us about the French conception of colonisation.

This chapter will first sketch out the ways through which the French Crown established its sovereignty over its overseas territories, giving particular attention to the letters of commission held by the *lieutenants généraux* of the King in these parts of the world.[7] Second, it will examine the administrative and legal structure of the overseas territories in comparison to those of the French provinces. And, finally, it will reflect on how these territories came to be considered as 'colonies' by placing them within an economic framework.

How did the kings of France seize America?[8]

The complex process by which kings of France progressively established their sovereignty over lands in America, Africa or India from the early 1500s onwards, is not well known.[9] Moreover, the establishment of the royal authority overseas has often been studied from the point of view of one territory but never comprehensively and nor from the point of view of the Crown. Yet integration of new territories situated in Europe but inside the Kingdom of France was a rather common operation.[10] Like his European cousins, the King of France exerted a wide range of powers and rights on the disparate parts of his kingdom, which were different according to the way these territories had been incorporated into the kingdom.

Inside the frontiers of four rivers – the Rhône, Saone, Meuse and Scheldt – the king was the successor of the Carolingian emperor. His sovereignty was then fully acknowledged over the *domaine royal*, that is to say the lands he directly owned, as well as over the lordships (*fiefs*) held by his great vassals.[11] Outside the Carolingian limits, the sovereignty of the French king over his territories could come from conquests, from cessions inscribed in peace treaties or from acquisitions made by marriage or bequest. The king swore then to respect the freedoms and privileges of the population that came under his rule. The Comté de Provence, on the left bank of the Rhône, was thus donated in 1481 by its last ruler, Charles III, who had no legitimate heir, to the King of France, Louis XI. Consequently, in 1487, Provence was permanently united to the realm and should have remained separate from the kingdom of France albeit living under the same sovereign. But, contrary to the Hapsburgs, for example, the kings of France were little concerned with deferring to the letter of treaties. In these new parts of their kingdom, they progressively set up the same institutions as in their former possessions, especially a *parlement*, the institution that embodied the justice of the King of France.[12]

The first half of the sixteenth century saw a tremendous expansion of the kingdom of France outside its old Carolingian limits, in addition to Brittany. At one time or another, Louis XII, François I and Henri II seized Lombardy and the kingdom of Naples and ruled the states of the Duke of Savoy – Savoy and Piedmont – from 1536–37 to 1559,[13] and Corsica, from 1553 to 1559. François II also briefly exercised viceregal authority over Scotland because of his marriage to Mary Stuart, Queen of Scots. After the end of the religious wars, the process of expansion restarted as early as 1601.[14] These European extensions of the kingdom can be compared with the first French overseas enterprises, that is to say, in Canada, under Jean-François de la Rocque de Roberval and, later, of Troilus de Mesgouez de La Roche, Aymar de Chastes and Pierre Dugua de Monts. There are also parallels in Brazil, with Nicolas Durand de Villegagnon's foundation of France Antarctique during the 1550s; in Florida, under Jean Ribault during the 1560s; and, in Brazil again, with the creation of France Equinoxiale, during the 1600s, by Daniel de La Touche de La Ravadière. Their actions have rarely been studied inside this wider frame, despite the fact that some of the well-known figures associated with them, such as Villegagnon, were involved in European as well as in overseas enterprises.[15]

The first official act organising an undertaking of French overseas expansion was the letters patent delivered on 15 January 1541 to Roberval,[16] who was granted the power to establish the sovereignty of his king over Canada, either by negotiation or by conquest.[17] For this mission, he was empowered to raise and equip an army and a fleet, to take with him soldiers and colonists, to legislate and to punish or pardon rebels and criminals; and he also had the authority to appoint his own lieutenants. Roberval was said to be the *lieutenant général* of François I: he thus had a personal delegation of power from the King and had the same powers and rights as the King himself. This point was made particularly clear in another commission, issued to La Roche, in 1578, which gave him the power to 'do in the aforesaid lands and country all that he think fit for the benefit of our service and the benefit of our realm, exactly as we could do ourselves if we were present personally'.[18] This title of *lieutenant général* was also granted to the other captains who went to America, including Villegagnon, Ribault,[19] La Roche,[20] Montbarrot and La Touche de la Ravardière,[21] Aymar de Chaste and Dugua de Monts.[22]

The letters patent issued to Roberval set up a framework for the development of the French overseas territories by asserting his right to conquer and to settle overseas territories on behalf of the King of France. The French sovereignty in America ultimately derived first from the *jus belli*, a legal base which was not robust in the European context,[23] but which was firmly established overseas.[24] Historians have generally failed to notice that these texts matched *le pays de Canada et Ochelaga* with other territories in Europe. The *gouverneurs* and *lieutenants généraux* who administered the French provinces on behalf of the King received such letters patent. Inside the kingdom, such letters were usually vague and generally stated that the holder had the same powers as his predecessors. But the letters patent given to Roberval were close to those given to the King's representatives acting in recently incorporated provinces such as Milan, Naples or Savoy and Piedmont. For example, Claude d'Annebault (c. 1495–1552), made *lieutenant général* of Piedmont two years before the nomination of Roberval,[25] Giordano Ursino (or Jordan Ursin), who represented Henri II in Corsica,[26] or René de Lorraine, Marquis d'Elbeuf, who was sent to Scotland in 1560,[27] all held powers close to those of Roberval. A comparative reading of these letters patent issued by the French kings to their captains in Europe and overseas shows continuity more than a separation between the two geographical spaces. The settlement founded by Roberval did not last, nor did the integration of Savoy and Piedmont to France, or the occupation of Corsica, which were surrendered to their former masters in 1559. But the influence of the letters patent, which had been conceded to Roberval, endured.

It is all the more striking that, at the beginning of the 1600s, the French Crown intensified its efforts to seize overseas territories. On 8 May 1602, a Breton nobleman, René Marec, Seigneur de Montbarrot, received letters patent as *lieutenant général* to establish a settlement on the coast of South America. Already Governor of Rennes, and embroiled in a plot against Henri IV, he immediately shared his commission with Daniel de La Touche, Sieur de la Ravardière.[28] The King established the latter 'his lieutenant general in America from the Amazon River to the Island of Trinidad' by letters patent delivered in July 1605, and renewed in 1610[29] and again in 1624.[30] The provisions of these letters patent correspond exactly to those given to Roberval. Meanwhile, the King tried to dispense with La Roche, who did not succeed in developing a permanent settlement on the Île de Sable, off the south-east coast of Acadia, and transferred authority over his territories to Pierre Dugua de Monts, who received letters patent as *lieutenant général* on 8 November 1603, again with the same powers as Roberval.[31]

By 1610, the French Crown had changed its strategy relating to New France because of the difficulties encountered by Dugua de Monts and also as a result of the evolution of politics in France after the death of Henri IV. The ultimate responsibility to develop New France was no longer given to a captain, who was directed to cross the Atlantic to organise settlements, but to a member of the king's court. It was, thus, a member of the royal family, Charles de Bourbon, Comte de Soissons, a Catholic cousin of Henri IV, who was nominated *lieutenant général* of New France on 8 October 1612. This nomination has been underestimated in the historiography,[32] especially because he held the charge only briefly due to his untimely death on 1 November 1612. It nevertheless represents an effective evolution in the French overseas enterprises for three key reasons. The first is that Charles de Bourbon, Governor of Normandy, was already interested in maritime affairs. Through his wife, he was linked to François de Razilly, an associate of La Touche, and was involved in the preparation of the expedition of Maragnan.[33] Second, Charles de Bourbon was an opponent of the pro-Spanish policy pursued by Marie de Médicis. He particularly despised the intended marriage between Louis XIII and the Spanish Princess Anne of Austria. The *lieutenance générale* of New France would give him leverage to act against Spain in America, just as Admiral Coligny had envisioned in his efforts in the 1560s. On Charles de Bourbon's death, his nephew, Henri II de Bourbon, Prince de Condé, also a cousin of Henri IV, then received the title of *lieutenant général*,[34] and he was also one of the most vocal and active opponents of Marie de Médicis and the new head of the anti-Spanish party at the court.[35] The best proof of the importance of his overseas charge is that he was deprived of it as soon as he was arrested for having led a rebellion. The third break represented by the nomination of Charles de Bourbon is linked to the structure of French politics at the beginning of the seventeenth century. In Bourbon France, different political factions were struggling to gain, or to keep, access to power and to material rewards, which included political offices (for example, governorships), as well as commercial monopolies, or lands. These factions were organised around a leader: either a junior member of the royal family, or a principal minister and favourite of the king, or a grandee, the head of a great noble family.[36] And they were made up of client networks constituted on a familial, regional and religious basis, united by political loyalties and interests. In the political game that these factions played, and in their quest for bounties, the boundaries between public and private interests were not well defined. From the 1610s, and following the nomination of Charles de Bourbon, positions of influence in overseas territories, like other plums in the kingdom, became stakes in the wider French political and religious game. The overseas territories, once the terrain of adventurers or rugged soldiers, began to move towards the heart of the early modern state.

A further step in this direction came in 1620, when Condé transferred his commission to Henri II (1595–1632), Duke of Montmorency, heir to one of the major noble houses in the kingdom, who held it until 1625. It is worth noting that the charge he received had been upgraded during the 1610s. In 1578, Troilus de Mesgouez de La Roche had been briefly said to be 'viceroy of the aforesaid new lands and countries that he will seize and conquer'. As far as we know, this was the first and only time that such a title appeared in the overseas context during the sixteenth century. But the viceregal title disappeared from the commission issued in 1598 by Henri IV, perhaps because it was too prestigious for a plain nobleman or perhaps because it was dangerous to accord such a dignity too freely. So although Dugua de Monts claimed the title in 1603, he did not receive it.[37] The viceregal title re-emerged in the 1610s when the *lieutenance générale* was held by a powerful courtier and when the Crown, weakened by aristocratic rebellions, needed to attract loyalty. The original letters patent delivered to Henri de Condé did not make him a viceroy, but the letters patent temporarily transferring his charge to Pons de Lauzières de Cardaillac, Marquis de Thémines and Maréchal de France, who had arrested Condé, and gave him the 'dignity and title of vice-roy and our lieutenant-general throughout the said country'.[38] When Montmorency received the title, the viceroyalty and *lieutenance générale* of New France was not at all an honorary position but gave to the holder the duty to license French undertakings in those parts of the world and a stake in the economic exploitation of the territories placed under his authority.

The management of overseas territories was thus characteristic of the organisation of the French state during the first decades of the seventeenth century with its strengths and weaknesses. The authority of the *lieutenants généraux*, and of their lieutenants in the field, was never uncontested because of the constant overlap of powers, rights and competencies. As Helen Dewar has shown, royal office-holders, such as an *Amiral de France*, or regional courts, especially *parlements* and admiralties in provinces such as Guyenne, Normandy or Brittany, were often upset to see their own authority superseded by those of the *lieutenants généraux* and sometimes helped the many merchants who were excluded from the overseas trade gain access to it through litigation. To overcome these difficulties, Henri de Montmorency tried to concentrate in his hands several responsibilities linked to maritime affairs: he had been appointed Amiral de France in 1612, on the death of his uncle, Charles de Montmorency, Duc de Damville, and then became viceroy of New France in 1620.

By the mid-1620s, Cardinal de Richelieu pushed to its limits the pattern established ten years before, and, coming from a family from western France deeply interested in America,[39] and following the advice of several of his councillors who specialised in overseas affairs,[40] he took three key steps. First, he centralised in his hands authority over French maritime affairs by assuming the office of Grand Maître, Chef et Surintendant Général de la Navigation et Commerce de France [Grand Master, Chief and Superintendent General of French Navigation and Commerce] created by Louis XIII in October 1626.[41] He abolished competing positions, including the Amiral de France hitherto held by Henri de Montmorency. And the title of 'Viceroy of America' was given to a loyalist, Henri de Lévis (1596–1651), Duc de

Ventadour, who was not an opponent of the cardinal's policies. Second, Richelieu set up the same kind of commercial companies as his predecessors but gave them stronger support from the State. And, third, he extended the reach of the French Crown to the Caribbean, while trying at the same time to pursue the development of Acadia and the St Lawrence River valley.

On 31 October 1626, the cardinal gathered at his residence the associates of the Compagnie des Îles de l'Amérique to negotiate a private contract.[42] The company, under Pierre Belain d'Esnambuc,[43] was to bring goods from Saint-Christophe (St Kitts) and surrounding islands to Le Havre. Richelieu personally invested 10,000 *livres tournois*, with Antoine Coeffier de Ruzé (1581–1632), Marquis d'Effiat, a client of Richelieu, then Surintendant des Finances, subscribing 2,000 *livres* and Isaac Martin, Sieur de Mauvoy, Secrétaire Ordinaire de la Marine, contributing the same sum. The very same day, Richelieu, as Grand Maître et Surintendant du Commerce de France, issued an official commission to Belain d'Esnambuc and Urbain du Roissey to colonise and to exploit these islands and ordered all civil servants and officers under his authority to aid them in this endeavour.

The process of creating the Compagnie de la Nouvelle-France followed exactly the same pattern a year later.[44] On 29 April 1627, in his own house, Richelieu supervised the drawing up by six partners of a project called *Articles accordés par le roi à la Compagnie de la Nouvelle-France*. The same day, a notarial deed certified that Richelieu and his partners had agreed on the project. On 7 May of the same year, the associates, now 100 in number, at least nominally, gathered again at Richelieu's residence to write and sign the *Articles et Conventions de Société et Compagnie* and committed themselves to respecting its provisions. Richelieu was the first to sign the act of accession to the company, followed by the Marquis d'Effiat and Isaac Martin. One year later, on 6 May 1628, the King transformed this private contract into an official *édit* (edict), and on 18 May Richelieu ordered all civil servants and officers under his authority to provide assistance to the company. This model was repeatedly used until the 1660s to sustain the French expansion. For example, letters patent dated 29 January 1642, which were granted to Jean Rigault, from Dieppe, gave him the power to take possession of the island of Madagascar in the name of the King, the right to settle colonists there and a commercial monopoly for the trade with the island for him and the associates of the Compagnie de l'Orient for ten years.[45] In light of this, it is clear that Richelieu innovated less than he improved the policy of his predecessors, but it is nevertheless certain that he put the colonies at the heart of the royal state.

Who holds French America?

The letters patent issued to Roberval instructed him to establish in New France the sovereignty of the King of France, which derived from the right of conquest. François I, like his successors, was also keen to respect the terms of the agreement that France had reached with the Pope in 1533. Clement VII at that time had acknowledged that Alexander VI's bull of 1493, which gave rights to Spain and Portugal over unconquered lands, applied only to 'known continents not to territories subsequently discovered by other powers'.[46] His letters patent made clear that Roberval should not infringe on the lands owned and peopled by the King of Spain. He was mandated to be the conqueror and the administrator of the new overseas territory for the King, but nothing was said about his own relation to the lands taken over. He was nevertheless allowed to keep one-third of the profits made during the enterprise, the hope being strong that gold and silver would flow from the conquered territories. Meanwhile, the letters patent issued to La Roche in 1577 gave him full property rights in the territories he would conquer, but, as we have seen with the title of viceroy, this gift did not last. In 1598, the terms of his last letters patent came back to those granted to Roberval and did not subsequently change.[47] The land thus belonged to the King and was administered by a *lieutenant général*, as with the other parts of his kingdom.

To encourage his followers, François I gave Roberval the authority to carve out, in the lands under royal sovereignty, *fiefs* and lordships for *seigneurs*, and tenures for commoners. La Roche was endowed with the same power, as was René Marec, Seigneur de Montbarrot, but Dugua de Monts received only the right to give away parts of the lands placed under his authority.[48] In these matters, as in others, Richelieu did not establish an entirely new relationship between the Crown and its overseas territories but nevertheless went a step further in that direction. In 1627, the Compagnie de la Nouvelle-France received the 'property, justice and lordship' of New France with the right to create lordships and to distribute the land.[49] As overlord of the land, the king retained only the fealty and homage for the territory with the obligation for its owners to pay a token duty on the accession of a new king. As early as 1605, the Crown also acknowledged that goods imported from New France were exempt from customs duties because the region constituted a territory dependent on the kingdom of France.[50] Richelieu again pushed to its limits the logic of the framework established for Roberval: the territory being firmly established by right of conquest in the King's hands, the Crown was now able to give it to a lord.

The same process occurred in the Caribbean as in New France but at a more rapid pace. In 1626, Belain d'Esnambuc had only been charged with the duty to 'hold the aforesaid islands under the king's authority and power and to bring the inhabitants to the obedience of the king'. On 12 February 1635, the second version of the Compagnie des Îles de l'Amérique accorded it the same extended rights as the Compagnie de la Nouvelle-France, including the ownership of the islands and the power to allocate lands.[51] In both cases, the King kept for himself only the appointments of judges as well as fealty and homage, and he pledged to deliver letters patent commissioning the governor and *lieutenant général* to those designated by the companies.[52] Overseas territories were thus placed within the framework of feudalism, which provided, notwithstanding the rise of the modern state, a useful structure and language for the expression of power.

During the 1640s, the difficulties of the Thirty Years' War and the period of the civil disorders called the *Fronde* captured the full attention of the government and dissociated the Crown from its distant possessions. In the early years of the decade, the heavily indebted Compagnie de la Nouvelle-France was obliged to delegate its rights to a *communauté des habitants*, composed of the principal settlers of New France. At the same time, the Compagnie des Îles de l'Amérique was forced to sell its islands to different lord-proprietors (*seigneurs-propriétaires*), who therefore acquired Martinique (Charles Houel), Guadeloupe (Dyel du Parquet, who also bought St Lucia and Grenada) and Saint-Christophe (Order of St John of Jerusalem or Order of Malta).[53] But the changes to overseas lords did not alter the relationships between the territories and the king, who remained the supreme authority. In 1664, the personal power of Louis XIV being firmly entrenched, the system of companies operating under a legal monopoly reached its climax with the creation of the Compagnie Française des Indes Occidentales. On 27 February 1663, the associates of the Compagnie de la Nouvelle-France had voluntarily ceded the proprietorship and lordship of New France to the king. Meanwhile, an order of the French Conseil d'État, on 17 April 1664, ordered the proprietors of the Caribbean islands formerly ceded by the Compagnie des Îles de l'Amérique to sell them back to the Crown. The lot was merged and handed on to a new Compagnie Française des Indes Occidentales, which again received the property, lordship and justice of all the French possessions in America. As in the 1620s, the king kept only the fealty and homage, together with the power to nominate governors-general and particular governors, who were chosen and presented to the king by the company.

However, this broad delegation of power given to the company created in 1664 should not mislead us since the overall context had changed. Whatever the status of the overseas territories, the Crown readily proceeded to establish the same political institutions there as in the metropole, in a similar way as when it tried to secure its grip on the lordships reintegrated to the *domaine royal*, or on the foreign provinces newly united to the kingdom.[54] In April 1663, the first action of the Crown, as soon as the Compagnie de la Nouvelle-France had been disbanded, was to reform the justice system in this territory and to create a *conseil souverain* (later called *conseil supérieur*), which played the role of an overseas *parlement*. Then the Crown dispatched a *lieutenant général*, Alexandre Prouville de Tracy, whose powers extended from Guiana in South America to New France in North America, and who acted as the direct representative of the king in Guiana, the French West Indies and New France. The first royal *intendant* nominated in America, Louis Robert, a member of the powerful Le Tellier family, received his *lettres de provisions* as Intendant of New France as early as 21 March 1663. Progressively the overseas territories came to be administered, with some differences, by the same diarchy as the French provinces with a governor and *lieutenant général*, who held all military authority, and a part of the civilian authority, and the *intendant* (or a *commissaire-ordonnateur* in the less important colonies), who held the primary civilian authority, particularly in financial matters. The last step of this process arrived when, faced with the commercial failure of the new company, Louis XIV and his minister Colbert brought about its disappearance in December 1674. At this stage, all the French overseas territories in America, including Guiana, were reincorporated into the *domaine royal* from which they had been removed forty years before.[55]

From overseas territories to colonies

If the French overseas territories were so clearly conceived as a part of the kingdom, what made them 'colonial' and, ultimately, susceptible to comments such as those uttered by Choiseul in 1765?[56] We must now, to conclude our analysis, examine more closely the clauses concerning the commercial regulations of the French presence in newly conquered parts of the world. In 1541, François I forbade his subjects (though for military reasons more than for commercial ones), who were not part of the army raised by Roberval, to go to Canada and to interfere with his actions there. The letters patent delivered to La Roche in 1577 and 1578 did not mention anything along similar lines, but this problem came to the fore in 1588 when the *état* (assembly) of Brittany echoed the claims of the merchants of Saint-Malo against Captain Jaunaye and Jacques Nouel, who claimed that they enjoyed a twelve-year monopoly with Canada.[57] None of these men had received a letter patent as *lieutenant général*, and the question of governance and commercial exploitation of New France appeared to be still unconnected.[58]

They were definitively linked in 1603, however, when the King gave to Dugua de Monts a monopoly on the fur trade in addition to his *lieutenance générale*.[59] This change was due to two factors. The first was the necessity of ensuring the economic viability of the settlement by reserving its profits to the patent-holder. The second was the rise of the fur trade, which gave to this region a greater economic value and increased competition between merchants.[60] Such commercial monopolies were common in France itself. In parallel with his overseas travels, Roberval received, 'alone', from Henri II, a patent to search and exploit mines 'in each and every country, land and fief giving us allegiance'.[61] In the 1600s, the draining of marshes throughout France was subjected to such a monopoly, given to a Flemish gentleman, Humphrey Bradley, and to his associates. Among those granted monopolies quickly appeared courtiers also linked to the French overseas enterprises, such as Antoine Coffier, Marquis d'Effiat and Isaac Martin, Sieur de Mauvoy.[62] These monopolies were always bitterly contested by those whose trade was thus hampered. Overseas business was not an exception, and the letters patent issued in 1598 and in 1603 triggered several years of struggle between La Roche, and then Dugua de Monts, and merchants from Saint-Malo, Rouen, Dieppe and the French Basque country. From the beginning of the 1610s, the attachment of trading monopolies to the devolution of political rights in America was nevertheless firmly entrenched. Henri de Condé as well as Henri de Montmorency patronised a set of commercial companies trading with indigenous people furs for wood and were supposed to organise the settlement of the newly acquired territories. The companies established by Richelieu were also based on a monopoly, as specified from the beginning for the Compagnie de la Nouvelle-France[63] and expressly added in 1634 in the case of the Compagnie des Îles de l'Amérique.[64]

Meanwhile, the discourse of political economy progressively gave to the French colonies a new status relating to the kingdom, envisioning them as mere economic dependencies of the metropole. Emerging in the first decades of the seventeenth century, and evident in memoirs or reports sent to Richelieu, this discourse was mainly synthesised, promoted and amplified by Colbert.[65] It stated that the colonies existed only to serve the commercial interests of the kingdom and that it was necessary to link them by a web of royal acts or declarations reserving their trade for the metropole. Colbert, more clearly than his predecessors, distinguished between internal and external monopolies. The first reserved trade to a group of French merchants to the exclusion of others, either nationals or foreigners. The second opened trade to all nationals but prohibited interference from foreigners. Colbert quickly recognised the necessity of opening colonial trade widely to all French merchants where and when he deemed it possible. So, as early as 1669, he abandoned the idea of reserving the American trade to the associates of the Compagnie des Indes Occidentales, and he obliged them to agree to deliver licences to merchants from other nations.[66] But Colbert strictly forbade the colonists to trade with foreigners and, especially, with the Dutch, who at this period represented the only European nation whose merchant fleet was able to satisfy the growing needs of the French colonies. To succeed, Colbert began to use royal orders-in-council, whose application in the colonies at the beginning of the 1670s triggered an array of revolts in the French West Indies as well as in the nascent colony of Saint-Domingue. And Colbert did not renounce encouraging monopolistic companies of the first kind, for example to foster the trade of undeveloped territories such as the south of Saint-Domingue, to ensure a steady flow of slaves from western Africa to the French West Indies, or, of course, to sustain the trade with Asia through the French East India Company, which was set up in 1664. Progressively, these orders-in-council formed the *Exclusif*, which regulated the commercial relations between the metropole and its colonies.[67]

There were many other examples of the territorial management of trade by the royal authorities. In regards to indirect taxation, for instance, the kingdom of France was thus divided into three parts.[68] The *étendue* comprised the central provinces where goods circulated freely and attracted duties only when they entered or exited the unified fiscal space of the *étendue*. The provinces 'considered as foreign' (*réputées étrangères*), situated at the periphery of the kingdom, paid duties according to special rates when they traded with the *étendue* or between themselves. Finally, Alsace, Franche-Comté and, later, Lorraine, stayed fiscally outside the kingdom: goods circulated freely with foreign states and faced a tariff barrier when entering the kingdom. But the main difference is that the *Exclusif* prohibited all trade with foreign countries and merchants. It accentuated the dependency on the metropole that the French overseas territories experienced especially for their basic provisions. And this dependency was founded on a political discourse which was produced to justify and amplify this dependency. The fiscal policy of the Crown joined with the colonial discourse to structure the colonial relationship between France and its overseas territories.

Conclusion

This chapter began by asking a question about the status of the French overseas territories: were they provinces of the kingdom or were they colonies in the modern meaning of the word? The final answer is that they were both. An anonymous defender of the *système de l'Exclusif* encapsulated this ambiguity in a striking formula: 'A commercial colony is a province [whose] full property belongs ... to the society to which it is incorporated; it is an estate of the Crown, and the people sent to populate and cultivate this province are mere concession-holders.'[69] Indeed, the way these territories came under the sovereignty of the king of France, and were integrated into the *domaine royal*, can be related to the integration, either successful or failed, of many continental parts of the kingdom at different periods. The Crown managed to deploy in its overseas territories the same structure of power as in its metropolitan provinces. It thus acted according to the value it gave to the overseas territories, and to its political aims, which were of course very different at the time of François I and Colbert, contrary to the everlasting impression given by the general narrative about the endless rise of the French modern state and the constant disinterest of French authorities towards the colonies. But the overseas territories were never given the chance to become ordinary 'provinces' of the kingdom. From the 1660s onwards, the Crown deployed commercial regulations, and also a process of juridical distinction between the populations, which inscribed them in a colonial relationship.[70] The processes that added overseas territories to the sovereignty of the King of France were not exactly the same as those that transformed them into colonies.[71]

Acknowledgement

I would like to thank my colleagues and friends Reynald Abad, Bertrand Haan, Marie Houllemare, Odile Jurbert, Jean-Marie Le Gall, Cédric Michon, David Richardson, Alain Tallon, Cécile Vidal and Thomas Wien, whose help and advice have been so important for me in the preparation of this chapter.

Notes

1 Quoted by Eugène Daubigny, *Choiseul et la France d'Outre-mer après le traité de Paris: étude sur la politique coloniale au XVIIIe siècle* (Paris: Hachette, 1892), p. 239.
2 See, for example, Pierre Pluchon, *Histoire de la colonisation française*, vol. I: *Le Premier Empire colonial: des origines à la Restauration* (Paris: Fayard, 1991).

3 James Pritchard, *In Search of Empire: The French in the Americas, 1670–1730* (Cambridge: Cambridge University Press, 2004); Philip Boucher, *France and the American Tropics to 1700: Tropics of Discontent?* (Baltimore, Md.: Johns Hopkins University Press, 2008); Dale Miquelon, 'Envisioning the French Empire: Utrecht, 1711–1713', *French Historical Studies*, 24:4 (2001), 653–77; Kenneth Banks, *Chasing Empire across the Sea: Communications and the State in the French Atlantic, 1713–1763* (Montreal: McGill-Queen's University Press, 2002).

4 Helen Dewar, 'Souveraineté dans les colonies, souveraineté dans la métropole: le role de la Nouvelle-France dans la consolidation de l'autorité maritime en France, 1620–1628', *Revue d'histoire de l'Amérique française*, 64:3/4 (2011), 63–92; and 'Litigating Empire: The Role of French Courts in Establishing Colonial Sovereignties', in Lauren Benton and Richard J. Ross (eds), *Legal Pluralism and Empires, 1500–1850* (New York: New York University Press, 2013), pp. 49–82. See also Catherine Desbarats, 'La Question de l'État en Nouvelle-France', in Philippe Joutard and Thomas Wien (eds), *Mémoires de la Nouvelle-France* (Rennes: Presses Universitaires de Rennes, 2005), pp. 187–98; and Catherine Desbarats and Allan Greer, 'Où est la Nouvelle-France?', *Revue d'histoire de l'Amérique française*, 64:3/4 (2011), 31–62.

5 Fanny Cosandey and Robert Descimon, *L'Absolutisme en France: histoire et historiographie* (Paris: Seuil, 2002).

6 Marcel Trudel, *Histoire de la Nouvelle-France, vol. I: Les Vaines tentatives, 1524–1603* (Montréal and Paris: Fides, 1963); Raymonde Litalien and Denis Vaugeois (eds), *Champlain: la naissance de l'Amérique française* (Sillery: Septentrion, 2004); Paul Butel, *Histoire des Antilles françaises: XVIIe–XXe siècle* (Paris:Perrin, 2007); Gilles Havard and Cécile Vidal, *Histoire de l'Amérique française* (Paris: Flammarion, 2014).

7 See Michel Antoine, 'Institutions françaises en Italie sous le règne de Henri II: gouverneurs et intendants (1547–1559)', *Mélanges de l'École française de Rome: moyen-age, temps modernes*, 94:2 (1982), 759–818.

8 See J. H. Elliott, 'The Seizure of Overseas Territories by the European Powers', in David Armitage (ed.), *Theories of Empire, 1450–1800* (Aldershot: Ashgate/Variorum, 1998), pp. 139–57; and Dominique Deslandres, '"Et loing de France, en l'une & l'atre mer, Les Fleurs de Liz, tu as fait renommer": quelques hypotheses touchant la religion, le genre et l'expansion de la souveraineté française en Amérique aux XVIe-XVIIIe siècles', *Revue d'histoire de l'Amérique française*, 64:3/4 (2011), 93–117.

9 On the cultural perspective of the ceremonies of possession, see Patricia Seed, *Ceremonies of Possession in Europe's Conquest of the New World, 1492–1640* (Cambridge: Cambridge University Press, 1995). For an analysis closer to my perspective on New France, see Michel Lavoie, *Le Domaine du roi, 1652–1859* (Sillery: Septentrion, 2010), pp. 1–62.

10 André Burguière and Jacques Revel (eds), *Histoire de la France, vol. I: L'Espace française* (Paris: Seuil, 1989); Léonard Dauphant, *Le Royaume des quatre rivières: l'espace politique français (1380–1515)* (Seyssel: Champ Vallon, 2012).

11 On the integration of Brittany into the kingdom of France, see Dominique Le Page and Michel Nassiet, *L'Union de la Bretagne à la France* (Morlaix: Skol Vreizh, 2003).

12 In 1501, at Aix-en-Provence, for example.

13 Marie Houllemare, 'Le Parlement de Savoie, un outil politique pour le roi de France (1536–1559), entre occupation pragmatique et intégration au royaume', *Revue Historique*, 315:1 (2013), 89–117.

14 Bertrand Haan, 'La Mise en application du traité de Lyon', *Cahiers René de Lucinge*, 37 (2003), 63–74.

15 Arthur Heulhard, *Villegagnon, roi d'Amérique: un homme de mer au XVIe siècle (1510–1572)* (Paris: E. Leroux, 1897); Marie-Noëlle Baudouid-Matuszek, 'Henri II et les expéditions françaises en Ecosse', *Bibliothèque de l'Ecole des Chartes*, 145:2 (1987), 339–82.

16 Bernard Allaire, *La Rumeur dorée: Roberval et l'Amérique* (Montréal: Les Éditions La Presse, 2013).

17 Henry P. Biggar, *A Collection of Documents Relating to Jacques Cartier and the Sieur de Roberval* (Ottawa: Public Archives of Canada, 1930), pp. 178–85.

18 Alfred Ramé, *Voyage de Jacques Cartier au Canada en 1534: Documents inédits sur Jacques Cartier et le Canada* (Paris: Tross, 1867), p. 9.
19 (Nicholas Le Challeux), *Discours de l'histoire de la Floride*, in *Les Français en Amérique pendant la deuxième moitié du XVIe siècle*, vol. II: *Les Français en Floride* (Paris: Presses Universitaires de France, 1958), p. 206; Mickaël Augeron, John de Bry and Annick Notter (eds), *Floride: un rêve français (1562–1565)* (La Rochelle: Musées d'Art et d'Histoire de La Rochelle, 2012), p. 91.
20 Letters patent, March 1577 and 3 January 1578, in Alfred Ramé, *Documents inédits*, pp. 5–10, at p. 9; Letters patent, 12 January 1598, in Marc Lescarbot, *Histoire de la Nouvelle-France* (Paris: Librairie Tross, 1866), vol. II, pp. 398–405.
21 Bibliothèque du Service Historique de la Défense (BSHD), G 193, no. 24–30. See Philippe Jarnoux, 'La France équinoxiale: les dernières velléités de colonisation française au Brésil 1612–1615', *Annales de Bretagne, et des Pays de l'Ouest*, 98:3 (1991), 273–96.
22 Letters patent, 8 November 1603, in Lescarbot, *Histoire de la Nouvelle-France*, vol. II, pp. 408–14.
23 Bertrand Haan, *Une paix pour l'éternité: la négociation du traité de Cateau-Cambrésis* (Madrid: Casa de Velázquez, 2010), pp. 116–17.
24 Anthony Pagden, *Lords of All the World: Ideologies of Empire in Spain, Britain and France, c. 1500–c. 1800* (New Haven, Conn.: Yale University Press, 1995).
25 Bibliothèque Nationale de France (BNF), Nouvelles Acquisitions Françaises 7229, pp. 185–90.
26 BNF, Français 16240, pp. 143r–5v.
27 BNF, Clairambault 295, pp. 473–6.
28 BSHD, G 193, no. 24–30.
29 Andrea Daher, *Les Singularités de la France equinoxiale: histoire de la mission des pères capucins au Brésil (1612–1615)* (Paris: Honoré Champion, 2002), p. 43.
30 BNF, Français 4254, pp. 23r–6v, 27 November 1624.
31 For a recent and comprehensive narrative of the complex dealings of La Roche, de Chaste and Dugua in New France, see Éric Thierry, *La France de Henri IV en Amérique du Nord: de la création de l'Acadie à la fondation de Québec* (Paris: Honoré Champion, 2008).
32 The nomination of Charles de Bourbon is sometimes presented as a clever move made by Champlain, yet a minor player, to secure the settlement of New France, an interpretation that goes against the working of the French court politics during the seventeenth century.
33 Maurice Pianzola, *Les Perroquets jaunes: des français à la conquête du Brésil: XVIIe siècle* (Paris: L'Harmattan, 1991), pp. 46–7.
34 Robert Le Blant and René Baudry, *Nouveaux Documents sur Champlain et son époque* (Ottawa: Publication des Archives Publiques d'Ottawa, 1867), p. 159.
35 Caroline Bitsch, *Vie et carrière d'Henri II de Bourbon, prince de Condé (1588–1646): exemple de comportement et d'idées politiques au début du XVIIe siècle* (Paris: Honoré Champion, 2008), pp. 125–32.
36 Sharon Kettering, *Patrons, Brokers, and Clients in Seventeenth-Century France* (Oxford: Oxford University Press, 1986).
37 'Dignité et tiltre de vice-roi et nostre lieutenant général en l'étendue dudit pays.' Thierry, *La France de Henri IV*, p. 126.
38 Le Blant and Baudry, *Nouveaux Documents*, p. 160.
39 Joseph Bergin, *The Rise of Richelieu* (New Haven, Conn.: Yale University Press, 1991), pp. 35–8.
40 Léon Deschamps, *Un colonisateur au temps de Richelieu: Isaac de Razilly – biographie, memoire inédit* (Paris: Institut Géographique de Paris, 1887).
41 Louis-Augustin Boiteux, *Richelieu, grand maître de la navigation et du commerce de France* (Paris: Editions Ozanne, 1955).
42 Jean-Baptiste du Tertre, *Histoire générale des Antilles habitées par les Français*, 4 vols. (Paris, 1667), vol. I, pp. 8–15.
43 Jacques Petitjean Roget, 'Saint-Christophe, première des isles françaises d'Amérique', *Annales des Antilles*, 24 (1981), 3–56.

44 Gervais Carpin, *Le Réseau du Canada: étude du mode migratoire de la France vers la Nouvelle-France, 1628–1662* (Sillery: Septentrion, 2001).
45 Arthur Malotet, *Etienne de Flacourt ou les origines de la colonisation française à Madagascar, 1648–1661* (Paris: Ernest Leroux, 1898), p. 40.
46 Robert J. Knecht, *Francis I* (Cambridge: Cambridge University Press, 1982), p. 331.
47 Lescarbot, *Histoire de la Nouvelle-France*, p. 398. BSHD, G 193, no. 24–30.
48 He was nevertheless the first to exercise it when he transferred the region of Port-Royal to Jean de Poutrincourt. Le Blant and Baudry, *Nouveaux Documents*, pp. 163–4.
49 *Edits, ordonnances royaux, déclarations et arrêts du conseil d'état du roi concernant le Canada* (Québec: De la Presse à Vapeur, 1854), pp. 5–11, article V.
50 Déclaration du roi, 8 February 1605: 'having ... enough suggested that these countries were recognized by us as being in our obedience, and to keep and acknowledge them as dependencies of our kingdom and crown of France', Thierry, *La France de Henri IV*, p. 207.
51 The Crown reserved a tenth of the profits of the islands. Tertre, *Histoire générale*, vol. I, p. 13.
52 Tertre, *Histoire générale*, vol. I, p. 48 (articles VI and IX).
53 Marcel Trudel, *Histoire de la Nouvelle-France*, vol. III: *La Seigneurie des cent-associés, 1627–1663* (Montréal: Fides, 1979–83).
54 Houllemare, 'Le Parlement de Savoie'; and Dauphant, *Le Royaume des quatre rivières*, pp. 379–81.
55 *Édit portant révocation de la Compagnie des Indes occidentales, décembre 1674*.
56 On the concept of 'colony', see Marie Houllemare, 'La Qualification du nouveau monde dans les textes législatifs français, XVIe–début XVIIe siècles', in Nicolas Lombart (ed.), *Les Nouveaux Mondes juridiques, dans la littérature et l'histoire (moyen âge–XVIIe siècle)* (Paris: Classiques Garnier, 2015), pp. 177–92.
57 Ramé, *Documents inédits*, p. 11.
58 In 1598, Henri IV only forbade people accompanying La Roche from trading independently. Lescarbot, *Histoire de la Nouvelle-France*, p. 402.
59 Thierry, *La France de Henri IV*, p. 131. The letters patent received by Henri II de Condé in 1613 are the first where the monopoly was directly incorporated into the text. Le Blant and Baudry, *Nouveaux Documents*, p. 235.
60 Bernard Allaire, *Pelleteries, manchons et chapeaux de castor: les fourrures nord-américaines à Paris, 1500–1632* (Sillery: Septentrion, 1999).
61 Biggar, *A Collection of Documents*, pp. 494–8 (30 September 1548) and pp. 508–31 (10/30 October 1552).
62 Raphaël Morera, *L'Assèchement des marais en France au XVIIe siècle* (Rennes: Presses Universitaires de Rennes, 2011), pp. 76–8.
63 *Edits, ordonnances royaux*, p. 8 (article VII).
64 Déclaration du roi, 25 November 1634, Le Tertre, *Histoire générale des Antilles*, pp. 41–3.
65 Morera, *L'Assèchement des marais*, pp. 51–110; Cornelius Jaenen, 'Le Colbertisme', *Revue d'Histoire de l'Amérique française*, 18:1 (1964), 64–85 and 18:2 (1964), 252–66.
66 Jaenen, 'Le Colbertisme', p. 258.
67 Charles Frostin, *Les Révoltes blanches à Saint-Domingue aux XVIIe et XVIIIe siècles: Haïti avant 1789* (Paris: L'École, 1975); Jean Tarrade, *Le Commerce colonial de la France à la fin de l'ancien régime*, thèse pour le doctorat d'État, 1972.
68 Jean-Pierre Poussou, 'Traites', in Lucien Bély (ed.), *Dictionnaire de l'ancien régime* (Paris: Presses Universitaires de France, 1996), pp. 1121–2.
69 'Observation sur le mémoire qui traite de l'étendue', *Journal de l'Agriculture*, 4:1 (1766), quoted by Tarrade, *Le Commerce colonial de la France*, vol. I, p. 86.
70 Cécile Vidal, 'Francité et situation coloniale: nation, empire et race en Louisiane française (1699–1769)', *Annales HSS*, 63:5 (2009), 1019–50.
71 Cécile Vidal, 'Introduction: nos ancêtres les Gaulois ou la francité dans le laboratoire colonial (XVIe–XIXe siècle)', in Vidal (ed.), *Français? La Nation en débat entre colonies et métropole, XVIe–XIXe siècle* (Paris: Éditions de l'EHESS, 2014), pp. 9–31.

CHAPTER ELEVEN

Napoleon III and France's colonial expansion: national grandeur, territorial conquests and colonial embellishment, 1852–70

Emmanuelle Guenot

Louis-Napoleon Bonaparte (1808–73) was proclaimed Napoleon III, Emperor of the French, in 1852, putting to an end a series of internal political turmoils in French regimes that had pitted monarchists, republicans and Bonapartists against one another. Napoleon III's authoritarian regime provided political stability that enabled the promotion of economic development and modernisation. His objective was to re-establish France as a great power capable of competing with its newly industrialised neighbours, Britain and Prussia. His vision of a powerful French nation included the expansion of French influence overseas based on the belief that great powers had a global reach, the need to continue a French tradition of overseas acquisitions (counterbalanced by losses) combined with a programme of *mise en valeur*, or wholesale development of newly conquered territories, and the drive to emulate the continental and overseas campaigns of his uncle, Napoleon I, in order to promote his own success as emperor. The increase in global trade, the advance in technology and the desire to establish Christian values and French civilisation also provided impetus for the Emperor's colonial interests and justification for the occupation of overseas lands. These were all interlinked elements that guided the Emperor in pursuing national prestige through campaigns on the European continent and abroad.

This chapter will first examine the character of Louis-Napoleon as a man of destiny who aspired to recreate his uncle's past glories and restore France to its former status among the world leaders. A man with a mission, he embodied modernity by his use of new political means to acquire power and his introduction of liberal reforms that drove France's new economic prosperity. Then, the chapter will explore how incursions into Asia and the South Pacific were driven by Napoleon III's spirit of competition with the British so as to establish new centres for trade under French control. This represented a desire to replicate his uncle's campaign in Egypt in the 1790s and to expand French influence across the Mediterranean and beyond, which had been initiated with the occupation of Algeria in 1830; for Napoleon III, this extended to establishing an autonomous Arab kingdom. But his ambitions also reached across the Atlantic, and his successes elsewhere were paralleled by an ill-fated campaign in Mexico. The final part of the chapter will examine the function of urban renewal, which not only strengthened the link between the *métropole* and its possessions but also colonised the indigenous space while promoting national prestige.

Setting the imperial scene

Napoleon III was born Charles-Louis-Napoleon in 1808, the youngest son of Louis-Bonaparte (brother of Napoleon I) and Hortense de Beauharnais (daughter of Napoleon's first wife, Joséphine de Beauharnais). He became the successor to his uncle after the death of his elder brother. Were it not for the rise of the Second Republic in 1848, he would have probably spent the rest of his life as an exiled prince dreaming of re-establishing the family dynasty and accomplishing great exploits for France, whose status had been diminished by the Treaty of Paris in 1814.[1] The proclamation of the short-lived Second Republic (1848–51) and the introduction of a new constitution based on universal (male) suffrage provided Louis-Napoleon with the means to gain popular legitimacy, and he was elected in December 1848 to the presidency of the Second Republic. His popularity was confirmed when, after a *coup d'état* in December 1851, a plebiscite held the following year established the Second Empire (1852–70) and bestowed on Louis-Napoleon the title of Napoleon III. He thus fulfilled his dream of becoming Emperor of the French.[2] He introduced a monarchy modelled on his uncle's regime, centred on the principles of authority and order, and embodied in a strong leader who sought national grandeur. The new emperor also expressed his determination to maintain the achievements of the Revolution and the value of meritocracy.[3]

Once on the throne, he endeavoured to restore France as a world leader by modernising the country through economic development. The first test of Napoleon III's leadership was the Crimean War of 1853–56, a Franco-British and Ottoman alliance against Russian territorial expansion at a time of Ottoman decline. The Emperor's involvement was based on his desire for a rapprochement with Britain to defend the commercial route to India, a policy of extending French influence in the Middle East and the Mediterranean, a challenge to Russian continental predominance and a spirit of revenge for his uncle's defeat by Russia in 1812. The victory against the Russian armies strengthened

Franco-British cooperation and affirmed Napoleon III's position as an international leader.

During Napoleon III's first decade in power, France experienced significant economic advancement, which distinguished his regime from that of his predecessors; this economic growth was also unmatched by any other state during the same period.[4] One of the main tools that drove France's economic development was the ratification of the Franco-British accord of 1860 (the Cobden–Chevalier treaty), which removed various prohibitions on British goods entering France that had previously prevented competition and stifled France's economic advancement.[5] This gesture pointed to the Emperor's determination to preserve peace with Britain and his belief in the British negotiator Cobden's words that 'free trade is God's own method of producing an entente cordiale and no other plan is worth a farthing' – the statement represented the first use of the phrase in this context.[6] At the same time, the British saw collaboration with France as a counterweight to the eastern European autocracies of Russia, Austria and particularly Prussia, against which the Emperor would fight and lose a war in 1870.[7]

The treaty aimed to eliminate or at least greatly lower taxes on sought-after products necessary to equip French industry with new technology. For example, steam-powered machinery was rare in the Lyon silk industry at the time of the treaty's signing.[8] The liberalisation of the silk trade was accompanied with new economic opportunities and a series of labour reforms that supported social relations between weavers and silk manufacturers, converting weavers to the economic liberalism of Napoleon III. These implemented changes also included freedom to strike and freedom to set up associations for industrial and commercial purposes.[9] The treaty aided France's economic development by fostering industry, trade and agriculture.[10] The transport, metallurgy, engineering and coal sectors soon thrived. The development of the telegraph offered a high-capacity means for the rapid transmission of information, and the development of the banking sector facilitated access to essential capital, especially for the completion of the national railway network.[11] Indeed, the railway master plan created under King Louis-Philippe in 1832 was finally brought to fruition with Napoleon III's authoritarian regime ensuring the reduction of conflicts and hesitation regarding the project.[12] While this drive to modernise and elevate France to the rank of a world power was hugely significant, it was not Napoleon III's only strategy; growing French influence overseas was considered equally essential to regaining national prestige.

CROWNS AND COLONIES

Territorial conquests and a passage to Asia-Pacific

In a speech delivered in Bordeaux on 15 October 1852, Napoleon III stated:

> The empire means peace, we have immense tracts of uncultivated lands to clear, roads to open, ports to create, rivers to make navigable, canals to finish, our railway network to complete. We have, opposite Marseille, a vast kingdom [Algeria] to assimilate to France. We have all the great ports of the west to connect with the American continent by modern communications, which we still lack. ... This is how I see the Empire, if the Empire is re-established. These are the conquests I am contemplating, and all of you are my soldiers.[13]

This statement provides a summary of Napoleon III's ideals for France and its colonies. The Emperor's vision was as much to bring peace to the motherland as to consolidate the French presence in North Africa and in the Americas, and he envisioned an empire extending far beyond France. When Napoleon III ascended the throne, however, French overseas possessions consisted only of slivers of lands, islands and ports of call scattered across the Atlantic, the Indian Ocean and the South Pacific. Some were remnants of the first French colonial empire, such as the West Indian sugar islands of Martinique and Guadeloupe, the fishing station of Saint-Pierre and Miquelon (off the coast of Newfoundland), French Guiana in South America, footholds in Senegal in West Africa and five trading posts on the coastline of India and Réunion Island in the Indian Ocean. Napoleon III's predecessor, Charles X (1824–30) had sent troops in Algeria to boost his prestige and secure a new colony, while Charles X's successor, Louis-Philippe (1830–48), acquired a foothold in Gabon (1839), the islands of Nossi-Bé (1840) and Mayotte (1841) off Madagascar in the Indian Ocean, Grand-Bassam and Assinie on the Ivory Coast (1842) and the Marquesas Islands and Tahiti (1842).[14]

Napoleon III's first consideration on becoming emperor was to acknowledge the relationship between the colonies and the mother country. A May 1854 decree divided the colonial domain into the 'great colonies', including Réunion Island and the West Indian islands, to be ruled by *senatus-consultum*, and the rest was placed under direct rule of the Emperor's government under the Ministry of Navy.[15] As in the past, French expansion under Napoleon III was not calculated on or underpinned by specific policies but was achieved in a rather piecemeal fashion and often as a result of the initiative of military men and missionaries in the field, as well as through specific geopolitical circumstances which offered new opportunities for interventions that led to formal acquisitions and centralised forms of administration.[16]

Above all, Napoleon III's colonial aspirations renewed a French tradition of overseas expansion, and he well understood that the economic development of newly acquired colonies was necessary to strengthen the positions established by the Navy and Army.[17] The most noticeable change from previous regimes, however, was that colonial expansion occurred simultaneously on four continents, demonstrating the Emperor's global ambition and inspiring the dream of linking these growing areas of French influence via waterways built across the isthmuses of Panama and Suez to meet the needs of a growing world market.

Napoleon I, during his Egyptian campaign of 1798–1801, had already contemplated the idea of a canal joining the Mediterranean and the Red Sea to support his designs in the East, especially in India.[18] Now, technological innovations (such as steamships) and investment capital could help connect Europe to the South Seas via America, and to Asia via the Middle East, showcasing France's engineering know-how, which would thereby greatly contribute to the nation's prestige.[19] While Napoleon III was inspired by his uncle's idea, the building of the Suez Canal was in fact ignited by the rising costs of coal needed to fuel the new steamships, a desire to outdo the British in bringing Asia closer to Europe and the circumstances of the Crimean War. Indeed, France's earlier reliance on Russia as a source of supply for jute and linseed sparked the need to turn to India for these essential commodities.[20] Furthermore, because of geographical factors, France had a greater interest in a commercial passageway through Egypt than the Cape route, which was dominated by Britain. The project also fitted with Napoleon III's idea of turning the Mediterranean into a 'French lake', where French influence extended across North Africa and the Middle East.

It took fifteen years of ceaseless diplomatic and engineering efforts from the creation of the Suez Canal Company in 1854 to the canal's eventual completion in 1869. The British were initially opposed to the project as they believed the French enterprise could undermine their Asian trade but finally recognised its benefits after they faced difficulties in transporting troops to suppress the Indian rebellion of 1857. While the French Emperor endorsed the Suez project and saw it as a means to reaffirm French mission to reclaim Egypt for the West, as had his uncle, he never gave his official support because of the newly formed alliance with Britain. The project was led by the French diplomat and engineer Ferdinand de Lesseps, who, as a cousin of the French Empress, enjoyed easy access to government circles. De Lesseps' father had served as the French Consul-General in Egypt, and he himself was posted there in the 1830s, befriending the would-be Egyptian ruler,

Muhammed Ali. The remarkable feat of engineering represented by the canal, which became the main artery for European-Asian trade, was celebrated during an ecstatic inauguration on 17 November 1869, over which Empress Eugénie reigned supreme, bringing triumph to the French nation and, more importantly in the long term, shortening distances to the Asia-Pacific region.[21]

A desire to emulate the success of Britain's imperial expansion, a general resentment of British global ambitions, a need to secure provisioning posts for the French Navy and merchant marine and the prestige that overseas acquisitions provided were all driving forces behind Napoleon III's conquest of new territories. While these motives were certainly present, there was in fact no written directive from Paris when a French naval officer took possession of New Caledonia in 1853 and transformed it into a penal colony modelled on the British colonies in Australia. The penal project reflected Napoleon's policy of removing recidivist offenders and other convicts from the French territory and sending them to penal colonies in an effort to prevent the continued political unrest that had plagued France since the Revolution of 1789.[22] Algeria had first been used for the exile of political opponents at the time of the Revolution of 1848 and the *coup d'état* of 1851, but a lack of established colonial policy and discord between Paris and the government in Algiers led to the pardoning of those who had been sent to agricultural work camps there.[23] New Caledonia also became a penal colony as an alternative to Guiana, where many Frenchmen, penal personnel and convicts alike succumbed to yellow fever and malaria.[24]

It took ten years for the new penal colony to see its first prisoners disembark. They arrived in 1864, and, despite France sending 30,000 prisoners to the South Pacific colony between 1864 and 1897, their number never surpassed those of French convicts sent to the detention centres of Guiana established in 1852. However, the effort did succeed in transforming the South Pacific island into a settler colony. Indeed, the policy of *doublage* (whereby convicts who received a sentence of a period of less than eight years were required to live in the colony for an additional period equal to their sentence) guaranteed a continuous flow of French settlers even if they were unwilling migrants. Only gradually did efforts to attract free settlers win success. Such a policy of convict settlement facilitated the economic and social development of the island, with the prisoners providing the heavy labour for the most demanding tasks of colonisation while offering, in the eyes of the government, a promising future to French prisoners undergoing rehabilitation.[25]

French expansion in Asia paralleled British moves in the region. Following the First Opium War of 1829–32 and the Treaty of Nanking in 1842, French merchants had established themselves in China. Their growing commercial interests and the murder of a French priest triggered the sending of French troops during the Second Opium War of 1856–60. The European bombardment of Canton (Guangzhou) and the sacking of the Qing Emperor's Summer Palace in Peking (Beijing) led to guarantees of protection for Christians in China and the granting of concessions to the foreigners; the setting up of consular representations in coastal ports facilitated the export of goods such as raw silk, a commodity of particular interest to Lyon's manufacturers in the mid-nineteenth century.[26] Similarly, efforts to acquire French footholds in South-East Asia were driven by economic interests and the desire to establish strategic naval outposts and commercial centres. The French, unlike the British in Singapore, lacked a territorial base in the region, and attempts to secure a colonial post had been in vain.

However, Vietnam offered a possibility for a French installation. French Catholic missionaries had been present intermittently in Vietnam since the seventeenth century. In early 1852, the missionaries' evangelisation came under new attacks from the Vietnamese government, forcing them to seek military assistance from the French government. A diplomatic mission was sent in 1856–57 but failed to secure the right of priests to practise their religion freely. The Emperor, influenced by his pious Catholic wife, agreed to a military intervention that lasted from 1857 to 1861. He saw the project in conjunction with France's expedition in China and the strategic role that Saigon could play in capturing a part of the growing traffic from southern China, an area that was already a well-established centre of rice trade, with the hope of reorienting it towards French control.[27] Moreover, the beginning of the construction of the Suez Canal supported the plan of French expansion and the possibility of transforming Saigon into a French Singapore or Hong Kong to rival British interests.[28]

By the early 1860s, through gunboat diplomacy, the French had forced the Vietnamese ruler to grant freedom of action to Catholic missionaries and to cede eastern provinces (the southern part of Vietnam) to France. The new colony of Cochinchina fulfilled the Emperor's dream of securing an outpost in South-East Asia. For good measure, the French brought the kingdom of Cambodia under their control as a protectorate.[29] The Chinese and South-East Asian campaigns were the crucial factors in modernising the French naval fleet, which had been undertaken in 1857 by equipping new vessels with the latest steam-power technology. This innovation combined with the Emperor's appointment of skilled naval officers transformed the French Navy into one of the most powerful in the world, making distant lands more accessible and threatening British naval superiority.[30] The new territorial acquisitions provided France with a large and fertile territory on the South China Sea and the Mekong river. They represented the first stage of France's conquest – completed after Napoleon III's fall – of a much larger empire in South-East Asia, extending to the protectorates of Annam (Central Vietnam), Tonkin (Northern Vietnam) and Laos, the three countries of Vietnam, Cambodia and Laos brought together under colonial administration in the 1880s and 1890s as French Indochina.

Expansion in Africa

Closer to home, Algeria became the most important French colonial possession and a favoured project of the Emperor.[31] The colonial policy of *ense et aratro* (by the sword and the plough) in the Maghreb, based on military conquest and agricultural development, was considerably advanced with the hard-fought submission of Greater Kabylia in 1857 and the introduction of European settler colonisation.[32] The importance of Algeria in the eyes of the Emperor was revealed by the imperial family's visit to Algiers in 1860, the first time a French monarch had ever visited a colony.[33] The trip was part of an imperial tour that included a stop at the newly annexed Duchy of Savoy and the County of Nice, ceded in 1860 after French troops had fought for Italian unification. The event marked the expansion of France's own continental borders and the re-establishment of French authority over territories that had once been occupied by the Emperor's uncle. Napoleon III and the imperial party travelled on the recently completed railways to reach their destinations and, along the way, opened the newly constructed Palais de la Bourse (commercial court and stock exchanges) in Lyon and Marseille as symbols of economic growth.

A military parade on the newly designed Place du Gouvernement in Algiers, where France had razed several pre-colonial buildings, including a mosque, showcased France's power and its hold on the region.[34] In his address to the population, Napoleon III thanked the French troops, destiny and God's protection for France's success in conquering the vast territory of Algeria. His reference to deity and providence aimed to legitimise France's occupation, and his call for France to uplift Arabs to the level of free men assigned the Emperor a humanitarian and paternalistic role. His call to extract the wealth of the land on behalf of the local population revealed more directly commercial intentions. In his speech, the Emperor guaranteed France's protection to settlers, and claimed that the establishment of French institutions and administration would make Algeria an integral part of the nation.[35]

In essence, Napoleon III's policy for Algeria aimed at continuing the promises made by Charles X, under whose administration Algeria had been invaded, with respect to religious practices and traditional land rights. He declared in a statement in 1863 that Algeria was an Arab kingdom where the indigenous population had the same rights as European setters.[36] Napoleon III was inspired in his pronouncement by the idea of utopian socialism, most particularly of the Saint-Simonian Prosper Enfantin, who envisioned Algeria becoming the meeting place between East and West and a place where French civilisation would be brought to the Arabs.[37] Napoleon III imagined Algeria as an autonomous kingdom – with himself as monarch – where Arab culture was respected while at the same time French military control was established and European immigration was supported.[38] Despite the Emperor's Arabophile policy, his imperial reforms, intended to maintain Algerian property rights, actually facilitated land appropriation by colonists, and the area of land in European hands increased sixfold between 1850 and 1870.[39] This change caused increasing tension between settlers and the indigenous population, and local opposition triggered the Emperor's second visit to Algeria in 1865. In an address on this occasion, the Emperor praised the economic development that was in progress; while he reassured the new settlers that the rebellious Arabs had been subjugated, he also urged them to treat the Arabs as fellow countrymen.[40] The somewhat contradictory statement thereby exposed the ongoing social tensions that would plague French occupation of Algeria for the next hundred years.

Further south, French occupation of Senegal, where the French had maintained slave-trading outposts and commercial entrepôts from the 1600s until the abolition of the slave trade in the mid-1800s, was driven by the energetic General Louis Faidherbe during two tours of duty in the 1850s and 1860s. Faidherbe became Governor of Senegal in 1854 and promoted the potential of West Africa as a French colonial and commercial centre.[41] He drew on his prior Algerian experience and exposure to Islam and extended French control from Gorée Island and coastal enclaves over the hinterland of Senegal. He also founded Dakar, which would become the capital of French West African federation and France's main base in sub-Saharan Africa. Dakar enjoyed one of Africa's best natural ports, and its location was ideal for drawing trade from Europe, Africa and South America, cohering with the Emperor's vision of a global network of trade under the French flag. Faidherbe also initiated a public works programme, set up a rudimentary school system, established a French-style centralised administrative system and formed the first permanent units of black African soldiers under French rule, the *tirailleurs sénégalais*, who would gain fame for their deployment in military action in other parts of the colonial domain – Indochina and North Africa – as well as in Europe.[42]

Misadventure in America

While Napoleon III consolidated France's colonial empire in Asia, North Africa, sub-Saharan Africa and the South Pacific, in 1867 he experienced a humiliating defeat in Mexico. The motives for the Mexican adventure included the Emperor's determination to establish a Latin, Catholic, monarchical presence there to thwart further advance from the USA. He envisaged that Mexico could form a strategic link between France and its South Pacific and Asian territories. Above all, the Emperor was desperately in need of silver.[43] Indeed, in 1851, the influx of Australian and American gold dramatically pushed up the value of silver, which meant that while three-quarters of French money was made of silver in the period from 1803 to 1847, during the following decade silver represented only one-fourth of the currency. Daily transactions, trade, the banks' reserves and the French economy as a whole were badly affected.[44] Consequently, France became increasingly interested in the exploitation of the silver mines of the state of Sonora in western Mexico.

French involvement in Mexico occurred at a time of political instability there and the beginning of the American Civil War (1861–65), an event that diverted the Americans from greater involvement in Mexican affairs or stronger reaction to the designs of the French. After a series of agreements between France and the Mexican government, the failure of the Mexican state to honour a debt to France triggered the sending of French troops in January 1862 and the takeover of the silver mines; the export of Mexican silver successfully allowed the re-establishment of a monetary balance in France for the first time since Napoleon III became emperor.[45] Napoleon III was also able to install his candidate, the Habsburg Prince Maximilian, as newly created Emperor of Mexico. At the end of the Civil War, however, the USA ramped up support for the Mexican government and warned France that it was determined to remove European influence from the area, in conformity with the Monroe Doctrine, thus driving Napoleon III's troops to a humiliating withdrawal in 1867; Maximilian was executed by Mexican nationalists.[46] Despite this resounding defeat, Napoleon III had elsewhere greatly extended France's colonial empire and, imbued by the spirit of grandeur, had erected new colonial cities modelled on the capital city to emphasise France's new global position.

Colonial embellishment

Napoleon III's determination to elevate France to the status of a great power included a programme of urban development at home and overseas.

NAPOLEON III AND FRANCE'S COLONIAL EXPANSION

His modernisation of Paris was aimed at displaying France's power and making the capital worthy of the new France (and its new emperor) in a way that would arouse envy and restore the nation to what the Emperor believed to be its rightful place in Europe. Paris's embellishment was driven as much by a need to control any potential threats from political dissidents as by a need to diminish insalubrity, overcrowding and health risks caused by rampant urbanisation while providing employment to local unskilled labour. The modernisation of Paris became an affair of state similar to a political campaign, and the magnitude of the project reflected the importance of Napoleon III's regime and his vision of a modernised France.[47] Monumental buildings, wide avenues, better transportation and water supply, cleaner neighbourhoods and the provision of parks and gardens all embodied the political strength of Napoleon III as a leader, who entrusted the urban reform undertaking to Georges-Eugène Haussmann. An authoritarian government aided in the realisation of Napoleon III's vision but not without social consequences, such as displacement of an increasing resentful working class that had lived in the revamped neighbourhood of old Paris.[48]

Similar programmes of urbanisation to showcase national grandeur took place in the colonies and functioned there, too, to promote and justify French colonialisation. Urban development occurred not only for the purpose of projecting the power of the *métropole* in the colonies but also to facilitate military deployment against any local opposition to colonial control. Moreover, such building programmes helped to provide a visual contrast between the European and indigenous quarters since this separation served to define 'otherness' and imposed a critical distance needed for surveillance.[49] The construction of grand buildings to affirm colonial power was not new, but, under the Second Empire, the aggrandisement of key colonial cities was carried out simultaneously in Saigon, Algiers, Pondicherry and Dakar, and such colonial 'Haussmannisation' helped consolidate colonial power.

The demolition of parts of pre-colonial Saigon in 1859 thus made way for a 'Paris on a small scale', developed to recreate 'French culture in a tropical guise' with European-style architecture and streets following a rectangular, grid-like pattern featuring city blocks, boulevards and avenues and a main axis running from north-west to south-west, turning Saigon's former citadel into a commercial and governmental centre.[50] Similarly, in Dakar, 'the expansion occurred by following the physical projection of power of the fort to the end of the southern harbor peninsula'.[51] The new street grid and the military structure established in the harbour peninsula formed an extension of colonial power northward from the fort and westward from the battery.[52] Because of its layout and architecturally grand style, Dakar was described, like Saigon, as a 'little Paris'.[53]

Algiers experienced a similar alteration in the built landscape, which saw the demarcation of a military and administrative zone, while the quarter located closest to the harbour and the administrative centre was transformed to accommodate European settlers. This remodelling of Algiers also exposed the dichotomy between the traditional/indigenous and the modern/European city, reflecting the asymmetry of power between colonised and colonisers and the existence of opposite worlds depicted as East and West.[54] In 1860, the imperial couple inaugurated the construction of a two-kilometre-long Boulevard de l'Impératrice, a wide thoroughfare that would link one end of the city with the other.[55] Within five years, the boulevard and other main arteries were completed, a monumental post office and palace of justice were erected, the railway line was in operation, and a new quay facilitated transhipment. These new imperial constructions were testimony to an ongoing urban colonisation of the indigenous city that reaffirmed France's authority and relegated the local population to the upper hills of the city and the warren of the old casbah.[56] Such urban changes accentuated the hierarchical and well laid-out European zone in contrast to the 'chaotic' and densely populated casbah.

Similarly, the old colonial territories also benefited from the Emperor's vision. It was under Napoleon III that French India reached its apogee. A neglected inheritance of France's first overseas empire, French India comprised five small and non-contiguous coastal enclaves. Though contrasting dramatically with the size and might of the newly consolidated British Raj, they were long-standing colonised possessions the French had been unwilling to quit but also reluctant to develop. But since the Treaty of Paris (1814) had limited the number of French troops in India, no territorial expansion was possible. The old trading regime based on the idea that the colonies were subordinated to the *métropole*, which had stifled the local economy since the late eighteenth century, was now removed. A rapprochement with the British nevertheless was reflected in a new Franco-British agreement in India which improved commercial activity, while local tax reforms helped finance a vast programme of irrigation improvement, thus increasing agricultural production in the two largest French Indian territories: Pondicherry and Karikal, located in the Tamil region.[57]

This new economic impetus provided the necessary funds to extend the road network across Karikal and Pondicherry; in other measures, a pier was constructed in Pondicherry in 1865 to cope with a sandbar that had made access difficult, and a quay was built in Karikal.[58] From 1862, travellers could reach Pondicherry on the Marseille–Saigon run of the Messageries Maritimes shipping line, although this was not a direct service as travellers had to change in Colombo (in British

Ceylon) to reach their final destination.[59] The construction of a railway line to join Pondicherry to the British railway network was initiated by the Emperor in 1858 to replicate the revolution in transport that had taken place in the *métropole*. However, difficulty in raising the necessary capital and in obtaining approval from British authorities reluctant to facilitate the transportation of goods to and from the port of Pondicherry, which could undermine their own economic advantages, resulted in the 38-kilometre Pondicherry junction line being opened only in 1879, after the overthrow of Napoleon III.[60] Nevertheless, such a project, even in the small French outposts in India, typified the grand visions of the Emperor.

By the time the Emperor faced his defeat against Prussian armies at Sedan in 1870, France's colonial domain had been significantly enlarged, growing from 300,000 square kilometres to over 1 million.[61] New overseas outposts and old territories had undergone major infrastructural changes, making way for proud colonial cities. The Emperor thereby left a colonial legacy that would provide the basis for further colonial expansion and become the source of great national pride for colonialists, particularly at times of political challenges in France.

Conclusion

During his twenty-one year reign, Napoleon III re-established France as a world power. While he embodied both tradition by his lineage and authoritarian policies, his determination and sense of duty to bring France back to what he considered to be its rightful place in the world drove him to initiate the necessary economic changes that propelled France into the modern industrial era. Although territorial acquisition formed part of a strategy that continued and renewed a French tradition of colonial expansion, never before had it been accomplished on such a large stage. The emulation of past colonial glories as much as the desire to compete with British interests in the race for world leadership resulted in the extension of France's colonial interests across Africa, Asia, the Americas and the South Pacific. The use of technological advancement enabled the realisation of the Suez Canal, an old dream of connecting East and West, and the modernisation and effective management of the Navy made distant lands more accessible for troops and settlers. The transformation of the urban space functioned as a means to project France's power and grandeur, and the Haussmannisation of Paris was replicated across the colonies, a development that helped reaffirm France's economic and political success and enhance the Emperor's personal prestige, thus leaving a legacy that would last well into the twentieth century.

Notes

1 Roger Price, *Napoleon III and the Second Empire* (London and New York: Routledge, 1997), p. 1; William H. C. Smith, *Napoleon III: The Pursuit of Prestige* (London: Collins & Brown, 1991), pp. 7–10; J. P. T. Bury, *Napoleon III and the Second Empire* (London: English University Press, 1964), p. 6.
2 J. M. Thompson, *Louis Napoleon and the Second Empire*, 4th edn (Oxford: Basil Blackwell, 1980), pp. 76–124; Theodore Zeldin, *France, 1848–1945* (Oxford: Clarendon Press, 1973), pp. 504–69.
3 Zeldin, *France, 1848–1945*, pp. 504–69.
4 Gabrielle Cadier, 'Les Conséquences du traité de 1860 sur le commerce franco-britannique', *Histoire, Économie et Société*, 7:3 (1988), 363–5; Alan B. Spitzer, 'The Good Napoleon III', *French Historical Studies*, 2:3 (1962), 308–29, at p. 315.
5 Cadier, 'Les Conséquences du traité de 1860', pp. 335–80; Arthur Louis Dunham, *The Anglo-French Treaty of Commerce of 1860 and the Progress of the Industrial Revolution in France* (Ann Arbor, Mich.: University of Michigan Press, 1930).
6 Thompson, *Louis Napoleon and the Second Empire*, pp. 240–1.
7 Jon Parry, 'The Impact of Napoleon III on British Politics, 1851–1880', *Transactions of the Royal Historical Society*, 6th series, 11 (2011): 147–75, at p. 149.
8 Cadier, 'Les Conséquences du traité de 1860', p. 379, n. 12.
9 George J. Sheridan Jr., 'The Political Economy of Artisan Industry: Government and the People in the Silk Trade of Lyon, 1830–1870', *French Historical Studies*, 11:2 (1979), 215–38.
10 Cadier, 'Les Conséquences du traité de 1860', pp. 357–74.
11 Roger Price, *People and Politics in France: 1848–1870* (Cambridge: Cambridge University Press, 2004), pp. 219, 229–30.
12 Frank Dobbin, *Forging Industrial Policy: The United States, Britain, and France in the Railway Age* (Cambridge: Cambridge University Press, 1994), pp. 95–157; Roger Price, *The Modernization of Rural France: Communications Networks and Agricultural Market Structures in Nineteenth-Century France* (New York: St Martin's Press, 1983), pp. 207–9.
13 'Discours du prince président au banquet offert par la chambre et le tribunal de commerce de Bordeaux, 19 octobre 1852', in *La Politique impériale exposée par les discours et proclamation de l'empereur Napoléon III depuis le 10 décembre 1848 jusqu'en février 1868* (Paris: Plon, 1868), pp. 157–60.
14 Robert Aldrich, *Greater France: A History of French Overseas Expansion* (Basingstoke: Macmillan, 1996), p. 95.
15 These were acts with the force of law, decided by the Senate, whose members were appointed for life by the Emperor.
16 C. M. Andrew and A. S. Kanya-Forstner, 'Centre and Periphery in the Making of the Second French Colonial Empire, 1815–1920', in Andrew Porter and Robert Holland (eds), *Theory and Practice in the History of European Expansion Overseas* (London: Frank Cass, 1988), pp. 9–35, at pp. 9–11. Jacques Weber, 'Un siècle de présence française en Chine (1843–1943)', in Jacques Weber (ed.), *La France en Chine (1843–1943)* (Nantes: Ouest Editions, 1997), pp. 7–33, at pp. 13–14.
17 James F. McMillan, *Napoleon III* (London: Longman, 1991), pp. 144–5.
18 Werner Baer, 'The Promoting and the Financing of the Suez Canal', *The Business History Review*, 30:4 (1956), 361–81, at p. 363.
19 The idea of a Central American canal as a means to connect the Atlantic and Pacific Oceans was mentioned as early as 1844, to improve access from Europe to the Pacific and to boost French expansion in the South Seas. C. W. Newbury, 'Aspects of French Policy in the Pacific, 1853–1906', *Pacific Historical Review*, 27:1 (1958), 45–56, at pp. 45–6. Thompson, *Louis Napoleon and the Second Empire*, p. 221.
20 D. A. Farnie, *East and West of Suez: The Suez Canal in History, 1854–1956* (Oxford: Clarendon, 1969), p. 32.
21 Farnie, *East and West of Suez*, pp. 81–93; Baer, 'The Promoting and the Financing of the Suez Canal', pp. 361–81.

22 Stephen A. Toth, *Beyond Papillon: The French Overseas Penal Colonies, 1854–1952* (Lincoln, Nebr.: University of Nebraska Press, 2006), p. 1; Isabelle Merle, 'Colonial Experiments, Colonial Experiences: The Theory and Practice of Penal Colonisation in New Caledonia', in Robert Aldrich and Isabelle Merle (eds), *France Abroad* (Sydney: University of Sydney Printing Services, 1997), pp. 19–20.
23 Frederick Quinn, *The French Overseas Empire* (Westport, Conn.: Praeger, 2000), p. 108; Aldrich, *Greater France*, p. 93; Stacey Renee Davis, 'Turning French Convicts into Colonists: The Second Empire's Political Prisoners in Algeria, 1852–1858', *French Colonial History*, 2 (2002), 93–113.
24 Davis, 'Turning French Convicts into Colonists', pp. 93–113; Karin Speedy, *Colons, créoles et coolies: l'immigration réunionnaise en Nouvelle-Calédonie (XIXe siècle) et le tayo de Saint-Louis* (Paris: L'Harmattan, 2007), pp. 35–9; Aldrich, *Greater France*, p. 89; Newbury, 'Aspects of French Policy in the Pacific', pp. 45–6; Jacqueline Dutton, 'Imperial Eyes on the Pacific Prize: French Visions of a Perfect Penal Colony in the South Seas', in John West-Sooby (ed.), *Discovery and Empire: The French in the South Seas* (Adelaide: University of Adelaide Press, 2013), pp. 245–82; Toth, *Beyond Papillon*, pp. xiv, 10, 13–17; Isabelle Merle, *Expériences coloniales: la Nouvelle-Calédonie (1853–1920)* (Paris: Belin, 1995), pp. 45–9.
25 Toth, *Beyond Papillon*, p. 1; Merle, *Expériences coloniales*, pp. 17–23.
26 Pierre Brocheux and Daniel Hémery, *Indochina: An Ambiguous Colonization, 1858–1954* (Berkeley, Calif.: University of California Press, 2009), p. 17; Andrew and Kanya-Forstner, 'Centre and Periphery in the Making of the Second French Colonial Empire', p. 11; Florence Perrais, 'Français et chinois à Shanghai (1850–1880)', in Jacques Weber (ed.), *La France en Chine (1843–1943)* (Nantes: Ouest Editions, 1997), pp. 209–14; Weber, 'Un siècle de présence française en Chine', pp. 9–13; Jian Tianyue, 'La Marine impériale dans l'expédition de Chine', *Revue Historique des Armées*, 273 (2014), 3–14.
27 Brocheux and Hémery, *Indochina*, p. 24.
28 Brocheux and Hémery, *Indochina*, pp. 14, 22.
29 Quinn, *The French Overseas Empire*, pp. 136–8, 162; Brocheux and Hémery, *Indochina*, pp. 17–20, 27, 70–3.
30 Étienne Taillemite, *L'Histoire ignorée de la marine française* (Paris: Librairie Académique Perrin, 1988), pp. 334–7; Brocheux and Hémery, *Indochina*, p. 21; Parry, 'The Impact of Napoleon III on British Politics', p. 157; Tianyue, 'La Marine impériale dans l'expédition de Chine'.
31 'Discours du prince président, Bordeaux, 19 octobre 1852', *La Politique impériale*, p. 160; McMillan, *Napoleon III*, p. 145.
32 Jennifer E. Sessions, *By Sword and Plow: France and the Conquest of Algeria* (Ithaca, NY: Cornell University Press, 2011), pp. 6–7, 183; McMillan, *Napoleon III*, p. 312.
33 McMillan, *Napoleon III*, pp. 144–7.
34 René Pillorget, 'Les Deux Voyages de Napoléon III en Algérie (1860 et 1865)', *Napoléonica*. Available online at http://www.napoleon.org/fr/salle_lecture/articles/files/deux_voyages_napoleon_iii.asp#informations (accessed 24 December 2014); Zeynep Çelik, *Urban Forms and Colonial Confrontations: Algiers under French Rule* (Berkeley, Calif.: University of California Press, 1997), pp. 27–8.
35 'Proclamation de l'Empereur aux habitants de l'Algérie, Alger, 3 mai 1865', in *La Politique impériale*, pp. 436–7.
36 'Lettre de l'empereur au gouverneur de l'Algérie, 6 février 1863', in *La Politique impériale*, pp. 390–4.
37 Sessions, *By Sword and Plow*, pp. 144–5; Charles-Robert Ageron, *'L'Algérie algérienne' de Napoléon III à de Gaulle* (Paris: Editions Sindbad, 1980), pp. 17–71.
38 Napoléon III, *Lettre sur la politique de la France en Algérie adressée par l'empereur au maréchal de Mac Mahon* (Paris: Imprimerie Impériale, 1865), pp. 7–85.
39 Sessions, *By Sword and Plow*, pp. 318–19; Quinn, *The French Overseas Empire*, p. 108; Aldrich, *Greater France*, p. 93; Davis, 'Turning French Convicts into Colonists', pp. 93–113.

40 'Proclamation de l'empereur aux habitants de l'Algérie, 3 mai 1865', in *La Politique impériale*, pp. 436–7; 'Proclamation de l'empereur aux peuple arabe, Alger, 5 mai 1865', in *La Politique impériale*, pp. 437–9.
41 French slave-trading officially ceased in the early 1800s, and slavery was abolished throughout the Empire in 1848.
42 Myron Echenberg, *Colonial Conscripts: The Tirailleurs Sénégalais in French West Africa, 1857–1960* (Portsmouth: Heinemann Educational Books, 1991), pp. 7–11; Quinn, *The French Overseas Empire*, pp. 155–7; Raymond F. Betts, 'Dakar: ville impériale (1857–1960)', in Robert J. Ross and Gerrard J. Telkamp (eds), *Colonial Cities* (Dordrecht: Martinus Nijhoff Publishers, 1985), pp. 193–6.
43 Michelle Cunningham, 'Introduction', in *Mexico and the Foreign Policy of Napoleon III* (Basingstoke: Palgrave Macmillan, 2001), pp. 1–15.
44 Shirley J. Black, 'Napoléon III et le Mexique: un triomphe monétaire', *Revue Historique*, 259:1 (1978), 55–73.
45 Black, 'Napoléon III et le Mexique', pp. 55–73.
46 McMillan, *Napoleon III*, pp. 149–52.
47 A. R. Gillis, 'Crime and State Surveillance in Nineteenth-Century France', *American Journal of Sociology*, 95:2 (1989), 307–41, at p. 314; Merle, *Expériences colonials*, pp. 55, 58.
48 Jeanne Gaillard, *Paris, la ville, 1852–1870* (Paris: Honoré Champion, 1977), pp. 22–3.
49 Çelik, *Urban Forms and Colonial Confrontations*, p. 5.
50 Anne Raffin, 'Imperial Nationhood and Its Impact on Colonial Cities: Issues of Inter-group Peace and Conflict in Pondicherry and Vietnam', in Diane E. David and Nora Libertun de Duren (eds), *Cities and Sovereignty: Identity Politics in Urban Spaces* (Indianapolis, Ind.: Indiana University Press, 2011), pp. 34–6; Howard Dick and Peter J. Rimmer, *Cities, Transport and Communications: The Integration of Southeast Asia since 1850* (Basingstoke: Palgrave Macmillan, 2003), pp. 298–300; Gwendolyn Wright, *The Politics of Design in French Colonial Urbanism* (Chicago, Ill.: Chicago University Press, 1991), pp. 161–75.
51 David Nelson, 'Defining the Urban: The Constructions of French-Dominated Colonial Dakar, 1857–1940', *Historical Reflections*, 33:2 (2007), 225–55, at p. 228.
52 Nelson, 'Defining the Urban', pp. 227–9.
53 Betts, 'Dakar: ville impériale', p. 193.
54 Shirine Hamadeh, 'Creating the Traditional City: A French Project', in Nezar AlSayyad (ed.), *Forms of Dominance on the Architecture and Urbanism of the Colonial Enterprise* (Aldershot: Avebury, 1992), pp. 241–59.
55 Pillorget, 'Les Deux Voyages de Napoléon III en Algérie'; Çelik, *Urban Forms and Colonial Confrontations*, pp. 27–8.
56 Çelik, *Urban Forms and Colonial Confrontations*, pp. 33, 35, 37, 58–9, 65.
57 The success was such that the idea was modelled by the British Indian authorities in 1854. Jacques Weber, *Pondichéry et les comptoirs de l'Inde, après Dupleix: la démocratie au pays des castes* (Paris: Denoël, 1996), pp. 121–32.
58 Weber, *Pondichéry et les comptoirs de l'Inde*, pp. 133–44.
59 Weber, *Pondichéry et les comptoirs de l'Inde*, pp. 185–6.
60 Edmond Maestri, 'Les Établissements français dans l'Inde et leurs chemins de fer: 1858–1934', in Michel Pousse (ed.), *L'Inde, études, et images* (Saint-Denis, La Réunion: L'Harmattan, 1993), pp. 211–41.
61 Tianyue, 'La Marine impériale dans l'expédition de Chine', p. 3.

CHAPTER TWELVE

The British, the Hashemites and monarchies in the Middle East

Matthieu Rey

When the future King of Iraq, Faisal I, landed in the southern city of Basra on 23 June 1921, he did not receive the warm welcome he had expected. He thus quickly moved towards Baghdad, the new capital of an as-yet-undefined country.[1] The inauspicious beginning to the Iraqi monarchy sheds light on the rocky path of the rule of the Hashemite dynasty under the British mandate and during the two decades that followed it. Several key features make up the background to the Hashemite monarchy in British-ruled Iraq and shaped the position of the monarchy in this newly created colonial or semi-colonial country.[2] The populations living in the three *wilâyât* (provinces or governorates), the territories which became Iraq in the 1920s, shared a common experience with many other Ottoman territories in the nineteenth century, and they had undergone a series of major political changes, though, at the time, they were not governed by a monarch, nor, apart from a few notables, were they in contact with the Hashemite family.[3] Yet, in the aftermath of the First World War, the British and the French drew up the map for a 'new Middle East' and created several new countries in the region.

It is not my purpose here to discuss whether Iraq had previous historical roots as a nation but how a new political entity emerged and was governed.[4] The British decided to make Faisal I the king of one of the new states of the Middle East, although the monarch was crowned before its constitution was established and the national boundaries were delimited, reflecting long-term British policy in the Persian Gulf. Studying the monarchy's evolution in Iraq points to three main issues. The first is the constitutional process that took place between 1918, when the Ottomans capitulated, and 1925, when the Iraqi constitution was adopted. The political history of the country during this period has been neglected in the scholarship, as studies of Iraq have focused on themes such as the Anglo-Iraqi Treaty and explanations for the failure of the state-building process.⁵ The second issue concerns nation- and state-building in the context of the creation of a monarchy.⁶ Rather than discussing the strength or weakness of the state, or the success or failure of nation-building, this chapter focuses on the dynamics of how the monarchy was established. The third point relates to the state as an institution. It has been argued by some that the very form of the state was imported into the Middle East, while others have identified the state as a product of modernity.⁷ However, building on Daniel Neep's work, I will investigate how a modern political framework can reshape traditional behaviours.⁸ From this perspective, monarchy as a regime can be conceived of as a series of agencies coordinated by formal and informal relations that govern the public sphere. While the British authorities built this framework, local dynamics also had an impact on it and gave it reality. Neo-institutional approaches identify the actors and their positioning as a key element of policy-building, and this approach allows us to assess the interaction between local and foreign actors in shaping a new polity.⁹

In order to understand how the monarchy ruled Iraq under British supervision, it is necessary to clarify the conditions of its establishment. The British had been present in the Gulf region for several centuries before the creation of Iraq. In the aftermath of the First World War, the British took control of Iraq and, during the Cairo conference of 1921, planned the organisation of their mandate over the country. This led to Iraq becoming part of Britain's 'informal' empire.¹⁰ However, the process was imposed on a highly politicised population. This encounter explains the main characteristics of the formal process undertaken to create the monarchy and of the constitutional form it produced. The parameters nevertheless changed after 1925 when the newly established authorities were faced with different issues than had confronted them at the outset of their rule. New practices thus emerged and remained in place and continued to be relevant until 1958, when a *coup d'état* led to the overthrow of the King and the abolition of the Iraqi monarchy.

The British in the Arabian and Persian Gulf

When Britain took control of the Iraqi territories, it had already been engaged in the Gulf region for several centuries. This presence did not proceed from the involvement of the British state but from the setting up by the East India Company, from the 1620s onwards, of a maritime trading route that encompassed the Gulf.¹¹ The East India Company successfully battled the Portuguese and displaced them from the Gulf, and their involvement in the region then grew steadily for the next two centuries. Several reasons have been put forward to explain this increasing power in the Gulf. Given the strategic position of the region on the route to India, the main objective of the British was to prevent any foreign, mostly continental European, power from encroaching on their interests, and they thus struggled successfully against the French, the Russians and, finally, the Germans.[12] However, controlling the route to India also meant preserving peace and security along the way. Echoing the humanitarian campaign against slavery, the British intended to curb piracy – or what they saw as such.[13] In this perspective, any independent actions by local sheikhs were interpreted either as attacks against British interests or as tokens of friendship for them. Gradually, the indigenous authorities and the British cooperated, even though they were guided by different agendas. Finally, technical improvements during this period, mostly in the field of transport, led to the integration of the region into the world economy and boosted its commercial potential.[14] British companies, such as the Euphrates and Tigris Steam Navigation Company, established by the Lynch brothers in 1861, competed to obtain concessions, and the British progressively gained control of several key positions in the Persian Gulf, though the region formally remained part of the Ottoman and Safavid empires.

British representatives slowly spread around the shores of the Gulf and made contact with various local figures. In 1723, the British established a residency in Bushire (in present-day Iran) under the aegis of the East India Company presidency of Bombay. As European threats to Britain's outposts grew, and Britain's own global interests expanded, monitoring the sea routes in the Gulf became crucial. London sent a special envoy to Basra (Iraq) and set up a legation there in 1798. At the end of the eighteenth century, the British thereby had firmly established their position in the Gulf, where the priority remained a struggle against piracy.[15] They soon understood that strategic requirements would not be met by simple legations, and John Malcolm, an East India Company official who was later appointed Governor of Bombay in 1827, devised a general blueprint for British control of the Gulf by conquering an island on which a naval base would be established, which, in turn, would allow the British to carry out surveillance over rival navies.[16] However, this plan was not implemented, as it quickly appeared obvious that the 'piracy' the British sought to control in fact reflected indigenous conflicts and actions. This nevertheless led the British to devote further attention to the region and to contract agreements with local chiefs in order to combat piracy.[17] The ultimate result was an accord signed in 1820 that defined a 'trucial peace' in the Gulf and that framed the relations between foreign and local interests.[18] The convention would have a strong impact on the political geography of the Gulf.

The aim of this chapter is not to explore in detail the diplomatic and political evolution of the British presence, but it is pertinent to pinpoint how British intervention affected local elites. As Frederick Anscombe has emphasised, the historiography has traditionally underestimated the role of these elites, seeing them as passive spectators rather than active players in the new circumstances produced by European involvement.[19] In contrast, recent research underlines the close connection between the sheikhs and their use of defined 'local activities' in order to strengthen the elites' role.[20] The political stage was shaped by three main protagonists: the Ottomans, the British and local chiefs. The tribal sheikhs competed against each other in order to dominate regional balances of power and flows of wealth. To achieve this, the sheikhs attempted to build alliances with foreign groups such as the British and the Ottomans, in return for which they agreed to various demands made by the foreigners. For example, when the Emir of Bahrain set out to curb the influence of the al-Thani, a tribe that had been settled in the territory of Qatar on the Arabian peninsula since the seventeenth century, the ruler of the al-Thani negotiated with the British in order to buttress his position. This marked the very beginnings of the rise of the al-Thani dynasty, which currently rules Qatar. The British recognised the al-Thani sheikh as the legitimate leader of the tribe, viewing him as the best protector of the coast and defender of British interests.[21] An 1868 agreement between the British Crown and the al-Thani represented the first step in the emergence of Qatar as an independent power. Such actions do not imply that the British were responsible for creating local leaders, nor that Qatar as a political entity was a British invention. Rather they indicate how manoeuvring between the British and local leaders in the context of tribal struggles and the resurgence of Ottoman power reshaped the political geography of the region.[22] Since the British wanted to control flows of goods and people in the Gulf, they sought to secure local partners. Their relationship institutionalised the power of the sheikhs and underpinned the emergence of the new political territories under British protection. The First World War confirmed this trend: several Gulf kingdoms were turned into protectorates, gaining de-facto independence from the Ottoman Empire. These local and international dynamics highlight how the British shaped the region and partly explain Britain's extended control of Iraq after 1918.

Establishing a monarchy in Iraq

A new country, Iraq, slowly emerged from the First World War and its diplomatic repercussions. Many studies highlight the importance of the correspondence between Henry MacMahon, British High Commissioner in Egypt and head of the Arab Bureau in Cairo, and Hussain, sheriff of Mecca, in the Arabs' agreeing to launch a revolt against the Ottomans in exchange for independence for an Arab kingdom.[23] Other scholars emphasise the impact of the warfare in Iraq.[24] Rather than focusing on these points, I would like to underline the main political changes that had been implemented since the mid-nineteenth century and the intense political debate that animated the Iraqi public sphere after 1908.

Faced with multiple challenges at the beginning of the twentieth century, Ottoman authorities introduced profound changes that affected the fiscal and military structures of the Empire. These reforms had an impact on the different provinces of the sultan, such as the *wilâya* of Baghdad, Mosul and Basra, which would be brought together as the state of Iraq after the First World War. Such developments in the early years of the 1900s constituted the underpinnings of the local political order during the war. Strengthening the centre of the Empire and reinforcing links between the provinces and the centre led to the reshaping of the local political sphere.[25] Political units, the region or *wilâya*, emerged, with councils established as local government authorities. In addition, a new system of patronage and election promoted a new elite, the 'notables' or *zu'âma*. A *zâ'im* headed a social network maintained thanks to his financial resources and revenues, and in which he secured a dominant political position. Two sorts of *zâ'im* appeared during the nineteenth century: the urban leaders from the great families and the tribal leaders, both of whom became key intermediaries between the centre and the periphery. During this period, meanwhile, a strong Shia movement emerged and demanded a new constitutional framework for the administration of the Ottoman Empire, part of a movement that spearheaded other reforms.[26]

When military officers launched a revolution in Istanbul in 1908, a new dual political system appeared. At the centre, a parliament was convened and began to concern itself with imperial issues. Elections in 1908 and 1912 gave a new status to the political elites by bringing their representatives into the capital; such men belonged to the group of the notables, even if they were not themselves the heads of families, and they mostly represented urban centres.[27] The revolution and the elections also triggered a new set of political dynamics at the provincial level in Iraq. The great growth of the local press, with more than 100 newspapers published within a year of the revolution, shows that the 1908 events led to the emergence of a vibrant public sphere.[28] Most of the issues that were tackled in these publications, and later in the electoral debates, revolved around the political organisation of the country and the control and use of its resources. It can be argued that the 1908 events led certain sections of the urban populations to become involved in political activities, though certainly not all did so. Furthermore, new topics were introduced for discussion, such as the optimal form of government for the country and the powers that should be granted to local communities. The high level of political awareness that existed in Iraq before the First World War should be underlined.

During the war, several major developments converged in Iraq. Ottoman imperial ties and the old regime in Istanbul gradually disappeared. As Ali Wardi has shown, local communities became more and more autonomous, and urban elites, mainly in the Shia-dominated centres, were able in the aftermath of warfare in 1915–17 to take control of such territories in collaboration with the tribal leaders grouped around them.[29] As a result, the old centralised imperial structure was transformed into a decentralised order in which certain notables strengthened their powers. Was Iraq divided by Sunni and Shia rivalries? Certainly, these two sectarian allegiances prevailed in the sharing out of power. The Ottomans, a Sunni dynasty, empowered local Sunni families. But, at the same time, Shia sacred cities became major centres for intellectual and political activities. In this context, sectarian division existed, but it was not the key element necessary to understand the aftermath of the war. War mobilisation led leaders of the Islamic holy cities to launch a struggle against the British. However, not until the end of the war did the British clearly attempt to promote their political or imperial hegemony over Iraq.

The British colonial order in the Middle East was not formulated by one government agency but involved three departments.[30] First, the War Office and, after the war, the Colonial Office supervised British policy for all the regions in which Britain maintained interests. A second source of policy-making was the colonial Indian government, as the Viceroy of India considered the Middle East as a part of its sphere of influence. When the First World War began, an Indian expeditionary corps was dispatched to occupy the port city of Basra, which was identified as a vital strategic point. From the conquest of this city until the end of the war, most of the decisions affecting Iraq were made by the government of India. However, as the war expanded and British officers decided to encourage the Arabs to take part in the fight against the

Ottomans, another department undertook responsibilities: the Arab Bureau in Cairo. Each of these departments had its own project for the future of Iraq.[31] It was the interplay between these institutions that structured British colonial power and the new political order in Iraq in the aftermath of the war.

When Iraq was occupied and became effectively a part of the British Empire in 1917, its future remained unclear. On his entry to Baghdad, General Frederick Stanley Maude declared that he had liberated the country from the Turks and that he would give power back to the Arabs. However, Maude did not put forward any proposal for an institutional set-up, and he died within a few months of his proclamation. The initial British response to the power vacuum created by the retreat of the Ottoman troops was to divide the country and to integrate the provinces into the British Empire as colonies.[32] Though this policy was initiated and monitored by the India Office, it quickly failed. The British never fully controlled the provinces, and their occupation ignited a major uprising. Moreover, in the aftermath of the war, Britain did not possess the financial capabilities or human resources necessary to counter an armed upheaval and to establish fully fledged colonies by complete occupation of the territory.[33] Finally, the international context had changed, and Woodrow Wilson's doctrine of self-determination prohibited this kind of arbitrary colonial rule over Iraq.[34] Consequently, the first British occupation ended two years after the war, though without any permanent institutional arrangement devised for the country. In order to resolve the issue, the new Colonial Secretary convened a conference in Cairo, in March 1921, where twenty-six senior British officials gathered to discuss the future of the Middle East.

When the conference opened, the British were faced with a choice between contradictory policies. In Iraq, as a consequence of the massive uprising, the plans of the Arab Bureau of Cairo became more relevant. During the war, in 1915, this British office had made contact with Sharif Hussain of Mecca. Hussain came from the old and prestigious Hashemite family, which for decades had ruled the two sacred cities of Medina and Mecca within the Ottoman Empire. Hussain became involved in politics during the last years of the Ottoman Empire, his involvement leading the Sultan to force him to reside in the capital. Hussain's son, Faisal, who was born in 1885 in the Hedjaz and received a traditional tribal education, became involved in politics at the beginning of the twentieth century. He first followed his father to Istanbul, then became a member of the Ottoman parliament after the revolution of 1908. When the war broke out, Faisal entered into discusssions with Arab nationalists in order to sound out public opinion in the Arab provinces. In 1916, the British Arab Bureau and

Sharif Hussain finally reached an agreement: the British would provide supplies for Hussain and his Hashemite revolt and recognise an independent Arab kingdom at the end of the war; Hussain's forces would launch a military revolt to weaken the Ottomans. Faisal commanded the troops when his father proclaimed the 'Arab revolt' in the company of Iraqi officers who had previously served under the Ottomans and now supported the uprising, the so-called *sherifian*. The famous T. E. Lawrence ('Lawrence of Arabia') became involved in promoting the Arab revolt against the Ottomans, and he became intimately associated with Faisal. In 1918, Faisal managed to force the Ottoman troops out of Syria. Faisal then established a constitutional monarchy in Damascus, with himself as king. His personal strategy nevertheless did not accord with the international agenda of the victorious Allies. In the secret 1916 Sykes–Picot Agreement,[35] the British and French decided to divide the lands of a dismembered Ottoman Empire at the end of the war. In 1920, at a conference in San Remo, the British and French reached a formal agreement on Middle Eastern issues. Officially under mandates of the League of Nations, the French would take Syria and Lebanon but would leave the neighbouring *sandjak* of Mosul to the British.[36] The British would control the territory of not only Iraq but also Palestine, which was placed under a colonial governor, as well as Transjordan, which became an emirate ruled by Abdallah, another son of Hussain and brother of Faisal. Subsequently, the French landed in Lebanon and moved towards Damascus. The French occupation of Syria resulted in the overthrow of the self-proclaimed King Faisal at the end of 1920; Faisal went into exile. When T. E. Lawrence went back to Europe, he served as a special adviser in the Colonial Office and accompanied Winston Churchill, when Churchill was Colonial Secretary, to the Cairo Conference of 1921, which proved crucial for the establishment of Faisal's kingdom in Iraq.[37]

The 1921 Cairo conference focused on Iraq and Palestine, the most contentious territories in the Middle East.[38] The British, with Lebanon and Syria in French hands, subsequently supported Faisal, the deposed king of Syria, as the future king of Iraq. Several issues were quickly settled. Iraq would become a constitutional monarchy under a parliamentary system, and Faisal appeared as the best candidate for the throne. The Kurds (the inhabitants of the *wilâya* of Mosul) would not be considered as a people, that is to say, as a political group that could request autonomy, so the *wilâya* of Mosul would become part of Iraq. The decision structured Iraq according to Western political lines while the British gave local notables an institutional role as rulers of this newly defined territory. When the conference ended and Faisal travelled to Iraq, none of the political institutions other than the monarchy had yet been established, and the British had not even clearly defined the future legal and international status of Iraq. They could put pressure on Iraqi authorities, however, by threatening to grant autonomy to Kurdistan (the *wilâya* of Mosul which was still administered separately), and they could remind Faisal that he might be overthrown with their consent if he did not safeguard British interests in the country.[39] Meanwhile, in addition to British pressure, from Faisal's point of view, the new monarchy had to face a variety of local demands that had been formulated ever since the turn of the century. The rocky path of the monarchy was therefore laid down through the circumstances in which it was created.

A monarch and country in search of a constitution

Pursuing the formalities for installation of the new regime, the British announced that a referendum would be held to recognise the Iraqi king and that a constitutional assembly would soon be elected, a strategy that allowed them to manage policy formulation, state-building and maintenance of imperial overlordship all at the same time. Indeed, in a referendum, Iraqi citizens were asked in the same question to agree to the nomination of the king and to recognise the mandate that established the British control, with the two issues not distinguished. In the event, local institutions were set up, notably a royal court headed by the king and a council of ministers. Neither could act without the consent of the British. The British also established another hierarchy of power through a multitude of agents, from the High Commissioner in Baghdad down to local British advisers and *mutassarif* (governors), even though, because of budget constraints, their number dropped drastically between 1918 and 1921. The formal administrative and political apparatus in Baghdad remained a twinned hierarchy in which each Iraqi minister had a British adviser, and the king was obliged to discuss all critical matters with the British High Commissioner. Moreover, several informal British advisers played an important role even if their influence depended on their personal relationships with the legal British representative.[40] Such non-official figures as Gertrude Bell – an explorer, writer and archaeologist who was sometimes referred to as the most powerful woman in the British colonies – played a significant role in British intervention in the events developing in Iraq.[41]

The texture of a constitution and the establishment of a state depended on several centres of power. The initial test for the British was the referendum that they organised and managed to win: King Faisal was indeed recognised as the legitimate monarch of the new Iraq. The process reveals the manner in which the British went about creating the state: abiding by the Western criteria of legitimacy to justify their new power as well as that of their Iraqi ally in the eyes of the international community. On the international stage, the first move aimed to guarantee the 'modernity' of the Iraqi monarch, a figure whose status was confirmed by a modern referendum on the basis of universal male suffrage. This meant in practice an intense campaign of intimidation and constraint against opponents of the British plan.[42] Such actions mainly targeted the Shia religious leaders and several notables who had been deeply involved in the constitutionalist struggle over the past decades. The manoeuvre thus shows how the British manipulated local individuals and groups to establish the monarchy.[43] A constitutional kingdom meant the exclusion of those who opposed the British order even if they might have been in favour of the constitutionalist principles that it implemented. A new relationship emerged between four pillars of the regime: the British, the King, the Council of Ministers and civil society. Yet, in order to settle the new order in place, a constitution had to be written.

The arrival of the King in his realm sheds light on the day-to-day practices and role of the monarch. As Ali Allawi explains, Faisal I both enjoyed support in the country and was aware of the difficulties he might face.[44] His schedule reveals how he behaved towards Iraqi society. When he arrived in Baghdad in July 1921, Faisal went to the residence of Sayyid Talib, the Naqib of Basra,[45] a key politician in the Ottoman provinces who remained the major rival to Faisal for the crown during the years 1920–21.[46] The invitation to Faisal from the Naqib and a banquet he hosted proved to be a reconciliation between the two figures.[47] It also underlined the nature of the political game: the King, like the other notables, paid visits to the leading men from all religious groups. During meetings that were both private and public, Faisal was able to strengthen his own power, but, at the same time, he had to recognise the other political players as legitimate interlocutors. Between 1921 and 1924, key issues shaped the dialogue between the four pillars of power in Iraq.[48] First, at the end of 1921, the British wanted Faisal to endorse a treaty that would establish their own pre-eminence in the country. A treaty was duly signed the following year, but it had to be ratified by the Council of Ministers. Second, Shia leaders continued to struggle against what they perceived as a foreign order and denounced the creation of the monarchy. Third, the future of northern Iraq, where the Kurdish presence was strong, remained uncertain, especially throughout 1923, and the British, mostly through their local agents, advocated a degree of autonomy for the region.[49] Fourth, in the south, the struggle between Wahhabi forces – a federated group of tribes driven by the religious call of Ibn Wahhab in favour of Sunni Islam and headed by Ibn

Saud, founder of Saudi Arabian Kingdom – and Iraqi troops revealed the fragility of the country. The British thus used the issue of security as a pretext to impose their rule over the newly established monarch. It became obvious to all the actors taking part that no arrangement could take root without the adoption of the new constitution.

These various constraints had a deep impact on political practice, though without fundamentally changing the way in which the monarchy was being created. In May 1924, a constitutional assembly was elected and, when it gathered for the first time, a subcommittee was quickly formed to consider the best form of government for Iraq. Several constitutional projects from all around the world were studied by this mixed committee composed of experts and politicians. As David Cannadine has put it, a new act in the imperial play could be performed.[50] Among all the constitutions considered, the Australian one seemed particularly relevant to the Iraqi situation, though requiring some alterations.[51] Picking one imperial model to apply to another territory was, Linda Colley argues, one of the most common practices employed to legalise and standardise the principal institutions around the Empire.[52] Following the advice of this committee, the Constitutional Assembly went on to ratify the proposal developed for the new constitution. In this organic law (*qânûn al-ta'sîs*), the king was granted a considerable number of powers though, as Article 19 proclaimed, he shared sovereignty with the people.[53] He was able to nominate the Senate (the upper house), call elections for the House of Representatives and postpone the implementation of new laws, among other prerogatives. In short, he became the central power in the institutional apparatus of the state. The Hashemite monarchy remained a parliamentary and constitutional regime, and, through the constitution, the British experts managed to strengthen the royal position since they saw the king as their main ally.

The most pressing issue of the new constitutional assembly remained the treaty between Iraq and Britain. The British put pressure on the King for the constitution to be ratified, but, while members of the assembly seemed to favour the monarchy, this did not mean that they supported the British order. When the British advisers intervened in the electoral processes, and in social and political policy, their actions produced undesired consequences. Most of the members of the constitutional assembly belonged to noble families, such as the Saaduns, who came from a great tribal confederation in southern Iraq. However, these figures were quickly able to bargain for their own institutional position rather than to bow to either the British or Faisal's will.[54] Eventually, the new system reinforced a pre-war model in which notables entered governing councils, discussed and amended the laws in order to gain resources for their own networks of power and clientelage and strengthened their symbolic capital. The Anglo-Iraqi Treaty of 1922 constituted the major plank in this framework, and, between 1924 and 1928, its workings revealed how 'democratic practices' emerged through the competitions between different centres of power.

A monarch under control? The prolonged ousting of the British

The first years of the monarchy witnessed the exercise of a heavy British hand over the country. The British nevertheless still negotiated their withdrawal from Iraq in return for the signing and ratification of the Anglo-Iraqi Treaty. The document enabled them to retain military bases in the country and to maintain control over its oil resources through the Iraq Petroleum Company. Oil became an important issue in the aftermath of 1928, when resources were discovered in Mosul. Even if production was much lower than in Iran, the British wanted to secure the Iraqi reserves. They associated American, French and Dutch companies into the new Iraq Petroleum Company, which also held a monopoly over production in all territories in the north of what is now Saudi Arabia. The British position on petroleum received support from the sherifian officers and the Iraqi army officers who had struggled with Faisal against the Ottoman rulers during the First World War.

The new elites had to build their own power base as they did not belong to the noble Iraqi families.[55] As a result, the balance of forces in Iraq between 1925 and 1932 remained unclear. The King obtained the main constitutional prerogatives, but he depended on British will to implement them. The British expected the King and the other institutions to be the true representatives of the Iraqi people and, at the same time, to be moderate, in other words to agree to British wishes and advice. The Prime Minister and members of the Council of Ministers were, on the one hand, powerful, thanks to their personal networks of power, but, on the other, they were weak because they were subject to royal and parliamentary pressure. Finally, parliament also had to face the instability of public opinion. In 1928, so much public pressure was exerted on Prime Minister Saadun, one of the most powerful politicians in Iraq, that he committed suicide, unable to face the dilemmas entailed in enforcing the Anglo-Iraqi Treaty.

A settlement of the ambiguous international situation of Iraq finally appeared on the eve of the 1930s. Britain would support Iraq's admission to the League of Nations and recognition of Iraq's independence (see Figure 20); in return, Iraq would endorse an arrangement allowing British forces to remain in the country to support the monarchy, and the boundaries of the country would be definitively established, which meant the integration of the largely Kurdish *wilâya* of Mosul.

This compromise resulted from the great bargain between, on the one hand, Iraq and Britain, and, on the other, that between the different groups that made up the Iraqi political elite. A new figure emerged from these negotiations, Nuri as-Said, who succeeded in having members of parliament who were favourable to him elected, men likely to ratify the Anglo-Iraqi Treaty.[56] In 1932, Nuri as-Said achieved his first success: Iraq under the Hashemite monarchy became fully independent, while the British nevertheless remained powerfully present in the country, operating two air bases and controlling the oil resources. The British were also allowed to send troops into the country in the case of war.

20. Photograph of King Faisal I and associates at the celebration of Iraq becoming a member of the League of Nations; Royal Palace, Baghdad, 6 October 1932. American Colony (Jerusalem), G. Eric and Edith Matson Photograph Collection, Library of Congress Prints and Photographs Division, Washington, DC, Wikimedians of Levant – GLAM Project. Wikimedia Commons

How did independence change the relationships between the British, the monarchy and the Iraqi territory? Iraq, in the imperial cartography, became part of Britain's informal empire. Although the formal British advisers left the country, most experts and foreign civil servants in Iraq remained British.[57] Therefore, if Britain's formal mandate over the country came to an end, the British retained a degree of effective control.[58] In 1933, Faisal I died, and his son Ghazzi succeeded him. The British saw him as a weak person, and they quickly feared that he could support the nationalist point of view.[59] As the British were facing new challenges in the mid-1930s, in particular the growing threat of Germany, they no longer saw Iraqi affairs from a strictly colonial point of view. Iraq acquired a more significant strategic position, and it was vital that the monarchy upheld the alliance with the British.[60] Even if the British authorities ended their direct involvement, they could nevertheless provide various sorts of benefits and exercise different types of pressure on the Iraqis. They agreed to support cabinets and politicians by promising military intervention in case of unrest. They did not oppose several coups that took place between 1936 and 1940. Certainly, the British expressed their preference for some politicians rather than others, but, overall, their hold over the country diminished, and they focused on the key tools the Treaty provided them. They looked upon the Hashemite monarchs as clients and dependents who were not able to challenge their international position, but they did not seek to interfere in the day-to-day running of the country. In 1939, Ghazzi died in a car accident. The four-year-old Faisal II succeeded him. The British saw the misfortune as an opportunity to nominate a regent who was friendly towards them. However, this position abruptly came to an end during the Second World War, when a coup overthrew the regent, Abdulillah, and brought to power a cabinet known for its anti-British stance.[61] British military forces then invaded the country, occupied it for the next three years (1941–44) and re-established the Hashemite regent. Once more, the Hashemite dynasty was brought to power, thanks to the British.

The relationship between the British and the Iraqi monarchy in the aftermath of the 1941 occupation and the Second World War has been well documented.[62] Several points can be underlined. Imperial control decreased: the British no longer sought, or were not able to seek, to determine day-to-day policies. What mattered was the flow of oil and the containment of Communism. The year 1948 marked a turning point as the Palestine war witnessed the retreat of British troops, leaving a dramatically negative effect on British prestige.[63] Political practice nevertheless continued as usual in Iraq. Men from the elite, cabinets and the royal court continued to negotiate among themselves on how to develop the country and increase the national wealth.[64] New demands supported by social classes that emerged in the aftermath of the war meanwhile shook the political order. Demonstrators in Baghdad in 1948 demanded the full implementation of the constitution, that is, a renewed constitutional monarchy founded on liberal practices.[65] These dynamics both undermined the monarchy and clashed with its innate interests. Finally, in 1958, the monarchy was overthrown by a military coup led by Colonels Aref and Qassem. A few years subsequently, the smaller Gulf kingdoms all won their independence, thus putting an end to British involvement in the region.[66]

When the British extended their influence in the Gulf, from Hormuz to Basra, they did not set out to implement a ready-made plan of domination. They intervened on particular issues, such as fighting against piracy or preventing foreign powers from gaining significant footholds. This effort led the British to enter into contact with local elites, particularly the sheikhs. The sheikhs defended their own agenda, which mainly focused on strengthening their position on the local stage. New actors also emerged from the relationship and they worked to institutionalise their control over the territory. Similar processes shaped modern Iraq. But, contrary to the rest of the Gulf, other dynamics had changed the local situation. The Ottoman imperial reforms produced a deep impact on politics and the elites. Therefore, notables reinforced their position by cooperating with the imperial power. The parliamentary system established in 1908 provided them an official institutional role, and they became partners in the policy-making process. When the British conquered Iraq during the First World War, they had to take this reality into account. They created a constitutional structure to rule the country, which was then used by the local actors to negotiate their new status. The formal framework built a parliamentary system and a constitutional monarchy. However, in practice, this architecture of power was controlled by local actors who used it for other purposes than those envisaged by the British. As a consequence, during the monarchical period, modernisation of the Iraqi state took place, and the monarchy set up by the British pursued a reinvention of traditional practices through new institutions and goals.

Notes

1 'Abd al-Razzâq al-Hassanî, *Târîkh al-Wuzârâ'al-'irâqîyya* [*History of the Iraqi Ministries*], 10 vols. (Baghdad: Wizâra al-thaqâfa, 1982), vol. I, pp. 77 ff.
2 Daniel Silverfarbe, *Britain's Informal Empire in the Middle East: A Case Study of Iraq, 1929–1941* (Oxford: Oxford University Press, 1986).

3 As Albert Hourani defines them, 'great families ... which reside mainly in the city, draw their strength from there, and because of their position in the city, were able also to dominate a rural hinterland, and ... these notables have some freedom of political action'. Albert Hourani, 'Ottoman Reforms and the Politics of Notables', in Albert Hourani, Philip Khoury and Mary Wilson (eds), *The Modern Middle East* (Berkeley, Calif.: University of California Press, 1993), p. 87.
4 On the historical roots of Iraq and nationalist claims, see Eric Davies, *Memories of States: Politics, Memories, and Collective Identity in Modern Iraq* (Berkeley, Calif.: University of California Press, 2005).
5 Toby Dodge, *Inventing Iraq: The Failure of the Nation Building and a History Denied* (New York: Columbia University Press, 2003); Michael Eppel, *Iraq from Monarchy to Tyranny: From the Hashimites to the Rise of Saddam* (Gainesville, Fla.: University Press of Florida, 2004).
6 Adham Saouil, *The Arab States: Dilemma of Late Formation* (London and New York: Routledge, 2014); Gokhan Bacik, *Hybrid Sovereignty in the Arab Middle East: The Case of Kuwait, Iraq and Jordan* (Basingstoke: Palgrave Macmillan, 2008).
7 Bertrand Badie, *L'État importé: essai sur l'occidentalisation de l'ordre politique* (Paris: Fayard, 1992); Nazih Ayubi, *Overstating the Arab States: Politics and Society in the Middle East* (London: I. B. Tauris, 1996).
8 Daniel Neep, *Occupying Syria under the French Mandate: Insurgency, Space and State Formation* (Cambridge: Cambridge University Press, 2014).
9 Paul DiMaggio and Walter Powell, *The New Institutionalism in Organizational Analysis* (Chicago, Ill.: University of Chicago Press, 1991).
10 For a discussion of the informal empire, see John Gallagher and Ronald Robinson, 'The Imperialism of Free Trade', *The Economic History Review*, 6:1 (1953), 1–15, p. 5. For a discussion of Iraq's status in the empire, see Majid A. Majid, *L'Émergence d'un état à l'ombre d'un empire: Grande-Bretagne – Irak* (Paris: Publication de la Sorbonne, 1996); and Silverfarbe, *Britain's Informal Empire*, pp. 14–18.
11 Malcolm Yapp, 'Nineteenth and Twentieth Centuries', in Alvin Cottrell (ed.), *The Persian Gulf States: A General Survey* (Baltimore, Md.: Johns Hopkins University Press, 1980), pp. 41–69; and 'British Policy in the Persian Gulf', in Alvin Cottrell (ed.), *The Persian Gulf States: A General Survey* (Baltimore, Md.: Johns Hopkins University Press, 1980), pp. 70–100, at p. 70; Hugh Arbunott, Terrence Clark and Richard Muir, *British Missions around the Gulf, 1575–2005* (Folkestone: Global Oriental, 2008), pp. 81–9.
12 Peter Sluglett, 'Formal and Informal Empire in the Middle East', in Robin Winks (ed.), *Historiography: The Oxford History of the British Empire* (Oxford: Oxford University Press, 2001), vol. V, pp. 417–18; Cottrell, *The Persian Gulf States*, pp. 74–7; David Commins, *The Gulf States: A Modern History* (London: I. B. Tauris, 2012), p. 58.
13 J. A. Saldanha (ed.), *The Persian Gulf Précis* (London: Archive Editions, 1986), pp. 93–7.
14 Zaki Saleh, *Britain and Iraq: A Study in British Foreign Affairs* (London: Books & Books, 1995), pp. 127–31; Hanna Batatu, *Old Classes and Revolutionary Movements of Iraq: A Study of Iraq's Old Landed and Commercial Classes and of Its Communists, Ba'athists, and Free Officers* (Princeton, NJ: Princeton University Press, 1979), pp. 73 ff.
15 J. B. Kelly, *Britain and the Persian Gulf, 1795–1880* (Oxford: Clarendon, 1968), p. 30 ff; Sultan bin Mohammadal-Qasimi, *John Malcolm and the British Commercial Base in the Gulf, 1800* (Sharjah: al-Khalīj lil-Ṣiḥāfah wa-al-Ṭibāʻah wa-al-Nashr, 1994).
16 Cottrell, *The Persian Gulf States*, pp. 73–6.
17 Daniel Foliard, 'La Terre vague: genèses du Moyen-Orient dans les savoirs et la culture britanniques, 1850–1914', Ph.D. thesis, University of Paris, 2011, pp. 67 ff.
18 Saldanha, *The Persian Gulf*, pp. 101–17; Kelly, *Britain and the Persian Gulf*, pp. 260–90.
19 Frederick Anscombe, *The Ottoman Gulf: The Creation of Kuwait, Saudi Arabia and Qatar* (New York: Columbia University Press, 1997), pp. 7 ff.

20 Commins, *The Gulf States*, pp. 71 ff.
21 Frederic Ascombe, 'The Ottoman Role in the Gulf', in Lawrence Potter (ed.), *The Persian Gulf in History* (Basingstoke: Palgrave Macmillan, 2009), pp. 265–7; Allen J. Fromherz, *Qatar: A Modern History* (London: I. B. Tauris, 2012), pp. 41–65.
22 This confirms James Onley's conclusions on mutual understanding. James Onley, *The Arabian Frontier of British Raj: Merchants, Rulers, and the British in the Nineteenth Century* (Oxford: Oxford University Press, 2007).
23 Georg Antonius, *The Arab Awakening: The Story of the Arab National Movement* (London: Simons Publications, 1965).
24 Ian Rutledge, *Enemy on the Euphrates: The British Occupation of Iraq and the Great Revolt, 1914–1920* (London: Saqi, 2014).
25 Gökhan Centisaya, *Ottoman Administration of Iraq, 1890–1908* (London and New York: Routledge, 2006); 'Alî al-Wardî, *Lamhât 'Ijtima'iyya mîn târîkh al 'iraq al hadîth* [*Sociological Elements on Modern Iraqi History*], 6 vols. (Baghdad: Dâr wa Maktaba al-mutanayya, 2005), vol. I.
26 Pierre-Jean Luizard, *La Formation de l'Irak contemporaine, le rôle politique des ulémas à la fin de la domination ottomane et au moment de la création de l'état irakien* (Paris: CNRS, 2002), pp. 140–85; Salâh 'Abd al-Razzâq, *Al-dustûr wa al-barlamân fî al-fikr al-siyâssî al-islâmî, 1905–1920* (*The Constitution and the Parliament in Islamic Political Ideas*) (Baghdad: al-'Ans, 2003), pp. 17–23.
27 Feroz Ahmad, *The Young Turks and the Ottoman Nationalities: Armenians, Greeks, Albanians, Jews and Arabs, 1908–1918* (Ann Arbor, Mich.: University of Michigan Press, 2014), pp. 114–20.
28 Orit Bashkin, *The Other Iraq: Pluralism and Culture in Hashemite Iraq* (Palo Alto, Calif.: Stanford University Press, 2009).
29 'Alî al-Wardî, *Lamhât 'Ijtima'iyya*, vol. IV.
30 Peter Sluglett, *Britain in Iraq: Contriving King and Country, 1914–1932* (London: Ithaca Press, 2007), p. 28 ff.
31 Several discussions nowadays argue that oil was the main goal of war. Were the British aware of the Iraqi wealth? Certainly, they viewed Iraq as a part of the strategic road towards Persian oil which had been discovered in 1908. They presumed that Mosul province could provide oil. But until 1945 oil remained mainly a Persian production. Moreover, the oil market, as Timothy Mitchell explains, was framed in a very particular way in which production was not the main goal. If the British were interested in oil, strategic considerations were more important: they needed air bases in the Middle East to refuel planes flying from Europe to Asia. Timothy Mitchell, *Carbon Democracy: Political Power in the Age of Oil* (New York: Verso, 2011).
32 Dodge, *Inventing Iraq*, pp. 4 ff.
33 Ian Rutledge, *Enemy on the Euphrates: The British Occupation of Iraq and the Great Arab Revolt, 1914–1921* (London: Saqi, 2014), pp. 237 ff.
34 Dodge, *Inventing Iraq*, pp. 6–7, 13–16; Thomas Knock, *To End All Wars: Woodrow Wilson and the Quest for a New World Order* (Princeton, NJ: Princeton University Press, 1992), pp. 168 ff.
35 Paul Cambon and Edward Grey signed the accord known as Sykes–Picot Agreement in the aftermath of the war. It allowed the British to refuse it.
36 Vincent Cloarec, *La France et la question de Syrie, 1914–1918* (Paris: CNRS, 1998), pp. 137–60.
37 See Scott Anderson, *Lawrence in Arabia: War, Deceit, Imperial Folly and the Making of the Modern Middle East* (New York: Doubleday, 2013), especially Chapter 9, 'The Man Who Would Be Kingmaker'.
38 Aaron Klieman, *Foundations of British Policy in the World: The Cairo Conference of 1921* (Baltimore, Md.: Johns Hopkins University Press, 1970).
39 'Abd al-Razzâq al-Hassanî, *Târîkh*, vol. III; Habibolah, Aratodi *Great Powers, Oil, and the Kurds in Mosul (Southern Kurdistan, Northern Iraq), 1910–1925* (Lanham, Md.: University Press of America, 2003).
40 The Iraqi Archives contains several files on the court record (no. 131 in the National Archive, in Iraqi National Library in Baghdad).

41 Janet Wallach, *Desert Queen: The Extraordinary Life of Gertrude Bell – Adventurer, Adviser to Kings, Ally of Lawrence of Arabia* (New York: Doubleday, 2005); Georgina Howell, *Gertrude Bell: Queen of the Desert, Shaper of Nations* (New York: Farrar, Straus & Giroux, 2008).
42 Luizard, *La Formation de l'Irak*.
43 Dodge, *Inventing Iraq*.
44 Allawi, *Faisal I*, p. 363.
45 The *naqib* was the head of the union of *ashraf* (plural of *sharif*), the heirs of the prophet. It was a very prestigious position.
46 Reidar Visser, *Basra, The Failed Gulf State: Separatism and Nationalism in Southern Iraq* (Munster: LIT Verlag, 2005).
47 Allawi, *Faisal I*, pp. 366–7.
48 Majlis al-Nuwwâb al-'irâqî, *Mahâdir majlis al-nuwwâb al-'irâqî*, 2 vols. (Baghdad: Majlis al-Nuwwab al-Iraqi, 1925–26).
49 Salah Jmor, *L'Origine de la question kurde* (Paris: L'Harmattan, 1994).
50 David Cannadine, 'Empire as Theatre', conference presentation at Empire of State of Mind: Articulations of British Culture in the Empire, 1707–1997, Lingnan University, Hong Kong, 24–6 May 2012.
51 Ra'd Nâjî al-Jada, *Al-Tatawwurât al-dustûriyya fî al-'irâq* (Baghdad: Bayt al-Hikma, 2004).
52 Linda Colley, 'Words and the World: Britain, Written Constitution and the Empire, 1780–1980', conference presentation at Empire of State of Mind: Articulations of British Culture in the Empire, 1707–1997, Lingnan University, Hong Kong, 24–6 May 2012.
53 See www.constitution.org/cons/iraq/iraqiconst19250321.html (accessed 11 February 2015).
54 'Ala Hussayn al-Rahînî, *Al-mu'ârada al-barlamâniyya fî al-'irâq fî 'ahd al-malik Faisal al-awwal* [*The Parliamentary Opposition in Iraq during the Reign of Faisal I*] (Baghdad: Bayt al-hikma, 2008), pp. 265 ff.
55 Interview with Fûlath Hadîd, London, 8 August 2009.
56 Khaîrî Amîn al-'Umrî, *Al-khilâf bayn al-balât al-malakî wa Nûrî al-Sa'îd 1921–1958 ma'a âham al-rasâ'îl allatî kâna yaktabuhâ Nûrî al-Saîd* [*Differences between the Monarchical Court and Nûrî al-Sa'îd*] (Beirut: Dâr al-'arabiyya lilmawsû'ât, 2008), pp. 32 ff.
57 Robert Jarman (ed.), *Political Diaries of the Arab World: Iraq*, 8 vols., vol. VI: *1932–1947* (Farnham Common, Slough: Archive Editions, 1998).
58 William Roger Louis, *The British Empire in the Middle East, 1945–1951: Arab Nationalism, the United States and Postwar Imperialism* (Oxford: Clarendon Press, 1984).
59 Gérard de Gaury, *Three Kings in Baghdad: The Tragedy of Iraq's Monarchy* (London: I. B. Tauris, 2008).
60 Silverfarbe, *Britain's Informal Empire*.
61 Daniel Silverfarbe, *The Twilight of British Ascendancy in the Middle East: A Case Study of Iraq, 1941–1950* (Basingstoke: Macmillan, 1994).
62 Matthew Elliot, *Independent Iraq, the Monarchy and British Influence* (London: Tauris Academic Studies, 1996).
63 Louis, *The British Empire*, pp. 89 ff.
64 Matthieu Rey, 'Le Parlementarisme en Irak et en Syrie entre 1946 et 1963: un temps de pluralisme au Moyen Orient', Ph.D. thesis, École des Hautes Études en Sciences Sociales, Paris, 2013, pp. 167–229.
65 Matthieu Rey, 'La Wathba, manifester en Irak en 1948', *Vingtième Siècle, Revue d'Histoire*, 4:108 (2010), 25–38.
66 Jeffrey Macris, *The Politics and Security of the Gulf: Anglo-American Hegemony and the Shaping of the Region* (London and New York: Routledge, 2012).

CHAPTER THIRTEEN

An empire for a kingdom: monarchy and Fascism in the Italian colonies

Alessandro Pes

The place of the royal house in the history of Italy has been mostly studied in terms of aspects of domestic policy. In particular, research has concentrated along two lines: first, the dynamics of the royal house's domestic life from the unification of Italy in 1861 until the abdication of the King in 1946; and, second, the interaction between the monarchy, the parliament and political parties. In the latter area, however, little attention has been given to the role that the royal house played in the determination of foreign policy, and especially in Italian expansion overseas. This lacuna can be partly explained by the lack of archival documents concerning the House of Savoy, particularly for the 1922–45 period. That phenomenon is connected with the way in which Italy passed from a monarchical to a republican regime; following the plebiscite, in which a majority of Italians voted in favour of a republic in 1946, the members of the royal family were exiled, and they took along with them a large part of the archives of the dynasty. Notwithstanding the scarcity of primary material, historical studies have used the relatively few available royal sources as well as the records of parliament, ministries and other administrative departments with which the royal family engaged during its reign. One of the key features in that history, and one of the least studied, concerns the relationship of the House of Savoy, and, in particular, King Vittorio Emanuele III, with the Fascist regime from 1922 to 1945.[1] This relationship has been primarily investigated from the perspective of constitutional law, with attempts to understand how the Fascist regime tried to appropriate various royal prerogatives and, in several situations, substituted the figure of the King with that of the head of government – that is, how it replaced Vittorio Emanuele III with Benito Mussolini. The dominant historiographical interpretation is that the Fascist regime placed itself in the symbolic and political role of the royal family during this period.

This chapter will take an approach to the relationship between the King and Duce that has seldom been used. Fascism managed to take the place of the monarchy as the main political and symbolic reference point for Italians, but to what extent did it use the colonies and the empire of Italian East Africa to position itself above the royal house? Were the colonies – about which, it must be emphasised, most Italians had little concrete knowledge – presented as a terrain for the concrete construction of Fascism and of Mussolini as the unique political symbol for the Italians? To answer these questions, the chapter will offer a brief sketch of the principal developments of Italian colonial expansion from 1861 to 1922, delineating the role of the royal house in the policy of expansion; it will then turn to colonialism in the Fascist period, focusing on the real and symbolic role played by the Italian monarchy in this era. It will demonstrate how, propagandistically, the colonies were represented as a Fascist achievement, with the King only a subsidiary actor in the process; this aspect of Fascist propaganda can best be witnessed through an examination of the way newspapers, especially the Rome daily *Il Messaggero*, represented Vittorio Emanuele III's tour of Libya in 1938. Analysing these accounts of the monarch's colonial journey helps illuminate the Fascist effort to displace the figure of the King with that of Mussolini. Finally, the chapter will consider Amedeo d'Aosta, a member of the royal house who was appointed Governor-General of Italian East Africa in December 1937, in light both of biographies of Amedeo and of a long and detailed report on him and his administration compiled by Katherine Fannin, a British journalist and friend of the Governor-General, based on her two trips to Italian East Africa, her interviews with Amedeo and her observations on the civil and military organisation of the empire.

A discussion of the administration of Amedeo d'Aosta in Italian East Africa is particularly significant here because of his unique position as a member of the royal family chosen by the Fascist regime to govern the colonies. His appointment marks the arrival in the Italian colonial domain of the diarchy that characterised the Kingdom of Italy itself – the parallel spheres of the monarchy, on the one hand, and the Fascist regime, on the other. Amedeo's very presence in the colonies, holding the most senior position in Italian East Africa, came to be a more or less insurmountable obstacle to the representation of the overseas empire as a solely Fascist realm. However, Italy's entry into the Second World War was to diminish the symbolic role that the regime's propaganda assigned to the colonial empire. As the war became the key catalyst for propaganda efforts, Amedeo d'Aosta and the imperial mission were drawn, via the wars on the African fronts, into the broader military and propaganda context of the world war.

AN EMPIRE FOR A KINGDOM

Colonial expansion of the Italian kingdom

By the time the Kingdom of Italy acquired its first colonial possession (Assab on the Red Sea coast of eastern Africa) in 1882, most of the other major European states had already initiated a policy of expansion in Africa and Asia. The Italian government, its unity secured in 1861 and completed with the annexation of Rome in 1870, undertook its first incursion in the colonial world without a clearly articulated project of overseas expansion. The takeover of Assab[2] was initially more the product of international dynamics and the political equilibrium among the European powers on the Horn of Africa than the result of a specific design for expansion in this area by the Italian government.[3] The Horn of Africa nevertheless became, from that date onwards, one of the two regions in which the Kingdom of Italy then planned its expansion. Between 1885 and 1896, an Italian colonial project in eastern Africa became reality through the conquest of the port of Massawa in 1885 and subsequent penetration of the hinterland. In 1890, Italy set up its first formal colony in eastern Africa, Eritrea, which became the base during the last decade of the nineteenth century for further expansion southwards, in the direction of Somalia, and westwards – with an effort to occupy the Ethiopian Empire.[4]

In the first phase of that effort, from 1889 to 1892, the Italian government employed diplomatic means to attempt to gain control over Ethiopia. The signing of the Treaty of Uccialli between the Kingdom of Italy and the Ethiopian Empire – represented by the future *Negusa Negast* (emperor) Menelik II – appeared at first as the formal establishment of an Italian protectorate over Ethiopia, which had been, along with Liberia, the only African state to retain its independence against the 'scramble for Africa'.[5] The treaty was nevertheless then denounced by Ethiopia because the version in Amharic contained no reference to a potential Italian protectorate over the Ethiopian Empire but only reference to the possibility of favoured trade relations. A long and unresolved diplomatic dispute convinced the Italian government, under Prime Minister Francesco Crispi, to prepare for a military campaign to occupy the Ethiopian Empire. But the effort to invade Ethiopia wound up in the worst military defeat suffered by a European country in a colonial war. In the battle of Adwa, on 1 March 1896, the Italian Army was soundly beaten by the Ethiopian forces, and so, too, was the political project of occupying Ethiopia.[6] Notwithstanding the failure of the expansionist endeavour in Ethiopia and the subsequent resignation of Prime Minister Crispi, succeeding governments continued to develop plans for expansion on the Horn of Africa.

From 1893, Somalia was subjected to Italian administration in the form of a chartered company, the Società Filonardi, though it produced such meagre results that three years later administration passed into the hands of the newly founded Società Commerciale Italiana del Benadir. That company's results were similarly far from positive, and from 1905, with the setting up of the commissariat of northern Somalia, the Kingdom of Italy took over direct administration of the Somali region.[7] Meanwhile, in 1900, in return for its participation in the war to suppress the Boxer rebellion in China, Italy was given its first and only Asian colony: a small 'concession' in the port city of Tianjin.[8] In the first years of the twentieth century, Italian colonial policy also turned to the coast of North Africa.

In fact, the southern shores of the Mediterranean had appeared as the prime objective for Italian expansion from the early days of the Kingdom of Italy. The first efforts were directed towards Tunisia, which played host to a substantial community of Italian migrants; the imposition of a French protectorate over the region in 1881, however, ended Italian hopes for expansion in that area. The disintegration of the Ottoman Empire in the early 1900s seemed to present possibilities for the Kingdom of Italy to acquire a colony in the Mediterranean, and Italian sights were directed there. Tripolitania and Cyrenaica were conquered in the Italo-Turkish War of 1911–12 and became the colony of Libya. At first, Italian control was limited to coastal regions, however, and only later, primarily in the Fascist era, did the Italians penetrate further south, into the Fezzan.[9]

With the advent of the Fascist regime, colonial expansion became one of the key planks in Italian foreign policy, concentrating until 1931 on the consolidation of Italian control over Libya.[10] After that date, the main thrust of Italian policy was directed towards a new project: the occupation of Ethiopia.[11] In 1935–36, in a military campaign that cost vast sums, the Kingdom of Italy conquered Ethiopia.[12] Uniting the newly conquered territory with the possessions of Eritrea and Somalia, the Fascist regime officially proclaimed the empire of Africa Orientale Italiana (Italian East Africa) in 1936.

The Royal House and the colonies in 'liberal' Italy

During the 'liberal' period (1861–1922), the royal house played a limited role in the birth and early development of a policy of colonial expansion. The House of Savoy had been involved from the beginning in the development of the Italian geographical societies that would be among the most influential actors in the emergence of expansionism.[13] Soon after the incorporation of Rome into the new Italian kingdom in

1870, the crown prince, Umberto, was named honorary president of the Società Geografica Italiana, implying a change of direction from a previously humanitarian mandate to a more political brief for the society. Nevertheless, the dynasty did not have a fundamental role in the decision by Italy to pursue an expansionist policy. As Angelo Del Boca has shown, even before he became king of a united Italy in 1860, Vittorio Emanuele – then King of Sardinia-Piedmont – had contacts with the Ethiopian elite, though he had used these to signal the complete lack of interest of Sardinia-Piedmont in negotiating trade agreements with Ethiopia.[14] After Italian unification, the 1889 Treaty of Uccialli ceded Eritrea to the Italians. The first official contact between the Italian royal family and Ethiopian dignitaries, however, took place only in August 1890, when a delegation of Ethiopian notables led by Ras Tafari Makonnen (the future *Negusa Negast* Haile Selassie) met King Umberto I. An official procession carried the dignitaries across Rome to the Quirinale, the royal palace. According to accounts of the meeting, Ras Tafari Makonnen asked for Italian protection over Ethiopia in order to guarantee peace in the country; the King of Italy responded that Italy had safeguarded the peace in its own colonial possessions and would do likewise in the Ethiopian Empire.

After their visit to the King, the Ethiopian delegation journeyed to various Italian cities, its tour organised by the Italian government so as to leave a positive impression on the visitors of the grandeur and modernity of the Kingdom of Italy. Just six years later, Italy declared war against the Ethiopian Empire, attempting to use the force of arms to subject the realm of Menelik II to its suzerainty.

The colonial empire, between monarchy and Fascism

With the rise to power of Fascism in 1922, and particularly with the beginning of Fascist moves towards a totalitarian state in 1925, the Italian royal house had to share both its real and symbolic power, as the figure of Mussolini became increasingly central to the way the regime exercised power over its citizens.[15] This diarchy – monarchy and Fascist regime – soon became apparent in the colonial sphere. Both Libya and the Italian territories in eastern Africa became the destination for a large number of Italian workers. Starting with the campaign of 'pacification' of Libya in the late 1920s and early 1930s, the peopling of these conquered colonies – and their transformation into Italian settler-colonies – became a clear and specific objective of the regime. The project was nurtured by the Fascist government through a complex and enduring propaganda campaign which discursively supported the regime's concrete projects. This particularity represented a distinctive characteristic of Italian colonialism, by comparison with other empires, in the administration and management of colonies.[16] Italian colonialism in the 1930s constructed around itself a kind of self-narration.

In this narrative, Italian settler colonialism was not to be considered a project of usurpation or exploitation but, rather, an endeavour that would secure a future unavailable for the masses of Italians who would otherwise remain on the Italian peninsula, a way of elevating them from their uncivilised status. This aim alone was sufficient, according to the propaganda, to distinguish Fascist Italy's form of colonialism from the sort practised by capitalist countries. For Italy, colonial possessions were a necessity, whereas for other countries they represented a means of accumulating a surplus of profits from the riches of the conquered lands, a strategy that would widen disparities between the colonising and subject populations. The difference between Fascist colonialism and that of other European governments was thus the very nature of the basis of conquest. As the poet, political figure and supporter of Fascism Gabriele D'Annunzio put it, the conquest of Ethiopia and the subsequent creation of the empire of Italian East Africa represented a fundamental stage in the struggle undertaken by the new Italy, 'the heir of ancient values, against the disastrous ideology and political action of Britain; the struggle, in sum, of a good imperialism, the vehicle of civilisation, against a bad imperialism, greedy, merely utilitarian and destructive'.[17]

Fascist imperialism, in short, through its propaganda, tried to set out a new model of colonial governance, different from the sorts of overlordship imposed by other European countries. Christopher Seton-Watson identified several major motives for Italian colonialism. The principal reason Italians undertook overseas expansion, both in the liberal and the Fascist periods, according to Seton-Watson, was the quest for glory and prestige. Industrial imperialism – the key agents for which were the bankers, the traders and the owners of small factories in northern Italy – translated as a search for markets, natural resources and opportunities for investment.[18] The demographic colonialism promoted by the politicians for the peasants of southern Italy became the search for land on which to settle the surplus population of the peninsula, in places where they could live their lives under the Italian flag.[19]

Certainly Seton-Watson has a point in his analysis about the significant traits that characterised Italian colonial policy, even if his explanation leaves out the racist element that formed one of the defining particularities of Italian colonial ideology and policy, at least in the Fascist period. However, in light of the historical scholarship since the 1980s, it is now difficult to sustain his emphasis that the quest for prestige and glory provided the key motive for Fascist colonialism. Italian plans for the complete occupation of Libya, the conquest of Ethiopia and the creation of a formal empire of Italian East Africa, and extension of Italian influence throughout the Mediterranean region, had little to do with a search for glory.[20] Rather, the plans were more practically oriented to gaining political and economic control over a clearly defined area. If the search for prestige did play a role in the colonial ideology developing in Italy, it was less a trigger for a policy of expansionism and more the most visible aspect of propaganda aiming to galvanise the nation in support of colonialism. The continual references in colonial propaganda to the ancient Roman past served the aim of recruiting Italian support for the regime and creating a sense of belonging to the nation. That nation entered the colonial arena with a very specific inheritance, that of ancient Rome, and, at the same time, was called upon to develop its own model of administration, one that distinguished it from other European colonial powers.

In addition to providing Fascism with a victory in an area where the previous regime had palpably failed, the conquest of Ethiopia also allowed Mussolini to portray Fascism as a movement for the regeneration of Italian society, the sole movement worthy of inheriting the imperial dignity of ancient Rome and of resurrecting it in the present day. In this sense, the colonial arena, and even more the wider imperial sphere, became one of the symbolic and concrete sites in which the Fascist regime sought to demonstrate to the Italians its own moral superiority with regards to the monarchy.

The military campaign that led to the Italian conquest of Ethiopia commenced on 3 October 1935 and concluded on 5 May 1936 with the entry of Marshal Pietro Badoglio into the capital of Addis Ababa. Preparations for the campaign had already highlighted the political will of the regime to cast the war in a Fascist mould; Mussolini had decided that the military contingents that would take part would become part of the Fascist militia.[21] This had a very specific meaning: the war of conquest would not be that simply of a royal army but also of a military corps linked to the political regime and thus would show at the end of the war that Ethiopia had been conquered on the battlefield of Fascism.[22] On 9 May 1936, Mussolini proclaimed the establishment of the Empire of Italian East Africa, using the historic moment to set before the Italians the hierarchical relationship between the regime and the monarchy, and between the Duce and the King. With the birth of the African Empire, Mussolini proclaimed Vittorio Emanuele III Emperor of Ethiopia, but underlined that the empire was a Fascist conquest. As Paolo Colombo has noted:

> In these words [of his speech] the references to the monarchy are minimal and hasty: a citation of the two succinct articles of the royal legislative decree of 9 May 1936 No. 754 and a telegraphic final phrase: 'Long live the king!' It was certainly not the new crown to be placed on the head of the 'little king' [Vittorio Emanuele III] that was being hailed.[23]

At the very moment of its birth, the Empire of Italian East Africa was thus characterised by the ambiguity of its nature: who was to be considered the real emperor? Mussolini, who had already represented this conquest as a gift that Fascism was making to the Crown and the nation, or Vittorio Emanuele III, who formally became Emperor of Ethiopia but who had received his imperial crown from the Fascist Duce? Fascist propaganda and rhetoric would use this ambiguity to promote among the Italians the idea that Mussolini was the sole person responsible for the new imperial dignity of which all could be proud. The Fascist newspapers were one of the principal conduits through which this ambiguity was presented to Italian society. Its key characteristics can be seen in the reports published by the Italian dailies regarding the tour of Vittorio Emanuele III to Libya in May 1938. Together with Queen Elena, the King had already undertaken several tours of the colonies prior to his being declared Emperor of Italian East Africa. In April 1928, they had visited Libya, and in 1932 and in 1934, respectively, they went to Eritrea and Somalia. Compared to these visits, the 1938 tour assumed greater propaganda value as the first by the royal couple to an overseas possession at the time when Mussolini was being publicly portrayed as the predominant Italian figure in the colonies.[24]

King Vittorio Emanuele's tour of Libya

The tour, and even more so the account presented in the Italian press, took place in two guises. The monarch, through his presence alone, asserted that Libya belonged to the Kingdom of Italy. However, the King's journey was portrayed as a continual peregrination to unveil achievements for which the Fascist regime was responsible. In this sense, the tour was a further phase in the effort by the Fascist regime to steal the King's thunder. In the Italian press, the reportage on the monarch and the royal family was predominantly linked to the inauguration of Fascist projects or to the monarch's presence at activities organised by the regime. For instance, there were articles on the sovereign at the 'exercises organised by the Gioventù italiana del Littorio' (a Fascist youth organisation) or for the inauguration of settler villages named in honour of the fallen of the 'Fascist revolution'.[25]

The major newspapers followed the travels of the King-Emperor Vittorio Emanuele III through the Libyan provinces. The royal steamer *Savoia* sailed from Syracuse, Sicily, on 19 May 1938 and moored in Tripoli on 21 May; accompanying the King were his wife, Queen Elena, and his daughters, Princess Mafalda and Princess Maria.[26] For the duration of his trip, the King would not be the only representative of the nation; alongside him and the other members of the royal family would be Biagio Vecchioni, a delegate of the National Fascist Party, and a group of Fascist soldiers from Cosenza, Ferrara and Turin.[27]

The king's arrival in Tripoli was announced in all the newspapers:

> The King-Emperor was in Tripoli and Tripolitania exactly ten years ago. Then the sun was rising over a Roman country of Mediterranean Africa. In the fullness of time, Italian authority has been affirmed, and under new auspices has begun the task of construction: now it is a question of the building on this fourth shore of the spiritual and material continuity of Italy; it is a question of extending the Fatherland into an Africa conquered and reconquered by our arms. ... It is advancing rapidly and encompasses the very borders of its life, it is beginning to be productive under the leadership of the great warriors who act in the name of the Duce.

The report continued:

> After the memorable visit of the Duce [the previous year], a new, proud stride has been taken towards the objectives of complete, literal Italianisation and Fascist strengthening, which are the clear goals of the civilisation of Rome. The Sovereign finds such impressive evidence of what has been accomplished over a decade through the conscious labour brought to fruition ever since the months of the triumphal visit of the Duce to today.[28]

Through such portrayals, the visit of Vittorio Emanuele III lost the character of an official tour by a head of state to colonial territories administered under his authority and assumed the appearance of a tour of Fascist achievements in the colony, a journey that was meant to confirm to the sovereign, and the world, the greatness of the Fascist regime.[29]

These journalistic accounts were little more than pretexts to present the colonies as a place that Fascism had made wealthy, fertile and Italian. The presence of the sovereign was recounted in the margins; the real stars of these reports were the Fascist projects, Fascist settlers, Fascist administrators, Fascist Italy. The King's visit to these territories provided a chance to write about him with fervour, but he was never presented as a genuine political agent or a symbolic reference point for the Italians.

In an article on the eve of the King's return to Italy, Francesco Maratea, a special correspondent for *Il Messaggero*, explained that

> The journey has been undertaken in an atmosphere of ardent Fascist passion. The Sovereign found himself in direct contact with the Blackshirts, was saluted by the most ardent and active Mussolinian youth, presided over the giving out to brigades of new, fasces [the fascist symbol] opened Case littorie [local Fascist Party headquarters], has felt the great striving that every hour acts as the resolute creative will of the Duce: Libya appears to him fully in the light of the civilisation of Fascism.[30]

In this sense, the colonies were portrayed as an exclusively Fascist space;[31] the figure of Vittorio Emanuele III remained in such descriptions on the sidelines. The King and the monarchy appeared as visitors to a colonial reality whose nature was described solely as Fascist.

The effort to show the colonies as uniquely Fascist during the King's tour is all the more evident when compared to reports of Mussolini's visit to Libya the year before. The description of Mussolini's entry to Tripoli on horseback left no doubt about the fact that the diarchy of King and Duce was something that did not involve the colonies, where the leader was indisputably Mussolini:

> Many writings hailed the Duce, founder of the Empire. Photographs of Mussolini were seen everywhere. ... The words of the Duce could be read everywhere: it was as if an acclamation could be heard repeated infinitely in Arabic. ... At 7.30 pm, the clamour of the immense multitude of indigenes, unleashing their own enthusiasm, announced the arrival of the Duce. ... When the Duce appeared, flanked by the most elegant mounted *zaptiè* [soldiers recruited from the colonised population], sergeants close by, the clamour became overwhelming. The founder of the Empire here has his triumph.[32]

The place of colonialism in the positioning of the figure of Mussolini vis-à-vis the monarch was also apparent in the representation of official moments in the life of the Empire. On the occasion of the celebrations for the second anniversary of the establishment of the eastern African empire, a delegation of fifty distinguished persons from all the colonial territories came to Rome for an official audience. On 11 May 1937, Mussolini, in the presence of the Secretary of the National Fascist Party, Achille Starace, and the Minister for Popular Culture, Dino Alfieri, received the delegation in the Salone delle Battaglie of the Palazzo Venezia. According to newspaper reports, the dignitaries were 'convened in Rome to pay homage to the King-Emperor and to the Founder of the Empire', but their first meeting was with Mussolini. Their reaction was presented thus by the papers: 'The eyes of all shone with ecstatic admiration and anxiety at finally being able to see and hear the great head of Fascist Italy, the Founder of the Empire.'³³ If the reports of the audience given by the Fascist leader to the fifty notables filled the first page of the newspapers, the reports of the swearing of obedience by these dignitaries before the King the following day did not garner equal coverage. The same newspaper, *Il Messaggero*, printed its report of that royal ceremony only on the second page; the oath-taking was presented more as an act of submission to the values of Fascism than as a swearing of fealty to the King-Emperor:

> Chiefs and notables gave the Roman salute, then knelt and finally processed out in profound acknowledgement, leaving the salons and descending the staircase of the royal palace. They will never forget: just as two thousand years ago pilgrims returned to their homes in distant lands of the Empire, so they brought back to their people and to their homes the firm conviction that nothing in the world could be seen greater than Rome.³⁴

Amedeo d'Aosta: a royal in the Fascist empire

The administration of the Empire was one of the central duties of the Fascist government. In 1936, this charge was conferred on Pietro Badoglio and, only several months later, on Rodolfo General Graziani, who would govern the empire of eastern Africa until December 1937. He was then replaced by Duke Amedeo d'Aosta, a member of the royal family. The choice of Amedeo by the Duce might appear to conflict with the effort to exclude the King and the royal house from the sphere of the colonies and the colonial imaginary of the Italians. The figure of Amedeo nevertheless can be seen as part of a functional strategy in Fascist design. The son of Emanuele Filiberto di Savoia-Aosta and Hélène d'Orléans, Amedeo came from the Savoia-Carignano branch of the royal family. His education was markedly different from the one generally undertaken by members of the Savoy royal house. At the age of nine, he had been sent to a London school, and he continued his education at Eton and Oxford. On his return to Italy, he entered the 'Nunziatella' Military College in Naples and then volunteered for active service during the First World War. After the end of the war, he left for Somalia with his uncle, Luis Amedeo di Savoia, the Duke of Abruzzi, with the aim of setting up an agricultural-industrial business on the Uebi-Scebeli river.³⁵ His Somali experience lasted for around six months before he went back to Italy, but he went to Africa again in 1922 and worked incognito as a labourer in a factory in the Congo. Back in Italy and in military service, Amedeo asked to be posted to Libya, where he served even after his marriage in 1927 to Princess Anna d'Orléans.³⁶

From 1929 to 1930, he took part in the 'pacification' of Libya, a military campaign under the command of General Graziani, whose mission was to suppress Libyan resistance to the Italian occupation.[37]

With the nomination of Amedeo as Viceroy of Ethiopia and Governor-General of Italian East Africa on 21 December 1937, the choice of Mussolini fell not only on a member of the royal family but also on a soldier with extensive experience of colonial affairs; on 29 December, Amedeo was also promoted to the rank of *generale di squadra aerea*.[38] 'Arriving in Addis Ababa the first task of the Viceroy was to put himself to work, the greatest and perhaps most arduous job which he could imagine.'[39] Taking up his post in Ethiopia, he stepped into the shoes of a predecessor, Graziani, whose rule had been characterised by great recourse to military repression to combat Ethiopian resistance and by the slaughter of civilians after an attempt was made on his life on 19 February 1937.

Amedeo's own administration was marked by a lesser use of military force and by an effort, at least ostensibly, to create conditions in the Empire conducive to the setting up of a civilian administration. An interesting perspective on his policies is offered by Katharine Fannin. Born into a family of tea planters in India in 1902, then educated in England and on the Continent, Fannin arrived in Kenya at the age of twenty-three. She married Charles Fannin, a South African Rhodes scholar who had been awarded a military cross in the First World War and who had gone to Kenya as a soldier-settler, though his farm had failed and he had become a government surveyor and town planner. In 1938, Katharine decided to tour Italian East Africa en route to home leave in England. The Italians, who had been castigated in the West and condemned by the League of Nations for their conquest of Ethiopia, saw in her visit the opportunity to present a favourable view of Fascist colonialism. For the British, her tour provided a useful means of gaining intelligence about the Italian colonies. Fannin was able to travel widely in Italian East Africa and interview numerous dignitaries about the methods of Italian colonial governance. She also had the chance to speak at length with Amedeo when she stayed at the Governor-General's palace in Addis Ababa.[40] On arriving in London, she wrote an extensive report on her travels for the Foreign Office. She then visited the Italian colonies and Amedeo once again on her return journey to Kenya and wrote a second report for the British government. The authorities expressed their gratitude for her valuable observations, which also came to public attention through a long letter in *The Times*. Partisans of the Ethiopian Emperor, Haile Selassie, then in exile in Britain, however, denounced her views as pro-Italian propaganda.[41]

Concerning the role of a member of the royal family as Viceroy of the Italian empire in eastern Africa, Fannin noted during her second visit:

> Two differences from November 1938 were quite outstanding. The first (and to my mind most important) was in the immense increase in the proportion of notices pasted and painted up all over the place especially between Assab and Dessie, in Eritrea, and in Italian Somaliland, and on the road to and in the town of Gondar, which supported the House of Savoy. 'Viva il Vice Re' 'Viva il Re Imperatore' 'Viva la Casa Savoia' 'Casa Savoia a Noi'. (I had not before seen the two last mentioned.) In November 'Viva il Duce', Mussoilni's name painted up on all available spaces, and his photograph everywhere had been largely in the majority. There are still, of course, a great number of 'Viva il Duce' notices, and colossal photographs and posters of Mussolini about, especially in the towns of Addis and Asmara where Fascists are particularly active; but I was impressed by what appears to me to be a definite swing in favour of the House of Savoy. This to me was particularly interesting on the Danakil road, because the 2800 Italians employed on that stretch are foremen, masons, clerks and technical workers: in fact those whose education probably makes them realise that the present lack of personal liberty which now obtains in Italy, and, to a lesser extent in the Empire, is due to the Fascist regime.[42]

In her travelogue, Fannin draws attention to the changes she had encountered in regards to the relationship between the Savoy royal house and the Fascist regime in the colonies. In her interpretation, the arrival of Amedeo d'Aosta in the colony has brought about a transformation in the representation of Empire as a creation of Fascism, revealing the active role played by the royal family and, in her view, establishing a new situation that would allow for greater individual freedom.

Notwithstanding the impressions of the British traveller, Amedeo did not publicly refrain from recognition of the colonial empire as a Fascist empire. On 9 May 1938, on the anniversary of the proclamation of the Empire of Italian East Africa, Amedeo sent a message to Mussolini in which he affirmed:

> To You, Founder of the Empire, rises manfully and powerfully the voice of all of us, which admits of no limits and with dedication accepts any sacrifice. We will know how to valorise these lands that You, Duce, gave to Fascist Italy and entrusted to our arms, to our minds, to our hearts.[43]

According to Fannin, the Viceroy would enjoy a popular consensus, at least until the spring of 1939. According to the British visitor:

> The Duke D'Aosta has a truly amazing hold on the personal affections of all the Italians, and so far as I could see, on that portion of the coloured

people with whom he has come in contact in Italian East Africa. This intelligent, generous, enlightened and essentially democratic man is, to my mind, perfect in the job in which he has been placed.[44]

In the lengthy transcripts of three meetings between Fannin and Amedeo appears the desire of the Viceroy to present evidence for the changes that had taken place in eastern Africa with the transfer of power from Graziani to him. In particular, recourse to violence as a method of maintaining control over the colonised population seemed to be explicitly condemned by Amedeo. In this sense, the Governor-General clearly marked out the distance between himself and a predecessor who had employed executions in public squares as the ultimate sanction to force the submission of the Ethiopian population to Italian authority.

Conclusion

Amedeo d'Aosta's policies in Italian East Africa may indeed be considered different from those of his predecessor. As shown by Nicola Labanca, the leading historian of Italian colonialism, Amedeo's arrival in Addis Ababa marked a major change in 'native policy', symbolised by the replacement of summary execution with court trials for those considered rebels. Nevertheless, Amedeo did not substantially modify the policy of racial segregation earlier imposed by Graziani. In 1940, the entry of Italy into the Second World War also brought its African possessions into the conflict. They soon became the launching pad for an attempted invasion of French Djibouti, British Somaliland and the Anglo-Egyptian Sudan. A British counter-attack resulted in British occupation of the Italian colonies the following year. On 5 May 1941, exactly five years after the triumphal entry into Addis Ababa of General Pietro Badoglio, Haile Selassie, the Emperor of Ethiopia, who had fled into exile with the Italian conquest in 1936, returned to the Ethiopian capital. The Italian colonies of eastern Africa were placed under British control as the Occupied Enemy Territory Administration. On 19 May 1941, Amedeo d'Aosta was captured by British forces, taken to Kenya and confined to a prison camp at Donyo Sobuk. After contracting tuberculosis, he died in Nairobi on 3 March 1942.

The competition between monarchy and Fascism was one of the key traits of Italian politics and society between 1922 and 1943.[45] The colonies constituted both symbolic and real sites in which this competition took place. The Fascist regime, especially in the 1930s, made colonial expansion one of its principal policies.[46] Once Ethiopia had been conquered, the establishment of the Empire of Italian East Africa gave an opportunity to put in place completely Fascist institutions, in which the king would occupy a merely formal and subsidiary position in comparison to that of the founder of the empire, Benito Mussolini. The appointment of Amedeo d'Aosta as Viceroy of Ethiopia apparently signified an imperial revival of the diarchy that existed in Italy itself. Notwithstanding the views of Katharine Fannin on the changes that had taken place in the colonies concerning propaganda in favour of the royal house, for most of Italian society, the character of the Empire remained Fascist; it did not undergo sudden alteration because of the nomination of a member of the House of Savoy as administrator. Fascist propaganda and rhetoric in Italy disseminated a Fascist portrayal of the colonial experience through the press, schools and cinema.[47] And the Duce was shown as the symbolic reference point for the colonial endeavour. The history of Amedeo d'Aosta's rule as Viceroy and Governor-General of the Empire of Italian East Africa reveals how the diarchy of the Italian state in this period – the parallel structures of the monarchy and the Fascist regime – became part of colonial dynamics as well. The presence of a royal duke at the helm of colonial administration in East Africa clearly undermined the portrayal by Mussolini's regime of an overseas empire that was a purely Fascist domain.

Notes

1 Paolo Colombo, *La Monarchia fascista* (Bologna: Mulino, 2010); Denis Mack Smith, *Italy and Its Monarchy* (New Haven, Conn.: Yale University Press, 1992).
2 Nicola Labanca, *Oltremare: Storia dell'espansione coloniale italiana* (Bologna: Mulino, 2002), p. 50.
3 Cf. Angelo Del Boca, *Gli italiani in Africa orientale: Dall'unità alla marcia su Roma* (Milan: Mondadori, 2001), p. 53.
4 For a detailed account of Italian colonialism in the late 1800s, see Giuseppe Finaldi, *Italian National Identity in the Scramble for Africa: Italy's African Wars in the Era of Nation-building, 1870–1900* (Bern: Peter Lang, 2009).
5 For a comprehensive discussion of the transformation of old Abyssinia into a new Ethiopian empire, see Bahru Zewde, *Pioneers of Change in Ethiopia: The Reformist Intellectuals of the Early Twentieth Century* (Athens, Ohio: Ohio University Press, 2002); Donald L. Donham and Wendy James (eds), *The Southern Marches of Imperial Ethiopia* (Athens, Ohio: Ohio University Press, 2002); Teshale Tibebu, *The Making of Modern Ethiopia, 1896–1974* (Ewing Township, NJ: Red Sea Press, 1995).
6 Angelo Del Boca (ed.), *Adua: le ragioni di una sconfitta* (Roma-Bari: Laterza, 1997).
7 Labanca, *Oltremare*, pp. 85–94.
8 Maurizio Marinelli, 'Projecting Italianità on the Chinese Space: The Construction of the "Aristocratic" Concession in Tianjin (1901–1947)', in Giovanni Andornino and Maurizio Marinelli (eds), *Italy's Encounters with Modern China: Imperial Dreams, Strategic Ambitions* (Basingstoke: Palgrave Macmillan, 2013), pp. 1–26.
9 Nicola Labanca, *La Guerra italiana per la Libia, 1911–1931* (Bologna: Mulino, 2012). See also Anna Baldinetti, *The Origins of the Libyan Nation* (London and New York: Routledge, 2010).
10 See Jacqueline Andall and Derek Duncan (eds), *Italian Colonialism: Legacy and Memory* (Bern: Peter Lang, 2005).
11 Cf. Riccardo Bottoni (ed.), *L'impero fascista: Italia ed Etiopia (1935–1941)* (Bologna: Mulino, 2008).

12 A revealing analysis of how the Fascist regime portrayed the conquest of Ethiopia and the subsequent creation of Italian East Africa in its propaganda is offered by R. J. B. Bosworth, *Mussolini's Italy: Life under the Dictatorship, 1915–1945* (London: Penguin, 2006).
13 Angelo Del Boca, *Gli italiani in Africa orientale: Dall'unità alla marcia su Roma* (Milan: Mondadori, 2001), p. 52. See also Valeria Deplano, *L'Africa in casa: propaganda e cultura coloniale nell'Italia fascista* (Milan: Le Monnier-Mondadori Education, 2015).
14 Cf. Del Boca, *Gli italiani in Africa orientale*, pp. 14–18.
15 Renzo De Felice, *Mussolini il duce: lo stato totalitario, 1936–1940* (Torino: Einaudi, 1996). See also Emilio Gentile, *Il culto del littorio: la sacralizzazione della politica nell'Italia fascista* (Roma-Bari: Laterza, 2009); Simonetta Falasca Zamponi, *Fascist Spectacle: The Aesthetics of Power in Mussolini's Italy* (Berkeley, Calif.: University of California Press, 1997).
16 Haile Larebo, 'Empire Building and Its Limitations: Ethiopia (1935–1941)', in Ruth Ben-Ghiat and Mia Fuller (eds), *Italian Colonialism* (Basingstoke: Palgrave Macmillan, 2008), pp. 83–94, at p. 83.
17 G. Tommasello, 'La Guerra d'Etiopia e il letterato: il disagio della scrittura', in Riccardo Bottoni (ed.), *L'Impero fascista: Italia ed Etiopia (1935–1941)* (Bologna: Mulino, 2008), pp. 215–32, at p. 219.
18 Christopher Seton-Watson, 'Italy's Imperial Hangover', *Journal of Contemporary History*, 15:1 (1980), 169–79, at pp. 169–70.
19 On the role of demographic colonisation in Italian colonial policy, see Aliza S. Wong, *Race and the Nation in Liberal Italy, 1861–1911: Meridionalism, Empire, and Diaspora* (Basingstoke: Palgrave Macmillan, 2006); and Mark Choate, *Emigrant Nation: The Making of Italy Abroad* (Cambridge, Mass.: Harvard University Press, 2008).
20 See, for example, Davide Rodogno, *Il nuovo ordine mediterraneo* (Torino: Bollati Boringhieri, 2006).
21 The Fascist Militia was a paramilitary organisation under the control of the Fascist Party.
22 Nicola Labanca, *Una guerra per l'impero: memorie della campagna d'Etiopia, 1935–36* (Bologna: Mulino, 2005). See also Eileen Ryan, 'Violence and the Politics of Prestige: The Fascist Turn in Colonial Libya', *Modern Italy*, 20:2 (2015), 123–35.
23 Colombo, *La Monarchia fascista*, p. 113.
24 Antonio Spinosa, *Vittorio Emanuele III: l'astuzia di un re* (Milano: Mondadori, 2015), p. 373.
25 'Il Re Imperatore tra i giovani del Campo Roma', *Il Messaggero*, 5 May 1938.
26 'Il Re Imperatore si imbarca oggi a Siracusa', *Il Messaggero*, 20 May 1938.
27 'Il Re Imperatore sbarca oggi a Tripoli', *Il Messaggero*, 21 May 1938.
28 F. Maratea, 'Bianco abbacinante', *Il Messaggero*, 22 May 1938.
29 For a still authoritative interpretation of Italian colonialism in Libya, see Claudio Segrè, *The Fourth Shore: The Italian Colonization of Libya* (Chicago, Ill.: University of Chicago Press, 1975).
30 F. Maratea, 'All'ultima tappa', *Il Messaggero*, 30 May 1938.
31 Cf. Christopher Duggan, *Fascist Voices: An Intimate History of Mussolini's Italy* (London: Bodley Head, 2012), pp. 249–82.
32 Guido Bardi, 'Cavalcata fantastica', *Il Messaggero*, 17 March 1937.
33 '50 capi della Libia e dell'Impero ricevuti dal Duce nel Salone delle Battaglie', *Il Messaggero*, 2 May 1938.
34 'Il Re Imperatore riceve il solenne giuramento di obbedienza e fedeltà dei capi e notabili di tutto l'Impero', *Il Messaggero*, 14 May 1938.
35 Edoardo Borra, *Amedeo di Savoia, terzo duca d'Aosta e viceré d'Etiopia* (Milano: Mursia, 1985), pp. 26–7.
36 Gigi Speroni, *Amedeo d'Aosta* (Milano: Fabbri, 2000), p. 57.
37 See Angelo Del Boca, *Gli italiani in Libia: Dal fascismo a Gheddafi* (Milan: Mondadori, 1997).

38 M. Leonardi (ed.), *Amedeo d'Aosta* (Rome: Organizzazione Editoriale Italiana, 1966), p. 155.
39 Leonardi, *Amedeo d'Aosta*, p. 158.
40 Judy Aldrick, 'An Ethiopian Escapade', *Africa*, 50:3 (1995), 387–9.
41 Judy Aldrick, *The Fannin Papers* (Kijabe: Old Africa Books, 2010), pp. 53–4.
42 FO 371/23382, National Archives of the United Kingdom.
43 'Il Duca d'Aosta al Duce nell'annuale dell'impero', *Il Messaggero*, 11 May 1938.
44 FO 371/23382.
45 See Colombo, *La Monarchia fascista*.
46 Valeria Deplano and Alessandro Pes (eds), *Quel che resta dell'impero: la cultura coloniale degli italiani* (Milan: Mimesis, 2014).
47 See Ruth Ben-Ghiat, *Italian Fascism's Empire Cinema* (Bloomington, Ind.: Indiana University Press, 2015); and Ben-Ghiat and Fuller (eds), *Italian Colonialism*.

CHAPTER FOURTEEN

'So brave Etruria grew': dividing the Crown in early colonial New South Wales, 1808–10

Bruce Baskerville

Great seals

'Historians seldom trouble themselves much about the Great Seal of England', wrote Sir Hilary Jenkinson in 1943.[1] His statement is just as true now for the great seals of England and all British and British-descended jurisdictions, including New South Wales. So, what is a Great Seal, and why should any historian 'trouble themself' about it all?[2]

What does an examination of great seals reveal about relationships between the Crown and the exercise of royal authority in settler colonies, and about the evolving relationships between British sovereigns, their viceregal representatives and loyal or rebellious subjects in overseas possessions at a crucial moment in British imperial history?

The Great Seal of the Realm forms the tangible expression, in a sigillographic form, of authenticating and expressing the decisions and decrees of a sovereign authority, whether by the sovereign herself or by agents acting in her name.[3] The word 'seal' can refer to either an impression attached to a document or the matrix or mould from which it is made.[4] It usually takes the form of a wax and resin (or similarly malleable material) disc into the surface of which has been impressed certain symbolic designs, patterns and inscriptions (on one or both sides), which has been attached in some way to a document. It is usually large, hence the term 'great seal'. When the seal is fixed to a document, the document is said to 'pass' the seal. Typical uses of a great seal are to authenticate proclamations, writs, appointments, summonses, land grants and documents freeing convicts. When used in such ways, a great seal functions as the 'signature' of a body politic.

When a sovereign dies or is otherwise succeeded, or there is a fundamental change in the constitutional character of a jurisdiction, a new great seal will be made, although there can be long delays in making such changes and the seal of a former sovereign may continue in use long after her demise. Such continuing use represents in a material form the cry 'The King is dead! Long live the King!' A great seal is *the* emblem of sovereignty.

The existence of multiple seals for the same sovereign or deputy sovereign, such as Great Seals Deputed, arose from a single sovereign administering more than one jurisdiction and were made for a 'deputy king' (such as a viceroy or governor) to use for administering a territory in the sovereign's name but physical absence. The terminology for this divisibility of the Great Seal refers to the Great Seal of the Realm as being for 'general purposes' with a Great Seal Deputed being for 'particular purposes'.[5] The 'general purposes' are the intangible supreme authority of sovereignty and prerogative vested in one person or office (rather than in a particular territory), and exercised in her name, which will be the same in any place subject to the same sovereign. The 'particular purposes' are so much of that intangible authority that is deputed or delegated to and exercised only within one jurisdiction, such as a palatinate or colony, rather than uniformly across every realm subject to the same sovereign.

From the thirteenth century, the English sovereigns used Great Seals Deputed in their various realms in the British Isles and France. The obverse (front) of these seals typically showed the sovereign mounted on horseback, against a local landscape, indicating the particular realm or seat of authority. The reverse, which initially showed the sovereign enthroned, was gradually replaced over time by the royal coat of arms and other heraldic devices.

This pattern of a divisible Great Seal representing divisible sovereign authority continued with the establishment of colonies in North America. The first Great Seal Deputed for the first English colony of Virginia was issued in 1606, with the royal arms (of 'general purpose') on the reverse and on the obverse a portrait of James I. The second seal issued in 1662 for Charles II was single-sided, with the royal arms surrounded by the motto 'Behold Virginia the Fifth Realm' (England, France, Ireland and Scotland being the others).[6] The Governor of Virginia proclaimed Charles II king in 1649, although the Virginians were forced to surrender their allegiance by a Commonwealth fleet in 1652.[7] The fifth seal, made in 1705 for the reign of Queen Anne, returned to the two-sided form, with the royal arms of 'general purpose' on the reverse, but the obverse now explicitly localised with an effigy of the Queen receiving from a kneeling Native American a sheaf of tobacco leaves and the motto 'Behold Virginia the Fourth Realm' (England and Scotland by now united as Great Britain).[8] This remained the design, with updated royal portraits, until Virginia's declaration of independence in 1776.

Great Seals and the popular imagination

The Virginia settler Richard Bland argued in 1766 that the Crown had, with every new governor, confirmed the rights of colonies under the Great Seal, and laws had been enacted by the 'king and Virginia Assembly', the 'proper Fountain' of authority in the colony. Now, however, the Parliament in London was taxing the colonists in the King's name. Bland argued that if the royal prerogative could not exempt the colonies from the powers of the 'king and British Parliament', then not only was the honour of the Crown impugned but colonial subjects were being deceived.[9] He recalled that in 1659 the Governor and Assembly had rebelled for a second time and had restored Charles II 'so that he was King in Virginia some Time before he had any certain Assurance of being restored to his Throne in England'.[10]

Bland was well aware of the idea of Virginia as a separate realm, with its own Great Seal Deputed expressing the particular sovereign authority in Virginia. That particular authority, he argued, was being subverted by the British ministry abusing the general authority of the Crown.

When the seal of George III was received in Virginia in 1767, it was engraved with greater crispness and beauty than earlier seals, but by that time the sovereign authority depicted on the seal was ebbing away.[11] Jenkinson argues that the attribution to a great seal of 'mystic talismanic' powers is undeserved, and, in the case of Virginia, the pinnacle in the aesthetic qualities of the Great Seal Deputed of 1767 certainly bore an inverse relationship to the constitutional authority it represented.[12] However, that is not to say that great seals did not acquire mythic characteristics that embedded them in common folklore.

Stories surrounding the Great Seal of James II, for instance, tell that on the night the King was fleeing London he threw the seal into the Thames, from where it was later recovered in a fisherman's net and returned to the new government. Nineteenth-century royal biographers claimed he had destroyed it with the aim of preventing the 'usurper' government from being able to function after the Glorious Revolution.[13] Whatever the mythology, the matrix was in the Royal Mint in London and roughly refashioned into the first Great Seal of William and Mary by March 1689.[14] These stories have their echoes in popular culture through stories such as those of the Seal of Solomon in Masonic and Kabalistic circles.[15] The Provincial Congress of Georgia in 1776 added a story to the preamble of a law setting out new administrative arrangements, of the fleeing Governor of Georgia who 'suddenly and unexpectedly carried off the great seal', as a justification for the new order.[16]

Whether these popular stories are more or less grounded in some truth, the metaphors for the loss of significant emblems being associated with the usurpation of sovereign authority would have been well known in early colonial New South Wales through published histories of the Glorious and American revolutions, stories told by locally resident American refugees and convicts, Masonic rituals (at least one lodge was well established by 1804) and nursery rhymes.[17]

Great Seals in the settler colonies

The British invasion of the Cadigal realm (present-day Sydney) began on 26 January 1788 and was formalised on 7 February when Governor Arthur Phillip formally proclaimed the colony of New South Wales. The ceremony included reading aloud his commission, made under the Great Seal of Great Britain, which appointed him governor and authorised him, as governor, to keep and use a public seal for 'all things whatsoever that shall pass the Great Seal of our said territory'.[18] Phillip, at this time, did not, however, possess the Seal, which the Commission stated would be delivered to him in due course. Until Phillip received a public seal, he used his own privy (or private) seal in its place. The use of such privy seals was characteristic of new colonies.[19] The Great Seal finally arrived in Sydney on the convict transport *Gorgon* on 21 September 1791, nearly four years after Phillip's proclamation of the colony.

In May 1790, the Privy Council had ordered the preparation of a great seal for New South Wales.[20] In August, the King approved a draft design,[21] and the Chief Engraver of Seals was ordered to prepare the matrices.[22] By January 1791, the new seal was ready to send to Phillip.[23] Of particular interest is the description of the allusory landscape and motto on the obverse of the seal (see Figure 21):

> Convicts landed at Botany Bay; their fetters taken off and received by Industry sitting on a bale of goods with her attributes, the distaff, bee-hive, pick-axe, and spade, pointing to oxen ploughing, the rising habitations, and a church on a hill at a distance, with a fort for their defence. Motto: Sic fortis Etruria crevit; with this inscription around the circumference: Sigillum Nov. Cam. Aust.[24]

The reverse of the seal depicted the royal arms and supporters within an encircling representation of the Order of the Garter and surmounted by an imperial Crown, with the royal motto, and around the circumference the King's titles (see Figure 22).

The seal designs were developed and made by the engravers at the Royal Mint. The Chief Engraver of Seals between 1769 and 1799 was Thomas Major, a renowned landscape engraver.[25] He enjoyed the

21. 1792 wax impression of the obverse of the Great Seal of New South Wales (1791 to 1817). Source: State Library of New South Wales, a1316004, Safe 1/4c. Reproduced with permission

patronage of the Duke of Cumberland (George III's uncle) and was an associate of the Royal Academy. He engraved several views of classical ruins and landscapes before being appointed to the Mint in 1768, and in 1784 produced a copy of the Great Seal of the Realm when the original was stolen from the Lord Chancellor's house. Major, the first great English landscape engraver, maintained the classical tastes in seal design of earlier engravers.[26] When placed in its temporal and cultural contexts, the New South Wales seal design is representative of its time. The depiction of imaginary landscapes on seals has long antecedents but had been developed along with the allusory motto under the influence of the Augustan literary styles and neoclassical arts then prevalent in British society, which included a conscious imitation of Roman writers such as Virgil and Horace.

22. 1792 wax impression of the reverse of the Great Seal of New South Wales (1791 to 1817). Source: State Library of New South Wales, a1316003, Safe 1/4c. Reproduced with permission

Between the accession of George III and the end of the Napoleonic wars, at least twenty new colonial great seals were made, with that for New South Wales falling roughly in the middle of this period. All bear Augustan or neoclassical influences in their mottoes and designs. They can be generally grouped into 'ancients' and 'moderns', a cultural distinction often made at the time in which 'moderns' favoured trade, empire and reason against the 'ancients', who stressed inheritance, localism and the value of society over the individual.[27] However, there is overlap between the ancient and modern designs, especially in the depiction of Arcadian townscapes with a church on a hill in both.[28]

The New South Wales seal appears unique, but, when placed in a sigillographic context, can been seen as representing the modern values of trade and industry and individual reform while also retaining ancient elements in the embracing town, fort and church on a hill depicting a social hierarchy in which an individual could reform both herself and her society. The New South Wales motto *Sic fortis Etruria crevit* taken from Virgil's *Georgics*, extolled the virtues of rural life and industry supposedly practised by the ancient Etruscans and from which Rome and its empire had grown.[29] The motto is usually translated as 'So, I suppose, brave Etruria grew', or 'So, this is how Etruria grew.' Simon Schama has commented on Virgil's description of the beehive, one of Industry's attributes, as the paragon of social and political virtue, located within depictions of antique landscapes that were an allegory for the humanistic landscapes of the 'moderns': diligent labour, placid livestock, bounteous orchards and fields, politically and visually overseen by the fathers of the city state on the hilltop.[30] Major's sigillographic representations of such landscapes, complete with Virgillian motto, is perhaps best realised in his seal for New South Wales.

The divisibility of royal sovereignty, tangibly expressed in multiple Great Seals Deputed already in existence in the British Isles, North America and the West and East Indies, extended to the South Seas with the arrival of the Great Seal of New South Wales. At some point, whether on 26 January 1788, 7 February 1788 or certainly from 22 September 1791, when the tangible representation of the 'particular purposes' of the Crown in New South Wales in the form of the Great Seal came into use, the territory of New South Wales became a separate realm. Although not ordinally numbered as on the seal of Virginia, a new body politic had been created by the royal prerogative. The 'general purposes' sovereignty of the Crown was represented by the Royal Arms and titles on the reverse of the seal, and the 'particular purposes' of the Crown's sovereignty in New South Wales were tangibly represented by the allusory landscape and motto on the obverse. Just as Governor Berkeley proclaimed Charles II king in Virginia in 1649 and 1659 quite independently of what was happening in England or any other realm, so now the deputed sovereign authority, exercised by the Governor in New South Wales, contained the nascent power to do the same things. The question now becomes one of what became of that power when the sovereign emblem was purloined and deputed royal authority usurped?

The Great Seal of New South Wales

In 1808, the Day of Landing on 26 January marked the twentieth anniversary of the invasion.[31] It was also the day in which the New South Wales Corps overthrew the Governor, Captain William Bligh. The usurpers were commanded by Major George Johnston of the Corps, and John Macarthur, the colony's leading businessman and conservative 'perturbator' who had resigned from the Corps in 1804 during an acrimonious dispute with the previous governor.[32] By the end of the Day of Landing, Bligh was detained, Major Johnston had assumed the title of Lieutenant Governor, Macarthur was Secretary to the Colony, and the military had taken possession of the Great Seal.

The usurpation lasted for nearly two years, covering almost the whole of 1808 and 1809. On 28 December 1809, Major Lachlan Macquarie and the 73rd Regiment sailed into Sydney Harbour.[33] There was no resistance from the Corps or the usurper administration. Macquarie reported that on his arrival he had 'found the colony in a state of perfect tranquillity, but in a great degree of anxiety for the long expected arrival of a new Governor'.[34]

Bligh had been imprisoned in Government House until February 1809, when he agreed to leave for England. Instead, he sailed for Hobart Town, where he remained onboard HMS *Porpoise* in the Derwent Estuary until the restoration.[35] The usurpation ended on New Year's Day 1810, when Macquarie restored the absent Bligh to office for twenty-four hours and then assumed the office of governor himself.

On the Day of Landing, the Corps marched from their barracks to Government House, where their only opposition came from Bligh's daughter, Mary Putnam, who tried to bar their entrance. After two hours of searching they eventually cornered Bligh and arrested him. Macarthur chaired a committee that interrogated all public officials to determine their allegiance, and all Bligh's personal and state papers were seized. Bligh wrote:

> I denied their Authority in any proceeding not authorized by myself, as to my King and Country only would I be answerable for any act of mine in this colony. At this time my Papers, Books and Private Instructions, which were locked up on the Evening of the 26th, were ordered to be examined, and with the Great Seal of the Colony were ordered to be taken away.[36]

Bligh objected to the seizure of the Great Seal and objected again as the Committee members were leaving Government House, to which the Committee bluntly responded, 'They could now command it; it was needless for me to make any opposition.'[37]

There followed various fallings-out between the usurpers, and their collective aims, never very cohesive apart from hatred of Bligh, shifted and changed over time. The loyalists had enunciated a set of ideals of sorts when they welcomed Bligh to the colony in 1806, but during the usurpation they gradually withdrew into a sullen silence when they were publicly ridiculed, ejected from public offices, had their properties appropriated and saw their leaders transported to the convict station at Coal River.[38] Nevertheless, ideological alignments can be discerned in the public statements, official actions and popular responses of the two camps.

The usurpers included the large landholders and merchants (later called Exclusives or Pure Merinos) who had mainly arrived as free men, along with their military supporters in the New South Wales Corps. The loyalists, on the other hand, were more disparate, consisting mainly of former convicts (sometimes called emancipists or expirees) and free migrants in the country districts of the Cumberland Plain around Sydney, as well as mid-level public officials.[39] Alan Atkinson argues that Macarthur conceived a political reform plan informed by Jeremy Bentham's 1803 anti-transportation pamphlet *A Plea for the Constitution*, and his antipathy to ex-convict advisers to Bligh, such as the attorney George Crossley, was well known.[40] Bligh evoked the 'small settlers', as he called them, as the true colonists, and explained his policies and actions in terms of the benefits to them.

The usurpers issued a brief manifesto on the first day of their new regime from the Corps' headquarters in the Sydney Barracks. After thanking 'the whole body of people' for their 'manly, firm and orderly conduct', they went on:

> In future no man shall have just cause to complain of violence, injustice or oppression; no free man shall be taken and imprisoned, or deprived of his house, land, or liberty, but by the law; justice shall be impartially administered, without regard to or respect of persons; and every man shall enjoy the fruits of his industry in security.[41]

The sentence 'no free man shall be taken and imprisoned, or deprived of his house, land, or liberty' is a literal translation of the twenty-ninth clause of Magna Carta.[42] Such baronial allusions allowed Macarthur and his allies to see themselves as nobles, with the Corps their knightly enforcers, and to regard their actions as preserving the legitimate (and limited) authority of the Crown.[43] The usurpers claimed they were rescuing the colony from a tyrannical governor under the influence of nefarious convict advisers.[44]

Bligh asserted that a jubilant Macarthur crowed on the night of the overthrow that 'Never was a revolution so completely affected, and with so much order and regularity.'[45] Some Sydney innkeepers rebadged their inns with 'revolutionary' signs. One showed Major Johnston driving a sword through a snake and receiving a cap of liberty from a female figure with the inscription 'The ever memorable 26th of January 1808.' Another was inscribed 'Success to Major George Johnston. May he live forever! Our deliverer and the suppressor of tyrants.' Yet another offered a more ambiguous depiction of Charles II hiding in an oak tree with the inscription 'The ever memorable 26th Jan'y 1808.'[46] The signs evoke American and Cromwellian ideas of a British revolutionary past, violent but constitutional.[47] None used the emancipatory symbolism of the Great Seal.

Supporters of the usurpation presented an address to Johnston in March 1808, stating that they admired Johnston's 'manly conduct', but that:

> We do not revolt against our King and Government but against those who have subverted the power delegated to them by our most revered sovereign. ... [W]e trust our conduct will continue such as may long entitle us to Great Britain's fostering breast, and such as will tend to prolong for ages a mutual interest and union with her.[48]

The constant references to the usurpers as 'manly' contrasted with their depiction of Bligh as a coward.[49] When Bligh was finally found, he was accused of hiding under a bed in what Johnston said 'was a situation too disgraceful to be mentioned'.[50] Atkinson suggests that one of the arresting officers was a 'deist radical' who sympathised with the French Revolution. He had cartoons vilifying Bligh distributed around Sydney and may have organised the revolutionary inn signs.[51]

While the usurpers did not refer to the Great Seal in their words or images, the use of the seal was necessary despite any antipathy to its allusions. A critical use to which it was put was sealing land grant documents, which proliferated during the usurpation. Some 27,500 hectares were granted during 1809, forming 34 per cent of all land granted since 1788 and the largest alienation of crown land up to that time.[52] Bligh warned against this when he issued a proclamation from Hobart Town, stating, 'That *I only* am empowered to keep and use the public seal for sealing all things whatsoever that shall pass the Great Seal of the territory.'[53] The usurpers ignored him.

The usurpers' 'platform' can be defined as supporting a regular administration in favour of the wealth-producing classes (including the large-scale granting of land), orderly control of the lower orders by the military (partly through control of the markets for food and alcohol), antipathy to convicts being rehabilitated into society and 'manliness', or, at least, Augustan ideals of martial courage, virtue, honour, reason and autonomy, all wrapped up in allusions to noble barons and chivalric supporters necessarily containing the excesses of royal authority deputed.

While the usurpers drew upon Magna Carta, the loyalists sought inspiration in the Bill of Rights of 1688. A welcome address to Bligh in 1806 included phrases and concepts of the impartial administration of the law, trial by jury and protection of property, that recalled the Bill as did the layout of the address. This was the closest to a formal manifesto articulated by 'the loyal people, settlers, landholders, cultivators and other principal inhabitants'. The 244 signatories looked to Bligh for 'such means as may be for the salvation, honor and interest of the colony'.[54] A further address just before the overthrow, with 833 signatures, petitioned Bligh to allow free trade within the colony and between other colonies, and for trial by jury.[55]

After the overthrow, publishing such addresses became dangerous, and Bligh and the loyalists turned to invoking the imagery of the French Revolution to describe the usurpers, citing their 'very Robesperian [sic] manner' and 'true spirit of Jacobinical equality'.[56] Local tavern songwriters emulated the Francophobia in 'pipes', such as *A New Song ... on the Rebellion*, written sometime in late 1808, that began 'The voice of rebellion resounds o'er the Plain'.[57]

The small settlers had a role in their self-governance through their local commons trusts and in the inclusion of their local magistrates in an informal viceregal 'privy council' of magistrates. They were the men brought before Macarthur's Committee at Government House, interrogated and dismissed from office.[58] The new usurper magistracy was planted in the country districts and policed the activities of the small settlers with enthusiasm.

Bligh had a large estate in the country named 'Blighton', which operated as a model farm to demonstrate new methods of agriculture and farming practices. Bligh's overseer, ex-convict Andrew Thompson, wrote in 1807 of Bligh's 'wisdom and attention to farming and improvement, which the Sovereign was pleased to practice at Home ... as an example to all others'.[59] The estate was notorious for the usurpers, who claimed the farm was evidence of Bligh's corruption in using convicts and crown livestock for his private gain.[60]

When the *Sydney Gazette* began publication in 1803, edited by convict George Howe, its masthead featured a woodblock print inspired by the Great Seal. It contained all the details of Major's sigillographic landscape except the convicts being freed. The surrounding motto was paraphrased in English as 'Thus We Hope to Prosper', with the convicts, now emancipated, in the role of ploughmen driving the oxen.[61] Although this woodblock had worn out within fifteen months and was replaced by the royal arms, it was the first device created in the colony depicting a symbolic local identity, and the visual transformation of the convicts in fetters to autonomous farmers would not have been lost on the small settlers.[62] The Great Seal had also inspired the first emblem of local identity in Van Diemen's Land (renamed Tasmania in 1856), where the Revd Knopwood slightly revised the motto to 'Sic fortis Hobartia crevit' and the Lieutenant Governor had it included in his privy seal.[63]

In the absence or loss of a great seal, such alternatives had to be invented. For Bligh, secretly issuing letters to the small settlers as well as proclamations and directives directly counter to those of the usurper regime in Sydney, his own privy seal provided the obvious instrument to authenticate documents. The loyalists were not persuaded by baronial allusions, derisory cartoons and iniquitous inn signs in Sydney. They countered by recalling the great kings who had survived by hiding, such as Charles II hiding in an oak tree near Worcester and Alfred hiding in the Somerset marshes.[64]

In about 1806, the small settlers developed an emblem of their own. The 'Trafalgar flag', made by the women of the Bowman household, displays a shield with the entwined rose, shamrock and thistle of England, Ireland and Scotland, supported by a kangaroo and emu, with two motto ribbons, the upper reading 'Unity', and the lower Nelson's signal at Trafalgar, 'England Expects Every Man to Do His Duty'. On one level, the flag celebrates Nelson's victory.[65] In the context of the usurpation, however, the flag's message to the loyalists took on a more subversive meaning.

Nelson was a naval hero and true patriot, unlike the usurpers who had overthrown the duly appointed governor for their personal ends. Unity among the settlers was vital if they were to resist the usurpers, as was their duty. The intertwined floral emblems suggest the mixing of ethnicities among the settlers, and placed upon a shield it further suggests that their unity gave them strength, just as the recent 1801 union of England, Scotland and Ireland had created the newer, greater Britain that Nelson defended. The kangaroo and emu supporters, their heads turned warily over their shoulders, indicate the new country where the new Britons were putting down roots and which they stood ready to defend.[66]

Like the *Gazette* woodblock, the flag reflects the loyalists' ideals. Free trade, the rule of law and possibilities for social and economic advancement were represented in Bligh's pre-usurpation trust of expirees, the role of Blighton as a demonstration farm and the informal privy council of settler-magistrates. The casting of the usurpers as French revolutionaries reflected the settlers' anguish at the curtailing of these advances, reinforced by acts of civil disobedience such as refusing to attend musters or acknowledge the usurper courts. Nelsonian patriotism provided a standard of Britishness untainted by the usurpers, and supported by viceregal influence, around which they could rally and support each other knowing that eventually relief would arrive from England.

Atkinson has argued that the usurpation involved working out certain political principles and that this took a form then understood as 'revolution'.[67] The usurpers invoked an understanding of revolution as being constitutional when rebelling against a tyrant. What the 'manifestos' show, however, is not two opposing ideologies of royalist versus revolutionary but two claims to legitimate authority derived from two understandings, neither particularly historically nor ideologically coherent, of royal authority deputed in New South Wales.

In terms of the ancients versus moderns paradigm, rather outdated by 1808 but still evident in official sigillography, the usurpers, with their military and landed estate interests, tend to align with the ancients and the loyalists are more inclined to align with the moderns, but the division is not clear-cut. Both still attributed sacredness to the sovereign. The loyalist John Jamieson declared Bligh's person to be as sacred as the King's.[68] But Johnston, in explaining his actions, claimed as justification 'how little [Bligh] regarded the honor of the sacred personage whom he represented'.[69] All seemed to agree on the sanctity of the King's person, but the loyalists went a step further and extended that sanctity to his deputy king, a sanctity enhanced during the usurpation by both king and deputy king being bodily absent.

Bligh was very clear that only he was the representative of the King. As such, only he could support the settlers' independence as loyal subjects, free from military subjugation and revolutionary excess. The usurpers rejected the loyalists' characterisation of them as Jacobin terrorists, claiming instead to free the respectable inhabitants from viceregal tyranny. Invoking the Magna Carta was an attempt to cloak usurpation with historical verisimilitude.

When Macquarie restored the royal authority deputed in 1810, he explicitly revoked and declared void every act of the usurper administration. He conducted an explicitly public ritual of reclaiming the Great Seal and displaying its return in the centre of the Parade Ground at the Barracks in Sydney, the very heart of the usurper administration, to legitimate his rule and establish the dominance of viceregal over military authority in the colony.[70]

Conclusion

Three questions have been posed in this chapter. The first is why should any historian trouble themselves with great seals? The historiography of the settler colonies or old dominions is dominated by twentieth-century nationalist writing. Examples of material culture such as great seals deputed, and their reflections in popular culture, suggest that that historiography, and its reliance upon the paper archive, is not sufficient for considering the relationships between crowns and colonists, especially in settler societies.

Great Seals Deputed need to be considered in an imperial or inter-colonial context and not in isolation or solely as antiquarian artefacts. They were designed and made in London, not the colonies, and they project an imperial ideal for each colony within an imperial network. Each colony is specialised, at least as a sigillographic ideal, in its functions, and that specialisation becomes evident when a seal is placed in the context of other colonial seals rather than considered alone as an illustration of *genius loci*.

Despite their seeming uniformity, each great seal deputed inherently contains an idea of separation as a new realm. Great Seals Deputed were not intended to instigate the development of new realms under new dynasties, but in the colonies could be read as such. In Virginia, the colonists tried to get the Crown to take its Virginian responsibilities seriously in 1649, 1659 and 1767, and the revolution of 1776 represents the failure of the royal authority projected in the seal, the loss of a capacity to imagine the new settler society alluded to in its seal design and motto. In 1810, the Crown did take the situation in New South Wales seriously, and its agents consciously and publicly restored the deputy king and the Great Seal. The ideals of convict redemption remained imaginable, and the allusory landscape remained capable of realisation.

Indeed, the idealised Etrurian landscape was, by 1808, beginning to portray a real place. The usurping Exclusives and military occupied the fort and the church (metaphorically the institutions of power) and claimed Industry and her bale of goods as their work. The loyalist small settlers, on the other hand, wielded Industry's attributes of pick-axe, spade, distaff, beehive and ploughing oxen, and the 'rising habitations' of the town, and saw in Industry their own actions in removing their fetters. Seals can be read, contextualised and interpreted just like any other document or material evidence.

The second question raised in this chapter is what became of deputed sovereign authority when the sovereign emblem was stolen and the deputed authority usurped? Bligh never surrendered his claims to the Great Seal. The usurpers made use of it to authenticate documents such as land grants, but Bligh persistently claimed they had never been duly authorised to use the seal, and Macquarie revoked every decision passed under the seal. The usurpers' 'authentications' were really forged signatures, ironic in a convict society. Usurpers and loyalists both invoked the sacredness of the King to justify their actions, but the attribution of that sacredness by the loyalists to the deputy king questions Jenkinson's claim that great seals lack any mystical qualities. The seal had to be applied by properly deputed authority, and the sanctity of the body politic of both the King and the Deputy King meant that an inhering sacredness was essential to the authenticity of actually using the seal. Application by anyone else, without the proper deputising, reduced it to no more than a blob of wax. Despite the usurpers' pretence of exercising deputed royal authority, Bligh's objections and Macquarie's revocations reveal that artifice. Royal authority in New South Wales during the usurpation was not really usurped, but lay dormant, waiting to be restored by proper authority.

The usurpers and the loyalists each invoked a version of British (or more specifically English) history to support their position. In doing so, they evoked two different pasts and two different futures. The usurpers invoked the possibility of an enduring union with Britain in which New South Wales would one day be represented in the royal arms as another realm under the one king. The fate of Virginia as the fourth realm, however, suggests that this ideal was already unlikely. The loyalists positioned New South Wales as a child of 1688, economically liberal, with royal authority locally controlled. That authority contained the potential to evolve from deputed to general authority in its own right. The royal arms on the reverse of the seal could be replaced by those of an autonomous British realm of New South Wales, ensigned by its own crown.[71] The divisions between the usurpers and loyalists, however, were not neatly binary. This is clearly seen in the localism of the ancients, not only reflected in the allusory landscapes of all the colonial seals, but also a feature of the modern loyalists' statements and emblems.

J. G. A. Pocock has described the period from 1660 to the 1830s as a 'long eighteenth century', in which the sixty-year reign of George III was a period of profound change in the monarchy and of transition to the modern period.[72] He describes the kingdom as a 'multiple monarchy' ruling in various jurisdictions in Europe and North America and permeated by vivid memories of the civil wars of the 1640s. These memories positioned the alternative to the Crown not as a republic but as the collapse of government, civil war and regicide. The American rebellion was an episode in the civil war that ended (in the Thirteen Colonies) when the Americans abandoned the Crown and converted civil war into war between sovereign bodies: the United Kingdom and the USA.

In New South Wales, the loyalists could see all around them the metaphoric collapse of government in usurper maladministration, civil war in military repression, and regicide in the public harrowing of Bligh. Macquarie restored both kingship and deputy kingship and brought to a close what was perhaps one of the final chapters in that civil war of the long eighteenth century. The reading of great seals deputed as 'documents' allow Pocock's argument to extend to the British South Seas and the usurpation in New South Wales to be recontextualised within the development of settler societies after 1783. No settler colony or dominion experienced a military usurpation of royal authority after 1810.

The final question posed is whether the disaggregation of a body politic and a body natural was only possible in a colonial state. Governors in Virginia and Maryland both proclaimed Charles II king in 1649, suggesting that one element of particular deputed authority is the right to proclaim a king in that realm. General authority can proclaim a sovereign simultaneously in every realm subject to that sovereign. However, within a particular realm, such a general proclamation can be countered if a deputy sovereign proclaims a different body as sovereign in that realm. This the Governor of Virginia did in 1649 and 1659 by proclaiming Charles II king in Virginia, contrary to the general proclamation in London of the Parliament as sovereign in every jurisdiction formerly subject to Charles I. The deputed authority could also be inverted, as the Georgia Assembly did in 1776 when it replaced the deputed authority exercised by the Governor and Assembly with a general authority exercised by the Assembly alone.[73]

Neither Virginia nor Maryland sought in 1649 to proclaim Charles II king in Britain, only in their particular realms. By contrast, the New South Wales Corps claimed to exercise the general authority of the sovereign by removing the particular authority of the Governor. Pocock says the Americans and later the Irish claimed their assemblies existed under the Crown but not the Parliament, claims that could not be sustained by the eighteenth century.[74] The usurpation, seen through the prism of the Great Seal, was unsustainable for the same reasons. Deputed, particular authority relied initially upon being deputed directly from the sovereign, but after 1810 it also needed support from the settlers' representatives to exercise that deputation. It laid a conceptual framework for the 'king in parliament (UK)' and a 'king in parliament (NSW)' to become increasingly separate bodies politic, even while the body natural of the sovereign remained singular.

When Phillip applied his privy seal and later the Great Seal to a document, he did so as an agent of the King, and within this agency he was also simultaneously Arthur Phillip the natural man and Governor Phillip RN, the fictive embodiment of the new colonial state.[75] The seal that he fixed to documents was, symbolically, both his personal (natural) and his corporate (politic) signature. The privy seal Bligh used in the absence of the Great Seal conveyed his personal and corporate authority. The metaphor of the King's two bodies extends to his viceroy. The dual bodies of the deputy king are a site in which a new realm can be imagined.

To paraphrase Ernst Kantorowicz, the usurpation was the moment in which the deputy king's two bodies, one his body natural and the other his body politic, became disaggregated.[76] This disaggregation is possible in any realm of deputed authority, and especially in a settler society, not just a colonial state. So brave Etruria grew.

Notes

1 Hilary Jenkinson, 'What Happened to the Great Seal of James II?', *The Antiquaries Journal*, 23:1–2 (1943), 1–13, at p. 1.
2 The study of seals, including their evaluation and use as historical records or documents, is called sigillography, from Latin *sigillum* (seal) and the anglicised ancient Greek *grapho* (denoting a personal agent and providing a personal designation correlative to the noun), first recorded in 1879, *Oxford English Dictionary*, online version dated June 2012 (accessed 22 March 2015).
3 Conrad Swan, *Canada: Symbols of Sovereignty* (Toronto: University of Toronto Press,1977), p. 15. In this chapter, the pronouns 'her' and 'she' refer to each and every gender unless the context indicates otherwise.
4 Hilary Jenkinson, *Guide to Seals in the Public Record Office* (London: Her Majesty's Stationery Office, 1968), p. 3.
5 Swan, *Canada: Symbols of Sovereignty*, p. 27.
6 Peter Walne, 'The Great Seal Deputed of Virginia', *The Virginia Magazine of History and Biography*, 66:1 (January 1958), 3–21; Jenkinson, *Guide to Seals in the Public Record Office*, pp. 335–9.
7 Robert Beverley, *The History of Virginia, in Four Parts* (London, 1722), reprinted with introduction by Charles Campbell (Richmond: J. W. Randolph, 1855), pp. 51–2; Brent Tarter, 'Old Dominion', *Encyclopedia of Virginia*. Available online at www.encyclopediavirginia.org/Old_Dominion#start_entry (accessed 11 January 2015). Similar actions occurred in Antigua, Barbados, Bermuda, Maryland and Newfoundland, after which the Commonwealth transported royalist prisoners as convicts to the West Indian colonies.
8 The term 'Native American' is anachronistic. 'American Indian' was the standard term used at the time, see Clyde Tucker, Brian Kojetin and Roderick Harrison, *A Statistical Analysis of the CPD Supplement on Race and Ethnic Origin* (Washington, DC: Bureau of Labour Statistics and Bureau of the Census, 1995), Table 4. Available online at http://www.census.gov/prod/2/gen/96arc/ivatuck.pdf (accessed 12 April 2015).
9 Richard Bland, *An Inquiry into the Rights of British Colonies* (Williamsburg: Alexander Purdie & Co., 1766). Available online at http://www.newrivernotes.com/topical_books_1766_virginia_rightsofthebritishcolonies.htm (accessed 11 January 2015).
10 Bland, *An Inquiry into the Rights of British Colonies*.
11 Marsh makes a similar point about the Georgia seal of 1767: B. J. Marsh, 'The Meanings of Georgia's Eighteenth-Century Great Seals', *Georgia Historical Quarterly*, 96:2 (2012), 195–232, at p. 216.
12 Jenkinson, *Guide to Seals in the Public Record Office*, p. 5.
13 Jenkinson, *Guide to Seals in the Public Record Office*, pp. 1–2, 4–5.
14 Jenkinson, *Guide to Seals in the Public Record Office*, pp. 5–6.
15 W. Kirk MacNulty, *Freemasonry: Symbols, Secrets, Significance* (London: Thames & Hudson, 2006), pp. 21–33, 66, 143–5. Marsh has identified the engraver of the

Great Seal of Georgia in 1754, John Pine, as extending his networks within the then developing Freemasonry movement: Marsh, 'The Meanings of Georgia's Eighteenth-Century Great Seals', p. 212 and note 49; 'Seal of Solomon', in Albert C. Mackey, *Encyclopedia of Freemasonry and Its Kindred Sciences* (New York: The Masonic History Company, 1914); James Panton, *Historical Dictionary of the British Monarchy* (Lanham, Md.: Scarecrow Press, 2011), pp. 462–3.

16 'Colony of Georgia: A Ground-Work of a More Stable and Formal Government', 15 April 1776, in Allen D. Candler (ed.), *The Revolutionary Records of the State of Georgia*, vol. I: *1769–1782* (Atlanta, Ga.: Franklin-Turner Co., 1908), pp. 274–5.

17 'Norfolk Island', *Sydney Gazette*, 9 September 1804, p. 2.

18 'Phillip's Commission', 2 April 1787, in *Historical Records of New South Wales*, 7 vols. (Sydney: Government Printing Office, 1892); vol. I, Part 2, pp. 61–7.

19 Swan, *Canada: Symbols of Sovereignty*, pp. 33, 114–15, 171–3.

20 'Device for Seal', Court of St James's, 21 May 1790, *Historical Records of New South Wales*, vol. I, Part 2, p. 340.

21 'Warrant for Seal', Court of St James's, 21 January 1791, *Historical Records of New South Wales*, vol. I, Part 2, p. 431.

22 'Device for Seal', Court of St James's, 4 August 1790, *Historical Records of New South Wales*, vol. I, Part 2, p. 389.

23 Governor Phillip to Lord Grenville, Sydney, 5 November 1791, *Historical Records of New South Wales*, vol. I, Part 2, p. 532.

24 'Device for Seal', Court of St James's, 4 August 1790, *Historical Records of New South Wales*, vol. I, Part 2, p. 389. 'Sigillum Nov. Cam. Aust.' is an abbreviation of the Latin phrase *Sigillum Nova Cambria Australis* (Seal of New South Wales).

25 Timothy Clayton and Anita McConnell, 'Major, Thomas (1720–1799)', *Oxford Dictionary of National Biography*, online edition January 2008. Available online at www.oxforddnb.com/index/17/101017847 (accessed 9 February 2015).

26 Leonard Forrer, *The Wyons* (London: Spink & Son Ltd., 1917), p. 73.

27 Leo Damrosch, *Jonathan Swift: His Life and His World* (New Haven, Conn.: Yale University Press, 2013), pp. 134–40, especially his analysis of Swift's *A Tale of a Tub [and] An Account of a Battel between the Antient and Modern Books in St James's Library* (London, 1704); Ian Jack, *Augustan Satire: Intention and Idiom in English Poetry, 1660–1750* (Oxford: Clarendon Press, 1952); Jacqueline Eales and Andrew Hopper, *The County Community in Seventeenth-Century England and Wales* (Hatfield: University of Hertforshire Press, 2012).

28 The ancient group includes the seals of West Florida (1764), Island of St John (later Prince Edward Island) (1769), New Brunswick (1784), Cape Breton Island (1785) and Lower Canada (1793). The modern group of seals is a little more expansive, covering Georgia (1754), Quebec (1763), East Florida (1764), New South Wales (1790) and Upper Canada (1792), with a later and more utilitarian group of Grenada (1795), Bahamas (1821) and Newfoundland (1827).

29 W. A. Gullick, *The New South Wales Coat of Arms with Notes on the Earlier Seals* (Sydney: Government Printer, 1907), pp. 31–5.

30 Simon Schama, *Landscape and Memory* (London: Fontana Press, 1996), pp. 528–9.

31 Alan Atkinson, 'The British Whigs and the Rum Rebellion', *Journal of the Royal Australian Historical Society*, 66:2 (1980), 73–90, at p. 86. The Day of Landing is now named Australia Day.

32 John Macarthur to Nicholas Vansittart Esq., London, 2 February 1804, *Historical Records of New South Wales*, vol. V, pp. 306–7.

33 'Proclamation', General Orders, 1 January 1810, Government House, Sydney, *Historical Records of New South Wales*, vol. VII, pp. 252–4.

34 Governor Lachlan Macquarie to Viscount Robert Castlereagh, 8 March 1810, Sydney, New South Wales, *Historical Records of New South Wales*, vol. VII, p. 303.

35 Governor William Bligh to Viscount Robert Castlereagh, 31 August 1808, Government House, Sydney, *Historical Records of New South Wales* vol. VI, pp. 711–12. Just before he sailed, Bligh demanded the return of the Great Seal and his state papers, but the usurper authorities ignored his demand and failed to discern

any plan he may have had to try and reclaim his authority from another location within the colony. See Governor William Bligh to Colonel William Paterson, 28 January 1808, Government House, Sydney, *Historical Records of New South Wales*, vol. VII, p. 11.
36 Bligh to Castlereagh, 31 August 1808, *Historical Records of New South Wales*, vol. VI, p. 624.
37 Bligh to Castlereagh, 30 June 1808, *Historical Records of New South Wales*, vol. VI, pp. 660–1.
38 Bruce Baskerville, '"Ready at All Times": The Hawkesbury Resistance to the Rum Rebels', 2008. Available online at https://historymatrix.wordpress.com/2013/08/06/ready-at-all-times-the-hawkesbury-resistance-to-the-rum-rebels (accessed 12 April 2015).
39 The terms 'Exclusives', 'Pure Merinos', 'Emancipists' and 'Expirees' really came into popular use just after the restoration: Amanda Laugesen (ed.), *Convict Words: Language in Early Colonial Australia* (Oxford: Oxford University Press, 2002). 'Pure Merino' was a reference to the pastoral elite and their flocks that included a strain of merino sheep descended from a flock kept by George III.
40 Alan Atkinson, 'Jeremy Bentham and the Rum Rebellion', *Journal of the Royal Australian Historical Society*, 64:1 (1978), 1–13, at pp. 2, 7–8. Bentham had originally intended to name the pamphlet *The True Bastille*.
41 'Proclamation', Headquarters, 27 January 1808, *Historical Records of New South Wales*, vol. VI, pp. 453–4.
42 F. M. Bladen, 'Introduction', *Historical Records of New South Wales*, vol. VI, pp. lxi–ii.
43 Atkinson, 'Jeremy Bentham and the Rum Rebellion', p. 83.
44 Anne-Maree Whitaker (ed.), *Distracted Settlement: New South Wales after Bligh from the Journal of Lieutenant James Finucane 1808–1810* (Carlton: Miegunyah Press, 1998), p. 54 (reproducing Finucane's diary entry for 28 July 1808).
45 Bligh to Castlereagh, 30 April 1808, *Historical Records of New South Wales*, vol. VI, p. 623.
46 Bligh to Castlereagh, 30 June 1808, *Historical Records of New South Wales*, vol. VI, p. 670. The 'ever memorable' line may be a double-edged reference to Charles I's last words, 'remember'.
47 Atkinson, 'Jeremy Bentham and the Rum Rebellion', p. 84 and notes 71, 72. Atkinson cites Macarthur in 1824 comparing his actions in 1808 with those of Cromwell.
48 'Address to Major Johnston', Sydney, 8 March 1808, *Historical Records of New South Wales*, vol. VI, pp. 534–5.
49 Isabel Karremann, 'Augustan Manliness and Its Anxieties: Shaftesbury and Swift', in Stefan Horlacher (ed.), *Constructions of Masculinity in British Literature from the Middle Ages to the Present* (Basinstoke: Palgrave Macmillan, 2011), Chapter 7 *passim*.
50 Major George Johnson to Viscount Robert Castlereagh, 11 April 1808, Headquarters, Sydney, *Historical Records of New South Wales*, vol. VI, p. 580.
51 Atkinson, 'Jeremy Bentham and the Rum Rebellion', p. 85.
52 Bligh to Castlereagh, Enclosure, 12 November 1808, *Historical Records of New South Wales*, vol. VI, p. 808 note.
53 'Proclamation', 29 April 1809, The Derwent, New South Wales, *Historical Records of New South Wales*, vol. VII, p. 109.
54 Hawkesbury Settlers' Address, Hawkesbury, 22 September 1806, *Historical Records of New South Wales*, vol. VI, p. 191.
55 Settlers' Address to Governor Bligh, New South Wales, 1 January 1808, *Historical Records of New South Wales*, vol. VI, p. 410.
56 Bligh to Castlereagh, 30 April 1808, *Historical Records of New South Wales*, vol. VI, p. 623; Provost-Marshal William Gore to Castlereagh, 27 March 1808, *Historical Records of New South Wales*, vol. VI, pp. 558–9.

57 George Mackaness (ed.), *A New Song, Made in New South Wales on the Rebellion, by Lawrence Davoren* (Dubbo: Review Publications, 1979). A 'pipe' was a form of popular song-writing, usually accompanied by a pipe or wind instrument.
58 The interrogations of the magistrates are at 'Examinations of Officers after the Arrest of Governor Bligh', 26 January 1808, and their dismissal at 'Government and General Order', Headquarters, 27 January 1808, *Historical Records of New South Wales*, vol. VI, pp. 435–53.
59 Andrew Thompson to Governor William Bligh, 26 March 1807, Hawkesbury, *Historical Records of New South Wales*, vol. VI, p. 263.
60 Brian Fletcher, 'The Hawkesbury Settlers and the Rum Rebellion', *Journal of the Royal Australian Historical Society*, 54:3 (1968), 217–37, at p. 220.
61 Gwenda Robb, *George Howe: Australia's First Publisher* (Kew: Arcadia/Australian Scholarly Publishing, 2003), p. 51.
62 The identity of the woodblock carver has been ascribed to various convict artisans, but the significant point is that it was authorised by the then Governor as suitable for the colony's first newspaper: Robb, *George Howe*, p. 51; *Thus We Hope To Prosper: The Colonial Pacific 1770–1901*, auction catalogue (Melbourne: Douglas Stewart Fine Books, 2014), item 16, pp. 22–3; Roger Butler, *Printed: Images in Colonial Australia, 1801–1901*, exhibition catalogue (Canberra: National Gallery of Australia, 2007), pp. 91–2.
63 Diary of Revd Robert Knopwood, Hobart Town, inside front cover, c. 1805. Available online at eprints.utas.edu.au/11149/1/rs_12_Robert_Knopwood_Diaries.pdf (accessed 26 January 2015). Knopwood was later accused of 'employing his altar against the throne' by supporting the usurpers: see letter to the Editor of the *Asiatic Mirror* (Calcutta), published in the *Madras Courier*, 29 May 1809, signed 'Clericus', in *Historical Records of New South Wales* vol. VII, p. 207.
64 F. M. Bladen, 'Introduction', *Historical Records of New South Wales*, vol. VI, pp. lxv–lxvii.
65 'Death of Admiral Lord Viscount Nelson', *Sydney Gazette*, 3 August 1806, p. 2; 'Sydney Gazette', *Sydney Gazette*, 24 August 1806, p. 4 (this is the first local publication of Nelson's 'England expects' signal, although the imported London and Indian papers may have already contained the story); Margot Riley, 'The Bowman Family's Trafalgar Flag: Symbol of Patriotism or Australian Nelsoniana?', *Australiana*, 27:3 (2005), 32–5.
66 Linda Colley, *Britons: Forging the Nation 1707–1837*, 2nd edn (New Haven, Conn.: Yale University Press, 2005), pp. 17–18, explores the links between the concept of a Briton and the 1801 Act of Union.
67 Atkinson, 'Jeremy Bentham and the Rum Rebellion', p. 74.
68 Principal Superintendant of Government Stock John Jamieson to Goverbnor William Bligh, 28 April 1808, Parramatta, *Historical Records of New South Wales*, vol. VI, p. 606.
69 Johnston to Castlereagh, 11 April 1808, *Historical Records of New South Wales*, vol. VI, pp. 580–2.
70 *Sydney Gazette*, 7 January 1810, pp. 2–3. Bligh had been imprisoned in the Barracks for some weeks until he agreed to leave the colony in early 1809. He was warned by the usurpers of his impending detention on 30 January, noted by Bligh as the anniversary of 'the martyrdom of King Charles': Bligh to Castlereagh, 10 June 1808, *Historical Records of New South Wales*, vol. VII, p. 172. Macquarie's public restoration of the Great Seal in the Barracks echoed that at the Banqueting House in London in 1660, when Charles II was symbolically restored to the throne in the same place as Charles I had been executed in 1649. The symbolism would have been apparent to the colonists, loyal and usurper.
71 Colley, *Britons: Forging the Nation*, pp. 17–18: the word 'Briton' during the eighteenth century had popular resonance as a self-definition, alongside regional identities and a common Protestantism, of dissimilarity with those beyond their shores, especially the French, and is used in such a sense in this chapter.

72 J. G. A. Pocock, 'Monarchy in the Name of Britain: The Case of George III', in Hans Blom, John Christian Laursen and Luisa Simonetti (eds), *Monarchisms in the Age of Enlightenment: Liberty, Patriotism and the Common Good* (Toronto: University of Toronto Press, 2007), pp. 286 and 301.
73 Hobbes argued that a sovereign could be either a single man (a monarch) or a more than one man (an assembly) and also that every man was obliged to obey a public official once he had heard his commission read and had seen the attached 'publique seal': Thomas Hobbes, *Leviathan* (London: Penguin Classics, 1985; first published 1651), pp. 239, 321.
74 Pocock, 'Monarchy in the Name of Britain', p. 295.
75 Quentin Skinner, 'Hobbes and the Purely Artificial Person of the State', *Journal of Political Philosophy*, 7:1 (1999), 1–29.
76 Ernst Kantorowicz, *The King's Two Bodies: A Study in Medieval Political Theology* (Princeton, NJ: Princeton University Press, 1957); Bernhard Jussen, 'The King's Two Bodies Today', *Representations*, 106:1 (2009), 102–17.

CHAPTER FIFTEEN

A new monarchy for a new commonwealth? Monarchy and the consequences of republican India

H. Kumarasingham

Can crowns be returned? Clement Attlee thought so. Only two months before Indian Independence in August 1947, the Prime Minister asked his sovereign, George VI, the last Emperor of India, whether the Imperial State Crown of India should be given back to the Indians (and Pakistanis) if they left the Commonwealth as they ultimately had paid for it.[1] The King, along with the potential loss of this headpiece, studded with over 6,000 diamonds, bought for his father's 1911 Durbar, had to deal with the more massive loss of the Empire's greatest jewel: India. *The Times* remarked that the Imperial State Crown of India 'on its velvet cushion in the Tower ... [was] the precious emblem of a tutelage outgrown'.[2] An imperial crown without an empire. India had marked Britain as the world's most formidable world power. The dissolution of the Indian Empire meant George VI had to surrender the Crown's pre-eminence and acknowledge the beginning of the end of Empire. Other, more personal, cuts had to be recognised, including an 'I' from his signature GRI (Georgius Rex Imperator), an evocation that adorned everything from coins to post boxes across every continent. The 'I', of course, recognised the British monarch's grandest title, which Victoria first took as Empress of India and proclaimed as such on 1 January 1877 at a lavish durbar in Delhi.

India transformed the monarchy, as its head knew only too well. Queen Victoria communicated via her private secretary to Earl Granville in January 1873 her impatience that no special mention of India had been made to the royal title since Britain assumed direct control after the Indian Mutiny of 1857. The Foreign Secretary was left with no illusion as to the Queen's belief in the importance of India and its significance for the Crown. Victoria believed India made her 'undoubtedly the Sovereign of Sovereigns, and consequently Empress'.[3] In 1949, 100 years after Britain seized the fabulous Koh-i-Noor diamond, India, famously known as the 'Jewel in the Crown', declared its intention to shed the monarchy and proclaim a republic – but within the Commonwealth. The monarchy, which had relied on India for its prestige, was now to be transformed by it once more with a new title. The monarch, no longer king-emperor, would be head of the Commonwealth. The move changed the constitutional and political nature of the British Empire and Commonwealth and drew attention to a monarchy with a fast-disappearing empire and the possibility of the crown going with it. Britain's Foreign Secretary, Ernest Bevin, like many of his officials, thought that the Commonwealth might itself be dissolved rather than compromise the Crown and Britain's position and pretensions.[4] Perhaps the phantasmagoria of monarchy would be swept aside and the Crown discarded as meaningless flummery, or it might be modernised for the post-war era of decolonisation as an internationalist institution unshackled by imperial expectations. Either way, Bagehot's warning not to let daylight in on monarchy hung over the deliberations.

For all the welcome and renewed scholarly attention to empires and decolonisation in recent years, there has been no commensurate growth in the analysis of the institution that ultimately symbolised the British Empire and presided over its dissolution. The massive five-volume *Oxford History of the British Empire* and its valuable companion series (with one exception covering a regional dimension) devotes not even a single chapter to the monarchy as a concept or institution.[5] If the word 'crown' is mentioned, it is employed, not unnaturally, as a metonym for the government and not for the royal individual who comes with it. In Volume IV, which covers the twentieth century, George VI earns two unremarkable mentions in the entire volume. Both John Darwin and W. David McIntyre have continued, through their prodigious and meticulous work, the sterling traditions set by Nicholas Mansergh in documenting the creation of the modern Commonwealth, but in all these accounts the monarchy, despite making purposeful appearances, does not draw the comprehensive focus it role justifies.[6] I have recently examined the reasons why India, Pakistan and Ceylon chose to be realms and not republics on Independence and their adoption of a political system that generally held the Crown as its basis.[7] Vernon Bogdanor has been one of the few scholars who has examined the constitutional realm of the monarchy, and his unparalleled 1995 work on the subject contains a beneficial chapter on the 'Sovereign and Commonwealth',[8] but the field on monarchical powers has generally ignored the Crown's Commonwealth position, and the British Crown has otherwise been left to a small band of public-law scholars, who make no attempt to examine the Imperial and Commonwealth history of the monarchy.[9] Philip Murphy has addressed this scholarly lacuna with his excellent *Monarchy and the End of Empire*, which provides much needed insights into the post-war British monarchy's involvement in Empire and the subsequent Commonwealth.[10]

This chapter seeks to build on Murphy's work but takes a different approach. Rather than using the monarchy to understand the end of Empire, it instead attempts to examine the reverse. Through the debates and issues that swirled around India's wish to become a republic and stay in the Commonwealth in 1947–49, we are able to discern the competing, original, reactionary and often bizarre ambitions for the post-imperial monarchy. This chapter does not attempt to retrace the reasons and details of the negotiations in 1949 over Commonwealth membership, but instead considers the monarchy from the positions of not only Britain and India but also Canada, Australia, New Zealand, South Africa, Pakistan, Ceylon, Ireland and Burma.[11] The brief period of the late 1940s opens a window to another age that reveals the identities and personalities of key figures in the end of Empire. The monarchy was emotive and exhausting for all concerned, at least when judged from the accounts of the time. In 1949, the Commonwealth and Crown were in jeopardy and risked dismantlement or promised restoration. Three hundred years after Cromwell had experimented with another commonwealth, the year 1949 would see its own version of Roundheads and Cavaliers, with the Crown's powers creating fissures that gave the Commonwealth its greatest test of survival in the twentieth century. The issue before the statesmen (no women were present) in April 1949 was not whether India could become a republic – that was axiomatic – but whether the monarchy was flexible enough to accommodate both latter-day Roundheads and Cavaliers under its banner.

A giraffe monarchy

The Commonwealth, with its complexities, contradictions and shifting characteristics, made it appear to some incredible. George VI appreciated this and thought the reaction of an outsider would 'surely be that of the man who, on first seeing a giraffe, exclaimed: "There ain't no such animal!" '.[12] The same could be said for the British monarchy's commonwealth extensions. Though there had been the dual monarchy of Austria-Hungary, the elected and collective crowns of the Holy Roman Empire, the Polish-Lithuanian Commonwealth and other examples of composite and multidimensional monarchies, including, of course, the royal ties between England, Scotland, Ireland and Wales, the British monarchy in its imperial-commonwealth facets is inimitable. This metaphysical and mystical royal chameleon offered across the globe, and continues to do so, a shared and yet divisible monarchy that never ceases to baffle. George V, jealously aware of these imperial manifestations, scrutinised all imperial legislation to guarantee the Crown's position and prerogatives.[13] During the Second World War, his son, George VI, would prove the conjectural texture of the Crown. George VI declared war a week apart as King in Canada from the King in Australia; the King in South Africa contemplated neutrality, but then found new ministers to carry out the declaration of war. The majority of the population of the Indian Empire was against the unilateral declaration of war committed by the King-Emperor's representative, which nonetheless compelled thousands to fight in his name. The King in Ireland remained neutral throughout, while the King's declaration in London of a state of war meant that colonies from Antigua to Zanzibar and from the Bismarck Archipelago to Malta were at war too. While at home, the King, as Duke of Normandy, had to accept foreign occupation of part of the British Isles with the Nazi conquest of the Channel Islands. The Commonwealth would, after the war, provide further monarchical mirages and mysteries drawn from history and utility. As Sir Percival Spear classically expressed it, the monarchy could become 'a new Athanasianism of many crowns in one monarchy'.[14] *The Times* seemed to agree, and, rather than wallowing in national self-pity at the loss of the Indian Empire, it thought the Crown, both as an institution and a physical signifier of royal power, could in fact have an opportunity to be refashioned for a new era:

> What has happened is that a symbol has been made obsolete by the emergence of the reality it was meant to foreshadow. ... If it can be regarded as a piece of jewellery emptied of its significance, to which a new meaning may now be given, it might suitably be used to typify the function of the Sovereign as the personal link of the entire Commonwealth, and carried before him when he opens his Parliaments overseas, as the Crown Imperial is carried on like occasions at Westminster.[15]

The editorial in the principal organ of the British Establishment commented that this intriguing remarketing of the crown would need the agreement of the states that paid for a historically laden symbol. By doing so, it suggested, perhaps, that for the monarchy to successfully act as a unifying institution across the Commonwealth it must, in particular, have the consent of the new members from South Asia.

Indeed, the South Asian leaders could compete at times with the sentiments of their settler dominion counterparts such as Robert Menzies, Prime Minister of Australia, who thought of the King as a 'father' of the imperial 'family'.[16] The Ceylonese leader, D. S. Senanayake, told his fellow prime ministers that he in fact represented the 'oldest continuous monarchy in the Commonwealth', since the 1815 Kandyan Convention vested the near 2,500-year-old Sinhalese crown on George III and his successors.[17] As Sir Ivor Jennings remarked, 'a good deal of ingenuity is required to prove the apostolic succession from Prince Vijaya to Queen Elizabeth, but nationalist history is not less influential through being as romantic as the story of King Arthur and the Knights of the Round Table'.[18]

For Pakistan, the acceptance of crown and commonwealth was weighted less on emotional searches for monarchical antecedents and more on the perceived practical advantages to be gained, which included military benefits and personnel.[19] Mohammad Ali Jinnah had always been in favour of Commonwealth membership and became, as the first governor-general, the King's representative in Pakistan (to Lord Mountbatten's disappointment, since the last viceroy wanted the job himself).[20] Alterations to the King's title, not just the Indian challenge, were viewed with considerable suspicion and sober calculation by the Pakistani leadership. On being asked to consider potential changes to the King's title in light of developments in Ireland, the Pakistani High Commissioner in London questioned the consequences of altering the bonds between Commonwealth states since in 'the final analysis it is the British crown that provides this link'. H. I. Rahimtoola further explained that if he took the issue to Pakistan's Constituent Assembly, where the country's future constitutional status was being debated, its members would 'naturally and quite legitimately ask me what particular advantage Pakistan will derive by retaining the link with the British Crown, which she would lose if that link were broken'.[21] Though these opinions of establishment figures in Ceylon and Pakistan were not necessarily representative of the views of their people, they were no less important for that. Their interest in the link with King and Commonwealth was, in foreign-policy terms, perceived as protecting Ceylonese and Pakistani interests vis-à-vis India. For all the member states, the Indian stance on Commonwealth membership would draw all of them well outside their comfort zone, and it was the monarchy that provided the context for their nostrums. If the monarchy had previously been judged a giraffe, it would seem an even more improbable creature through the debates covering the new Commonwealth.

The Indian challenge

It was a matter of great regret to George VI that he never visited Britain's Indian Empire. As with his father, a durbar had been thought vital not only to proclaim the new king-emperor but also to personally affirm a connection with his Indian subjects and to allow *darshan*. This ancient Indian principle was the practice for certain priests, kings and other leaders to be seen and to see their followers in a reverential and near spiritual manner. A durbar had indeed been organised for 1937–38, intended for Edward VIII, whose abdication in 1936 annulled plans for both his coronation and a durbar. George VI was impatient to visit, but the precariousness of the monarchy after the abdication and the Indian political situation meant it was constantly postponed; with the outbreak of war a royal tour was rendered near impossible. The Indian National Congress had declared in Lahore on 26 January 1930 – a date that from 1950 would be celebrated as Republic Day – *Puna Swaraj*, complete independence, and a severance from Britain became the objective of the party. Though the situation would change since India, Pakistan and Ceylon would all become realms and not republics on independence, this pronouncement, and Gandhi's mobilisation of the masses over the limited reforms expressed in the Government of India Act 1935, created a potentially combustible context for a royal visit, especially when it was unclear what, if any, reform George VI's Delhi Durbar would offer, as had been the tradition in earlier durbars.[22]

George VI realised, however, the desire for the Indians to achieve Independence, and he hoped this would occur within the Commonwealth. The possibility of secession that was mentioned as a chance to entice Congress's support for the war effort appalled the monarch, since to the King-Emperor it was against the interests not only of Britain but also many outside the Congress camp. The King confided to his diary on 3 March 1942, 'Why mention secession as it is what Congress has always wanted to do. Many Provinces won't want to join it, or the Indian Princes either. Many Indians still want to owe allegiance to me as King Emperor.'[23]

There was something to what the King said, as there were several parts of India that were dismayed at the thought of a Congress Raj. Rather than pure emotional attachment to the monarchy, certain sections of Indian society viewed the Crown as a protector of their interests. Remembering that over one-third of India was governed by local potentates with personal and treaty arrangements directly with the Crown rather than with the British government in India, this sentiment also had constitutional significance. The princely states were convinced and cajoled to join either of the successor dominions of

India and Pakistan, and they were courted to take this dramatic step by being assured by the King's cousin and Viceroy, Lord Mountbatten, that the Crown would continue as an institution in the region.

An exchange Mountbatten had with the Maharaj-Rana of Dholpur on 29 July 1947, just over a fortnight before Indian Independence, is representative of the uses of the Indian Crown for decolonisation, on the one hand, and republican Congress pragmatism in 'inheriting' the Raj, on the other. Mountbatten explained to the reluctant ruler of Dholpur that he had

> never been able to understand Your Highness's point of view that if you sign the Instrument of Accession you will find yourself linked against your will to an independent Government without a monarchical head. If you accede now you will be joining a Dominion with the King as Head. If they change the constitution to republic and leave the British Empire, the Instrument of Accession does not bind you in any way to remain with the republic.

Mountbatten added a personal royal gloss by claiming, 'I know that His Majesty would personally be grieved if you elected to sever your connection with him while he was still King of India.'[24] On the eve of Independence, after the accession documents had been duly signed, the Maharaj-Rana '[w]ith tears in his eyes' told the last Viceroy of India that it pained him to sign, but Mountbatten consoled him that the King's role had not gone but merely changed.[25]

Such scenes, with varying lachrymose levels, were repeated across the subcontinent where rulers were promised that not only would their relationship with the King endure but that if the successor dominions became republics and consequently broke the royal connection, they could leave at will. On both these assertions, Mountbatten was wrong and dangerously deceptive. The Indian and Pakistani governments and their constitutions would confer no such powers to recently acceded princely territories. However, the secessionist threat remained strong enough for the sentiment of royal association to remain burning. Harold Macmillan, representing Winston Churchill as Leader of the Opposition, in the second reading of the India Independence Bill debate in the House of Commons, said that the princely states had 'firm and devoted association with the glorious reigns of the Empress Victoria the Great and succeeding Emperors'. He hoped, therefore, that a 'flexible instrument of British constitutional development ... is capable of finding a suitable formula of association by which their loyalty and devotion to the Crown may find a new expression in harmonious association with the British Commonwealth, and with the United Nations'.[26] As Ian Copland argues, though George VI reigned under the conventions of constitutional monarchy, he nonetheless 'had the capacity to cause a lot of headaches for the government if he chose to make an issue of the rulers' dynastic connection with his house'.[27]

The great-grandson of the Queen-Empress was 'saddened' by the loss of his imperial title of 'Emperor of India', but, in the words of his official biographer, he 'was no Bourbon', as he never 'confused the substance with the shadow'.[28] No longer Emperor after 15 August 1947, George VI was able to reassure his supporters in India and the Empire-Commonwealth that he was formally King of India till January 1950. The fiery and heartfelt polemics of Indian nationalists against the Crown and Empire had briefly to be quelled and republicanism kept at bay, however. The Congress leadership engaged in the negotiations for their new state in order to attract the princely states and to prevent India being isolated and surrounded by Commonwealth realms, especially, of course, Pakistan. Nevertheless, the republican sentiment was embedded in their methods. As a Canadian diplomat observed accurately of at least the Congress Party,

> one thing certain amid so many uncertainties is that India is determinedly republican in spirit. An essential feature of republicanism as the Indians understand it, is that the individual citizen is subject to no person. To ask Indians to accept allegiance to any man is bad enough, and it becomes far worse when that man happens also to be the King of Great Britain.[29]

The Indian Communists and socialists were joined by leftist sections of the Congress Party in accusing the Commonwealth of racism and imperialism. Having the King anywhere near their independent constitution was anathema and contradicted their rejection of colonialism.[30] Yet even Harold Laski, 'the last of the republicans',[31] failed to find a substitute for the Crown as the basis of Commonwealth association.[32] The King-Emperor had also experienced bouts of frustration.[33] Even George VI's request to receive for the Royal Collection the seals of the Secretary of State for India from their last holder, Lord Listowel, ended in disappointment, as the India Office could not find them, but his wish to have the Union Jack that had flown night and day since the 1857 siege over the famous ruins of the Lucknow residency was fulfilled.[34] Artefacts of the past could be held in privileged custody, but the future of the monarchy was open to further rebellion and ridicule.

The 'Commonwealth Nexus', as documents from Whitehall and Commonwealth capitals called it, was viewed as an important network for the South Asians to secure arms, aid and access to all manner of diplomatic intelligence and economic information and preference. For Indian moderates, especially those trained in English law, such as

Sir Tej Bahadur Sapru, and members of the famed Indian Civil Service, such as Sir Girja Bajpai, the Commonwealth offered security and, in New Zealand Prime Minster Peter Fraser's phrase, 'independence plus'.[35] Unlike Fraser, however, and despite personal sympathy for constitutional monarchy, they saw that the writing on the wall spelled an Indian republic. The highly respected Sapru wrote in April 1948 of his belief 'that the republican form of government about which eloquent speeches were made in the Constituent Assembly was by no means inconsistent with alliance with England' via the Commonwealth. Nehru agreed with this argument, and, as Nicholas Mansergh, scholar of Ireland and India, remarked, the Indian form of republicanism did not 'possess the doctrinaire, uncompromising character of Irish republicanism' despite comparable distaste for British rule.[36] For the 'old Dominions' the addition of the 'brown Dominions',[37] as *The Times* termed them, saw an opportunity to rebrand and legitimise the older Commonwealth in a new age but, nonetheless, to maintain their cultural and symbiotic relationship under the mantle of the Crown.[38] The tune would change when India decided to become a republic and disrupt and possibly displace the hallowed relationship between crown and commonwealth.

The foreign king

Inevitably, there were grave reservations about breaking the Crown as the constitutional link in the Commonwealth chain and forsaking allegiance to its suzerainty. Within all the states involved, multiple perspectives and passions rose as for few other constitutional issues. Yet this was for all the members the crux of the issue: the subject of the monarchy was not one of legalism or constitutional metaphysics, but it was one of identity and community. Each state had its own version of these debates. The Irish, in 1946, with their flammable relationship with Britain and the Crown, saw their constitutional obligations to the King as purely 'facultative' and 'tenuous' and already acted like 'in effect … a Republic' before this was achieved a few years later. Nonetheless the same memorandum on Irish foreign policy, in which these points appear, also saw the usefulness of keeping the link with the Crown not only for diplomatic relations with Commonwealth states, but also, closer to home, seeing the Crown as helpful in the ambition to bring about 'restitution of the occupied area of the six counties' of Northern Ireland. The same memorandum also prefigured the formulation that would arrive in 1949: 'The position of the King in Ireland has become so attenuated that in fact and in law he is now nothing more than a symbol of our external association with the nations of the Commonwealth.'[39]

That position had long been argued by Eamon de Valera and J. A. Costello as the working methodology under which Ireland existed independently before being acknowledged as such. Dublin finally removed the sovereign from the constitution when the Republic of Ireland was proclaimed on 18 April 1949, and the republic consequently left the Commonwealth. However, like much in Anglo-Irish relations, this was not quite the full picture. By mutual agreement, both states created a treaty relationship that provided a privileged relationship for citizens of both countries whereby they were not treated as 'foreigners', and Anglo-Irish relations remained the bailiwick of the Commonwealth Relations Office. George VI, meeting the Irish Minister of External Affairs, Seán MacBride, a few weeks later, quipped, 'What does this new legislation of yours make me in Ireland, an undesirable alien?'[40] Nonetheless, the Irish Ambassador was placed immediately after the Commonwealth High Commissioners and before all other heads of foreign delegations at the King's funeral in 1952.[41]

The path of Burma held something of a dangerous precedent for the 1949 Commonwealth meeting. To expedite independence, the Burmese had originally showed mild interest in remaining in the Commonwealth. After the end of Japanese occupation, the British hoped to convince Burma onto the traditional dominion road to independence, but local leaders such as Thakin Nu and Maung Gale said that they had been 'fighting the British for 100 years' and could not stomach the 'British' before 'Commonwealth of Nations'. David Rees-Williams, the Minister for Colonial Affairs, sympathised and thought 'United Commonwealth of Nations' a better formulation.[42] However, the main hurdle, as for the 'Southern Irish', was allegiance to the Crown, which the Governor of Burma, Sir Hubert Rance, believed would prevent Burmese membership. The Burmese leaders, in common with many others across the world, believed India would never join. When India and Pakistan in fact did become dominions and consequently kept George VI as their head of state, the *New Times of Burma* reacted that the announcement that the 'two Indias ... will have to swear allegiance to the British Crown has simply taken our breath away'.[43] Rance believed in June 1947 that the 'time was ripe for a new conception' of the Commonwealth for countries that had 'no ties of blood, culture or religion' and saw 'with humble respect to His Majesty' that the Crown 'may prove not immediately but ultimately a difficulty'.[44] Lord Listowel, last Secretary of the State of India and Burma, recalled that if it were not for the communists and greater effort from the British Cabinet, the Burmese Independence leader Aung San might have tolerated the royal link and thus stayed in the Commonwealth.[45] Thakin Nu, however, incredibly suggested that as an alternative to the Commonwealth there might instead be a lead from Britain's Labour government to create 'a political Federation based on the integration of Socialist Parties throughout the world'.[46] The 'Crimson Thread of Kinship', which Sir Henry Parkes believed bound the British world, would have taken on a new meaning, and one can only imagine where the King would sit in this Red Commonwealth!

The settler king

The core members of the Commonwealth club, a metaphor like that of the family constantly used to describe and explain the Commonwealth, were the Britannic Realms of Australia, New Zealand, South Africa (especially under Smuts) and Canada. In 1949, these states could be described as having near fanatical followers of 'British Shintoism', the concept Murphy employs to describe the 'pseudo-religious' reverence the British monarchy generated.[47] The settler states had long held domestic and external autonomy but chose through self-interest and emotion the 'Britannic Vision' of their identity. As David McIntyre suggests, the concept of Sir Sidney Low's idea of a 'Britannic Alliance' of Crowns gained wide currency that demonstrated the Crown's multifaceted capacities but ultimate unity.[48] As John Darwin argues, the settler states saw the dilemma that any loosening of the 'monarchical bond' to allow a republican India was likely to break their 'solidarity'.[49] During discussions following India's Independence, the divisibility of the Crown was debated as well as the possibility of establishing a governor-general of the United Kingdom to act when the sovereign was abroad. Sir Norman Brook recorded that 'the King himself thought that it would be good idea in that it would remind the people of the United Kingdom that he was King of other places beside the United Kingdom'.[50]

For the Australians and New Zealanders in particular, and irrespective of party lines, their crown was sacred to their identity. Fraser's successor, Sid Holland, was speaking to the converted when he told a dinner in honour of the Australian Prime Minister, Robert Menzies, in August 1950 that 'Our allegiance to the British Crown, our membership of the Commonwealth and Empire, our attachment to the British name in general, are absolute. They are not subject to considerations of expediency and relative value. They are postulates which lie at the very basis of our national life.'[51] Menzies, unlike Fraser, who developed a close relationship with Nehru, was 'not unduly oppressed by the alleged or real sensitivities of our Asian colleagues'.[52] As Walter Crocker, Menzies' High Commissioner in Delhi (and biographer of Nehru), noted, the Australian Prime Minister 'had no curiosity about and no interest in India or Indians' and long simmered in the company of Nehru during their long tenures in office.[53] Nehru was contemptuous of Labor External Affairs Minister H. V. Evatt's belief, like his Liberal Party opponent Menzies, that 'British' must precede 'Commonwealth of Nations' and that 'kingship' and 'kinship' were of 'supreme significance' to the Commonwealth. This 'old' styling of the relationship did not find favour in India.[54] Nehru witheringly described Evatt's 'approach' to the future of the Commonwealth as 'simple and childlike'.[55]

South Africa, with its large Indian population and racialist policies, had complex objections concerning Indian membership in the Commonwealth. As Prime Minister and, from June 1948, Leader of the Opposition, Jan Smuts was incensed at Indian membership on republican terms. Leo Amery soothed his old friend Smuts' fears about the Asian members not long after the London Declaration in 1949: 'I realize all the difficulties which may arise in a partly coloured Commonwealth [but] if that Commonwealth can hold together it may avert an ultimate war of races.' The move could open the way, he added, for Iceland, Norway and even the USA to join. Amery thought the move had removed a serious conflict and pondered, is 'it inconceivable that one of these days republicanism may become the black man's slogan and all whites stand together as monarchists?'[56] Smuts confided to Churchill that India should not have been accommodated. The South African field marshal believed his opponents, the Nationalists, were 'jubilant' with the republican issue and that the new prime minister, Daniel Malan, would use the Commonwealth conference as a 'stepping-stone to full secession'. There was also the issue of Indian pressure for changes to South Africa's segregationist policies. However, Churchill was 'distressed' to disagree with his old friend and ally as he preferred India in and thought Nehru 'magnanimous'. Another key reason for Churchill was that if India had been excluded it would 'place the crown in an invidious light if it appear an exclusive rather than inclusive symbol'.[57]

Canada had a better relationship with the Indian leadership than other core members, and Nehru felt close to Louis St Laurent and Lester Pearson especially. However, they also had their concerns. Apart from sharing the other settler dominions' duty to protect their own relationship with the Crown, they also disliked the Indian-proposed substitute 'Commonwealth Citizenship'. As their External Affairs Department recognised, an 'embarrassing position' would be inevitable for Canada if this followed:

> It must be borne in mind that at present Indians, though British subjects in our law, are excluded as immigrants to Canada, in exactly the same way as other persons of Asiatic race, such as the Chinese, while United

States citizens and French citizens are placed in a preferred category with white British subjects. Rights and privileges are thus accorded to some aliens which are denied to some Commonwealth citizens. It would seem inevitable that we should find ourselves eventually in an embarrassing position regarding our immigration policy if we agreed to a scheme under which the essential feature of the Commonwealth connection would be the common status of Commonwealth citizenship.[58]

On the Crown itself, a record of a meeting of the Indian High Commissioner in Ottawa, Sardar Malik, stated 'that while he could appreciate the sentiment of the Canadian public towards the Crown, the position in India was quite different. The Crown and the personality of the King had not, under British rule in India, endeared themselves to the Indian public.' The meeting recorded India's belief that

> the Royal visit to South Africa early in 1947 had created a bad impression in India. It was felt that the King was in this way being too closely associated with the South African Government with which India was then at a serious stage in its dispute over the treatment of the Indian community in South Africa. Malik mentioned that in this way the King had been publicly linked with the policies of one Commonwealth government and that, therefore, there was a danger that the King should be dragged into controversial public issues.[59]

As Stuart Ward has argued, no matter the supposed elasticity and efforts to claim British identity, few outsiders succeeded in gaining acceptance of the '"core" Anglo-Saxon constituency', and the monarchy was viewed by this community as their possession.[60] The Round Table tried to justify with theological fervour the Commonwealth redemption of the Crown in the new order that would have found meaning with the 'core':

> [T]he Crown, as the liturgical formulae of its imposition make clear, is not an emblem of power. That position belongs to the Sceptre, the rod of justice, descending no doubt from the first bough torn from a tree by prehistoric man as a weapon to impose his will upon his fellows. The Crown stands, according to the liturgy, for glory and for righteousness. Now India has chosen to remove the King as bearer of the Sceptre from her political system. But she still participates in the glory and righteousness of the Commonwealth, that is, in the ideals and the way of life for which it stands, and in that sense continues to pay respect to the King as wearer of the Crown.[61]

It is not difficult to deduce what the secular Nehru would have thought of this religious allegory.

The road to 1949: royal embellishments and republican antecedents

The Burmese route to complete severance with Britain and the Commonwealth when it became independent in January 1948 had major sympathisers across the region. Nehru, however, explained to the first Prime Minister of Burma, Thakin Nu, on 14 April 1949, that India was 'unafraid of a little unpopularity' by staying in what was then an essentially monarchical association if India's broader objectives could be met. Due to 'disruptive tendencies', presumably that of the princes and others, especially secessionist non-Congress groups, India had elected to maintain the Commonwealth nexus 'deliberately' in order to build up 'our strength till we can stand completely alone, if necessary' and to protect Indian minorities abroad.[62] The failure to hold or attract Burma to the Commonwealth raised major questions from senior British figures who harboured sympathy for the Burmese dislike of allegiance and developed ideas for reform. Malcolm MacDonald, then serving as Governor-General of the Malayan Union, responded in late June 1947 to Rance's plea for a 'new conception' of the Commonwealth and the Crown's place within it. MacDonald sent a long memorandum on the issue to Arthur Creech Jones, the Secretary of State for the Colonies. The problem must be faced 'realistically' since the Burmese

> reluctance ... to accept the rule of a 'foreign King' has, of course nothing to do with the personality of His Majesty. If that were the issue, we would have all our Asiatic friends wholly with us. The personal and official qualities of the King and Queen are regarded with as deep respect and liking in these countries as they are in the present self-governing Dominions. The objection is to the institution of 'a foreign Crown'.
> ... I wonder if we can find a solution to this problem which, in part at any rate, abolishes the institution of the Crown whilst fully preserving the personality of the King throughout the Asiatic nations of the Commonwealth.

MacDonald thought that the King might instead be recognised in the Commonwealth 'as the supreme constitutional authority' in terms of carrying out diplomatic and external affairs in his name by each member state. This seasoned politician and proconsul insisted that making the way open for the Asian colonies to enter the Commonwealth would make 'the position of His Majesty ... much stronger than it would otherwise be. The alternative is the gradual withdrawal of various peoples from the Empire, and a consequent diminution of his sovereignty.' The 'foreign' elements of both Canada and South Africa had been convinced and courted towards loyalty to the Crown in return for practicable autonomy in internal affairs. The monarchy offered, in MacDonald's view, a similar path to reclamation of the region. George VI, in an undefined mixture of personal and constitutional roles, could point the way:

> If we can arrange that these same countries stay in the Commonwealth acknowledging him as its head in all questions of external relations, his personal sway will remain widespread. As the heads of an increasingly large and varied family of great peoples, British monarchs will maintain a position of unexampled glory.[63]

MacDonald's call in the case of Burma went unheeded as it entered Independence in January 1948 as a republic outside the Commonwealth since the British Cabinet, at that stage and for that case, were unwilling to compromise over the Crown. Not long afterwards, in late 1948, Patrick Gordon Walker took up MacDonald's ideas for South Asia with zest. In a paper entitled 'Link with India', Gordon Walker argued that if an Indian republic was given membership of the Commonwealth then the organisation in terms of the Crown link should create 'all ... possible embellishments, for they would then serve to adorn and add to a link that was in itself sufficiently substantial'.[64] The Under-Secretary of State for Commonwealth Relations envisaged even more powers for the King than the Governor-General of Malaya proposed. Gordon Walker believed 'a "gossamer" tie will not do' and that the Crown must be 'capable of being shown ... to be a real link'. In preparing these papers, Gordon Walker and officials from the Commonwealth Relations Office then produced a list of potential 'solid' links and embellishments for the Crown:

- Having the King formally confirm the presidents of India.
- Acceptance of the King as the person, as had been the case in Ireland, to accredit ambassadors.
- A 'delegation' of authority from the King to the president to perform certain acts (unspecified what these would be).
- The King would formally summon Commonwealth prime ministers' meetings and other Commonwealth occasions.
- The King, as head of the Commonwealth, could act on behalf of 'two or more' member states where there was a common action required.
- A Commonwealth tribunal, in the nature of the Judicial Committee of the Privy Council sitting 'under the King's authority and advising His Majesty'.

- Commonwealth citizenship, where a citizen was 'accepted as identical with a British subject, and that a British subject owed allegiance to the Crown'.

Two 'less solid' links were also suggested:

- That the King be recognised as 'the fountain of honour' by not only the realms but also the republics. This could be strengthened with the 'invention of some Commonwealth mark of distinction to be conferred by the King on the recommendation of all Commonwealth Prime Ministers acting jointly'.
- The president of India in the protection of Commonwealth citizens when in India was doing so 'in exercise of powers delegated to him by the King'.[65]

Gordon Walker took these extraordinary ideas on his mission to South Asia, where he was tasked by the Cabinet to stress the advantages of keeping the King as the link. The minutes of the meeting between Gordon Walker and Nehru in New Delhi on 30 March 1949 record four related, but still more distinctive, 'embellishments' for the King from the list developed three months earlier:

- The King 'should have the power to appoint the President of the Indian Republic, which would be renewable each time a President assumed office'.
- The King should be 'empowered to appoint [an] "Arbitral" Tribunal, on the recommendation of the Prime Ministers of the Commonwealth, to settle political disputes'.
- The King could establish and bestow distinct Commonwealth Honours.
- The King 'would appoint and also preside over, from time to time, a Commonwealth Privy Council'.[66]

The acceptance of any of these embellishments would have given the monarchy extraordinary international influence for a constitutional head of state. Such authority would have been made Commonwealth King George VI more powerful than the Imperial King-Emperor George VI.

Constitutional monarchy is governed by the critical convention of responsible advice from the government of the day. This reasons that the prime minister and cabinet exercise power and take responsibility for actions carried out in the sovereign's name. The 'embellishments', as suggested by Gordon Walker, would open the question from whom and how does the head of the Commonwealth derive responsible advice when there would be not only several realms where the Crown had a different legal and political personality but also a republic where the King was not head of state. How would the Crown act collectively? How would it act when conflicting advice and actions occurred and when the King acted in a commonwealth capacity? There is no definitive answer to any of these important questions; instead, a measure of placation can be gleaned from Vernon Bogdanor's comment that the sovereign should 'exercise great tact and forbearance. There is no way theoretically of resolving conflicts which might arise, but they can nevertheless be resolved in practice if there is a spirit of goodwill and cooperation. In the last resort, the ultimate test of any constitutional arrangement can only be that it works.'[67]

Titles and limitations

Nehru, unsurprisingly, had problems with the above 'links' and 'embellishments'; though some were logical, he was not sure whether these would be 'acceptable to Indian sentiment'.[68] Pearson recorded that

> I am given to understand that the reason why the suggestion that the King might delegate his prerogative power of accreditation to the President of the Indian Republic has been allowed to recede into the background of current thinking about possible forms and symbols of Commonwealth association is that the King himself was not at all receptive to the idea.[69]

Other ideas included giving every Commonwealth head of state, including republican members, membership of the Privy Council in order to maintain a link with the Crown.[70] Churchill apparently 'found a precedent from Roman history' that led to the incredible idea that George VI be made 'President of India'.[71] Further titles emerged. Gordon Walker, thinking the term 'president' too republican, suggested 'Lord Protector', which, as Murphy argues, would have had 'darkly Cromwellian overtones for ardent monarchists'.[72] Churchill's suspicion would have picked up on this suggestion as he believed '[f]or some years the tendency of Socialist and Left-Wing forces has been to gird at the word "Empire" and to espouse the word "Commonwealth" – because Oliver Cromwell cut off King Charles' head and all that.'[73]

The Canadians, in preparation for London, came up with many novel suggestions for the King's title in India and the Commonwealth, including 'Patron of the Republic of India', 'Honorary (or Royal) Patron of the Commonwealth' or 'perhaps an Indian term in keeping with India's historical tradition'.[74] The Indian president, in order to preserve some royal link, might be called 'President and Regent of India' or 'President and Governor General of India'.[75] They also hoped 'use could be made of the historical connection of the Crown with parliamentary institutions when the desirability of retaining the Crown connection' was discussed, with acknowledgement for the Indians. Intriguingly, they also put forward 'that the idea might be informally hinted to Mr. Nehru that the Crown could serve as a possible basis for the eventual reunion of India and Pakistan'.[76] Instead, India and Pakistan would make Commonwealth history by being the first independent members to go to war with each other.

The constitutional adviser to the Indian government, Sir Benegal Rau, meanwhile brought up a case from ancient India where the 'republic of the Licchavis was in partnership with the Gupta Empire in the time of Chandra Gupta I' as an Indian precedent for 1949.[77] Such thinking also pushed this eminent Indian jurist to suggest that the Crown could have some 'dormant sovereignty' role in India – *ex silentio*, as R. J. Moore termed it – where the King would have but 'not exercise any of the functions of sovereignty'.[78] The Indians, in October 1948, prepared a ten-point memorandum that attempted to find agreement with the other Commonwealth members while maintaining their republican position within the organisation. Authored by Bajpai and Rau, the document suggested as point 5 that the King become 'first Citizen of the Commonwealth' and 'fountain of honour' and that reciprocal powers be exchanged between the Indian president and the monarch.[79] Whether the Indians intended to draw on the Roman *princeps* practice of making their emperors 'first citizens' is unknown, but it does indicate the willingness not only to accommodate monarchy but also to admit its status. In New Delhi it was suggested that the neo-imperial 'King of Commonwealth' could be suitable.[80] 'The King of the Commonwealth' was also the title Krishna Menon, as High Commissioner in London, thought a suitable replacement for 'King of India', without explaining what that title would entail.[81] Perhaps for this reason the British Cabinet Committee examining the issue ruled out the suggestion just days before the Commonwealth prime ministers arrived, as they believed that formulation was most likely to be 'unacceptable to certain Commonwealth Governments'.[82] However, as late as 22 April 1949, the Canadian Secretary of External Affairs expressed his preference for 'King of the Commonwealth' over 'Head of the Commonwealth'.[83]

Attlee examined republics in the German and Dutch empires, while the Palace itself unearthed the republican cases of Danzig and Lübeck in the Holy Roman Empire.[84] This search for a formula included the British Prime Minister still trying to convince Nehru of the natural place of monarchy in India. Attlee, in an uncharacteristically long letter on 20 March 1949, containing 'unofficial and only personal ideas', stated to Nehru, whose father had written a famous report in 1928 advocating dominion status for India, that in the Commonwealth the link is the King. Attlee then turned to the unsuitability of republicanism for Asia and the dangers it could bring to India and the world:

A NEW MONARCHY FOR A NEW COMMONWEALTH?

I should have said that the general tradition in Asia is in favour of monarchy. I think this is true of India historically. ... Republicanism is an alien importation from Europe. ... The Asiatic republics are few and of recent establishment. Their record is not very encouraging. They tend to degenerate into dictatorships or oligarchies. ... You may object that The King is an Englishman, a man of alien race, representing a domination now past and over. I wonder if this objection is entirely valid. I am an Englishman, but for centuries the English have had Kings who have been Angevin, Welsh, Scottish, Dutch and German, and we have not worried about it. ... I think there are, therefore, solid advantages in retaining The King in the Indian Constitution.[85]

Nehru, confiding to the Deputy Prime Minister, Vallabhbhai Patel, dismissed all of these long entreaties with pithy disdain. It was, Nehru the old Harrovian exclaimed, a 'surprisingly naïve document'.[86] Even 'Head of the Commonwealth', which, of course, became the settled title, generated apprehension from the Indians and Canadians, while Malan was worried that it connoted that the King had power over a 'super-state' and head of a 'centralised empire', which Nehru also feared.[87] The final declaration stated, 'The Government of India have however declared and affirmed India's desire to continue her full membership of the Commonwealth of Nations and her acceptance of The King as the symbol of the free association of its independent member nations and as such the Head of the Commonwealth.'

The insertion of 'as such' appeased those concerned about making it seem the King had powers over the organisation but pacified the other side in the acknowledgement of him as the head of this peculiar organisation. The King's prime ministers collectively mobbed the palace to avail their head of state in his new designation as 'Head of the Commonwealth'. The King thanked his prime ministers and, consciously or not, used the now politically incorrect phrase 'British Commonwealth of Nations' in thanking them.[88] It was left to the mandarins of Whitehall to agree on the Latin designation. The use of 'republica' was rejected outright. As Murphy describes the scene, they were 'like nervous schoolboys handing in their Latin homework' to Oxford don Colin Hardie. Suggested changes to connote 'nations' not 'races' were accepted but not, interestingly, Hardie's recommendation for 'caput' over 'princeps'.[89] 'Consortionis Populorum Princeps' was the final designation, which S. A. de Smith thought 'an ingenious version of the untranslatable'.[90] The same could be said for the position itself. The classics of Western civilisation were not the only sources consulted. At the Prime Minister's suggestion, Philip Noel-Baker, Secretary of State for Commonwealth Relations, and his office sought advice from Sanskrit scholars to find a title from Indian

[301]

history that could give the King a title in an Indian language and not exclude either monarchical headship of a republic. Janata-Raj was suggested since it 'would express the idea of ... a conception of Kingship from the popular will'.[91] Nothing eventuated from this intriguing idea.

A king not a crown

An interesting commonality between the key protagonists, the Roundheads and Cavaliers, the courtiers and counsellors, was the emphasis on the king and not the crown. Evatt described for Australia that 'intimate relationship with the King' and the corollary that he preferred the word 'king' to 'crown'. For this controversial tower of Australian politics, 'A crown is a chattel which is stowed in the Tower of London except on ceremonial occasions, but the King is the head and pivot of the British Commonwealth of Nations.' Evatt continued that the crown was an 'abstraction', but the King 'stands for something reaching far beyond politics. He is the head of the society of the Commonwealth ... and in loyal allegiance to his person they are able to feel at one with one another without compromising their political separateness.'[92] Nehru told the Constituent Assembly, from which he sought approval for India's Commonwealth membership, that the King's symbolic status was critical since it conferred no powers over the Indian state. He pointed out that the London Declaration 'is to the King and not to the Crown'.[93] Malan, in his speech to the South African House of Assembly, constantly referred to 'Kingship' in reference to the Commonwealth, but also stressed that it meant something different for states of 'British descent' than it did for South Africa.[94] The King's Private Secretary, Sir Alan Lascelles, thought the solution dealing with the King was 'very wise' and that George VI would 'be pleased'. As Krishna Menon recorded years afterwards, the King could have made life very difficult for them and obstructed the changes.[95] Perhaps this gives evidence to the second part of Sir Stafford Cripps' private comment that George VI was 'not bright but progressive'.[96] The King became the personal, and not constitutional, link for the Commonwealth. *The Times* reported that the 'informal personal influence of the King has taken on new life and meaning' and now 'constitutional monarchy has become a representative monarchy'.[97] Dwelling on the personal, it can only be imagined how some of George VI's more assertive predecessors would have acted had they been on the throne.

Bogdanor notes that these were transformative years for the monarchy: 'the concept of a single *Crown* uniting the members of the Commonwealth was coming to be replaced by that of several crowns linked by the *person* of the sovereign.'[98] Attlee expressed his own opinion on the matter in a letter to Nehru and on the value of thinking of the King and not the Crown:

> I say The King rather than the Crown. King George has often stressed this point to me. The Crown is an abstract symbol connoting authority. ... But the real link is a person, The King. At the head of the Commonwealth is a family. ... It is something universal, transcending creeds and races. ... The existence therefore, of a King and Royal Family provides us a mystique which is appreciated by a very wide range of people, and a mystique is a valuable point of unity, of stability. Their very remoteness from the play of politics and the clash of creeds makes them a unifying influence.

Churchill, no friend of India and no ally of republicanism, conveyed to the House of Commons his opinion that accepting India in the Commonwealth was the right decision and one that uplifted the monarchy:

> It seems to me that the personal dignity of the King is not impaired by the conditions under which India remains in the Commonwealth. The final significance and value of the Monarchy seems to be enhanced by the way in which the King is acknowledged by the Republic of India and by the Commonwealth monarchies alike. ... It seems to me that, far from being any derogation of the Monarchy, the proof of the attachment and importance that all the Dominions gives to it has shown the strength and vitality of that institution.[99]

Conclusion

Despite having a reign nearly four times as long as her father, we are unable, as Murphy has stated, to get a fulsomely documented picture of Queen Elizabeth's reign.[100] As such, this piece has confined itself to the relatively short, but important, period from 1947 to 1949, where more documents are available, to see how the monarchy was affected, defined and adjusted to post-war changes in the Commonwealth. This chapter, by extricating the elements from the well-documented debates surrounding Indian membership of the Commonwealth, has sought to depict how monarchy needed to change for a new age and survive the inclusion of republics. The analysis provides crucial material for imperial, commonwealth and monarchy scholars to understand the complex and curious relationship between crown and commonwealth. George VI confided 'that he hoped there wouldn't be too many Republican stars in his Crown!'[101] In fact, thanks to republican India, the King's daughter was later proclaimed 'Head of Commonwealth', a post which is not bestowed by hereditary right. Nehru was beseeched by both the British and his high commissioner in London to issue a proclamation welcoming, as the prime minister of the only republic, the Queen as Head of the Commonwealth. The Indian Prime Minister thought any such proclamation would 'evoke surprise and criticism' since the royal titles and the succession had nothing to do with the Indian Constitution, unlike the realms. Nehru did consent, however, to sending a personal telegram to the Queen, where 'we accepted her as Head of the Commonwealth'.[102] This telegram was given significance by constitutional authorities in settling the issue of the Queen's assumption of the title.[103] Nehru told Menon:

> Our adherence to [the] Commonwealth is in [the] nature of an unwritten treaty which continues till it is terminated. Death of a sovereign does not and cannot terminate this association if parties concerned do not take any such step. From our adherence to [the] Commonwealth it also follows that King or Queen is accepted as a symbol as the Head of Commonwealth.[104]

The Commonwealth in this rendering places the monarchy below itself, but nonetheless as an automatic part of it. The monarchy had shown itself, fascinatingly, to follow earlier Indian royal precedents by being adaptable to the diversity and complexity of their times. As C. A. Bayly argues in an analysis of pre-British Asia:

> In Muslim and Asian societies a broad recognition of the supremacy of the emperor's cult, not uniformity of belief, was what was required. Everywhere, therefore, the panoply of state and imperial power rested in longer term on the co-option and honouring of local elites or self-governing local communities. Rulers had to accept and make the most of the political forms and religious beliefs of the localities and leave them to their own devices.[105]

This approach of leaving the politicians to their 'own devices' in the context of the immediate post-war Commonwealth allowed the monarchy to endure for another reign at least. Passions were subdued in favour of pragmatism, with the result that crown and commonwealth could mean all things to all people and, in the process, revealed the monarchy as both an unlikely and obvious survivor well aware of its own limitations.

Notes

1 Clement Attlee to King's Assistant Private Secretary, 12 June 1947, PREM 8/802, National Archives of the United Kingdom.
2 *The Times*, 24 June 1948.

A NEW MONARCHY FOR A NEW COMMONWEALTH?

3 Colonel Henry Ponsonby to Earl Granville, 26 January 1873, in George Earle Buckle (ed.), *The Letters of Queen Victoria*, second series, vol. II: *1870–78* (London: John Murray, 1926), p. 238.
4 Diary of Patrick Gordon Walker, 7 January 1949, cited in Ronald Hyam (ed.), *The Labour Government and the End of Empire 1945–1951: Part IV: Race Relations and the Commonwealth, British Documents on the End of Empire* (London: Her Majesty's Stationery Office, 1992), p. 180.
5 W. Roger Louis (ed.), *Oxford History of the British Empire*, 5 vols. (Oxford: Oxford University Press, 1998–99). The exception is an insightful chapter by Mark McKenna, 'Monarchy: From Reverence to Indifference', in a companion volume, D. M. Schreuder and S. Ward (eds.), *Australia's Empire* (Oxford: Oxford University Press, 2008), pp. 261–87.
6 For some of their more recent accounts, see John Darwin, *The Empire Project: The Rise and Fall of the British World-System, 1830–1970* (Cambridge: Cambridge University Press, 2009); and W. David McIntyre, *The Britannic Vision: Historians and the Making of the British Commonwealth of Nations, 1907–48* (Basingstoke: Palgrave Macmillan, 2009). For a lasting overview on the subject and his writings, see Nicholas Mansergh, *The Commonwealth Experience* (London: Weidenfeld & Nicholson, 1969).
7 H. Kumarasingham, 'The "Tropical Dominions": The Appeal of Dominion Status in the Decolonisation of India, Pakistan and Ceylon', *Transactions of the Royal Historical Society*, 23, 6th ser. (2013), 223–45; and H. Kumarasingham, *A Political Legacy of the British Empire: Power and the Parliamentary System in Post-colonial India and Sri Lanka* (London: I. B. Tauris, 2013).
8 Vernon Bogdanor, *The Monarchy and the Constitution* (Oxford: Oxford University Press, 1995).
9 For example, Maurice Sunkin and Sebastian Payne (eds), *The Nature of the Crown: A Legal and Political Analysis* (Oxford: Oxford University Press, 1999).
10 Philip Murphy, *Monarchy and the End of Empire: The House of Windsor, the British Government and the Postwar Commonwealth* (Oxford: Oxford University Press, 2013).
11 The best account is R. J. Moore, *Making the New Commonwealth* (Oxford: Oxford University Press, 1987).
12 John Wheeler-Bennett, *King George VI: His Life and Reign* (London: Macmillan, 1958), p. 379.
13 Robert Holland, 'Britain, Commonwealth and the End of Empire', in Vernon Bogdanor (ed.), *The British Constitution in the Twentieth Century* (Oxford: Oxford University Press, 2002), p. 639.
14 Spear quoted in Nicholas Mansergh, *Survey of British Commonwealth Affairs: Problems of Wartime Co-operation and Post-war Change, 1939–1952* (Oxford: Oxford University Press, 1958), p. 370.
15 *The Times*, 24 June 1948.
16 Frank Bongiorno, 'Commonwealthmen and Republicans: Dr. H. V. Evatt, the Monarchy and India', *Australian Journal of Politics and History*, 46:1 (2000), 36.
17 Ivor Jennings, 'Republicanism in Asia', in H. Kumarasingham (ed.), *Constitution-Maker: Selected Writings of Sir Ivor Jennings* (Cambridge: Cambridge University Press, 2015), p. 220.
18 Cited in Kumarasingham, *A Political Legacy of the British Empire*, pp. 128–9.
19 Kumarasingham, *Tropical Dominions*, pp. 237–42.
20 See Ayesha Jalal, 'Inheriting the Raj: Jinnah and the Governor-Generalship Issue', *Modern Asian Studies*, 19:1 (1985), 29–53.
21 Telegram from H. I. Rahimtoola, Pakistan High Commissioner, 19 January 1949, CAB 134/119, National Archives.
22 See Kumarasingham, *Tropical Dominions*.
23 Wheeler-Bennett, *King George VI*, p. 696.
24 Lord Mountbatten to the Maharaj-Rana of Dholpur, 29 July 1947, in Nicholas Mansergh (ed.), *The Mountbatten Viceroyalty: Princes, Partition and Independence, July 8–Aug. 15, 1947* (London: Her Majesty's Stationery Office, 1983), vol. XII, p. 392.

25 Viceroy's Personal Report No. 17, 16 August 1947, in Mansergh, *The Mountbatten Viceroyalty*, p. 769.
26 House of Commons Debates, 10 July 1947, vol. 439, cols. 2441–550. This, perhaps, was Macmillan's subtle way of pointing to attempts by the princely state of Hyderabad, with Conservative sympathy, to get UN and British assistance to achieve independence against New Delhi's determination to prevent it.
27 Ian Copland, *The Princes of India in the Endgame of Empire, 1917–1947* (Cambridge: Cambridge University Press, 1997), p. 218.
28 Wheeler-Bennett, *King George VI*, p. 720.
29 High Commissioner to Secretary of State for External Affairs, 13 January 1949, *Documents on Canadian External Relations*, vol. XV, p. 773.
30 Michael Brecher, 'India's Decision to Remain in the Commonwealth', *Journal of Commonwealth and Comparative Politics*, 12:1 (1974), 79. Notable opponents of Commonwealth membership in the Indian Constituent Assembly included K. T. Shah, H. V. Kamath, Damodar Swarup Seth, L. S. Saxsena and Maulana Mohani.
31 Kumarasingham, *Constitution Maker*, p. 218.
32 Harold Laski to Clement Attlee, 1 February 1948, PREM 8/735, National Archives.
33 Edward VIII, as Prince of Wales, had confessed to his father of being 'depressed about my work in British India', partly due to his inability to win over the nationalists and being unable to do 'a scrap of good'. David Cannadine, *Ornamentalism: How the British Saw Their Empire* (London: Penguin, 2002), p. 146.
34 Lord Listowel, *Memoirs*, unpublished; Sir Francis Wylie to Lord Mountbatten, 14 August 1947, in Mansergh, *The Mountbatten Viceroyalty*, p. 725.
35 H. Kumarasingham, 'The "New Commonwealth", 1947–49: A New Zealand Perspective on India Joining the Commonwealth', *Round Table: The Commonwealth Journal of International Affairs*, 95:385 (2006), 441–52.
36 Mansergh, *Commonwealth Experience*, pp. 329–30.
37 *The Times*, 3 January 1949.
38 In October 1948, Peter Fraser exclaimed that he 'derived great pleasure from the presence of the representatives of India, Pakistan and Ceylon'. Fraser believed that it 'had been an inspiration to them all'. The Commonwealth had shown 'courage and enlightenment ... in recognising the rights of these peoples who had so long been struggling to achieve their independent destiny. This indeed was an example which had been an inspiration to the world.' Imperial Conference Papers 1948, Fraser, Concluding Speech at 10 Downing St, 22 October 1948, EA1, 153/26/4, Archives New Zealand/Te Whare Tohu Tuhituhinga O Aotearoa, Head Office, Wellington.
39 Memorandum, 'The Present Position of the King in Irish Law', July 1946, *Documents of Irish Foreign Policy*, vol. VIII: *1945–1948* (Dublin: Royal Irish Academy, 2014), pp. 195–7.
40 Wheeler-Bennett, *King George VI*, p. 719.
41 Lorna Lloyd, *Diplomacy with a Difference: The Commonwealth Office of High Commissioner, 1880–2006* (Leiden: Martinus Nijhoff, 2007), p. 172.
42 D. R. Rees-Williams to Lord Pethick-Lawrence, 15 April 1947, in Hugh Tinker (ed.), *Constitutional Relations between Britain and Burma: The Struggle for Independence 1944–1948*, vol. II (London: Her Majesty's Stationery Office, 1984), pp. 482–3.
43 *New Times of Burma*, 5 June 1947; and Note 2, 5 June 1947, in Tinker, *The Struggle for Independence*, pp. 563–5.
44 Sir Hubert Rance to the Earl of Listowel, 9 June 1947, in Tinker, *The Struggle for Independence*, pp. 574–5.
45 Listowel, *Memoirs*.
46 'Burma Goodwill Mission', Minutes of Meeting of the Burma Committee, 25 June 1947 in Tinker, *The Struggle for Independence*, document 412.
47 Murphy, *Monarchy and the End of Empire*, pp. 3–5.
48 McIntyre, *The Britannic Vision*, pp. 220–21.
49 Darwin, *The Empire Project*, p. 553.

A NEW MONARCHY FOR A NEW COMMONWEALTH?

50 H, Kumarasingham, *Onward with Executive Power: Lessons from New Zealand, 1947–57* (Wellington: Institute of Policy Studies/Victoria University of Wellington, 2010), pp. 43–4.
51 Kumarasingham, *Onward with Executive Power*, pp. 106–7.
52 David Lowe, 'Cold War London: Harrison and White', in Carl Bridge, Frank Bongiorno and David Lee (eds), *The High Commissioners: Australia's Representatives in the United Kingdom, 1910–2010* (Canberra: Department of Foreign Affairs and Trade, 2010), p. 128.
53 Meg Gurry, 'Leadership and Bilateral Relations: Menzies and Nehru, Australia and India, 1949–1964', *Pacific Affairs*, 65:4 (1992–93), 513.
54 Frank Bongiorno, 'Commonwealth and Republicans: Dr H. V. Evatt, the Monarchy and India', *Australian Journal of Politics and History*, 46:1 (2000), 46.
55 Jawaharlal Nehru to V. Patel, 26 March 1949, in Jawaharlal Nehru, *Selected Works of Jawaharlal Nehru*, vol. X, ed. S. Gopal (New Delhi: Jawaharlal Nehru Memorial Fund, 1990), p. 151.
56 Leopold Amery to Jan Christiaan Smuts, 2 May 1949, in Jean van der Poel (ed.), *Selections of the Smuts Papers* (Cambridge: Cambridge University Press, 1973), vol. VII, pp. 290–1.
57 Jan Christiaan Smuts to Winston Churchill, 21 May 1949, and Churchill to Smuts, 22 May 1949, in Jan Christiaan Smuts, *Selections from the Smuts Papers*, vol. VII: *August 1945–October 1950*, ed. Jan van der Poel (London: Cambridge University Press 1973), pp. 296–9.
58 Memorandum by Department of External Affairs, 3 March 1949, *Documents on Canadian External Relations*, vol. XV, p. 780.
59 Memorandum by Commonwealth Division, 4 April 1949, *Documents on Canadian External Relations*, vol. XV, p. 794.
60 Stuart Ward, 'Imperial Identities Abroad', in Sarah Stockwell (ed.), *The British Empire: Themes and Perspectives* (Oxford: Blackwell, 2008), p. 230.
61 Dermot Morrah, 'Crown without Sceptre', *The Round Table: The Commonwealth Journal of International Affairs*, 39 (1948), 207.
62 Jawaharlal Nehru to Thakin Nu, 14 April 1949, in *Selected Works of Jawaharlal Nehru*, vol. X, p. 411.
63 Malcolm MacDonald to Arthur Creech Jones, 26 June 1947, in Tinker, *The Struggle for Independence*, pp. 615–18, in the opinion of Lord Killearn, Special Commissioner in South East Asia, raised similar issues 'as those which in their day confronted Lord Durham and Mr Campbell-Bannerman'.
64 'The Link with India', 31 December 1948, CAB 134/119, National Archives.
65 Notes, 23 December 1948, GNWR 1/7, Patrick Gordon Walker Papers, Churchill College, Cambridge.
66 Minutes of interview between Nehru and Gordon Walker, 30 March 1949, *Selected Works of Jawaharlal Nehru*, vol. X, p. 152.
67 Bogdanor, *Monarchy and the Constitution*, p. 267.
68 Minutes of interview between Nehru and Gordon Walker, 30 March 1949, *Selected Works of Jawaharlal Nehru*, 10, p. 152.
69 Norman Robertson to Lester Pearson, 26 January 1949, *Documents on Canadian External Relations*, vol. XV, p. 775.
70 Memorandum by Under-Secretary of State for External Affairs, 17 August 1948, *Documents on Canadian External Relations*, vol. XIV, p. 868.
71 Sarvepalli Gopal, 'Nehru and the Commonwealth', in David Dilks (ed.), *Retreat from Power: Studies in Britain's Foreign Policy of the Twentieth Century*, 2 vols. (London: Macmillan, 1981), vol. II, p. 140.
72 Murphy, *Monarchy and the End of Empire*, p. 44.
73 Hansard, 28 October 1948, vol. 457, cols. 242–3.
74 Memorandum by Head of Commonwealth Division, 20 April 1949, *Documents on Canadian External Relations*, vol. XV, p. 800.
75 Memorandum, 20 April 1949, p. 798.

76 Memorandum by Commonwealth Division, 23 March 1949, *Documents on Canadian External Relations*, vol. XV, p. 789.
77 Cited in Kumarasingham, *A Political Legacy of the British Empire*, p. 42.
78 Moore, *Making the New Commonwealth*, pp. 144–5.
79 Ten Point Memorandum, 28 October 1948, in *Selected Works of Jawaharlal Nehru*, vol. VIII, pp. 248–50.
80 Cable to Krishna Menon, 19 November 1948, in *Selected Works of Jawaharlal Nehru*, vol. VIII, p. 256.
81 'The King's Title', Note by Sir Norman Brook, 2 April 1949, CAB 134/119, National Archives.
82 Cabinet Committee Minutes, 12 April 1949, CAB 134/119, National Archives.
83 Memorandum by Commonwealth Division, 22 April 1949, CAB 134/119, National Archives.
84 McIntyre, *Britannic Vision*, p. 248; and see footnote 101, p. 336.
85 Clement Attlee to Jawaharlal Nehru, 20 March, CAB 127/344, National Archives.
86 Jawaharlal Nehru to V. Patel, 26 March 1949, in *Selected Works of Jawaharlal Nehru*, vol. X, p. 151.
87 D. F. Malan, speech to South African House of Assembly, 11 May 1949, in Nicholas Mansergh (ed.), *Documents and Speeches on British Commonwealth Affairs, 1931–1952*, 2 vols. (London: Oxford University Press, 1953), vol. II, p. 863.
88 Notes by Lester Pearson from London Conference, 19–30 April 1949, *Documents on Canadian External Relations*, vol. XV, p. 799.
89 Murphy, *Monarchy and the End of Empire*, pp. 47–8.
90 S. A. de Smith, *The Vocabulary of Commonwealth Relations* (London: University of London, 1954), p. 27.
91 Philip Noel-Baker to Clement Attlee, 12 April 1949, PREM 8/1468, National Archives.
92 *The Times*, 14 January 1949.
93 Nehru's speech to the Indian Constituent Assembly, 16 May 1949, in *Selected Works of Jawaharlal Nehru*, vol. XI, p. 326.
94 Daniel Malan, 11 May 1949, in Mansergh (ed.), *Documents and Speeches*, vol. II, pp. 863, 859–71.
95 Brecher, 'India's Decision to Remain in the Commonwealth', note 55, p. 88.
96 Peter Clarke, *The Cripps Version: The Life of Sir Stafford Cripps 1889–1952* (London: Penguin, 2002), p. 268.
97 *The Times*, 28 April 1949.
98 Bogdanor, *Monarchy and the Constitution*, p. 252. Italics in original.
99 Hansard, 28 April 1949, vol. 464, cols. 369–75.
100 Aside from Murphy, this has, nonetheless, been attempted in R. Craggs and H. Kumarasingham, 'Losing an Empire and Building a Role: The Queen, Geopolitics and the Construction of the Commonwealth Headship at the Lusaka Commonwealth Heads of Government Meeting, 1979', *Journal of Imperial and Commonwealth History*, 43:1 (2015), 80–98.
101 Notes by Lester Pearson from London Conference, 19–30 April 1949, *Documents on Canadian External Relations*, vol. XV, p. 799.
102 *Selected Works of Jawaharlal Nehru*.
103 See Bogdanor, *Monarchy and the Constitution*, pp. 263–4. The Indian High Commissioner, Krishna Menon, even joined the Accession Council on the condition that he could sign the Accession Proclamation if the title 'Head of the Commonwealth' were inserted. See Murphy, *Monarchy and End of Empire*, p. 50.
104 Jawaharlal Nehru to Krishna Menon, 13 February 1952, *Selected Works of Jawaharlal Nehru*, vol. XVII, pp. 500–2.
105 C. A. Bayly, *The Birth of the Modern World, 1780–1914* (Oxford: Blackwell, 2004), p. 32.

CHAPTER SIXTEEN

Waiting to die? The British monarchy in Australia, New Zealand and Canada, 1991–2016

Mark McKenna

In the former British colonies of Australia, Canada and New Zealand, one could be forgiven for ascribing perpetual qualities to the British monarchical connection. Since the mid-nineteenth century, prophecies of the demise of constitutional monarchy governance have far outnumbered the political initiatives taken to remove it. The end of the monarchical connection has repeatedly been pronounced as inevitable, yet the institution's long-demonstrated capacity for adaptability and reinvention has continually defied predictions of its imminent death. Nonetheless, terminal images prevail. In Australia, Canada and New Zealand, the prospect of Queen Elizabeth II's death has framed much of the recent public discussion regarding the future of constitutional monarchy. Nowhere more so, perhaps, than in Australia, where many republicans who led the 'yes' campaign in the 1999 referendum seem to have fallen in line with conventional wisdom: the declaration of an Australian republic cannot take place before royal rigor mortis occurs.[1]

In 2016, Australia remains one of only sixteen (from a total of fifty-three) Commonwealth countries that continue to retain the Queen as their head of state. This is despite the fact that from the mid-1960s there has been a marked decline in what historian John Hirst described in 1994 as the monarch's 'civic personality'.[2] Monarchical symbolism, which once dominated political, legal and cultural institutions, had by the end of the century gradually evaporated to the point of near invisibility. At the same time, however, constitutional monarchy survived the changing historical circumstances that caused many historians and commentators to predict its demise; chief among them were decolonisation, Britain's entry into the European Common Market in 1973 and the decline of the British race patriotism that had for so long defined colonial identities. Moreover, constitutional monarchy survived the crisis in the royal family's public image in the early 1990s that preceded the referendum and ultimately remained without serious challenge for a further two decades. In light of this enduring presence, how can we explain constitutional monarchy's extraordinary longevity?

This chapter seeks to understand the changing arguments for the retention of constitutional monarchy in Australia since the inception of the movement for an Australian republic in 1991. While it makes comparative reference to Canada and New Zealand, its primary focus is Australia. It suggests that traditional arguments employed to support constitutional monarchy since the mid-nineteenth century have lost much of their cultural and political power. Indeed, the survival of constitutional monarchy in the twenty-first century rests on entirely new ground. Today, the strongest arguments for the continuation of constitutional monarchy are negative. That is, the monarchy is to be retained for what it is not (political) rather than for what it is (a hereditary head of state). This represents a fundamental change, not only in the characterisation of monarchy but also in the representation of liberal democracy in Australia, which is increasingly alienated from the central symbolic power that underwrites the state's constitutional and legal authority. The prospect of an eviscerated monarchical connection continuing indefinitely has potentially profound consequences for the parliamentary democracies of Canada and New Zealand, but more so of Australia.

Identifying the source of constitutional monarchy's appeal presents several challenges. The scripted, tightly managed public relations exercise that constitutes royal tours and the increasingly contrived packaging of monarchy in a consumer market economy makes monarchy's public resonance difficult to assess. Attempting to understand the public response to the 2014 tour of Prince William and the Duchess of Cambridge to Australia and New Zealand, for example, in which the royal couple were accompanied by 450 journalists who tracked their every move, throws up similar methodological challenges to those faced by historians seeking to understand the world tour of Queen Victoria's second son, Prince Alfred, in the late 1860s.[3] Media reports of official royal public engagements, replete with detailed discussion of fashion trends and gushing protestations of loyalty, quickly become repetitious. Because so much evidence of popular monarchism is mediated through the commercial imperatives of the media, it is extremely difficult to disentangle the celebrity culture with which contemporary monarchy is entwined from genuine support for the institution of monarchy itself. In order to reach beyond the surface ripples of state-sponsored choreography and public loyalty displays, important as they are, and to understand why constitutional monarchy continues, it is necessary to focus specifically on the arguments employed in the public domain in support of the monarchy. This is not to suggest that popular monarchism and emotional attachment to the Crown are irrelevant. On the contrary, in early twenty-first-century Australia especially, waning emotional attachment and irrelevance constitute the last remaining arguments *for* constitutional monarchy.

While there are many shared historical explanations for the relative strength of constitutional monarchy in post-war Australia, New Zealand and Canada, there are also substantial differences. In both New Zealand and Canada, traditional explanations have generally relied on demographic and cultural arguments. In contrast to Australia, New Zealand, with relatively little Irish immigration and a predominantly European population (still at approximately 75 per cent, with 16 per cent Maori), saw itself as an isolated British community which was economically dependent on Britain. Because of the signing of the Treaty of Waitangi in 1840 between the Crown and the Maori, many Maori have long held reservations regarding any move to a republic. Rightly or wrongly, they have perceived their personal relationship with the Crown that flowed from the Treaty as offering them more protection than that provided by the New Zealand government.[4]

The Treaty of Waitangi has also provided a foundational narrative of historical origin in New Zealand for which Australia has no comparable example. The special relationship between Maori and the Crown is reflected in 2016 on the British monarchy's website, which relies on the Treaty narrative to explain how British sovereignty over New Zealand was acquired. The same website also emphasises the close relationship between the Crown and Canada's indigenous people, explaining that British sovereignty over Canada was acquired through a combination of 'settlement, war or cession'. Significantly, these narratives stand in stark contrast to the royal website's statements regarding the Crown's acquisition of sovereignty over Australia, which, after explaining that James Cook claimed sovereignty over the east coast of Australia in 1770, skips conveniently to Australian federation in 1901. The silence is deafening. So is the failure to acknowledge any special relationship between the Crown and Australia's indigenous people, for which there is considerable evidence, as recent historical scholarship has shown. In 1999, at the very time the republic referendum was being held in Australia, indigenous leaders travelled to London to press their claims for land rights and social justice, rights which they believed Australian governments had denied them.[5]

The relative absence of political and constitutional crises surrounding the role of the Governor-General in New Zealand, together with what legal scholar Peter Boyce has described as the country's slowness to assert its independence from Britain, have also contributed to the resilience of constitutional monarchy in New Zealand.[6] New Zealand did not ratify the Statute of Westminster until 1947. It ended appeals to the Privy Council as late as 2004 and did not abolish imperial honours until 2000, only to see titular honours reinstated under Prime Minister John Key in 2009.[7]

The fact that New Zealand is a unitary and unicameral state in which an act of parliament alone would *legally* suffice in order for the country to become a republic, points to an ingrained cultural reluctance to end constitutional monarchy. New Zealand's legislative path to a republic is relatively straightforward when compared to Australia, where the Constitution requires both a national majority and a majority of states in a referendum, or Canada, where it is necessary to secure a majority of both the House of Commons and Senate and each of the ten provincial legislatures.

Historical explanations for the retention of Canada's constitutional monarchy have often referred to the strong British character of Anglo-Canadian society until the late twentieth century, its fundamental conservatism, and the fact that retaining the link to the Crown has been a means of differentiating Canadian identity from that of the USA. Although republican sentiment has naturally been far stronger in Quebec, monarchy, because of its joint Anglo-French heritage, has also been depicted as more deeply ingrained in Canadian history, one that goes back to the kings of France in the sixteenth, seventeenth and eighteenth centuries.

Despite Canada's strong record of asserting its independence when compared to Australia or New Zealand (Canada ended imperial honours, for example, in 1919, six decades before Australia and nearly a century before New Zealand) and the fact that it was far less dependent on Britain economically than either Australia or New Zealand, attachment to both 'the Crown' as a legal and political entity, and to the person of the monarch, has remained strong and varied, differing from one province to the next.[8]

In Australia, from as early as the late eighteenth century until at least the 1950s, by far the strongest and most enduring argument in support of constitutional monarchy was the monarch's pivotal role as the symbol of the nation's fundamentally British character. As in Canada and New Zealand and other former colonies within the British Commonwealth, the monarchy was the Empire's metaphysical core. For Australian Britons, the monarchy called up an ancient and sacred language in which religious, political, spiritual and imperial narratives meshed to form what one Sydney newspaper described in 1911 as Australia's *'British faith'*.[9]

This 'faith', steeped in the language of human feeling and grounded in the spiritual bond between sovereign and people, was so deep that it was said to be beyond the powers of human expression. Robert Menzies, Australian Prime Minister at the time of the death of King George VI, in 1952, tried to explain the unexplainable. The 'commonwealth', he said, was 'united not by legal bonds, not by the Crown as an abstract notion, not by fine-spun constitutional theories, but by a common and all powerful human emotion which discards form and penetrates instantly to the substantial truth'.[10] The 1954 royal tour of the newly crowned Queen Elizabeth II and Prince Philip was, in Menzies' words, the occasion for an outpouring of 'nation wide emotion'.[11] The presence of the Queen on Australian soil in 1954 was a powerful vehicle for national communion. In hindsight, it represented the zenith of mass displays of monarchical allegiance in Australia. The feverish expressions of loyalty to the monarch (in a population of 9 million, more than 5 million Australians were estimated to have 'seen' the Queen) suggested that Australia's relationship with the motherland was about to enter a new golden age. In fact, the interests of the two countries had already begun to drift apart. As non-British immigration to Australia increased significantly in the post-war period in tandem with the Empire's decline and a burgeoning cultural nationalism, Australia's previous status as a white mono-cultural British enclave in the South Pacific quickly disintegrated. Australian conservatives, however, were not yet prepared to relinquish their emotional allegiance to the Crown.[12]

In 1979, Sir Paul Hasluck, former Liberal minister and Governor-General, published a small, inconspicuous book: *The Office of Governor-General*. It was one of the first works from a former politician to explicitly address the question of Australia's allegiance to the Crown since the writings of Robert Menzies. Hasluck, who possessed a sharp intellect and a deep commitment to social justice, was also an astute judge of Australian political culture. His commitment to the Crown was genuine and considered. Reflecting on the position of the Crown in Australia, Hasluck wrote of 'the wealth of tradition and patriotism' that helped 'the Crown to attract to itself the loyalty and affection of the people in a way in which an elected leader, backed by little more than half the voters, and opposed by others, may not be able to do'. 'The Crown', he observed, 'being outside politics, attracts the same loyalty from all subjects all the time and stands for those matters on which the nation is undivided.'[13] Even in 1979, Hasluck's conclusions were questionable. Governor-General Sir John Kerr had already divided Australians in 1975 when he dismissed Labor Prime Minister Gough Whitlam and provoked a vocal republican movement.

By the 1990s, however, all of the arguments Hasluck outlined to explain Australia's allegiance to the Crown had evaporated. In 1999,

5 million Australians (45 per cent of the electorate) voted to sever the last connection with the British Crown and become a republic. Queen Elizabeth II no longer attracted the *undivided* allegiance of Australians, nor did she 'attract *the same loyalty* from all subjects all the time'. Only months before the republic referendum, the High Court of Australia handed down a judgement in which Britain was deemed to be a 'foreign power'. The end of Australia as a 'British' society also signalled the end of a particular kind of monarchical allegiance in which the monarch stood for racial homogeneity and unified emotional attachment to a 'British faith'. By the 1990s, if Queen Elizabeth II embodied national unity, then it was Britain's not Australia's.[14]

In June 1991, the Australian Labor Party (ALP) passed a motion at its federal conference in Hobart committing the party to facilitating community discussion on the issue of a republic. The following month, the Australian Republican Movement (ARM) was established in Sydney. Both the ALP and the ARM nominated the centenary of Australian federation (1 January 2001) as the date by which the republic would be achieved. The decade-long debate that ensued in the lead-up to the 1999 referendum dramatically shifted the political context in which arguments in support of constitutional monarchy appeared. While there had been earlier examples of republicanism in the 1970s, the 1990s republican movement, led as it ultimately was by Labor Prime Minister Paul Keating (1991-96), and a wide cross-section of Australians from the worlds of business, media and the arts, constituted the most serious challenge yet to constitutional monarchy in Australia. No longer able to rely on traditional arguments, which appealed to Australia's Britishness or common emotional attachment to the Crown, supporters of the monarchy were forced to invent new ways of defending the institution that were both politically effective and more relevant to contemporary society. In doing so, they fundamentally altered the grounds of constitutional monarchy's appeal.[15]

Throughout the 1990s, there were two broad categories of defence marshalled by supporters of constitutional monarchy – positive arguments for the retention of the monarchy and negative arguments regarding the threat to Australia's constitutional system posed by the prospect of a republic. The launch of Australians for Constitutional Monarchy at Sydney Town Hall in 1992, which closed with a rousing rendition of 'God Save the Queen', demonstrated that residues of allegiance to Britain still remained. The movement's name was accompanied by the sub-title 'Leadership Beyond Politics', which drew on the well-worn argument that monarchy was above politics. Thus, the monarch's allegedly non-partisan leadership was the only safeguard against politicians who sought to gather more power for themselves and usurp the Constitution. The chief virtue of the monarchy was consequently its non-political status.[16] Closely related to the notion of a monarchy that hovered gloriously above the sullied world of day-to-day politics was a second, positive, argument, one that drew on Walter Bagehot's classic elucidation of monarchy's core appeal: its mystery.[17]

While the following arguments were rare, and existed predominantly in the corridors of the Liberal and National parties, they nonetheless bore resemblance to the much more widespread popular affection for the public spectacle of royalty (period costume, cathedral-length bridal trains, glittering tiaras, discreet, white-gloved hands waving from horse-drawn carriages, stirring Handel anthems, sackbutt fanfares and sacred vows uttered on bended knee, all watched by millions on TV, sanctioned by God and the sponsors). Speaking in 1994, Alexander Downer, later minister for foreign affairs in the Howard Liberal government (1996–2007), claimed that to bear allegiance to the monarchy was to recognise 'the limits of human reason' and to accept human fallibility.[18] To be a monarchist was therefore an act of intellectual humility. Or, in Liberal Party minister Tony Abbott's words, it was a 'reminder of the transcendent in the life of the world'. For, as Pascal observed, mused Abbott in 2006, 'the heart has reasons that reason cannot know. The monarchy is unlikely to disappear while human beings retain their respect for order, continuity, ceremony and that which summons us to be our best selves.'[19] In Abbott's mystical view, support for the monarchy became a demonstration of one's social conscience and spirituality. Associated with such arguments is the far more plausible explanation given by Justice Michael Kirby, a former High Court judge, social progressive and law reformer, who explained his allegiance to the Crown by reflecting on his background:

> I must acknowledge the forces which have fashioned my own approach to the issue of republicanism. My ethnicity is Irish but with a healthy corrective against the excesses of anti-English attitude by links to Northern Ireland. There is also my religion. I was brought up in the Anglican Church. Every Sunday I spoke, or sang, the prayers of the King's Majesty and later for the Queen's. In formative years these ideas enter one's sensibilities. That is not to say that in maturity, we cannot throw off early allegiances. But many of them become part of our spirits.[20]

Kirby was one of the founding members of Australians for Constitutional Monarchy and also one of the few monarchists who refrained from indulging in the negative politics of the 1999 referendum. His commitment to the monarchy was both personal and constitutional. He was one of the leading proponents of the third and final positive argument for constitutional monarchy – the constitution has served us well – and the related contention that Australia was already a crowned republic or a republic in disguise. The conclusions that flowed from these propositions – that Australia was a peaceful, stable democracy, already fully independent from Britain and blessed with a constitution comprised of checks and balances traditionally associated with republican government in which the people were sovereign – implied that the monarchy was the keystone of constitutional stability and, *ipso facto*, that its removal would result in constitutional chaos. Thus, the final clarion call: 'if it ain't broke, don't fix it'. Less sober arguments flowed from the mistaken belief that the monarchy was essential to the future stability of Australian democracy, including suggestions that the removal of the monarchy would destroy 'the essence of order and community', tear down the one source of 'reverence and awe' in public life, usher in the triumph of 'Kentucky Fried culture', result in unfettered democracy, empower stockbrokers and a new market elite, end civilisation and sever Australia from history itself.[21]

As the republic referendum approached, monarchists increasingly referred to the potential denigration of Australia's heritage (a thinly veiled euphemism for British culture) under a republican government. They also sought to refute the nationalist arguments of republicans by pointing to the Australian nature of the monarchy and the Queen's formal title – 'Queen of Australia' – and stressing that monarchists were no less Australian than republicans. By November 1999, when the time came for the formal 'No' case to be put to voters by monarchists and other opponents of the republic (including a large section of the electorate that was attracted to a popularly elected president rather than the minimalist model of a president appointed by parliament that was on offer) the mere mention of constitutional monarchy had become a political liability. Voters entered the polling booth confronted with the following proposal:

> Write Yes or No in the space provided opposite the question set out below. A PROPOSED LAW: To alter the Constitution to establish the Commonwealth of Australia as a republic with the Queen and Governor-General being replaced by a president appointed by a two-thirds majority of the members of the Commonwealth Parliament.[22]

The 'No' case leaflet handed to voters appealed to the electorate's preference for a popularly elected president ('No Say – No Way'), pandered to popular mistrust of politicians ('Vote No to the Politicians' Republic') and revelled in the ignorance of sections of the electorate ('Don't Know? – Vote No'). The only positive argument put was that 'Australia is already an independent nation.'[23] Given that the republican proposal was attempting to remove both the Governor-General and the Queen and thereby end constitutional monarchy, it seemed remarkable that the formal 'No' case made not one mention of the Queen or the monarchy. As former Labor Prime Minister Paul Keating tellingly observed: this was 'the love that dare not speak its name'.[24] By successfully prosecuting an overwhelmingly negative case in the referendum, supporters of constitutional monarchy had not only distanced themselves from monarchy, they had undermined any positive grounds for the retention of constitutional monarchy in the future.

In the wake of the referendum, the retreat from serious defence of constitutional monarchy became even more noticeable. In post-colonial societies with increasingly multicultural populations, such as Australia, appeals to common heritage and representations of the monarch as a vehicle of national cohesion had little or no traction. Gone, too, was any pretence that the royal family could be seen as the paragon of family values or moral rectitude, while outside of Britain itself, the concept of the welfare monarchy no longer had meaning. The once widely held view that the monarch's role was to provide leadership beyond politics by acting as a constitutional safeguard was demolished in 2001. Sir William Heseltine, Assistant Private Secretary to the Queen during the 1975 constitutional crisis, which ended when Governor-General John Kerr dismissed the Labor Prime Minister Gough Whitlam, admitted that the Queen was disappointed not to have been consulted by Kerr. 'It would be true to say', Heseltine acknowledged, 'that none of us at that time thought that this was an ideal solution to the crisis.' He believed that the Queen, if consulted, would have advised Kerr not to dismiss Whitlam. Heseltine's remarks confirmed that the Queen had no constitutional role to play in Australia. Any suggestion that the monarch continued to act as a constitutional safeguard was now exposed as fiction.[25]

It was also significant that both during and after the republic referendum, the very term 'constitutional monarchy' was jettisoned in favour of euphemisms such as 'the current system'. The platform of the Liberal Party of Australia makes no mention of the monarchy, referring instead to the party's commitment to a 'constitutional head of state', while the ALP's platform is committed to Australia becoming an 'independent republic'.[26] In order to negate the republican argument for an Australian head of state, monarchists have increasingly referred to the Queen as the 'sovereign'. They have consistently argued that the Governor-General is Australia's head of state. This is despite the fact that Section 2 of Australia's constitution states clearly that the Governor-General is the Queen's 'representative' and that the Queen has herself employed the term 'head of state' to describe her constitutional status in Australia and New Zealand.[27]

Finally, the once mystical justifications for monarchy's existence have completely evaporated. In Australia, the mystery of hereditary monarchy has been supplanted by the acknowledgement of a different source of mystery and historical depth. From the mid-1990s, the widespread acceptance of 'Acknowledgement' and 'Welcome to [Indigenous] Country' protocols has revealed a deep, pre-1788, indigenous past. 'Time immemorial' and the 'ancient past', once seen as the sole domain of a distant British homeland from which Australians were exiled, are now found on Australian soil through public acknowledgement of the indigenous past. When Australians pay their respects to 'elders past and present' during 'Welcome to Country' ceremonies, they implicitly acknowledge another historical and cultural authority – more deeply connected with 'country' and more attuned to the intricate particularities of place. Both the 'Acknowledgement' and 'Welcome to Country' protocols dissolve the borders and territorial boundaries of the nation-state and expose them as fictions. Protean enough to be both local and universal, the protocols transform the Commonwealth's six states and two territories into their original state – a mosaic of indigenous countries. Crown land is nominally, if not legally, revealed as an invention.[28]

If so many traditional arguments used to sustain the existence of constitutional monarchy have vanished or weakened substantially, and if there is no longer a deep affinity in Australian culture with the institution of monarchy, what is left? The only remaining arguments are negative. The monarchy no longer hovers above or beyond politics, it is merely distant, usually absent and *non-political*, which is now considered by its proponents to be its main advantage. In Australia, New Zealand and Canada, by far the most common descriptors for constitutional monarchy are words such as 'outdated', 'foreign' and 'anachronism', which point to monarchy's other remaining virtue, its glorious irrelevance, an irrelevance that is frequently lauded as preferable to the difficulties of framing a republican constitution. At a time when public disenchantment with institutional politics is widespread in liberal democracies, the monarchy appears by comparison to be untainted by corruption and political cynicism.[29]

Fear of losing the monarchy is no longer a barrier for Canada, New Zealand or Australia to become republics. Rather, it is the electoral fear that can easily be created around proposals for constitutional change, fear that results in what Canadian historian Michael Bliss has rightly described as the constitutional 'inertia factor'.[30] Hence, Tony Abbott's mischievous warning that 'in the same way that the beating of butterflies' wings is said to have unknown consequences for the weather half a world away, becoming a republic may set up cultural dissonances Australians will live to regret'.[31] Lurking not far under the surface of the negative arguments that champion the monarchy as harmless and non-political is a fundamentally patronising and pessimistic view of politics and human potential, which suggests that the existence of hereditary monarchy protects the people from an excess of democracy.

From the 1990s, Australia, Canada and New Zealand have entered a period in which the central symbolic power that once personified the state has lost its political and cultural resonance. The monarchy has become a hollow symbol that has outlived its relevance and utility. This lingering colonial hangover has resulted in serious consequences for the practice of democratic government. Australia has in fact drifted further and further away from the Westminster system of parliament. The ceremonial power and symbolic authority that was once exercised by the British monarch has since fallen into the hands of the prime minister. The very danger the monarchy was meant to protect against – the centralisation of legislative and ceremonial power in one political office – is now occurring in the context of its retreat. With the monarch 'irrelevant' and the office of governor-general trapped in a halfway house between Buckingham Palace and Yarralumla, the office of prime minister has become more presidential. Until the declaration of the Australian republic, this trend is likely to continue.[32]

In both Canada and New Zealand, similar concerns have been raised in recent years regarding greater concentration of power in the office of the prime minister. As Michael Bliss has pointed out,

> There is a serious flaw in [Canada's] Constitution related to the monarchy, and the flaw is that the monarchy is so completely ceremonial and toothless that it is nothing more than a creature of the government of the day ... the Governor General having no legitimacy to be a serious check on prime ministerial power.[33]

In New Zealand, especially because of the country's unicameral parliament, the disappearance of the monarchy as a countervailing force in the country's constitution has also resulted in fears regarding the potential concentration of prime ministerial power. In all three countries there is growing confusion as to exactly who is the head of state, the governor-general or the monarch, a vacuum that has again allowed the office of prime minister to command greater authority.[34]

From the perspective of post-republic referendum Australia, sixteen years after the last serious debate regarding the removal of constitutional monarchy, it is telling to observe the same arguments for a republic now surfacing in Canada and New Zealand. In both countries, republican sentiment has grown stronger over the past two decades.

Republicans point to the inevitability of change – the growing numbers of non-British migrants and their descendants who owe no allegiance to the monarchy, the decreasing number of committed monarchists, who will politely 'die off' to be replaced by younger generations who will be of a naturally republican disposition – and they employ well-worn arguments of national interest and identity. The Australian experience, however, suggests that these arguments provide false comfort. Since the 1970s, Australian republicans have comforted themselves with the thought that geopolitical and demographic change would eventually result in the declaration of a republic. They were lulled into a false sense of security. As predicted, Australia and Britain's political and economic interests diverged. The numbers of die-hard monarchists have dwindled. And there has been a rapid increase in non-British immigration. These changes all occurred, but none have brought about the end of constitutional monarchy. Aware of the need to actively maintain its relevance to contemporary society, monarchy has also taken steps to modernise its public image. The 2013 changes to the laws governing succession to the British throne, which ended male primogeniture, were yet another example of the monarchy's infinite capacity for adaptability and its ingenious instinct for survival.[35]

Despite the disappearance of monarchy as a meaningful and relevant institution in post-referendum Australia, the question of the monarchy's future has turned increasingly on the person of Queen Elizabeth II and the undeniably widespread public respect and affection for her many years of service. The former executive director of the ARM and Liberal minister Malcolm Turnbull reflected on this position in 2013:

> It may be that there are two questions. What does Elizabeth mean to Australia? What does the institution of the monarchy mean? There have always been more Elizabethans than monarchists in Australia ... she is a human link from one generation to another ... the end of the Queen's reign will be a momentous historical watershed – she has been part of the historical landscape for so long that I don't believe we will know quite what the reaction will be to her death or abdication until after it occurs. ... The issue of timing is absolutely fundamental to the republican cause and it seems to me that the next best opportunity to create that sense of timeliness is after the end of the Queen's reign.[36]

As the Queen approaches her ninetieth birthday, republicans in both major political parties have reached a consensus in recent years that there will be no move towards a republic until the post-Elizabethan era. Agreeing to wait until the monarch dies, they hope that the last residue of attachment to the monarchy will die with her, if it has not died already. During the Queen's past four visits to Australia (2000, 2002, 2006 and 2011), her presence has been a catalyst for nostalgia and public admiration of her long reign. Her visits have repeatedly been characterised as the 'last hurrah' or 'suffused with a sense of transition, as of an image fading'.[37] More recent examples of the monarchy's presence in public life, such as Prime Minister Tony Abbott's decision in January 2015 to award a knighthood to Prince Philip, resulted in overwhelming condemnation and public ridicule.[38] Although Australians have not found a way to agree on the particular form of republic they wish to introduce after the Queen's death, a slow-burning consensus appears to have emerged that Australia is in spirit, if not in name, already a republic.

Speaking in her 1953 Christmas broadcast from New Zealand, Queen Elizabeth II provided something of a mission statement for her reign. 'I want to show you', she said, 'that the Crown is not merely an abstract symbol of our unity but a personal and living bond between you and me.'[39] In that ambition, she has largely succeeded, as residual respect for her years of service attests. Yet her personal success has also meant that the future of constitutional monarchy in Australia, and perhaps to a slightly lesser extent in New Zealand and Canada, now rests largely on her continued existence. When she is gone, the disappearing, anachronistic, irrelevant and non-political monarchy will finally have to be replaced. Yet the end of constitutional monarchy in Australia, New Zealand and Canada will likely be formulated not only on the grounds of national identity but also on the need to address the far more urgent and practical necessity of providing a ceremonial counterweight to prime-ministerial power.

Notes

1 On recent debate in Australia, see Benjamin T. Jones and Mark McKenna (eds), *Project Republic: Plans and Arguments for a New Australia* (Melbourne: Black Inc., 2013); see also Peter Boyce, *The Queen's Other Realms, the Crown and Its Legacy in Australia, Canada and New Zealand* (Sydney: The Federation Press, 2008). Boyce points out that polls in Australia, Canada and New Zealand since the 1990s show that 'a clear majority would support a termination of monarchy at the expiry of the Queen's reign'. Boyce, *The Queen's Other Realms*, p. 2.
2 John Hirst, 'The Conservative Case for an Australian Republic', *Quadrant* (September 1991), pp. 9–11.
3 Adam Dudding, 'William and Kate Beguile New Zealand's Republicans into Amnesia', *The Guardian*, 12 April 2014. Available online at www.theguardian.com/world/2014/apr/11/william-kate-new-zealand-republicans-amnesia-prince-george (accessed 12 April 2014).
4 For New Zealand's population statistics, see the New Zealand government website, http://nzdotstat.stats.govt.nz/wbos/Index.aspx?DataSetCode=TABLECODE7511 (accessed 23 January 2016). On New Zealand and monarchy, see Boyce, *The Queen's Other Realms*; also Noel Cox, 'The Evolution of the New Zealand Monarchy: The Recognition of an Autochthonous Polity', Ph.D. thesis, University of Auckland, 2001; and the historian, Philippa Mein Smith, 'Cheering Prince George but Planning to Do Away with the Queen?' CNN, 8 April 2014. Available at http://edition.cnn.com/2014/04/08/opinion/uk-royal-visit-republicanism-philippa-mein-smith (accessed 23 January 2016).

5 See http://www.royal.gov.uk/MonarchAndCommonwealth/Australia/Australia.aspx (accessed 1 March 2015).
6 Boyce, 'Preface', in *The Queen's Other Realms*.
7 On John Key and titular honours, see Adam Dudding, *The Guardian*, 12 April 2014. On New Zealand and Privy Council, see www.justice.govt.nz/courts/the-supreme-court (accessed 24 January 2016).
8 On Canada and the monarchy, see Colin M. Coates (ed.), *Majesty in Canada: Essays on the Role of Royalty* (Toronto: Dundurn, 2006); Boyce, *The Queen's Other Realms*; David E. Smith, *The Republican Option in Canada, Past and Present* (Toronto: University of Toronto Press, 1999); see also the Canadian Government website, www.parl.gc.ca/About/Senate/Monarchy/SenMonarchy_00-e.htm (accessed 23 January 2016); and the royal family's website, www.royal.gov.uk (accessed 23 January 2016).
9 *Daily Telegraph*, 23 June 1911, p. 12.
10 Menzies, quoted in Paul Keating, Address by the Prime Minister, the Hon. P. J. Keating, MP, National Press Club, Canberra, 22 July 1993. Available online at http://pmtranscripts.dpmc.gov.au/release/transcript-8921 (accessed 16 February 2016).
11 Robert Menzies, 'The Function of the Crown', Introduction to Rex Ingamells, *Royalty and Australia* (Melbourne: Hallcraft, 1954), unpaginated.
12 Mark McKenna, 'Monarchy: From Reverence to Indifference', in D. Schreuder and S. Ward (eds), *Australia's Empire* (Oxford: Oxford University Press, 2008), pp. 261–87; see also John Coakley and Mark McKenna, 'Whatever Happened to Republicanism?' in Katie Holmes and Stuart Ward (eds), *Exhuming Passions: The Pressure of the Past in Ireland and Australia* (Dublin: Irish Academic Press, 2011), pp. 271–94.
13 Paul Hasluck, *The Office of the Governor-General* (Melbourne: Melbourne University Press, 1979), pp. 7–8.
14 On the republic referendum, see John Warhurst and Malcolm Mackerras (eds), *Constitutional Politics: The Republic Referendum and the Future* (St Lucia: University of Queensland Press, 2002). On the High Court decision (*Sue v. Hill*, 1999), see James McConvill, 'The United Kingdom Is a Foreign Power', *Deakin Law Review*, 4:2 (1999), 151–8, available online at www.austlii.edu.au/au/journals/DeakinLawRw/1999/8.pdf (accessed 23 January 2011).
15 Mark McKenna, *The Captive Republic: A History of Republicanism in Australia* (Cambridge: Cambridge University Press, 1996).
16 By far the best outline of the arguments put forward by Australia's monarchists is Gareth Grainger and Kerry Jones (eds), *The Australian Constitutional Monarchy* (Sydney: ACM Publishing, 2000).
17 Walter Bagehot, *The English Constitution* (Oxford: Oxford University Press, 1955; first published 1867).
18 Alexander Downer, *Australian Conservatives and the Monarchy* (Sydney: Monarchist League, 1993).
19 Tony Abbott, foreword to David Flint, *Her Majesty at 80: Impeccable Service in an Indispensable Office* (Sydney: ACM Publishing, 2006), unpaginated.
20 Justice Michael Kirby, 'The Australian Monarchy and Its Likely Survival', Address to the Australian Society of Labour Lawyers, Adelaide, 12 March 1993. Available online at www.michaelkirby.com.au/images/stories/ speeches/1990s/vol28/998-Aus_Society_of_Labour_ Lawyers_-_The_Aus_ Constitutional_Monarchy_and_ Its_ Likely_Survival.pdf (accessed 23 January 2016).
21 'Reverence and Awe' and 'Kentucky Fried Culture', in Tony Abbott, *The Minimal Monarchy and Why It Still Makes Sense for Australia* (Kent Town: Wakefield Press, 1995), pp. 141–2. On the loss of 'essence and order', etc., see A. Atkinson, *The Muddle-Headed Republic* (Melbourne: Oxford University Press, 1993), p. 46.
22 Australian Electoral Commission, 1999 Referendum, www.aec.gov.au/elections/referendums/1999_Referendum_Reports_Statistics/1999.htm (accessed 23 January 2016).

23 Australian Electoral Commission, *Yes/No Referendum '99: Your Official Referendum Pamphlet* (Canberra: Australian Electoral Commission, 1999).
24 Paul Keating, *The Australian*, 28 October 1999; quoted in Mark McKenna, 'The Australian Republic: Still Captive After All These Years', in John Warhurst and Malcolm Mackerras (eds), *Constitutional Politics: The Republic Referendum and the Future* (St Lucia: University of Queensland Press, 2002), pp. 145–62, at p. 155.
25 William Heseltine, *Sydney Morning Herald*, 10–11 March 2001, p. 1.
26 Liberal platform, http://share.liberal.org.au/info/docs/federalplatform.pdf (accessed 23 January 2016). Labor platform, www.alp.org.au/national_platform (accessed 23 January 2016).
27 See David Flint, in Senate Legal and Constitutional References Committee, *The Road to a Republic* (Canberra: Parliament of the Commonwealth of Australia, 2004), p. 49; and Mark McKenna and Wayne Hudson (eds), *Australian Republicanism: A Reader* (Melbourne: Melbourne University Publishing, 2004), pp. 257 and 268.
28 Mark McKenna, 'Tokenism or Belated Recognition? Welcome to Country and the Emergence of Indigenous Protocol in Australia, 1991–2014', *Journal of Australian Studies*, 38:4 (2014), 476–89.
29 On Canada, see Jeffrey Simpson, 'Why the Monarchy (Sigh) Still Survives in Canada', *The Globe and Mail*, 1 July 2011: 'Over the years, public opinion surveys have shown similar results. The monarchy is considered irrelevant or of little interest to the largest number of Canadians. Those who care passionately about it, one way or the other, are in a minority.' On Australia, see Jones and McKenna, *Project Republic*. On New Zealand, see Morgan Godfrey, 'The Monarchy Has Lost Meaning', *New Zealand Herald*, 13 April 2014, available online at www.nzherald.co.nz/opinion/news/article.cfm?c_id=466&objectid=11237269 (accessed 23 January 2016); and Patrick Dougan, 'New Zealand Ditching Monarchy Is Inevitable: Mackinnon', *New Zealand Herald*, 6 April 2014, available online at www.nzherald.co.nz/nz/news/article.cfm?c_id=1&objectid=11233254 (accessed 23 January 2016).
30 Bliss, quoted in Daniel Schwartz, 'Will Baby Prince George Ever Become King of Canada? The Future of Monarchy in Canada', CBC, 30 July 2013. Available online at www.cbc.ca/news/canada/will-baby-prince-george-ever-become-king-of-canada-1.1305652 (accessed 23 January 2016).
31 Abbott, *The Minimal Monarchy*, p. 93.
32 On the increasingly presidential nature of the office of prime minister, see Mark McKenna, 'Howard's Warriors', in Raimond Gaita (ed.), *Why the War was Wrong* (Melbourne: Text, 2003), pp. 167–200.
33 Bliss, quoted in Schwartz, 'Will Baby Prince George Ever Become King of Canada?'
34 On New Zealand and increased prime ministerial power, see Bruce Jesson, 'Republicanism in New Zealand', in Luke Trainor (ed.), *Republicanism in New Zealand* (Palmerston North: Dunmore Press, 1996), pp. 47–60, at p. 58. (Jesson argues that one constant complaint about New Zealand's form of government is 'the power of the Prime Minister and Cabinet', which is connected in turn to the disappearance of the monarch and the relatively invisible constitutional role of the governor-general.) See also Boyce, *The Queen's Other Realms*, p. 5. ('As in Britain, the enshrining of state authority in the Crown has provided an effective mask for the steady expansion of power within the political executives of Canada, Australia and New Zealand.')
35 On changes to laws of succession, see 'Law Ending Exclusively Male Royal Succession Now Law', BBC News, 25 April 2013. Available online at www.bbc.com/news/uk-22300293 (accessed 23 January 2016).
36 Malcolm Turnbull, 'Foreword' to Jones and McKenna, *Project Republic*, pp. x–xii.
37 'Last Hurrah', *Sydney Morning Herald*, 20 March 2000, p. 5; 'Image Fading', Editorial, *Sydney Morning Herald*, 3 April 2000.
38 For more about Abbott's knighthood for Prince Philip, see Michael Safi, 'How Giving Prince Philip a Knighthood Left Australia's PM Fighting for Survival', *The Guardian*,

3 February 2015. Available online at www.theguardian.com/australia-news/2015/feb/03/how-giving-prince-philip-a-knighthood-left-australias-pm-fighting-for-survival (accessed 23 January 2016).

39 The text of the Queen's broadcast is available at www.royal.gov.uk/ImagesandBroadcasts/TheQueensChristmasBroadcasts/Queen's%20Christmas%20Broadcasts%20listing/Christmasbroadcast1953.aspx.

INDEX

Page numbers in **bold** type denote illustrations; those followed by the letter 'n' indicate notes.

Abbott, Tony 15, 315, 318
Abdulillah 240
Afrikaans language 104–6, 111
Afrikaner identity 102–7
Alauddin, Sultan 119, 122
Albert, King of the Belgians 19
Albert, Prince Consort 40
Alfred, Prince, Duke of Edinburgh
   assassination attempt on 71
   breach of good manners by 62–3
   colonial depictions of 60–1
   as naval officer 57–8, 69, 70–1
   visit to Australia and New Zealand 27, 167
   see also Prince Alfred's visits to Victoria
Algeria 214, 216, 218–19
Algiers 222
Amedeo d'Aosta 246, 255–8
Amery, Leo 294
Anglican Church *see* Church of England
Anglo-Iraqi Treaty 238
Annam 21, 218
Anne, Queen 31
ANV (Algemeen Nederlandsch Verbond) 104
Apartheid policy 106
Arab Bureau 231, 233–4
Arab revolt 234
architecture 220–2
Army, British 34–5
Assab 247
Assinie 214
Attlee, Clement 300–1
Australia
   acknowledgement of indigenous past 318

   acquisition of Crown's sovereignty over 311
   allegiance to Crown 293–4, 302, 313
   Constitution 237
   constitutional crisis 15, 313, 317
   future of constitutional monarchy in 309, 320–1
   imperial honours 15, 312
   republic referendum 314, 316
Australian Labor Party 314
Australian Republican Movement 314
Australians for Constitutional Monarchy 314

Belgium 8, 18
Bell, Francis Dillon 168, 169
betel sets **126**, 126–7
Bligh, William 268–74
Board of Ministers (Ceylon) 153–4
Boers, Wilhelmina's assistance to 101
Bourbon France 199
Boxer Rebellion 77–8, 80, 248
Brazil 14, 197
British Crown *see* Crown, British
brothels 64, 66, 68, 71
Browne, Thomas Gore 166
Brunei 16
Bülow, Bernhard von 77–8, 81, 84, 87–90
Burma 9, 11, 159, 292–3, 296, 297
Buwono VII, Sultan **127**, 128
Buwono VIII, Sultan Hamengku **127**, 127–9
Buwono X, Paku 127, 129, 130, 131, 133

[325]

Cairo Conference (1921) 233–4
Cambodia 21, 217
Canada
  attachment to Crown 311–12
  explanations for monarchy's survival in 311–12
  as federal dominion 40
  future of constitutional monarchy 319–21
  and Indian membership of Commonwealth 294–5
  as New France 198–200, 202–4
Candler, Samuel Curtis 62, 64–9
Caribbean, French colonisation in 201, 203
carte-de-visite portraits 56
Céleste, Céline 65–6
Ceylon
  becomes a republic 16
  and Commonwealth 287
  deposition of Kandyan king 140–1, 142
  Independence 154–7
  loyalist sentiments 142
  Queen as head of state 16
  see also Kandyan regalia
Charles de Bourbon, Comte de Soissons 198–9
Charles II 263–4, 268, 271, 273, 277
Charles V 13
China 217
Church of England 33–4
Churchill, Winston 4, 234, 294, 303
Cobden-Chevalier treaty 213
Cochinchina 217
Colbert. Jean-Baptiste 204, 205–6
Colenso, John 33–4
colonies, association with monarchies 6–7
Commonwealth of Nations
  concern about republics as members 297–303
  debates on monarch's role 285–303
  impact of Indian Independence on 287–95

  monarch as titular Head of 5, 16, 41, 301–4
  pragmatic reasons for membership 287–91
  and prefix 'British' 292, 294, 301
  reverence in Anglo-Saxon dominions for 293–5
  secession from 288, 292, 296
  viceregal assent to legislation 15
Compagnie de la Nouvelle-France 201, 202–3
Compagnie des Iles de l'Amérique 203
Congo Free State 18
constitutional monarchy in Australia
  evaporation of relevance 309, 311, 318–19
  future of 309, 320–1
  implications of continuance for parliamentary democracy 319, 321
  negative arguments for retention 316–19
  positive arguments for retention 314–16
constitutional monarchy in Canada and New Zealand 319–21
convict settlements 216
coronations, British 1–5
Corsica 196, 198
Council of State (Ceylon) 146–7, 152
Crimean War 212–13
Crown, British
  appropriation of land in name of 15
  Canada's attachment to 311–12
  civil war as antithesis to 275–6
  as 'composite kingdom' 31, 276, 285–6
  contemporary relevance in Australia 16, 318–19
  creation of crown colonies 32
  divisibility of 15, 277–8, 286, 293
  imperial evolution under Tudors and Stuarts 30–1
  imperial expansion (1688–1837) 30–3

as inheritor of Kandyan
 crown 141–2
and metaphor of King's Two
 Bodies 277–8
New Zealand's attachment
 to 311–12
petitions and appeals to 31, 36–40,
 69–71, 167–9
as physical object 283, 286
role in colonial government 35–6
role in post-war Commonwealth,
 debates on 287–303
sacred character of 274, 275–6, 295
scholarship on 28–30, 41, 284–5
see also Commonwealth of Nations;
 Great Seals; monarchy, British
Crown, French
 delegation of powers through
  letters patent 197–8,
  200–3, 204–5
 delegation of powers to chartered
  companies 202–4
 fiscal policy 206
 overseas expansion during *ancien
  régime* 197–9
 territorial expansion in Europe
  196–7
 see also French territories
crown colonies, creation of 322
Curzon, Lord 14
Cyrenaica 248

De Silva, George 153
decolonisation 8
Delhi Durbars 19, **19**, 178–9
deposition of rulers
 India and Burma 9
 King of Kandy 9, 140–1, 142
 King of Portugal 21
 Napoleon III 21
diarchy
 in French overseas territories 204
 of Italian Fascist state 246,
  252–5, 258–9
Downer, Alexander 315
Dugua de Monts, Pierre 198, 202, 205

durbars
 Ceylon 142
 India 14, 19, **19**, 178–9, 288
Dutch East Indies Company 99
Dutch monarchs and Indonesian
 royalty 123, 124–30
 see also Wilhelmina, Queen

East India Company 120, 228–9
Edward, Prince of Wales 169, 170
Ehelepola 140–1, 143
Elizabeth II
 and Australia's constitutional
  crisis 317
 coronation 4–5
 as Head of Commonwealth 5, 16
 and monarchy's future in Australia
  309, 320–1
 royal visits by 27, 170–3, **173**, 320–1
 and Waikato apology 172, 173
embassies as 'courtly encounters'
 10, 131
Emma, Queen 128
Eritrea 247, 252
Ethiopia
 as Empire of Italian East Africa
  251–2, 255–8
 failed Italian invasion (1896) 247
 Italian conquest (1936) 251
 return of crown and cap 159
 Treaty of Uccialli 247
Evatt, H.V. 294, 302
exile
 Faisal I of Syria, then Iraq 234
 Haile Selassie of Ethiopia 21,
  256, 258
 Thibaw of Burma 11, 159
 Vikrama Rajasinha, Sri, of
  Kandy 141

Faidherbe, Louis 219
Faisal I
 family background 233–4
 as king of Iraq 227, 234–6
 as king of Syria 231
 photo **239**

[327]

Faisal II 240
Fannin, Katherine 256–8
Fascism
  Churchill's warnings about 4
  Italian 248, 249–58
federal schemes 40–1
feudatories 11
First World War
  impact in Middle East 232–4
  and loss of thrones and empires 7–8
Florida 197
Franco-British accord (1860) 213
French Crown *see* Crown, French
French Guinea 214
French territories
  delegation of power to chartered companies 202–4
  expansion in Europe 196–7
  expansion under Napoleon III 214–20, 223
  in India 222
  overseas expansion (1824–48) 214
  overseas expansion during *ancien régime* 197–9
  as provinces 194, 204–7
  sovereignty based on right of conquest 202

Gabon 214
gender issues *see* women
George, Duke of Cambridge 34
George, Prince 27
George III 31–2
George IV 36, 144, 164
George V 19, **19**, 148, 169
George VI
  coronation 1–4
  declarations of war by 286
  and Indian independence 283, 288, 299
  role in post-imperial Commonwealth 283, 284, 285, 290, 302
German Constitution, Kaiser's prerogative powers 78, 79–81
German South-West Africa
  exercise of Kaiser's prerogative power 79–85, 87–90
  extent of Kaiser's prerogative power 78, 79–81
  'Hottentot Election' 90–1
  Protectorate Law 82, 90
  see also Herero War
Ghazzi 240
gift-giving 20
  by indigenous royals 20, 31, 123, 124–30
  as performance 131–2
gifts
  from Dutch monarchs to Indonesian royals 133
  educative and exhortatory motives 124–5, 128–9
  from Indonesian royals to Dutch royals 123, 125–30
  method of presentation 124, 130–1
  sending of photographs as 130
  symbolic aspects 124–8, 130
Gloucester, Duke of 148, 149–50, 155
Gordon Walker, Gordon 297–8
governors and governors-general
  French *lieutenants généraux* 197, 202–4
  and metaphor of King's Two Bodies 277–8
  'reserve powers' 15
  royal appointments 35–6
  sacredness as 'deputy kings' 275–6
  Yogyakarta Sultan as hereditary governor 134
  see also Great Seal of New South Wales; viceroys
Grand-Bassam 214
Graziani, Rodolfo 255–6
Great Seal of New South Wales
  design and motto 265–6, **266**, **267**, 267–8
  as inspiration for emblem of local identity 272–3
  reclamation of 276
  usurpation of 264, 268–74, 271, 275–6

INDEX

Great Seals
  and divisibiity of royal sovereignty 263, 268, 275–6
  function and design 262–4, 267, 279n28
  implications of usurpation 275–6
  mythic characteristics 264–5
  use and significance of Great Seals disputed 263–4, 267, 275
  see also Great Seal of New South Wales
Grey, Sir George 166
Grubb, Frederick 145–8
Guadeloupe 214
Guiana 216
Gulf region, British involvement in 228–30
Gulf states, emirs of 22

Haile Selassie, Emperor 21, 249, 256, 258
Hare Pomare 37
Hashemite monarchy in Iraq
  constitutional status and powers 236–7, 238
  establishment 227–8, 233–5
  evolution (post-1925) 238–40
  as 'informal' British colony 238–41
  overthrow 241
  see also Faisal I
Hasluck, Paul 313
'Haussmannisation' 221
Hawaiian royal family 39–40
Hennessy, Ann 69–70
Henri de Lévis, Duc de Ventadour 200–1
Henri II, Duke of Montmorency 199–200, 205
Henri II de Bourbon, Prince de Condé 199
Herero War
  genocidal aspect 78, 86–7, 88–9, 91
  German electorate's support of 90–1
  Kaiser's lack of active involvement in 79, 83–7, 89

  see also Trotha, Lothar von; Wilhelm II
Heseltine, William 317
Hicks, Ann 69–70
Hobson, J.A. 7
'Home Rule' 40
House of Orange
  Afrikaner identification with 106–7
  Indonesian sultans and 125, 133
House of Savoy 245, 248, 252–8
Hull, Isobel V. 80, 84
Hun Speech *(Hunnenrede)* 77–8
Hussain, Sharif of Mecca 231, 233

immigration issues 294–5
imperial federation 40–1
imperial honours
  in Australia 15, 312, 321
  export of 29
Independence ceremonies 154–7
India (post-Indepenence)
  decision to remain in Commonwealth 292, 296
  as republic within the Commonwealth 297–302
  return of Imperial State Crown of India 283
  role of monarch in Indian republic 297–303
India (pre-Independence)
  1858 Proclamation 38–9, 177
  allegiance of Indian princes to British Crown 39, 41, **42**
  becomes a republic 16
  durbars and royal visits 14, 19, **19**, 178–9, 288
  French India 222
  importance of Middle East for 232
  Queen Victoria and 18, 29, 38–9, **42**, 178, 283–4, 287
  status of princely territories 178
  viceregal pageantry 14

INDEX

India (princely states)
  impact of Indian independence on 22, 288–9
  status of 178
  see also Maharani of Kutch
indigenous rulers
  deposition of 9, 11, 21, 140–1, 142, 159, 256
  preservation of Indonesian royalty 123, 124–30
  retention of customary power 10–11
  sub-national, in former colonies 21–2
  visits to European courts by 20
Indonesia *see* sultans (Indonesia)
Iraq
  adoption of constitution 235–7
  British invasion (1941) 240
  British occupation (1917) 233
  creation as state 232–5
  establishment of monarchy 227–8, 233–5
  impact of Ottoman reforms 231–2
  independence and admission to League of Nations 238–9
  as 'informal' British colony 233, 237–41
  overthrow of monarchy 241
  political awareness before First World War 231–2
  role of noble elites 230, 237–8
  see also Faisal I; Hashemite monarchy in Iraq
Iraq Petroleum Company 238
Ireland 291–2
Italian colonialism
  creation of Empire of Italian East Africa 251–2
  under Fascist regime 248, 249–58
  under Kingdom of Italy 247–9
  relationship of House of Savoy with Fascist imperialism 251–9
  royal powers and prerogatives 14
Italian East Africa 248
Italo-Turkish War 248

James II 264
Jayatilaka, Don Baron 153
Johnston, George 268, 270
jubilees
  Queen Victoria 29, 39, 142
  Queen Wilhelmina 99, 106, 126
Juliana, Princess 127, 128, 129, 131–2

Kaiser Wilhelm II *see* Wilhelm II
Kandyan king, deposition of 140–1, 142
Kandyan regalia
  British capture of 143–5
  ceremonial reappearance at Independence 154–7
  description and illustration 143–4, **144**
  issues concerning restitution 151–4
  return to Ceylon of 145–54
  symbolic significance 154, 157–8, 157–9
Keating, Paul 314, 317
Kerr, John 313, 317
Key, John 27
King's Two Bodies 277–8
Kirby, Michael 315
Knight, Alice 66–7
Koroki Te Rata Mahuta 170
krises (daggers) 121, 125, **126**
Kruger, Paul 101
Kurds 234–5, 236, 239
Kutch *see* Maharani of Kutch

La Roche de Mesgouez, Troilus de 199–200
La Rocque de Roberval, Jean-François de 197, 202
La Touche, Daniel de 197, 198, 202
Laos 21, 218
Lawrence, T.E. 234
Leopold II 18
Lesotho 16
Lesseps, Ferdinand de 215
letters patent 197–8
Leutwein, Theodor 83, 84, 85–6, 87
Libya 248, 252–4

[330]

INDEX

lieutenants généraux 197,
    198–200, 202
Louis XIV 10, 204
Louis XVI 20

Macarthur, John 269–70, 272
MacDonald, Malcolm 296
Macquarie, Lachlan 269, 274, 275–6
Madansinhji (Maharao of Kutch)
    182–3, 188–90
Magna Carta 270
Maharani of Kutch
    betrothal, marriage and children
        182–4, 191
    daily life in the *zenana* 184–6
    family lineage 181–2
    purdah and 179, 183–5, 188–91
Major, Thomas 265–6
Makonnen, Tafari 249
Malan, D.F. 106, 294, 301, 302
Malaysia 16, 22
Manners-Sutton, Mabel 64
Maori King movement
    lack of legal status 171
    loyalty to British Crown 163,
        165–7, 172–3
    official rebuffs and snubs
        163, 167–70
    origins 164–5
    recognition by Elizabeth II 171–2
    as threat to settler hegemony 166,
        168–9, 171
    Waikato War and 166–7
Maori peoples
    relationship to Crown 311
    Treaty of Waitangi 37–8
    Waikato War 166, 172
Marec, René 198, 202
Marquesas Islands 214
Martinique 214
Maryland 277
Massawa 247
Maude, Frederick Stanley 233
Mauritius 16
Maurits of Orange-Nassau 119, 122
Maximilian I 220

Mayotte 214
Melbourne *see* Prince Alfred's visits
    to Victoria; Victoria (colony)
Melbourne Club 64–5, 66,
    68–9, 70, 71
Melbourne Punch 60–1
Menzies, Robert 287, 293, 313
Mexico 220
military appointments 18, 34–5,
    83–6
missionary proselytising 34
Mombauer, Annika 80
monarchs, European
    composite character 285
    sacral aspect 7
    symbolic visibility of 17, 22, 33
    see also Crown, British; *names of
        individual monarchs*
monarchs, non-European
    Queen Victoria's meetings
        with 39–40
    'sub-national', in former
        colonies 21–2
monarchy, association with
    imperialism 7–9
monarchy, British
    capacity to adapt and survive 320
    as constitutional safeguard
        314–15, 317
    debates on monarch's role in
        post-war Commonwealth
        285–303
    as Head of Commonwealth 5,
        16, 300–3
    reverence in settler states
        for 293–5
    role in Indian republic 297–302
    sacred character 295
    see also constitutional monarchy
Montmorency, Charles de 200
monuments and statues **2**, 27–8,
    33, 157
Mountbatten, Lord 22, 289
'museumification' 154, 158
Mussolini, Benito 245–6, 249, 251–2,
    254–5, 257

Nagapuhi tribe 163, 167–8, 170, 171
Napoleon III
  African expansion under 218–19
  Asian and Pacific expansion under 216–18
  background 212
  Crimean War and 212–13
  economic liberalisation under 213
  Franco-British accord 213
  imperial motives and vision 214–16
  Mexican misadventure 220
  overseas military intervention 217
  overthrow 21
  royal visits by 18
  Suez Canal project 215–16
  urban embellishment 220–3
Nehru, Jawaharlal 5, 294, 298, 299, 301, 302
Netherlands
  Caribbean islands 8
  loss of East Indies 8
  non-official support for Boers 101
  see also sultans (Indonesia); Wilhelmina, Queen
New Caledonia 216
New France 198–200, 202–4
New South Wales
  creation as colony 265, 268
  design of Great Seal 265–6, **266**, **267**, 267–8
  usurpation of Great Seal 264, 268–74, 271
New South Wales Corps 268, 270, 277
New Zealand
  attachment to Crown 293, 311–12
  explanations for constitutional monarchy 311–12
  future of constitutional monarchy 27, 319–21
  Treaty of Waitangi 37–8, 311
  see also Maori king movement; Maori peoples
Newry, Lord 64–5, 66
Nice 218

Nossi-Bé 214
Nuri as-Said 239
NZAV (Nederlandisch Zuid-Afrikaansche Vereniging) 102, 104, 107

oorkonden (illuminated greetings) 20–1, 97, 99
oorkonden to Queen Wilhelmina
  anti-British subtext 109–11, 114
  from first *Apartheid* government to 106–7
  illustrations **98**, **108**, **109**, **110**, **111**
  linguistic issues 103–4, 111
  number and source 99
  ornamental components 107–11
  from South African women 108–13
  use of *stamverwantschap* in 105–6
Opium War 217
orders-in-council 32

pageantry
  durbars 14, 19, **19**, 178–9
  Indonesian sultans and 121–2, 131–2, 133
Pakistan 287
Palestine 234
Paris 221
parliamentary democracy 319, 321
Pearson, Lester 299
penal colonies 216
Penang 4–5
Persian Gulf region, British involvement in 228–30
petitions and appeals
  to British royals 31, 36–40, 69–71, 167–9
  by Maori 37, 168–9
Philip, Prince, Duke of Edinburgh 15, 312, 321
Phillip, Arthur 265, 277
photographs as gifts 130
Piedmont 196, 198
piracy 229
Pondicherry 222–3
Portugal
  overthrow of monarchy 21

INDEX

royal rule in Brazil 14
prerogatives, royal
  assent to legislation 15
  divisibility of the Crown and 15, 263, 268, 277–8
  expansion under Queen Victoria 33–6
  of French *lieutenants généraux* 197, 202
  of French monarch 202
  of French viceroys 199–200
  of German Kaiser over colonies 14, 78, 79–85, 87–90
  in Italian East Africa 14
  of Yogyakarta's sultans 134
prime ministerial power 319–20, 321
Prince Alfred's visits to Victoria
  1869 return visit 71–2
  banquets and balls 62–4
  local depictions of the prince 56–8, 60–1, 71
  local depictions of Queen Victoria 53–6, 58–9, 71
  local representations of the colony 58–60
  his unrespectable private pastimes 64–9
Privy Council 32, 265, 299, 312
privy seals 265, 273, 277–8
protectorates 9–10, 217–18, 230, 247, 248
purdah 179, 183–5, 188–9

Qatar 230

Rance, Hubert 292
referendums
  on Australia becoming a republic 314, 316
  to recognise Iraqi king 23, 25
regalia
  Burmese throne 159
  crown as 'chattel' 302
  Ethiopian crown and cap 159
  Imperial State Crown of India 283
  of Indonesian sultans 121
  symbolic significance 139, 157–9

  see also Kandyan regalia
Reichstag, powers over colonial matters 82, 87, 90
republicanism
  Canada 319–20
  debate in Australia over 27, 314–21
  India 290, 295
  Ireland 292
  New Zealand 319–20
  rise of 21
republics
  compatibility with Commonwealth membership 16, 297–303
  as nineteenth-century anomaly 6
Réunion Island 214
Richelieu, Cardinal 200–1
Roberval, Jean François de La Roque de 197, 202
royal family portraits 56
royal visits
  to Australia 27–8, 51–72, 310, 313, 320–1
  Belgian 19
  to Ceylon 19, 141–2, 149–50, 155
  Dutch 98–9
  by Elizabeth II 27, 170–3, **173**, 320–1
  French 18, 218
  to India 12, 14, 19, **19**, 36, 178–9, 288
  Italian 19, 252–4
  local hostility towards 12
  to New Zealand 163, 167, 169–73, **173**
  to South Africa 295
  symbolic significance 18–20, 27–8
  see also Prince Alfred's visits to Victoria

Saigon 221
Saint-Pierre and Miquelon 214
Sarkin, Jeremy 86, 88, 91
Savoy 196, 198, 218
  see also House of Savoy
Schlieffen, Alfred von 79, 83, 84, 87
Scotland 196, 198

seals
  colonial great seals 267
  defined 262
  privy seals 265, 273, 277–8
  of Secretary of State for India 290
  sigillography and 278n2
  see also Great Seal of New South Wales; Great Seals
Second World War
  declaration by George VI of 286
  Iraq and 240
Senanayake, Don Stephen 5, 156–7, 287
Senegal 214, 219
serempi dances 131–2
sigillography 278n2
Sihanouk, King 21
Siti Nurul Kusumowardhani, Gusti Raden Ajeng 131–2, **132**
Smith, Louis L. 62, 63
Smuts, Jan 294
Società Commerciale Italiana del Benadir 248
Società Filonardi 248
Society for the Propagation of the Gospel (SPG) 33
Somalia 248, 252
South Africa
  attempt at federation 41
  concern at Indian membership of Commonwealth 294, 302
  Dutch-descended settlers' identity 101–11
  formal establishment 100
  royal visit to 295
  support in Netherlands for Boers 101
South African Republic (SAR) 100, 101, 102, 107–8
South African War 101–2
South-West Africa *see* German South-West Africa
Spain
  post-Franco overseas possessions 8
  Spanish empire 13–14
Sri Lanka *see* Ceylon
stamverwantschap 105–6

Standish, Frederick 62–6, 64–6, 68, 71
State Council *see* Council of State (Ceylon)
statues *see* monuments and statues
Statute of Westminster 2, 312
Stuart monarchs 31
Stubbs, Reginald 147, 152–3, 160n25
Suez Canal 215–16
sultans (Indonesia)
  artistic representation of the Dutch 123
  early dealings with the Dutch 121–4, 134–5
  expressions of alliance with Dutch monarchy by 125, 130–3
  gifts to Dutch royals from 123, 125–30
  in independent Indonesia 133–4
  and marks of Islamic kingship 121–2
  representation at Wilhelmina's investiture 131
  self-presentation to local audiences 121–2, 133
  Yogyakarta Sultanate 134
sultans (Malaysia) 22
Suriname 7
Swaziland 16
Sydney Gazette 272
Sykes-Picot Agreement 234
Syria 21, 234–5

Tahiti 214
Taingakawa, Tupu 169
Tawhiao, Matutaera 166, 167–9
Te Atairangikaahu 172, **173**
Te Hipango 37
Te Rata Mahuta 169, 170, 171
Te Rauparaha 37–8, 165
Te Wherowhero, Potatau 38, 165–6
Thani dynasty 230
Thibaw 159
Tianjin 248
Tonga 5, 21
Tonkin 218
Trafalgar flag 273

INDEX

Transjordan 234
Transvaal
  ookonden to Dutch monarch from 97, 100
  political history of 100, 101
Treaty of Waitangi 37–8, 164, 172, 311
Tripolitania 248
Trollope, Anthony 65
Trotha, Lothar von
  appointment as commander of expeditionary force 83–6
  campaign of expulsion and genocide by 86–7
  failure as military commander 86–7
  recall of 89–90
Tudor monarchs 30–1
Tunisia 248
Tupu Taingakawa 169
Turnbull, Malcolm 320

Uccialli Treaty 247
urban aggrandisement 220–3

viceroys
  Ethiopia 255–8
  India 14, 22, 29, 35, 178, 232
  influence of ex-viceroys 22
  New France 199–200
Victoria, Queen
  African wooden sculpure of 11–12, **12**
  attention to imperial affairs 18
  as Empress of India 18, 29, 178, 283–4, 287
  favours imperial federation 40
  golden and diamond jubilees 29, 39, 142
  Indian Proclamation (1858) and 38–9
  monuments and place names as legacy **2**, 27–8 33, 51, 157
  relations with Maori 37–8, 164, 167–9
  role in Army appointments 18, 34–5
  role in Church appointments 18, 33–4
  royal appointments to colonial posts 35–6
  royal audiences 37, 39–40
  symbolic visibility of 33
  Treaty of Waitangi and 164
Victoria (colony)
  concern with reputation and self-representation 58–60, 62–3, 72
  establishment 51
  respectable *versus* unrespectable aspects 61, 64–8
  see also Prince Alfred's visits to Victoria
Vietnam 21, 217
Vikrama Rajasinha, King Sri 140–1, 142
Virginia 263–4, 275, 277
Vittorio Emanuele III
  as Emperor of Italian East Africa 14, 251–2
  and legitimation of Fascist Empire 252–4
  royal visits by 19
VOC (Verenigde Oostindische Compagnie) *see* Dutch East Indies Company

Waikato Raupatu Claims Settlement Act 172
Waikato War 166, 172
Waitangi *see* Treaty of Waitangi
'Welcome to Country' protocols 318
Whitlam, Gough 313, 317
Whitlam government 15
Wigram, Clive 147
Wilhelm II
  chooses Trotha to lead expeditionary force 83–6
  constitutional powers and prerogatives 79, 81–2
  countermands Trotha's annihilation order 85–7
  exercise of powers and prerogatives 79–85, 87–90

INDEX

Wilhelm II (*cont.*)
  Hun Speech 77–8
  lack of active role in Herero War 79, 83–7, 89
  relations with Chancellor 87–90
  see also Herero War
Wilhelmina, Queen
  assistance to the Boers 101
  as embodiment of *stamverwantschap* 105
  as 'female king' *(koningin)* 100, 111–13
  gifts from Indonesian royalty to 126, 127, 128, 129
  investiture 131
  jubilees 99, 106, 126
  significance for Dutch-descended South Africans 100–7, 111–13
  see also oorkonden to Queen Wilhelmina
William, Prince, Duke of Cambridge 27, 163, 310

William III 31
William IV 36, 164
Wilson, James 70–1
women
  as adornments of Melbourne society 54
  Afrikaner women's use of *oorkonden* 108–13
  female representaions of states and colonies 59–60
  gift-giving by royal women 129–30
  purdah and female segregation 179, 183–5, 188–9
  Wilhelmina's appeal as 'female king' 112–13

Yogyakarta, Sultan of 22, 126–7, **127**
Yorke, Eliot 64

zenana
  daily life in 184–6
  formal gatherings in 186–7
Zulu monarchs 22, 34, 39